ASSIGNMENT

Due Date: First day of class

Instructions: Please print and complete the form below using a black or contract to your instructor.

D1490114

Student's Name: Carmen O'Brien-Thomas

Instructor's Name: Ms. Carliss Riddick

Section: ORED

Morgan Email Address: Caobr1@morgan.edu

Personal Email Address: Ct.dcgirl1996@gmail.com

Local Address: _____

_____

Local Telephone Number _____ - _____ - _____

Cell Phone Number 240 - 691 - 9097

Major: Elementary Education

Student ID Number: 00180076

As a freshman student at **Morgan State University,** I am committed to the following:

1) attendance at all classes, activities, enrichment programs, seminars, cultural activities, etc.
2) the purchase of the required textbook and planner
3) adherence to all college policies, including the honor code, code of conduct, and plagiarism policy

Carmen O'Brien-Thomas   February 3, 2015

Signature   Date

STRATEGIES FOR COLLEGE SUCCESS

Janet A. Amos

This Textbook Belongs to:

Name _Carmen O'Brien-Thomas_

Campus/Local Address _____

City/State/Zip _____

Phone Number _240-691-9097_

EDITED BY

BRENDA J. JAMES, PH.D.
CENTER FOR ACADEMIC SUCCESS
AND ACHIEVEMENT (CASA)

Tapestry Press, Ltd.
Littleton, Massachusetts 01460

2014 – 2015

Printed in the United States of America.

ISBN 978-1-59830-679-8

Cover Photos: John Moore, Morgan State University campus photographer
Additional Photos: William Carson, Joanna Crosby, The Beulah C. Davis Special Collections Room, Morgan State University, MSU Sports Information, Becky Verzinski, Evan Richardson, Dwain Pruitt.

Acknowledgments:
Pages 1–12, 17–23, 37–82 and Sections 2–10: *The Successful Student's Guide to College* by Janet A. Amos. Copyright © 2014 Tapestry Press, Ltd. All rights reserved.

The policies and regulations contained herein are meant to supplement that which is written in your catalog, not to replace them. Where there is a difference between the catalog and this publication, the catalog will take precedence.

Janet A. Amos is recently retired Dean for Teaching and Learning Excellence and former Dean of Academic Affairs for Kanawha Valley Community and Technical College. She has an Education Specialist degree in Developmental Education from Appalachian State University in North Carolina, a Master of Arts in Counseling and Guidance, and two Bachelor of Science degrees in Psychology and Recreation Therapy. Janet designed the three-credit hour College 101 (college success and retention course) for WVSCCTC in 1989. Janet is married and the mother of four children.

CONTENTS

SECTION 3: MAKING THE CLASSROOM WORK FOR YOU 107

SECTION 4: IMPROVING YOUR MEMORY AND LEARNING SKILLS 131

SECTION 6: LEARNING TO THINK CRITICALLY

SECTION 7: PRESENTING YOUR BEST WORK

PREFACE TO THE STUDENT AND INSTRUCTOR

Strategies for College Success is a student-friendly text and workbook that offers the student a wealth of tools and strategies for college, career, and personal success. The concepts taught in this course will help students to develop self-discipline to succeed in the critical first weeks and months of college and will give them the tools to stay motivated until graduation.

Course Description

Freshman Orientation is designed to retain new students and to help them make a successful transition to University life. The course will provide students with essential information about the academic demands of the University and its rules, procedures, and resources. Students will be introduced to academic, social and personal survival skills that will contribute to academic and personal success. The course curriculum will encourage students to establish supportive relationships with peers and faculty and will help them to become a part of the academic community. Freshman Orientation is a course that is a University requirement for graduation.

Standardized Testing

Morgan State University administers a number of standardized assessments to entering freshmen through the orientation course and to graduating seniors. The University uses the results from these assessments to understand better the computer, information management, and general education skills that students bring to college and to measure the change in these skills from the first year to the senior year. A student's performance on these assessments will not impact his/her grade for orientation, grades for the semester, or overall grade point average.

Achievement in Orientation

Any student who earns a 92% or higher in the orientation course will be featured in a group cover photo for the 2015–2016 orientation textbook. To be eligible for the cover photo, students must also demonstrate that they have purchased the 2014–2015 orientation textbook, by submitting the first ASSIGNMENT page to their instructor. The cover photo will be taken during the spring semester.

NOTE: The policies and regulations contained herein are meant to supplement that which is written in the Morgan State University catalog, not to replace them. Where there is a difference between the catalog and this publication, the catalog will take precedence.

Preparing for Success in College

WHAT'S IN IT FOR YOU

The fact that you've opened this book and begun reading this section shows that you want to succeed in your education. The purpose of this section is to help you learn the ropes of your college and the services offered to help you succeed in your educational goals. You'll clarify the reasons you're in college and the advantages of a college education. You'll examine common obstacles to college success and strategies to conquer them. Many students just like you have used the strategies offered in this book to make the most of their education and move on to successful careers.

There's more to succeeding in college than understanding English, math, technology, or other subjects. Often it's more important to stay motivated in school and find effective ways to solve problems. Motivation is the energy and the desire you need to meet the challenges of college. You can learn skills to help you stay motivated, just as you can learn skills to master your courses. With these skills, your mind can become a toolbox for smoothing out some of the rough parts of school.

This section shares the secrets that can give you a solid start in your education. It gives you a chance to learn and practice some important skills that will help you get through school.

In this section you'll explore:

- The reasons you're in college
- The advantages of a college education
- The benefits of getting involved in your college community
- Your school's resources and services
- Transportation possibilities and backup plans
- Ways to finance your education
- Strategies for balancing school, work, family, and friends
- Your own vision of success
- Strategies for accomplishing goals
- How to boost your self-esteem
- How to create positive self-talk to motivate yourself
- The importance of creating a successful self-image
- Tips to improve your self-discipline
- Strategies for creative problem solving and decision making
- Benefits and risks of online social networking

THE ADVANTAGES OF A COLLEGE EDUCATION

A college education offers you a multitude of advantages from improved employment opportunities to an increase in self-esteem. You will boost your employability, have more jobs to choose from, earn more money, be more likely to receive promotions, obtain necessary skills for today's workforce, be better able to support your family, and have a higher standard of living. Probably even more important is the sense of personal accomplishment you will gain from achieving your educational goals and the enrichment you will gain from socializing with a diverse population of students who share similar educational goals.

Improved Opportunities for Financial Security

Financial security is probably the single greatest reason that students give for attending college. The more education you have, the higher your salary. Look at the average weekly salaries for U.S. workers with various levels of education shown in Table 1-1.

Table 1-1

Gross Weekly Salaries for U.S. Workers with Various Levels of Education at age 25 and Over	
$471—	Less than a high school diploma
$652—	High school graduate
$727—	Some college
$785—	Associate's degree
$1,066—	Bachelor's degree
$1,300—	Master's degree
$1,735—	Professional degree
$1,624—	Doctoral degree
Source: Bureau of Labor Statistics, 2012	

These weekly salary listings are only averages—some people make a lot more, some less. Beyond salary figures, don't forget the employability factor. A college education provides professional training, greater knowledge and, therefore, greater employment potential. The U.S. Bureau of Labor Statistics claims that there will be a significant increase in job opportunities for those with college degrees and a decrease in opportunities for those without. Greater financial security is more achievable not only when you have your degree, but also when you are equipped with the skills and personal qualities needed in today's job market.

Obtaining the Necessary Skills for Today's Workforce

Your college works closely with business and industry to keep abreast of the required skills for today's workforce. As you prepare for your career, it helps to know what kinds of skills employers want you to have. A survey of necessary skills for the workplace was conducted by the U.S. Department of Labor. The Secretary's Commission on Achieving Necessary Skills (SCANS), under the Secretary of Labor, spent 12 months surveying business owners, public employers, people who manage employees daily, union officials, and workers on the line and at their desks to find out what skills employers want their employees to have. From these surveys, the commission identified five workforce competencies which, in conjunction with a three-part foundation of skills and personal qualities, lie at the heart of job performance today. A list and explanation of the five competencies and the three-part foundation are shown in Tables 1-2 and 1-3. These two documents are now part of what is called the SCANS Report. This report identifies many skills that you will want to develop and improve on throughout your education to prepare for your career. Exercise 1-2 asks you to identify some of your courses that will help you develop the SCANS workforce competencies. When you realize the workforce competencies that you can gain from your courses, you will have a better understanding of their importance to your career.

Table 1-2

FIVE WORKFORCE COMPETENCIES

Resources: Identifies, organizes, plans, and allocates resources
- A. *Time*—Selects goal-relevant activities, ranks them, allocates time, and prepares and follows schedules
- B. *Money*—Uses or prepares budgets, makes forecasts, keeps records, and makes adjustments to meet objectives
- C. *Material and Facilities*—Acquires, stores, allocates, and uses materials or space efficiently
- D. *Human Resources*—Assesses skills and distributes work accordingly, evaluates performance and provides feedback

Interpersonal: Works with others
- A. *Participates as Member of a Team*—contributes to group effort
- B. *Teaches Others New Skills*
- C. *Serves Clients/Customers*—works to satisfy customers' expectations
- D. *Exercises Leadership*—communicates ideas to justify position, persuades and convinces others, responsibly challenges existing procedures and policies
- E. *Negotiates*—works toward agreements involving exchange of resources, resolves divergent interests
- F. *Works with Diversity*—works well with men and women from diverse backgrounds

Information: Acquires and uses information
- A. *Acquires and Evaluates Information*
- B. *Organizes and Maintains Information*
- C. *Interprets and Communicates Information*
- D. *Uses Computers to Process Information*

Systems: Understands complex inter-relationships
- A. *Understands Systems*—knows how social, organizational, and technological systems work and operates effectively with them
- B. *Monitors and Corrects Performance*—distinguishes trends, predicts impacts on system operations, diagnoses deviations in systems' performance and corrects malfunctions
- C. *Improves or Designs Systems*—suggests modifications to existing systems and develops new or alternative systems to improve performance

Technology: Works with a variety of technologies
- A. *Selects Technology*—chooses procedures, tools or equipment including computers and related technologies
- B. *Applies Technology to Task*—Understands overall intent and proper procedures for setup and operation of equipment
- C. *Maintains and Troubleshoots Equipment*—Prevents, identifies, or solves problems with equipment, including computers and other technologies

---

Table 1-3

A THREE-PART FOUNDATION: WORKFORCE SKILLS AND PERSONAL QUALITIES

Basic Skills: Reads, writes, performs arithmetic and mathematical operations, listens, and speaks
  A. *Reading*—locates, understands, and interprets written information in prose and in documents such as manuals, graphs, and schedules
  B. *Writing*—communicates thoughts, ideas, information, and messages in writing; and creates documents such as letters, directions, manuals, reports, graphs, and flow charts
  C. *Arithmetic/Mathematics*—performs basic computations and approaches practical problems by choosing appropriately from a variety of mathematical techniques
  D. *Listening*—receives, attends to, interprets, and responds to verbal messages and other cues
  E. *Speaking*—organizes ideas and communicates orally

Thinking Skills: Thinks creatively, makes decisions, solves problems, visualizes, knows how to learn and reason
  A. *Creative Thinking*—generates new ideas
  B. *Decision Making*—specifies goals and constraints, generates alternatives, considers risks, and evaluates and chooses best alternative
  C. *Problem Solving*—recognizes problems and devises and implements plan of action
  D. *Seeing Things in the Mind's Eye*—organizes, and processes symbols, pictures, graphs, objects and other information
  E. *Knowing How to Learn*—uses efficient learning techniques to acquire and apply new knowledge and skills
  F. *Reasoning*—discovers a rule or principle underlying the relationship between two or more objects and applies it in solving a problem

Personal Qualities: Displays responsibility, self-esteem, sociability, self-management, and integrity and honesty
  A. *Responsibility*—exerts a high level of effort and perseveres towards goal attainment
  B. *Self-Esteem*—believes in own self-worth and maintains a positive view of self
  C. *Sociability*—demonstrates understanding, friendliness, adaptability, empathy, and politeness in group settings
  D. *Self-Management*—assesses self accurately, sets personal goals, monitors progress, and exhibits self-control
  E. *Integrity/Honesty*—chooses ethical courses of action

Exercise 1-2 Identifying workforce skills and personal qualities stressed in this course

After reading about the Three-Part Foundation: Workforce Skills and Personal Qualities described in Table 1-3, review the table of contents of this text and check the workforce skills and personal qualities that are included in this course in Table 1-3.

Colleges have, as a major mission, education and training that prepares you for today's workforce. As you can see, some of the same skills and qualities that make you a successful student also help you become a successful employee. Knowing how your courses and class projects relate to your career preparation should also motivate you to succeed in your college education.

GETTING INVOLVED IN YOUR COLLEGE COMMUNITY

Today's student is busy trying to meet the demands of school, work, friends, and/or family. The more demands you have competing for your time, the more you may feel you don't have time to get involved in your college community. Yet getting involved, even in small ways, will help you further invest yourself in your college education. Generally, when students invest themselves in school-related activities, for socialization or for learning, they become more attached to their school and achieve their educational goals. Of course, it's easier for students who live in college dorms to get involved in campus activities. However, whether you live on campus or at home, there are many ways to involve yourself both socially and academically and become more a part of your college community. As you involve yourself in college activities from major clubs to lunch, you are developing educational networks that can also serve to advance your professional goals.

Getting Socially Involved

Part of the challenge and reward of attending college is making new friends and meeting people who share your interest and excitement about college study and building a career. Social involvement is essential for success in your education as well as your career. Good social skills make you a better candidate for jobs, improve your chances for advancement in your career, and make your career life more fulfilling.

Perhaps for the first time in your life, you're in school with people who share your commitment to learning and growing—to making life more rewarding. They also share your desire to succeed. Your fellow students are in college because they want to be. They know college opens new opportunities for personal and professional growth. You might recall playing on a sports team or other group activity in the past, in which all the members wanted the same thing. In the case of sports, everyone wants to play well and win. The individuals on the team draw on the group's common goal for guidance and motivation to work hard. You can use the common bond with your fellow students as a source of guidance and motivation as well.

You'll also learn valuable life skills from socializing that are difficult to learn anywhere else. You'll be mixing with students from different backgrounds and varying degrees of seriousness and maturity. You may learn many things from others with professional or college experience. You'll find that discussing your studies with fellow students makes learning easier and more interesting.

Your college may attract some of the richest cultural activity from around your area. Depending on your school, you may have access to some of your area's most interesting music, theater, and other arts. Some of the greatest talents that your community and this nation have to offer may appear on your campus to present their ideas. And, most likely, there's a student organization meeting regularly to discuss the issues most important to you, helping to shape your school and your community. Alicia, an accounting major, remembers how important her college women's network was for staying on track in her studies. "I think it was the first

---

Tips . . . For Getting Socially Involved

The way to make new friends is simply to spend time with people at school. Even if you have little extra time, sharing a snack or discussing assignments with some other students can lead to new friendships. Make the time for these new relationships, and the rest will take care of itself. Consider some of these activities to begin building social involvement in your college.

- Go to classes early, even if it's only a few minutes early. Make conversation with other students who have arrived early. If your professor arrives early, you could discuss the latest assignment or an issue related to the course.

- Whenever possible, eat meals on campus. Buy lunch or bring a sandwich from home and sit down with classmates or school staff.

- Share your commute to and from campus with classmates, whether by offering rides, if you have a car, or by keeping each other company on public transportation. Just mentioning in class where you live often leads to an interesting friendship and makes your commute more enjoyable and productive.

- Volunteer for student activities and projects, such as student get-togethers or cookouts, fairs for displaying student work, student clubs, or tutoring services if you have a certain skill. If you have an idea for an activity, talk to your fellow students and a student services administrator to see about making it happen.

- Participate as much as possible in such college activities as orientation sessions, social gatherings, and ceremonies. Join student organizations or try to start your own major club.

time I sat in a room with 10 or so women that all shared a clear commitment to education and a career," she says. "We'd meet every couple of weeks just to talk, give each other moral support and encouragement. I made some really great friends." And if you have an idea for a new organization, your college may support you in your efforts to create a new student organization.

Getting Academically Involved

The first and most important step in academic involvement is attending **all** of your classes. Some students assume that, since so much of college work takes place outside the regular classroom, regular attendance is optional. Nothing could be further from the truth. The work you do outside the class is putting into effect the information you have learned in class.

Remember that class time is the core of your college experience. All your other learning experiences will focus on the materials you studied in class. And **every** class is important. Regular attendance means attending every class, not just most of them. You might not think you're missing anything by missing a class or two. But, invariably, the day you're absent is the day the instructor reviews important information or gives a pop quiz. Many instructors will not let you make up a pop quiz, so your grade will be zero. Also, by skipping classes, you reduce your opportunities to participate in class, and many instructors base at least part of your grade on how much you contribute to the class. Besides, missing class is wasting your own money.

When you need to, you can pick up information you missed in class by borrowing notes from other students; but that's no substitute for being in class yourself. You can't ask questions if you're not in the classroom; your classmates won't know all the answers. Being in class is also the best way to benefit from other students' questions and ideas—learning in a group environment is very effective for most people.

> ### ~Jayleen~
>
> *I remember skipping a lot of my math classes in the first term. I figured I could just make up the work by borrowing notes and putting in a little extra study time. One night I spent hours working on a problem only to find the next day that it had been solved in the last class I missed. By skipping classes, I think I put in more time and effort than most students and still didn't get the grades I was really capable of.*

When you show up to class, be on time. Despite what you may have heard, the first few minutes are just as important as the rest of the class. Instructors often use the first few minutes of class to clarify confusing points, to answer questions, and to make important announcements about upcoming assignments and exams. Keep in mind that many instructors take careful note of who's on time to class and who isn't. They even notice who sits up front and who contributes to the class. You want to show your instructors that you are eager to learn and are taking responsibility for your education.

Make class time your priority. Work other appointments around class, not the other way around. Treat class attendance the way you would treat attendance at work. You wouldn't just decide to skip work, would you? In a college situation, you're the boss **and** the employee. You owe it to your "boss" to show up for class every day, on time, prepared, and ready to work. Not only will you reap all the benefits a college has to offer, you'll benefit from making a commitment to your education and sticking to it. Refer to Section 3, Making the Classroom Work for You, for more information on the importance of attending class.

Academic involvement means more than just attending classes and completing assignments. It means learning how all the facts you learn in class relate to one another, actively building a better understanding of your field, and pursuing your greatest interests.

In short, take charge of your education and make the most of every academic opportunity. If you're bored by a particular assignment, try to figure out why. Many students discover that they find an assignment boring when they don't understand it completely or know how it relates to the rest of the material they're studying.

Rosa, a first-term computer science student at a college, could hardly keep herself awake during her weekly college math class. "It really seemed like a waste of time," she says. "I'm here to learn about computers, not to become a math whiz. I never liked math in high school, and now I just sit in class and stare at the clock."

Tips . . . For Getting Academically Involved

Successful students strive to make the most of their academic work. Try the following strategies to maximize your academic involvement in college.

- Discuss assignments with fellow students before or after class, or at any other time. Assist other students and seek assistance whenever, and as soon as, necessary.

- Discuss a point with your instructor during a break or after class. Instructors will appreciate your interest and admire your extra effort. In return, you're likely to be rewarded with interesting new insights and more motivation to work hard.

- Prepare questions for class on issues that confuse you. Asking questions is the key to learning. It's the only way your professor can know which topics need further discussion. Other students are likely to share your confusion, so everybody benefits when you ask questions.

- Find out how to improve skills you think you need to work on. For example, find a tutor or a math skills class. If you're not sure which of your skills needs strengthening the most, ask one of your instructors to help you evaluate your abilities.

- Join study groups to prepare for tests. Even a couple of brief meetings will lead to new friendships and help you stay motivated to study.

When Rosa starting doing badly in her business spreadsheet class, though, she began to change her mind. "Math was boring because it seemed so pointless. But after fouling up the first four spreadsheet assignments, I realized that I needed to understand math formulas in order to use spreadsheets. Suddenly, I began to see how all my classes related to each other. And believe it or not, math didn't seem so boring anymore!"

Now that you've explored tips for getting academically involved in your college, it's time to think about what you believe will help you succeed in college. Try Exercise 1-3 to identify factors important to your academic success.

Exercise 1-3 Factors important to my academic success

Indicate the degree to which each of these statements will be important to your academic success.

1 = Highly unlikely
2 = Unlikely
3 = Equally unlikely and likely, or not sure
4 = Likely
5 = Highly likely

The most important factors for my college success will be my:

1.	ability to prioritize tasks and use my time effectively.	1	2	3	4	5
2.	ability to solve problems effectively.	1	2	3	4	5
3.	regular attendance in all my classes.	1	2	3	4	5
4.	understanding of how my courses relate to my future career.	1	2	3	4	5
5.	willingness to ask my instructors or seek tutoring when I need assistance.	1	2	3	4	5
6.	involvement in community services and activities related to my field.	1	2	3	4	5
7.	management of personal matters outside of class.	1	2	3	4	5
8.	ability to concentrate and learn what I read.	1	2	3	4	5
9.	ability to manage my money.	1	2	3	4	5
10.	previous work experience.	1	2	3	4	5
11.	ability to work with a group/team.	1	2	3	4	5
12.	completing assignments on time.	1	2	3	4	5
13.	maintaining an optimum level of health.	1	2	3	4	5
14.	determination to work hard.	1	2	3	4	5
15.	developing more self-discipline.	1	2	3	4	5
16.	ability to motivate/inspire myself.	1	2	3	4	5
17.	ability to take charge of my education.	1	2	3	4	5
18.	Other _____	1	2	3	4	5
19.	Other _____	1	2	3	4	5

Examine each of the statements from Exercise 1-3 again. Circle the number of each statement that would apply to your success at work. Based on this exercise, discuss any improvements you can make while in college that will strengthen your work performance.

_____
_____
_____
_____
_____
_____
_____
_____
_____

Finding the Right Balance

Academically involved students generally make many friends in college, just as the socially involved students spend much of their social time discussing their coursework. Academic and social involvement go hand in hand, creating the ideal community for college learning. Since the people at your school share your interests in learning and growing, they can become your best source of support and motivation.

Finding the right balance between social and academic life is a challenge most students face. If you choose to party all the time, rather than study, nobody's going to stop you. Nor will anyone force you to make friends, get involved in student organizations, or attend special school events. Finding the right balance for you is *your* job, and each student's balance will be a little different. Sometimes finding the right balance is a rough process. Sally, now about to graduate from an electrical technology program, has a typical story to tell.

> ### ~Shari~
>
> *I remember my first term. I started partying a lot with my friends at school. We had a great time, but I really fouled up on my first midterms. I settled down enough to survive my finals, but I didn't get the grades I wanted. Eventually, I became one of those students who showed up a little later for parties. I'd study up to the last minute before my friends were going out on the town. Mainly, I think I learned to squeeze more study time out of each day. I don't think I really missed that much in the way of social life, but I do think I got more out of my classes than most people.*

Shari's experience reveals two of the important secrets of balancing social and academic life: making sacrifices and managing time. With all the wonderful opportunities of college life, you'll have to sacrifice some very tempting activities to find enough time for your studies. But if you manage your time effectively, you'll keep the hardest sacrifices to a minimum. In Section 2, you will learn many effective strategies for setting priorities and for making the most of your time.

Getting Off to a Good Start in Your Classes

Making the most of your first classes is the key to getting off to a good start toward academic success. Here are some practical suggestions to help you get organized right away.

The first session

Bring paper, pens, and pencils to your first class. Be ready to start learning right away. Listen carefully to your instructor's description of himself or herself and look for interesting aspects of his or her background. You may find that your instructor shares some of your interests. And all instructors can share some personal hints about how they succeeded in college and in their careers. If the instructor asks for student introductions, listen carefully to these as well and write down names if this will help you remember them. Knowing someone's name and a little about their background is a great way to start a friendship.

Make a list of the texts, supplies, equipment, and other resources necessary for the course. Include in your list any resources your instructor suggests as optional; ask where you can purchase these materials. Note any assignments that may require time in your college library.

Keep a copy of the course syllabus or study plan or take notes about your instructor's description of the course and its contents. As much as possible, include any description of specific assignments or exams and their due dates. Take note of office hours or other times when the instructor is available to answer questions or provide assistance.

Know your instructor's policies, requirements, and expectations regarding attendance, grading, class participation, group work, and independent assignments. Find out your instructor's policy for making up work or submitting work late. Now is your chance to ask any questions about the course. Listen carefully to your instructor's responses to questions. You may want to stay for a few minutes after class to ask additional questions or to listen in on your professor's responses to other students' questions.

The first week

Purchase all the necessary supplies as soon as possible—supplies may be limited. Used textbooks may be available at your school or a local bookstore, but a fresh and unmarked text is generally worth the money. Never buy a used workbook—pages may be missing. If you do buy used texts, be sure they are complete, readable, and the correct edition. If you're trying to save money, think about buying other school supplies, such as paper, notebooks, pens, and pencils, at a discount store rather than at your college bookstore. In addition to the items required for your courses, the following items will help you get off to a solid start in most college programs: a dictionary, thesaurus, writing handbook, personal computer, and a calculator. You may decide that it's worth buying a computer. Some schools require you to have a specific computer that will network with their system. You may also find that your school's computer labs give you all the computer access you need.

Make a habit of beginning your assignments right away. Completing your first assignments on time will give you an immediate sense of accomplishment and confidence—an important part of your school success. Schedule time for each assignment, including the first stages of longer-term projects, papers, or test preparation. Start assignments early—you'll find that it feels better to be ahead than behind. You'll want to review the time management tips found in Section 2.

Establish one or more study areas: a quiet space at home, the college library or study area, a community library, or a place to hide during your breaks at work. Make sure you have readily available all the necessary supplies for completing assignments, such as paper, pens and pencils, an eraser, a calculator, drawing tools, and a dictionary. Many of these supplies can be carried with you wherever you go, so you can study on the run.

If you want to make any changes in your courseload, meet with your advisor as soon as possible to discuss your options. She or he will be able to clarify what courseload would be best, given your educational plan and personal circumstances. The more quickly you can resolve these matters with your advisor, the more likely you'll find the courses you want, and the sooner you can get down to work.

Get to know your library, either at your school or elsewhere in your community. Learning to use its many services and resources is a critical step toward academic success. Today's libraries are truly remarkable, storing more information within their walls than most people imagined possible just ten years ago. Beyond books, magazines, journals, and microfiche, more and more libraries offer CD-ROM technology, which allows you to search through hundreds—even thousands—of journal articles in seconds on compact disk. Most libraries have adopted computer catalog systems, which lead you to all of the library's resources using a single computer terminal. Multimedia centers give you access to sights and sounds from around the world. And as the Internet use expands across the world, more and more students are able to use not only their own library, but far away libraries as well.

Today's reference librarians are highly skilled information experts trained to help you unlock the doors to this incredible wealth of information. They can offer quick help in locating materials for your topic. They probably offer several different orientation sessions and tutorials on mastering the art of library research. Ask them which ones would be most appropriate for you and schedule them as soon as possible. Mastering today's library skills will save you many hours and greatly improve your work.

Often, everyday issues and concerns relating to transportation, finances, family, work, and friends interfere with the kind of social and academic involvement in college that helps you succeed. The following sections suggest the steps you can take to clear the way for success in college.

BENEFITING FROM CAMPUS RESOURCES AND SERVICES

> **~Candace~**
>
> *I was having a lot of trouble with my college writing course—English and grammar have always been tough subjects for me. My advisor told me about the writing tutoring program on campus—I hadn't even known it existed. I'm glad I found out about it, though. My tutor suggested a brief manual that covered the basic rules of writing. We decided that each week I'd write her a one-page essay on any topic I chose and then we'd discuss it and improve it. I wrote about my kids, my mother, what I thought about college. I've really seen an improvement in my work, and so has my tutor. What's more, I'm feeling more relaxed and confident about writing assignments.*

Your college is familiar with just about every challenge you'll face during your program. In most cases, instructors or school staff can offer helpful advice and often just the right services to help you meet those challenges. The time you spend in college will be more successful and rewarding if you make the most of what your school has to offer. That means taking charge of your education and finding whatever support you need to help you concentrate on it.

Using Your College Catalog/Student Handbook

As a first step, let's examine what your college has to offer. You'll find that most of your college's requirements and regulations, as well as the services your college offers, are described in your college catalog or student handbook.

ACADEMIC ADVISING SYLLABUS

Advising Mission

Academic advising is an intentional, collaborative, and ongoing partnership between students and the university based on sharing timely information that enables students to navigate the educational system and to identify and reach educational, personal, and career goals. Faculty, professional academic advisors, and retention staff who are charged with advising-related duties establish an engaging and challenging learning and mentoring relationship which supports the mutual trust and respect of both parties.

Philosophy

The philosophy is based on the following beliefs:

- Students are often unaware of the demands and expectations of the university and therefore need to learn the culture of higher education. Academic advising plays a key role in your understanding of the collegiate environment.

- Academic advising is not an isolated event but an ongoing communication between you and your advisor in which mutual trust and respect must be established.

- Academic advisors recognize and accept that all students are unique and enter the learning process at varying points, learn at different rates and through a variety of methods. To that extent, your advisor will work closely with you to identify and make your educational experience one that fits your needs, goals, and plans.

- At the heart of academic advising is the development of an educational plan that will enhance your intellectual and personal growth, including the selection of appropriate classes to satisfy degree requirements in an efficient and effective manner. While your advisor will help you define your educational goals, the primary responsibility for decision-making rests with YOU, the student.

Advisor/Advisee Responsibilities

Your advisor will:

- Help you to understand the meaning and relevance of the college experience.

- Assist you in developing and achieving realistic academic and career goals based on your interests, abilities, values, and needs.

- Interpret university policies, procedures, and requirements.

- Refer you to the appropriate resources, including the Counseling Center, tutoring services, the Office of Student Accessibility Services, the Career Center, etc.

- Address your academic questions and concerns.

- Adhere to the highest principles of ethical behavior and maintain confidentiality. Your advisor will not discuss issues with parents or non-university persons without your written permission.

- Guide you in your selection of courses.

YOU will:

- Take responsibility for your educational experience.

- Learn how to access, use, and check your university email often as well as WebSIS.

- Become familiar with campus resources, including the Counseling Center, campus tutoring services, the Office of Student Accessibility Services, the Career Center, etc.

- Maintain contact with your advisor throughout the semester.

- Come to each advising appointment prepared to ask questions and discuss concerns.

- Know how and when to check holds on WebSIS and which offices to contact to rectify or remove the hold.

- Assess your interests, abilities, values, and needs utilizing the Career Center or other resources to discuss these with your advisor.

- Use the Undergraduate Catalog and other resources to become knowledgeable of academic requirements, policies, and procedures.

- Know important dates and deadlines (registration, drop/add, final exams, etc.) as listed on the university's Academic Calendar.

- Discuss your selection of courses with your advisor.

- Accept responsibility for your decisions and actions which affect your educational progress and goals.

Student Learning and Expectations of Advising

The following are skills that your advisor and you will work together to gain by the end of each year in your academic program. Please review them periodically to assess your understanding. If at any time you have questions or concerns, please contact your advisor who will explain what you do not understand or who will advise you as to your next step.

_____ Know who your advisor is and how to contact him/her.

_____ Learn and accept the differences between high school and college.

_____ Become familiar with the General Education requirements.

_____ Know the core requirements for you major, if declared.

_____ Become familiar with MSU academic calendar/deadlines, add/drop, registration dates, etc.

_____ Develop a high degree of academic integrity.

_____ Understand the University's expectation for student behavior (the Morgan State University Student Code of Conduct) and the consequences of behavior on your future.

_____ Learn to manage your time successfully so that you are able to complete assignments and still manage personal responsibilities.

_____ Learn to budget and manage finances effectively.

_____ Learn to ask for help when you need it rather than attempting to deal with overwhelming situations alone.

_____ Learn about/take care of financial aid responsibilities, including filing FAFSA on time.

_____ Discover your own personal learning style and learn how you can use it to be a more successful student (become aware of your STRENGTHS).

_____ Become familiar with campus services.

_____ Become familiar with the Undergraduate Catalog.

_____ Learn what future employers expect of their employees and adopt a level of academic integrity that will provide a foundation of ethical behavior in the career arena.

_____ Be able to navigate WebSIS.

Demonstrating Your Achievement of Learning Outcomes

Through the advising experience at Morgan State University:

_____ Students will demonstrate the ability to make effective decisions concerning their degrees and career goals.

_____ Students will develop an educational plan for successfully achieving their goals and select courses each semester to progress toward fulfilling that educational plan.

_____ Students will demonstrate an understanding of the value of the General Education requirements.

_____ Students will fulfill all contractual stipulations for academic probation when appropriate.

_____ Students will understand University policies related to dismissal, academic dishonesty, and the appeal process.

_____ Students will understand how to calculate grade point averages.

_____ Students will understand the impact that withdrawing from classes has on their educational plan and financial aid.

_____ Students will utilize the resources and services on campus to assist them in achieving their academic, personal, and career goals.

_____ Students will make use of referrals to campus resources as needed and provide feedback to their advisor.

_____ Students will be able to read and utilize their EARS report accurately.

CONFIRMING, SELECTING, OR CHANGING A MAJOR

Choosing a major is an important academic decision and one that is more complicated than many students think. Some students select their major based on their high school interests and strengths. Others select a major based on their impressions of the jobs that seem related. For example, students may declare a major in nursing because they think it will lead to a specific type of work after graduation. Most business curricula provide a broad education including all facets of business, but some students only think in terms of specialization, such as majoring in accounting or marketing. Many liberal arts majors (e.g., psychology, French, cell biology) will not prepare them to enter many possible career fields.

Many students feel pressured to declare a major upon entering college. If students have accurate information about the type of course work required by the major, know their personal interests and abilities are a good match, and understand the career implications related to it, declaring a major immediately is probably the correct decision. Making an official declaration of major depends on the institution's system. Students' academic advisors can instruct them in the required procedure.

Major-Changers

A common event on many campuses is when "decided" students need or want to change their majors. There are many reasons for changing a major, such as lack of interest, inability to perform at a certain level in the major's course work, or the discovery of another academic area that is more appealing. If your student has doubts about her choice, she should contact her advisor for a referral to either an advisor who is a specialist in exploring alternatives or an advisor in her new area of interest. After collecting the information needed to confirm that a new alternative is viable and realistic, her advisor can help her with the institutional procedure for officially changing her major.

Undecided Students

Students who are not sure of their choice, have several ideas about majors, or are totally undecided, will want to explore many options in an organized way. Depending on the institution's advising system, undeclared students may be assigned to a faculty member from any discipline, or a professional advisor who specializes in working with undecided students. A generalist advisor has information about all the college's majors and curricula, can help students access resources for assessing their interests and strengths, and can help them relate these to general career fields.

Some colleges set a certain number of credit hours when "undecided" students must declare a major, while others do not. Since most students begin their college careers enrolling in required general education courses, they have the opportunity to explore a variety of academic disciplines. This often opens up new areas of interest to which they have not been previously exposed. Since waiting too long to declare a major may delay graduation, it is important that you encourage your student to seek the advising and career services that can help her make a decision regarding her major in a timely way.

Developing an Academic Plan

One of the first tasks that students and advisors will want to do is formulate an academic plan tailored to the individual student's interests, abilities, and goals. Devising a plan will help her organize a tentative path to graduation. During this planning session, your student will set academic goals and organize her course of study. The academic plan is a flexible document that may change every term, but the general plan provides a base for her to follow and alter as necessary. Rather than just randomly selecting and scheduling courses every term, the plan will help your student understand how a degree is structured and will reassure her that she is on the right track. Even if your student has selected a major, she will benefit from developing a tentative plan. Since a large percentage of students change their academic direction, this exercise teaches your student the basic information needed to rewrite or alter her plan later.

Pre-registration

Since registering for classes can be a busy time for both advisors and students, most colleges encourage discussing and choosing next term's courses during the current one. Quality time is more likely to be available with the advisor during this period. Your student and her advisor can discuss how current classes are progressing, since this may influence the courses chosen for the coming term. Many advisors use a checklist or degree audit sheet from the student's chosen curriculum to review what courses students have taken and what courses are appropriate for the future. This is also a time to review the student's academic plan and make adjustments if necessary. The pre-registration system is designed to lower the stress of registering for courses and increases the likelihood of making good decisions.

ACADEMIC REQUIREMENTS AND PROCEDURES

Exercise 1-4 is designed to introduce you to your college's academic requirements and procedures and to answer some of the questions that students commonly ask. Knowing your college's rules can help you avoid costly mistakes. For example, Jeremy got a new job which conflicted with one of his classes. He stopped attending the class after the third week and received an "F" in the course because he failed to complete an official withdrawal form. If Jeremy had known the rules, he wouldn't find himself with an "F" on his transcript—instead he would have received a "W" for "withdrawal."

Exercise 1-4 Getting acquainted with your college's academic requirements and procedures

Use your college's catalog and/or student handbook to answer the following questions. As you respond to each question, write in the margin any additional questions that come to mind. Try to answer each question even if doesn't immediately apply to you; it may apply to you at some point in the future or to a student you'd like to help some day.

1. What is the last day you can add a class?

2. What is the last day you can drop a class?

3. What is the school's procedure on dropping classes? What is the refund policy after dropping a class?

4. Sidney completed 85% of his course before he was hospitalized with pneumonia. He did not complete his final paper or final exam. Explain your school's policy on handling situations like Sidney's.

5. What is your college's policy about repeating courses to improve a grade?

6. Does your college have an appeal process that allows you to challenge a grade you feel you have wrongfully received? If so, explain the policy.

7. Does your college offer CLEP (College Level Examination Program) tests or "test-out" exams? If so, explain what they are and what office(s) administer(s) them.

8. Does your college allow you to "audit" or participate in a class without the obligation of grading but rather just for the opportunity to benefit from the class participation? If so, explain the procedure to "audit" a class.

    _____

    _____

    _____

    _____

    _____

9. What is your college's attendance policy?

    _____

    _____

10. What college office would you talk to to get information about transferring courses from another college to this college?

    _____

    _____

11. What is your college's policy on cheating and plagiarism?

    _____

    _____

    _____

    _____

12. Explain the grading system your college uses (letter grades, withdrawal, incomplete, test-out, CLEP, etc.).

    _____

    _____

    _____

13. Imagine that you received the following grades this term: English—A, Math—B, College 101—C, Fundamentals of Business Computers—D, and Management—F. Use your college's system for calculating grade point average (GPA) and calculate your GPA for the five courses.

    _____

    _____

    _____

    _____

14. What is meant by a cumulative GPA?

    _____

    _____

15. What is the minimum GPA you can have to graduate?

    _____

    _____

16. What are the graduation requirements for your major?

    _____

    _____

17. Does your school have probation and suspension policies? If so, explain them.

    _____

    _____

    _____

18. List all the courses you must take to complete your major. If they must be completed in any particular order, list them in that order.

_____
_____
_____
_____
_____
_____
_____
_____
_____
_____

19. Does your college offer any special recognition to students who demonstrate academic excellence (dean's list, scholarships, honors awards)? List at least three.

_____
_____
_____

20. Review your college's calendar and complete the following.

a. List all holidays the school will be closed this term.

_____
_____
_____

b. List the times and dates of your final exams.

_____
_____
_____

c. What is the first day of school next term?

_____

d. What are the registration dates for the next term?

_____
_____

21. What is the tuition of your college per course? Per term? What is the tuition per year?

_____
_____
_____

22. Explain the difference between associate and bachelor degrees. How many credit hours are required for each degree?

_____
_____
_____
_____
_____

23. Review the associate and bachelor degree programs your college offers. List three associate degree programs and three bachelor degree programs that are appealing to you.

_____

_____

_____

_____

24. What is developmental education?

_____

_____

25. What developmental education courses does your college offer?

_____

_____

_____

_____

26. What is the difference in the general education requirements between an associate and a bachelor degree program?

_____

_____

_____

27. Does your college offer cooperative education? If so, explain the program and the admission requirements.

_____

_____

_____

STUDENT SERVICES

Most colleges offer a wide variety of services that are already paid for in your activity fee. Most of the services are free of charge or have minimal fees simply because the college wants to help you stay in college and succeed. These services may include counseling, tutoring, medical exams and prescriptions, assistance to disabled students, transportation, child care, financial aid, reading, writing, and math assistance centers, computer labs and assistants, career services, extracurricular activities, and student organizations and activities. Latisha had a sore throat and stopped by the student health center to see if she could get some cold medicine. To her surprise, there was a physician on staff who diagnosed strep throat and filled an antibiotic prescription for Latisha. She didn't realize that her college activity fee covered this service at no extra charge. The following exercise will help you get acquainted with your college's services.

Exercise 1-5 Getting acquainted with your college's student services

1. Does your college provide career services? Where is the office, what are the hours, and what services do they provide?

_____

_____

_____

_____

_____

2. Does your college offer services for disabled students? If so, where do you apply for these services?

_____
_____

3. What transportation systems serve your college?

_____
_____

4. Are child care services available at your college? If so, explain what services are available.

_____
_____
_____

5. What tutoring services does your college offer? How do you apply for tutoring?

_____
_____
_____
_____

6. List all computer labs and briefly describe their services.

_____
_____
_____
_____
_____
_____
_____
_____

7. If you have difficulty with math, what services does your college provide to assist you? Who do you contact for assistance?

_____
_____
_____

8. If you have difficulty with writing or reading, what services does your college provide to assist you? Who do you contact for assistance?

_____
_____
_____

9. What assistance does your college provide for ESL (English as a Second Language) students? Who do you contact for assistance?

_____
_____
_____

10. Where is your financial aid office located? Briefly describe the types of financial aid available through this office.

_____

_____

_____

_____

_____

_____

11. What health services does your college offer?

_____

_____

_____

_____

_____

_____

12. What counseling services does your college offer?

_____

_____

_____

_____

_____

_____

13. What activities and services are available at your college's student union or activity center?

_____

_____

_____

_____

_____

_____

_____

_____

14. What extracurricular activities are available at your college?

_____

_____

_____

_____

_____

15. What intercollegiate sports are available at your college?

_____

_____

_____

_____

16. Does your college have a student government body? Where are they located? How do you get involved?

    _____

    _____

    _____

17. Of all the student organizations available at your college, list the three that interest you most and how you can contact them.

    _____

    _____

    _____

18. Who would you contact to start a new student organization?

    _____

19. List the hours of your college library.

    _____

    _____

    _____

20. What types of recreational facilities are available on your campus (gym, weight room, track, tennis courts, pool room, swimming pool, racquet ball)?

    _____

    _____

    _____

    _____

    _____

Whatever challenges you're facing, you're not alone. Many students hesitate to seek services from their college, or even just talk to a friend, because they are embarrassed or doubt that anyone can help them. An important part of achieving success, though, is knowing how to ask for help and support when you need it. Jaime was losing a lot of sleep over his English exam before he decided to talk to his professor. "He stayed after class with me for twenty minutes, helping me review the material," says Jaime. "That was a big help." Another student, Gina, was confused by her financial aid forms and even considered dropping out of school, rather than admit she was having trouble with them. She mentioned her feelings to a friend—who, it turned out, had had the same problem. She convinced Gina to get help from the financial aid office. "As soon as I confided in someone, I felt better—like a weight was lifted off my shoulders," Gina says. "I don't know why I kept it bottled up for so long." Remember, asking for help isn't a weakness; it's a strength. Successful students know when to ask for help.

Exercise 1-6 Getting to know your campus support services

Working with another student, choose one of the services mentioned in the previous exercise. Contact the service and set up an appointment to learn more about the services offered. Take notes on what you learn and report your findings back to the class. As other students report their findings, and as you progress through the remainder of this section, create a directory for as many of the services as possible. Part of the purpose of this exercise is to get to know your fellow students and begin building a support system that can help all of you meet any challenge.

YOUR MORGAN NETWORK ACCOUNT

All Morgan students need a Morgan Network Account in order to use campus computers, email and Blackboard. You will also need this account if you bring a wireless computer/device to campus and wish to use Morgan's wireless network. It is very important that you keep your account up to date. Your user name will always remain the same. Your password expires every 90 days; *you* must make an effort to change your password before it expires.

Your Username and Password

Your **user name** is the same as the beginning part of your Morgan email address (before the @ sign). If you do not know your user name do the following:

- Access WebSIS via the Morgan home page: http://www.morgan.edu
- Enter the Secure Area: User Name = Student ID#, PIN = Date of Birth MMDDYY
- Click on the Personal Information Menu
- Click on View Email Address
- Your Morgan Network user name is the same as the beginning part of your Morgan email address—the part before the @ sign.

For Example: Jason Smith's user name is jasmi89

If you have never used your account, your initial **Password** is the **first 3 letters of your first name, the last four digits of your Student ID#, the last 3 letters of your last name.** Capitalize the first letter of the string. Using the example above, Jason Smith's password would be Jas8876ith.

Keep Your Morgan Network Account Up to Date:

Use **http://resetmypwd.morgan.edu** to keep your account up to date. Passwords expire every 90 days! Make sure you use this website to keep your password current. You MUST set up your security questions in order to use this website! Follow these instructions to set up your security questions:

Self-Service Password Management

The Morgan State University e-mail password system is a self-service system similar to those commonly used for commercial websites. Once you have answered two security questions from a list of choices and entered a third question and answer that are personal to you (this is your profile), you will be able to:

- Create a new password if you forgot your password or if your password expired. (Passwords expire every 90 days or 4 times a year)
- Change your password.
- Unlock your account if you tried more than 3 times to enter your password

NOTE: Passwords must be at least 8 characters in length with at least one capital letter and one number. If you are unable to resolve your password problem, call the HELP Desk at 443-885-4357 or e-mail helpdesk@morgan.edu.

**Forgot My Password or
Change My Password**

Unlock My Account   **My Security Questions**

- Click on "My Security Questions"
- Log in
- Complete the three security questions

• **Make sure you remember the answers to your questions. Write them down!**

Once you have set up your security questions you should return to http://resetmypwd.morgan.edu to change your password. Click "Change My Password" to change your password. If you attempt to log in unsuccessfully three times, you will get locked out. You can use the reset site to unlock your account. If you accidentally let your password expire, you can still use the reset site to change it.

Accessing Technology Resources

Use your Morgan Network user name/password for:

Blackboard: http://morgan.blackboard.com

Email: http://email.morgan.edu

Computer Labs: Found in *all* academic buildings, the library, and several residence halls. The Student Center has an internet café on the first floor near the information desk.

Your Morgan Email

Your Morgan email address is username@morgan.edu. You are required to use your Morgan email address for all Morgan business, including communicating with your professors, classmates and Blackboard administrators. University departments such as Financial Aid and Residence Life will contact you via your Morgan email address.

Getting HELP

Morgan Network Account/Passwords:

HELP Desk 443.885.4357

For Blackboard Account Issues, your Blackboard Administrators:

Karen Rubinstein: karen.rubinstein@morgan.edu, x1103
Sabah Karam: sabah.karam@morgan.edu, x4597 or text/voice 443.267.8885
Office Location: Library 212

Lavern Woodland: lavern.woodland@morgan.edu, x3512
Office Location: Calloway 313

For General Questions

Ask the Bear http://www.morgan.edu. Look for the Ask the Bear logo on any Morgan webpage! The bear has answers to your technology questions, as well as questions about other services on campus.

BLACKBOARD 9

Blackboard is Morgan's Learning Management System (LMS). You'll use Blackboard to access your course syllabus, course material, as well as to interact and communicate with classmates. Use your Morgan Network account user name/password to log on to Blackboard.

All new Morgan students automatically receive a Blackboard account at the start of the fall semester. However, there will occasionally be students who do not yet have an account. If you are able to log in to your Morgan email but get an "authentification error" when you try to log in to Blackboard, you may need to get a Blackboard account. Send an email to any of the Blackboard administrators with your Morgan user name, and specify that you need a Blackboard account.

Logging in to Bb9

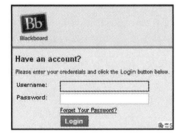

Enter your Morgan User Name and Password. Click the "Login" button.

The Blackboard Welcome Screen

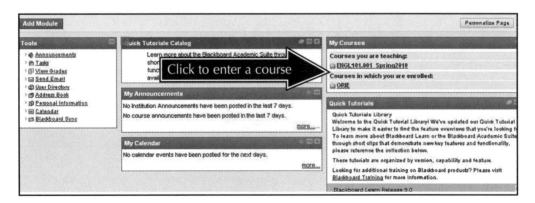

Get Blackboard Announcements and Notifications on Facebook or on Your iPhone

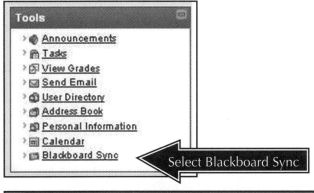

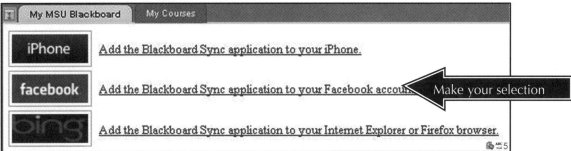

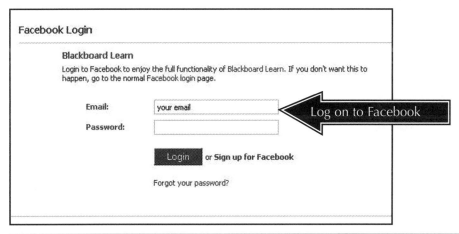

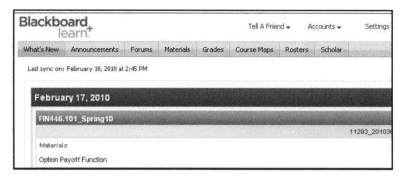

In Facebook you will see a list of your Blackboard courses. Use the tabs at the top to select announcements, materials, grades etc.

The next time you log into Facebook, click Applications. Then click the Blackboard Application. You will see your course list, as shown above.

Tour of a Blackboard Course

Click on the menu areas to view them.

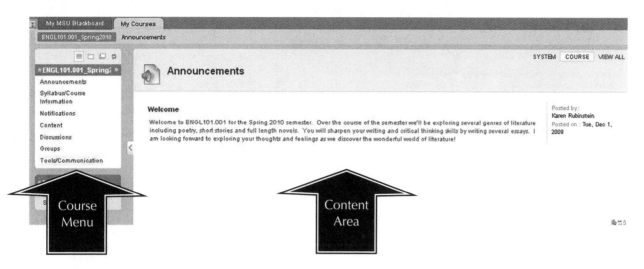

Tour of the Course Menu

Announcements	View timely Announcements by day, week, or month
Syllabus/Course Information	View your syllabus and other information about the course
Notifications	View a To-Do List, Task List, Course Calendar, Alerts
Content	Contains content related material
Discussions	The Blackboard Discussion board—interact w/classmates
Groups	Participate in small groups
Tools/Communication	Find your Grades, Email, Blogs, Journals and other tools used in the course

Tour of the Content Area

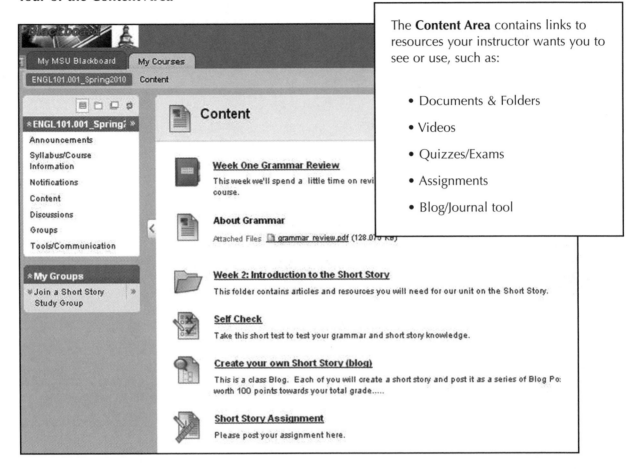

Note: Some instructors may add additional content areas to the course menu, or rename existing content areas.

Turn in an Assignment

You will find your assignments in the Content area. Your instructor should inform you if the assignments are located in another content area he/she has added.

worth 100 points towards your total grade.....

Short Story Assignment
Please post your assignment here.

Click the Assignment Link

The Assignment Tool opens with the Name and other information about the assignment.

Name:	Short Story Assignment
Instructions	Please post your assignment here.
Due Date	February 19, 2010 1:34:00 PM EST
Points Possible	100

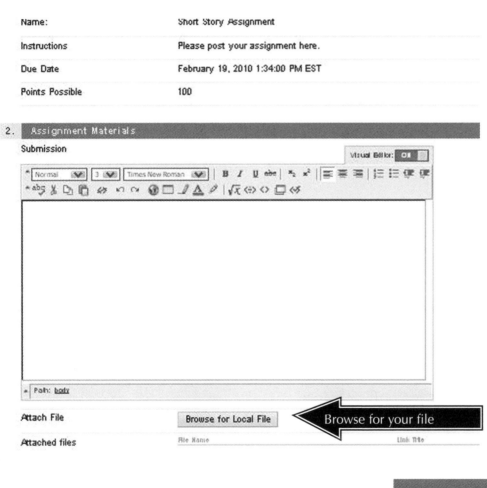

Use Email

Use the email feature to contact your instructor or other classmates. **Blackboard only sends email.** Use your Morgan email (http://webmail.morgan.edu) to view email from your instructor or classmates.

The email tool is located in the Tools/Communication area.

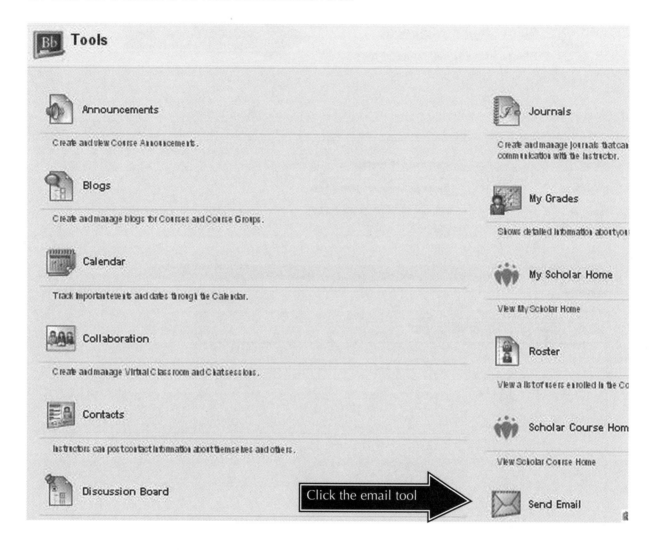

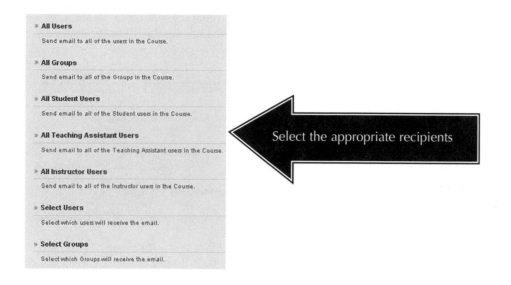

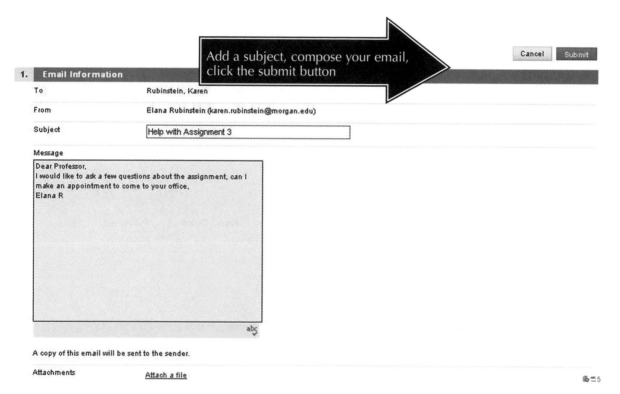

You can also add an attachment to any email.

Use the Discussion Board

Click the Discussions link from the course menu. The Discussion board is organized into forums. You will see the forums listed on the Discussion Board page, as well as a description, the total number of posts, any unread posts and the number of participants.

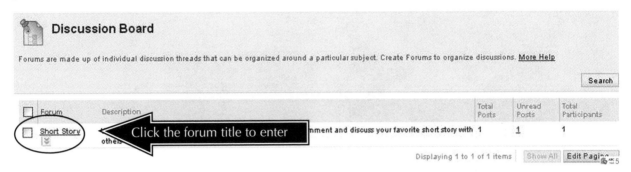

Once you open the forum you will see any threads that have been posted. A thread is like a conversation; several students can post messages in a thread. You can reply to posts w/in a thread, or create your own thread.

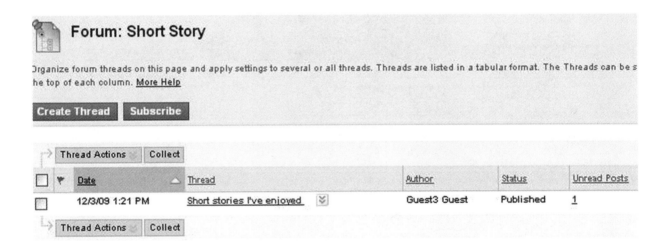

Create a Thread

Click the Create Thread button. Provide a subject and your message text. Click the Submit button when you have finished.

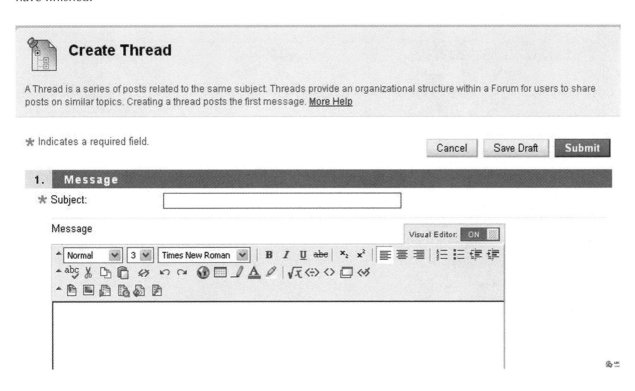

You will see your thread added to the forum screen:

Viewing a Thread

Click a thread title to view any posts in the thread.

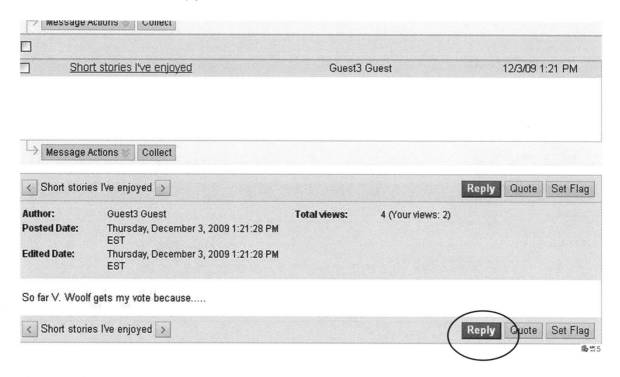

The image below illustrates a thread with one post in it. Use the **reply** button to respond to that post.

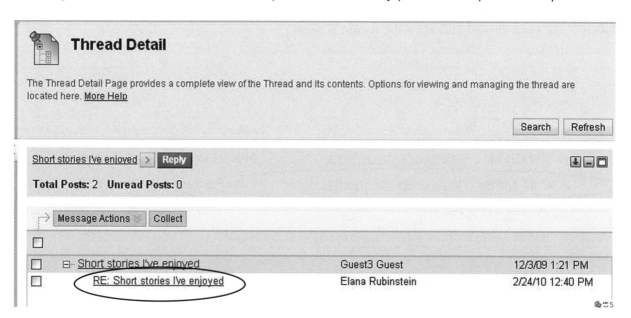

Your response will display on the Thread Detail screen. Notice it is slightly indented.

LEARNING CAMPUS CULTURE

Using Your Placement Office

One of the greatest benefits of a college is its placement services. Your college's placement staff members are experts at helping you conduct a job search in your field, either while in school or after graduation. If starting or advancing a career is part of your plan, your placement office has the know-how to make it happen. Some schools offer a career development program, class, or seminar. Sometimes these courses are required and sometimes they are optional.

Start taking advantage of your placement office's services right away. Talk to the staff about finding a job, while you're a student, if you need to find one. Even if you're not looking for a job right away, your placement office will offer services to help you develop the all-important job search skills that can help anyone—at any stage of life—make the most of their career potential. These skills take time to develop, and the sooner you start learning them, the sooner you'll become an expert. You can begin developing a first-class resume or portfolio. You can develop interview skills and learn about the employers in your area and elsewhere. You can begin practicing for any licensing or hiring exams you might be required to take.

Developing these skills will begin paying off right away. If you're on a new career path, examining the job prospects in your field will help you see how your coursework relates to what these employers want—a key to staying motivated as a student. Through your placement office, you have access to the best resource for developing the skills you'll need to build the career you want. If it's a job you want, make your placement office one of the first stops during your first couple of weeks in school. Section 9 will focus in depth on career assessment and job search skills.

Working with the System

Finding and using services in your college, as with most organizations, means dealing with a system of many rules and regulations. Sometimes it may seem as if all the rules and regulations get in the way of your education. Perhaps you simply want to change classes, and you can't understand why you have to run around

---

Tips . . . For Making the System Work for You

- Know the rules. Review the guidelines for student behavior and academic performance in your college catalog or in the exercise earlier in this section. Take note of deadlines for class registration and for adding and dropping. Know your college's refund policy. Check these deadlines at the start of each term.

- Keep a file containing your student handbook, college catalog, financial aid information, and enrollment information. Save copies of all of your tests, papers, and project evaluations in case you have questions in the future about your grades.

- Get to know the administrators and staff on campus. Administrative staff often can be a great help when you really need it, and you never know when that will be.

- Keep trying. Sometimes you'll have trouble getting what you want from your college, even though you have your objective clearly in mind. You may get the feeling that the staff person you're dealing with just might be having a bad day or may not have the power to get around the rules. Try coming back when another staff person is on duty. Ask to speak to a higher-level administrator. Speak with your advisor or other students to see if they know of a way to help you. Remain calm, courteous, and patient. A positive attitude will help you succeed in the long run.

---

school collecting signatures, filling out forms, and applying for refunds. But the college administration views this differently. Each form is necessary to keep every student's information straight and to ensure that one office knows what another office is doing with your record. Breaking one of the rules or omitting a signature throws off the whole record-keeping system. For example, if your class drop forms aren't filled out correctly, you may end up with an "F" on your record automatically.

If you need assistance that your school can't offer directly, you'll probably find the services you need in your local community. For example, local organizations, churches, and governments frequently offer such services as child care assistance, crisis hotlines, health services, and substance abuse counseling. The student services personnel at your school can help you find these and other services.

So far, you've seen how social and academic involvement in your education are keys to success. The next step is to carefully think about the challenges that you're likely to face, then to develop strategies to deal with them.

FINANCING YOUR EDUCATION

Continuing your education creates numerous financial challenges. First, there is the challenge of paying tuition for your educational program. If you're like most students, you've reached deeply into whatever savings you have, and, in addition, you may have taken out a loan—perhaps going deeply into debt for the first time in your life.

Second, you may have given up income by cutting back on work hours, reasoning it's better to focus on education to get a job that you really want when you finish. This lost income places even greater demands on your finances, particularly if you live on your own or if you have a family to support. And just like most students, your success in college, and in the rest of your life, may depend on improving your money management skills.

Know Where Your Money Goes

Have you ever asked yourself, "Where does all my money go?" Knowing where your money goes is a first step to effective money management. Exercise 1-7 will engage you in a personal accounting and evaluation of your expenditures for one week.

Exercise 1-7 Where my money goes

Over the next week, record every item that you purchase. Keep a small notebook with you at all times to record each purchase at the time you make it. Create columns in your notebook to write down the date of your purchase, the name of the item, and the cost. At the end of the week, total the amount you spent that week.

After recording your expenditures for one week, answer the following questions to evaluate your spending habits.

1. List the most frequently purchased items and the total amount you spent on that item for the week. Note April's list for an example.

    April: <u>Drinks and snacks: $42.50, gas: $75.84, eating out with kids: $58.78, groceries: $77.90</u>

    Your list:

    _____
    _____
    _____
    _____

2. What important discoveries did you make about how you spent your money last week?

    _____

    _____

    _____

    _____

3. Are there any changes you would like to make in the way you spend your money? If so, what are they?

    _____

    _____

    _____

    _____

You just had a brief look at your expenditures in a typical week while you're in college. Sometimes, just becoming aware of your spending habits can encourage you to make better plans and budget how you want to spend your money. The next step to managing your money is to develop a budget that compares your expenses with the money you bring in. Exercise 1-8 will help you get started on a budget.

Exercise 1-8 My monthly budget

Complete the monthly budget form that follows. Add other budget items as necessary. You can use the same form to create a yearly budget.

Ideally, you're spending less money than you're bringing in. If this is not the case, you need to find ways to reduce your expenditures. Many students find that, by reducing expenses, they can work fewer hours, freeing up more time and energy for college study.

Your college's financial aid office may offer additional advice on managing your money better. The advice will cover skills like budgeting and understanding student financial aid alternatives. Your college knows how financial troubles can cause students to drop out of school. Even after you graduate, your school is interested in seeing that you have the financial skills necessary for success, especially if you've used a federally guaranteed student loan. Your school is eager to help you develop financial skills. Take advantage of this unique opportunity to learn these lifelong skills.

Budget Planning Worksheet			
Estimated Income	**Monthly Amount**	**Estimated Expenses**	**Monthly Amount**
Income Sources		**Housing**	
• Net Salary		• Rent/Mortgage	
• Grants		• Gas/Electricity	
• Scholarships		• Water	
• Loans		• Telephone/Cell Phone	
• Family		• Other	
• Other		**Food**	
		• Groceries	
		• Misc.	
		Transportation	
		• Car Payment	
		• Car Repair	
		• Car Insurance	
		• Bus/Subway	
		• Other	
		Health	
		• Doctors	
		• Insurance	
		• Prescriptions	
		• Other	
		Dependent Care	
		• Child Care	
		Personal/Miscellaneous	
		• Clothing	
		• Laundry	
		• Dry Cleaning	
		• Personal Items (toiletries, etc.)	
		• Other	
		Entertainment	
		• Movies/Concerts	
		• Eating Out	
		• Other	
		Debt Obligations	
		• Student Loans	
		• Credit Cards	
		• Other	
		Emergencies	
TOTAL INCOME		**TOTAL EXPENSES**	

Adapted from the U.S. Department of Education, "Budget Planning Worksheet,"
http:www.studentaid.ed.gov/students/publications/repaying_loans/2003_2004/english/pdf/budgetworksheet.pdf.

Tips . . . For Reducing Expenses

- Save time and money on meals by bringing them from home. If you cook your meals, try to cook enough food for several days so you can take advantage of bulk prices and spend less time cooking.

- Think about the long-term costs of small expenses. Kelly was shocked to realize that, over the course of a semester, she had spent over $200 on soda, candy, and chips—money that could have gone, instead, toward tuition or school supplies.

- Make a list of expenses and identify any items that you can do without. Decide whether there are less expensive alternatives to the items you buy.

- Number each item on your list of expenses according to how important it is to you. When money gets tight, you'll know which items need to be taken care of first. For example, Harold listed some of his expenses in the following order: (1) rent, (2) meals, (3) transportation, (4) school supplies, (5) new car stereo speakers, (6) new sneakers. When money got tight during his first term in school, he realized that new sneakers and his new car speakers would have to wait a while.

- Continue writing down your purchases. Simply keeping track may discourage unnecessary buying.

- Clip coupons and watch for sales. If you shop for groceries regularly, you may be able to save quite a lot by clipping coupons from the newspaper. Watch for clothing sales as well. Remember, though, that buying an item you don't really need, just because it's on sale, is still a waste when money's short.

- Avoid using credit cards. Although many credit cards don't charge interest if you pay all of your charges each month, most people let their credit debt build up from month to month. The interest on even a small amount of credit card debt can add up to hundreds of dollars a year. If you must use credit cards, watch for cards with lower interest rates and lower annual fees. But paying cash makes you more aware of spending and keeps you out of debt.

- Look for free entertainment, such as activities on campus.

When I called my friend at his dorm, I was somewhat surprised by his answering machine message: "Hi, this is Dave," it began. "If it's the phone company, I sent the money. If it's Mom or Dad, please send me money. If it's a friend, you still owe me money. If it's financial aid, you didn't loan me enough money. If it's a female, leave a message. . . and don't worry, I've got plenty of money!"

—Source Unknown

Coping with Credit Cards: Going Plastic

Garret Jones went plastic when he was a freshman. He already had one credit card from his parents, but he signed up for a second credit card at the student union. The credit card marketer offered him a free CD and told him he could even pay for his spring break trip with his new card. It was almost as if someone else would be paying for the trip. Garret funded his Daytona Beach spring break trip with his new credit card. He charged the hotel, food, gas, and partying expenses. Sounds like something a young college kid would do, doesn't it? Do you know any older adults who have stretched or exceeded their credit limit by buying a car, home entertainment system, a vacation, or a house that was beyond their budget?

Garret not only had his spring break trip on his card; he had his books, some GAP clothes, a restaurant bill, and concert tickets. He reached his credit card limit of $2,000. Let's calculate how long it would take Garret to pay off his $2,000 debt by paying his minimum monthly payment and $10 extra each month.

If Garret Paid Minimum Payment*		If Garret Paid $10 Extra Per Month*	
Current Balance:	$2,000.00	Current Balance:	$2,000.00
Minimum Monthly Payment:	$40.00	Minimum Monthly Payment:	$50.00
Annual Percentage Rate (APR):	19.00%	Annual Percentage Rate (APR):	19.00%
Total Number of Monthly Payments Until Payoff:	335	Total Number of Monthly Payments Until Payoff:	122
Time Until Payoff:	27 Years 11 Months	Time Until Payoff:	10 Years 2 Months
Total Interest Paid:	$5,497.80	Total Interest Paid:	$1,983.88
Total Amount Paid:	$7,497.80	Total Amount Paid:	$3,983.88

*These calculations assume that Garret doesn't make additional charges.

Garret did not realize how much extra he would have to pay if he couldn't afford to pay off his credit card quickly. It's easy to see why the credit card business is a lucrative one.

Now Garret is in a dilemma; he has no extra income, and he can't afford the minimum monthly payments. Suddenly, he's facing the darker side of credit cards. Garret was able to pay two minimum monthly payments, but he missed the third payment. The card company slapped him with a $20 late fee. Then Garret bounced a couple of checks, and his bank charged him $20 for each overdraft fee. His credit card monthly payments kept adding late fees. The credit card company wasn't worried, because they expected Garret to call mom or dad to bail him out—surely mom and dad didn't want him to have a bad credit rating. Garret's mom and dad were struggling with their own bill before they inherited this new debt from Garret.

Do you think this won't happen to you? Even Garret's credit card debt was a little lower than the average college student credit card debt. According to a December 2000 study by the Nellie Mae Corporation, a leading national provider of higher education loans, the average student (aged 18–25) credit card debt was $2,738, up from $1,879 in 1998. The study also indicated that the more credit cards students had, the higher their credit card debt.

All this bad news does not mean that credit cards are all bad. You need credit cards to make hotel reservations, to rent a car, make on-line or phone purchases. It's also important to establish a good credit history. A good credit history is important to your financial stability when starting a family, buying a home, starting a business, buying a car and, in some cases, getting that first professional job. A bad credit rating may seem less important now, but it may keep you from opening a new checking account, getting another credit card, renting a car, moving into an apartment, getting a home mortgage, purchasing furniture, computers or anything on credit. If a company does extend credit to you, it may be at double the interest rate when you are identified as a high risk.

Credit card companies do not send you a card because they're trying to help you with your finances. They send you credit cards because they want to make their shareholders happy. And their shareholders are happy when you have to pay 18–20+% interest. What this means is that the clothes you charged at Abercrombie and Fitch might be out of style before you finish paying for them. Read the following tips for coping with credit cards.

The more you can pay, the less interest you will pay. Let's take a look at what Garret's payoff might look like if he could afford to double his payments.

If Garret Paid Minimum Payment*		If Garret Paid $40 Extra Per Month*	
Current Balance:	$2,000.00	Current Balance:	$2,000.00
Minimum Monthly Payment:	$40.00	Minimum Monthly Payment:	$80.00
Annual Percentage Rate (APR):	19.00%	Annual Percentage Rate (APR):	19.00%
Total Number of Monthly Payments Until Payoff:	335	Total Number of Monthly Payments Until Payoff:	43
Time Until Payoff:	**27 Years 11 Months**	**Time Until Payoff:**	**3 Years 7 Months**
Total Interest Paid:	**$5,497.80**	**Total Interest Paid:**	**$700.90**
Total Amount Paid:	**$7,497.80**	**Total Amount Paid:**	**$2700.90**

It makes an incredible difference if you can either afford to or discipline yourself to make extra payments. If Garret could have paid his minimum monthly at $40 per month and also pay an extra $40 per month, his interest would be only $700.90, compared to $5,497.80 in interest, paying only the minimum monthly payment. Of course, if Garret could have paid the entire amount within the allotted 25 days, he would pay no interest. The best policy is not to use credit cards if you can't pay off the entire bill, except in emergencies.

Tips . . . For Coping with Credit Cards

- Make your credit card payments on time. Many credit cards charge you late fees.

- Pay your entire bill, or as much as you can. Minimum monthly payments on many major credit cards are only about 2 percent of what you owe. It will take you years to pay them off at that rate, and if you keep using the card meanwhile, your debt is guaranteed to grow.

- If you max out your card, don't start another credit card—pay off your current one.

- If you do have more than one credit card debt, pay off the debt with the highest rate of interest first. Then attack the debt with the next highest rate.

- Avoid frequent trips to the ATM. Especially avoid those that charge $1–$2 fees just to use them.

- Try to get into the habit of using a debit card rather than your credit card. Your debit card withdraws money you have in your checking or savings account.

- Consider purchasing a SmartCard. SmartCards are prepaid cards, and you can't spend more than you paid for them.

- If you can't afford your purchase in cash, you probably can't afford to use a credit card either.

- Call your credit card company and ask for a lower rate. If you have a good payment history, you may qualify for a lower promotional rate. If that doesn't work, tell them your other credit cards charge a lower fee and that if they won't, you will cancel the account.

- When in debt, consider using your income tax refund, bonuses, or birthday money to pay off your debt. Paying off your debt will give you greater benefits—less interest to pay and less stress as you drive down your debt.

- Next time you think about using a credit card to pay for your tuition and books, consider applying for a federally guaranteed student loan. These loans may require more paperwork but, in the long run, they are more cost effective.

- If the credit card company sends you checks, don't use them. Companies can charge you fees to use these checks and later charge you interest on an unpaid balance.

- Remember that financial responsibility pays you. The more you pay off, the less interest you pay. Outsmart the card companies—make it your goal to never pay interest.

- Calculate your credit card pay-off options and much more at www.bankrate.com/calculators/managing-debt/credit-card-payoff-calculator.aspx.

- Learn more about establishing good credit and credit reports at Money Matters (http://money.usnews.com/money/blogs/my-money/2014/01/02/4-things-credit-card-newbies-should-do-to-establish-good-credit).

Working Through School

Many students work while attending college classes. Although working may be necessary, it also takes time away from your studying. If you're working full-time or part-time, or if you're considering it, think about how you might adjust your work to make the most of your education.

Why work? Perhaps you must work to cover necessary expenses. Review your budget and list of expenses to determine if you can reduce the amount of money you have to make, even if it means putting off saving for a car or a new stereo. You might discover that you can get by with a little less. You might consider reducing the hours you work, if a lower income will still cover the essentials.

Is the job right for you? It's best if your job fits into your career plans. If you're in a job that doesn't relate to your education, it may be worth giving up some income to switch to a job that fits your interests and career goals—that is, if you can spare the income. Working in a relevant job allows you to start applying what you're learning in college. You're also more likely to find support from your employer in terms of adapting your work hours to your college demands. Some employers may even offer salary incentives, a job promotion, or tuition aid to help you through your program. Whatever the job, consider whether the work environment will hinder your performance in school. If you leave work too emotionally or physically exhausted to deal with your studies, perhaps it's worth finding a different job with the same or a different employer. Your financial aid office, student services office, or placement office probably will have helpful information about jobs to fit your needs.

Are you using your work time wisely? If you work while you're in college, make the most of your work time. First, maintain an upbeat and committed attitude toward work. An upbeat attitude on the job will carry over into your studies. You're more likely to see interesting connections between what you're learning in school and the workplace. Make the most of it by practicing people skills: cooperation, teamwork, conflict resolution, and leadership techniques. Tanya's experience in sharing responsibilities with three other workers at an insurance company helped her coordinate group projects in her office technology coursework. "I remember the first day our group met to work on our word processing project," she says. "For a minute, the four of us just sat there wondering where to start. It was clear that we needed a leader. I figured if I can organize a four-person team to do photocopying at the office, I should be able to coordinate this. The whole group seemed relieved when I started making a plan that we could follow."

Second, become the best employee you can be. Employers are always looking for great employees and are frequently willing to take big risks for those who show promise. And a glowing recommendation from your current employer may be the key to getting the job you really want.

Finally, if you're looking for a job, it's worth talking with your placement office about strategies for finding the job you want. Be clear about how much money you need to make and about how many hours you want to work. In addition to the posting of advertised jobs, your placement office can help you find out about good companies in the local area that might be interested in you. In Section 9 you'll find detailed suggestions about how to find a job. In particular, you'll find valuable tips on preparing for an interview, including questions to ask, what to say, and how to dress—suggestions that can pay off right away.

IDENTITY THEFT: WHAT YOU SHOULD KNOW*

How can someone steal your identity? Identity theft occurs when someone uses your personal information such as your name, Social Security Number (SSN), credit card number or other identifying information without your permission to commit fraud or other crimes.

Identity theft is a serious crime. People whose identities have been stolen can spend months or years—and their hard-earned money—cleaning up the mess thieves have made of their good name and credit record. In the meantime, victims may lose job opportunities, be refused loans, education, housing or cars, or even get arrested for crimes they didn't commit.

Can you prevent identity theft from occurring? As with any crime, you cannot completely control whether you will become a victim. But, according to the Federal Trade Commission (FTC), you can minimize your risk by managing your personal information cautiously and with heightened sensitivity.

How identity theft occurs

Skilled identity thieves use a variety of methods to gain access to your personal information. For example:

- They get information from businesses or other institutions by stealing records from their employer, bribing an employee who has access to these records, or hacking into the organization's computers.

- They rummage through your trash, or the trash of businesses or dumps in a practice known as "dumpster diving."

- They obtain credit reports by abusing their employer's authorized access to credit reports or by posing as a landlord, employer or someone else who may have a legal right to the information.

- They steal credit and debit card numbers as your card is processed by using a special information storage device in a practice known as "skimming."

- They steal wallets and purses containing identification and credit and bank cards.

- They steal mail, including bank and credit card statements, pre-approved credit offers, new checks, or tax information.
- They complete a "change of address" form to divert your mail to another location.

- They steal personal information from you by posing as a legitimate business person or government official.

Once identity thieves have your personal information, they may go on spending sprees using your credit and debit cards, open a new credit card account in your name, take out auto loans in your name, establish phone or wireless service in your name, counterfeit checks or debit cards and drain your bank account, file for bankruptcy under your name, or give your name to the police during an arrest. (If they are released and don't show up for their court date, an arrest warrant could be issued in your name.) The following tips will help you minimize your risk of falling victim to identity thieves.

---

*Sources: "Federal Trade Commission Consumer Information: Identity Theft" (http://www.consumer.ftc.gov/features/feature-0014-identity-theft) and "ID Theft: What's It All About" (www.bbb.org/us/article/ftc--id-theft-what-its-all-about-4789)

Tips . . . For Minimizing Your Risk for Identity Theft

- Order a copy of your credit report from any of the three major credit bureaus and examine it for suspicious activity.

- Place passwords on your credit card, bank and phone accounts. Avoid using easily available information like your mother's maiden name, your birth date, or the last four digits of your SSN or phone number.

- Secure personal information in your home, especially if you have roommates.

- Ask about information security procedures in your workplace. Find out who has access to your personal information and verify that your records are kept in a secure location.

- Don't give out personal information over the phone, through the mail, or over the Internet unless you've initiated the contact or are sure you know who you're dealing with.

- Guard your mail and trash from theft by depositing outgoing mail in post office collection boxes (not an unsecured mailbox), removing mail from your mailbox promptly, and tearing or shredding charge receipts, copies of credit card applications or offers, insurance forms, checks and bank statements, and expired charge cards.

- Before revealing any identifying information (for example, on an application), ask how it will be used and secured and whether it will be shared with others.

- Keep your Social Security card in a secure place and give your SSN only when absolutely necessary.

- Limit the identification information and the number of credit and debit cards that you carry to what you'll actually need.

- On your computer: Update your virus protection software regularly, don't download files from strangers or click on hyperlinks from people you don't know, use a firewall and secure browser, and avoid using an automatic log-in feature that saves your user name and password.

If you think your identity has been stolen, here's what to do now:

1. Contact the fraud departments of any one of the **three major credit bureaus** to place a fraud alert on your credit file. The fraud alert requests creditors to contact you before opening any new accounts or making any changes to your existing accounts. As soon as the credit bureau confirms your fraud alert, the other two credit bureaus will be automatically notified to place fraud alerts, and all three credit reports will be sent to you free of charge. To report fraud, call and write:

    *   **Equifax**—1-800-525-6285; P.O. Box 740241, Atlanta, GA 30374-0241
    *   **Experian**—1-888-397-3742; P.O. Box 4500, Allen, TX 75013
    *   **TransUnion**—1-800-680-7289; Fraud Victim Assistance Division, TransUnion LLC, P.O. Box 2000, Chester, PA 19022-2000

2. Close the accounts that you know or believe have been tampered with or opened fraudulently. Use the **ID Theft Affidavit** (available at www.consumer.ftc.gov/articles/pdf-0094-identity-theft-affadavit.pdf) when disputing new unauthorized accounts.

3. **File a police report.** Get a copy of the report to submit to your creditors and others that may require proof of the crime.

4. **File your complaint** with the FTC. The FTC maintains a database of identity theft cases used by law enforcement agencies for investigations. Filing a complaint also helps us learn more about identity theft and the problems victims are having so that we can better assist you. You can call the FTC's Identity Theft Hotline toll-free at 1-877-IDTHEFT (438-4338).

For more in-depth information on recovering from identity theft and help with specific problems, see http://www.consumer.ftc.gov/features/feature-0014-identity-theft.

FINANCIAL AID

Education is one of the smartest investments you'll ever make, but it's also a serious investment that may affect your life for many years to come. Fortunately, by choosing a college, you're getting one of the best bargains in higher education. But using financial aid wisely can ease the financial strain of college so you can devote more time and energy to your studies. Your financial aid options may include grants that you **don't** have to pay back, loans that you **do** have to pay back, and subsidized work-study jobs.

The major source of these funds for most students is the federal government, but some funding may also be available from the state, local community, your college, or possibly your employer. Your college's financial aid office is committed to helping you find the funding you're eligible for and can help you through the process. Eligibility is based primarily on financial need and satisfactory progress through your program. In some cases, academic achievement, physical disability, and minority status can play a role.

Grants. Grants are gifts that don't have to be repaid. They generally are offered to students with the greatest financial need. The federal government is the major source of grants for college students; but it's worth checking with your financial aid officer about community, state, or college grants. If your college participates in the federal government Job Training Partnership Act program, for example, you may be eligible for a grant or other tuition assistance.

Scholarships. In some instances, scholarships are available for college students based on merit, academic achievement, or other special circumstances. These scholarships may be available from your college or be offered by foundations, government agencies, religious groups, businesses, and community organizations. Check with your financial aid officer if any scholarships are available.

Loans. For many students, loans are a major source of education funding. Education loans have the advantage of long repayment periods, of up to 10 years, and low interest rates, usually below 10 percent. The largest source of education loans, the federal guaranteed student loan program, is based mostly on need. Some loans allow you to put off repayment until after you complete your education; others require some repayment while you're in college. Other education loan options are available for parents of dependent students, although the interest rates on these loans are substantially higher.

It's important to remember that student loans must be paid back, even if you choose not to complete the program! Although your coursework may require only a number of months or a few years, if you take a loan you may be paying monthly loan payments for the next 10 years. Although studies regularly show that students who complete education beyond high school earn substantially higher wages than people who don't, the cost of your education and the financial strain it may cause should be taken very seriously. Failure to repay loans may make it difficult or impossible to rent housing or to find home mortgage or car loans, and it ultimately could lead to confiscation of your wages and your income tax refund. Carefully consider your budget and use student loans only when absolutely necessary for you to stay in school.

Work-Study. Your college may offer job opportunities for students with financial need. It may participate in the federal government's work-study program or offer other work opportunities to its students. Ask your financial aid officer if such opportunities exist at your school.

The most important financial decision regarding your education is being sure that your educational program fits your goals. A substantial number of students leave college study early in their program. In the first few weeks of each term, think seriously about your commitment to succeeding in the program. If you have doubts, either about whether the program is right for you, or whether you have the time and commitment necessary to do your best, consult with your advisor, a counselor, or some other school official. Speak to administrators in the student accounts office and in the financial aid office during the early weeks of your program and tell them about your concerns. If you then decide to leave early in the term, you may be able to back out of loan obligations or recover much of your tuition money.

Student Financial Aid and Scholarship Information on the Web. The federal government publishes an annual student guide for financial aid on the web as well as in print form. The address for the annual Funding Your Education: The Guide to Federal Student Aid is located at https://studentaid.ed.gov/sites/default/files/funding-your-education.pdf. This guide provides information on eligibility, application, deadlines, grants, loans, work-study, loan deferment, borrower responsibilities, telephone numbers, and websites. Federal Student Aid (studentaid.ed.gov), an office of the U.S. Department of Education, provides publications, fact sheets, online tools, and other resources to help you prepare and pay for college or career school.

There are also several websites that search for college scholarships. One of the Internet's largest scholarship search sites is Fastweb. It is an excellent online resource for preparing, evaluating, selecting, applying for, and financing education. The address for Fastweb is http://www.fastweb.com.

Applying for Federal Student Aid on the Web. You can complete your Free Application for Federal Student Aid (FAFSA) online at https://fafsa.ed.gov. Applying online is faster than mailing in a paper application, and you'll get your results in 7–14 days. Many times the printed application forms are mailed in with errors, but applications online will be edited for errors immediately, so you'll make fewer mistakes and you'll be able to learn sooner if you qualify for aid.

Use the FAFSA address (https://fafsa.ed.gov) and follow the onscreen instructions to complete the application. When you have completed your application, print out and sign a signature page. You and one parent (if you are a dependent) need to sign the application form. Mail the signature page to the address provided. After printing the signature page, click the "Submit My FAFSA" button. Then your screen will read, "Your application has been submitted." Note the confirmation stamp number. Also note your Expected Family Contribution (EFC). This number represents the estimated amount that you and your family will be expected to contribute toward your educational expenses for one academic year.

If you are interested in learning more about federal student aid programs, call 1-800-4-FED-AID (1-800-433-3243).

Exercise 1-9 Understanding your student loan

If you have taken a student loan, answer the following questions to clarify the conditions of your loan. If you have difficulty answering any of the questions, contact your financial aid office and set up an appointment to review your financial aid file.

1.   What kind of student loan do you have?

2.   When is the last day you may withdraw from school without owing money on your student loan?

3.   How much is your student loan for?

4.   When must you begin making payments on your loan?

5.   What will your monthly payments be when you begin repayment?

6.   How long will you be making monthly payments on your loan?

BALANCING SCHOOL, WORK, FAMILY, AND FRIENDS

Success in college requires a balance among all the demands on your time and energy, especially the demands of work, family, and friends. In the following sections are some tips from students who managed to find that balance in and out of school. You'll find additional strategies for making the most of your busy schedule in Section 2. Feel free to skip ahead to that section after you read this section.

Strategies for Work and School

Working while going to school is a necessity for many. It's challenging to maintain your best performance at both work and school. Sometimes slight adjustments can help you keep up with the demands of work and school.

Tips . . . For Managing Work and School

Many students succeed in college while working part-time and even full-time. If you are working your way through school, consider some of these suggestions for managing work and school.

- Use small blocks of free time during your workday for studying: commuting time, breaks, and meals.

- Explain your education plans to your employer and emphasize how much college means to you and that you are looking for ways to succeed in your studies and on the job.

- Consider rearranging your shifts to better fit your college schedule. Fellow employees may be willing to trade shifts or cover for you in an emergency.

- Keep your employer and fellow employees up-to-date about your schoolwork. They can be good sources of encouragement and guidance.

- Consider employment that might better fit your life as a student and your career goals if you need a job or if you're thinking of changing jobs.

- Look for opportunities on the job that may help you succeed in college, such as working more with computers, writing, or practicing a second language.

Strategies for Family and School

Many college graduates point out how important family support and cooperation were to their success in college. Depending on your family situation, a number of strategies may be helpful.

Living at home

Attending a college while living at home with parent(s) or guardian(s) presents special challenges. The demands of college study often require an adjustment to your home lifestyle. For example, if you've recently left high school, you may discover that both you and your parents are struggling to adjust to your new life. Your parent(s) may be unsure what your educational goals are. Your feelings about home, your independence, and your parents may all be changing. Your parents' feelings about you and their relationship with you may be changing as well. If you have siblings, you may have less time to spend with them. To make your home life work best for your success in school, you'll have to work through some of these adjustments.

If your parent(s) is/are unsure about your educational plans, perhaps the most important step is to gain their support for the educational goals you're trying to reach. Parents are sometimes skeptical about their child's education, especially if they don't know much about the program. Discuss with them the type of education you're pursuing. Describe the career opportunities that will be open to you when you graduate. Often parents feel better about college programs after visiting the facilities and meeting staff. Most important, let them know you're committed to working hard and graduating. If at all possible, get your parents' support. The same advice applies to siblings and extended family support.

A second major challenge for college students living at home is to create a good study environment. You'll need a quiet place to study, a place in which you can be comfortable and productive and avoid the interruptions that often occur in a home. This may mean negotiating with other family members for private time and space; for example, having a bedroom to yourself for several hours every day. Perhaps you'll need to negotiate time when the television and music will be kept turned off or on low volume so you can concentrate on your studies. Let family members know what your needs are and how important studying is to you. Keep in mind, however, that they have needs of their own. It's best if you can manage time and space for studying without asking for too great a sacrifice from others. Sometimes, when home is too distracting, it's easier and more productive to do your studying at school or at a local library. Keep trying alternate arrangements until you find a place where you can get your studying finished efficiently. Check Section 3 for suggestions on how to set up a study area, including tips on portable supplies that will make it easier to study outside your home.

For couples

Occasionally, spouses may feel threatened by your dedication to school work and therefore may not be as supportive. To remedy this, get your partner involved in your educational plans as much as possible. Share your goals and discuss the benefits of your program. This way you'll both be prepared to face the challenges that college will bring. Remember to schedule recreational time for just the two of you, and create opportunities for your partner to get to know your fellow students. Schedule time each week to share dinner and a movie, for example. Anthony used a cookout sponsored by the African-American Student Union to introduce his wife to some of his campus friends. "Before the cookout, I felt like I was living two completely separate lives," he says. "My wife didn't have any idea what my college life was like. Now that she's seen the school and met some of my classmates, she gives me more encouragement and even looks forward to hosting study sessions at our apartment."

For parents

Sharing your educational plans and goals with your children is also important. This is especially true if you're a single parent. Explain to them how important school is to your happiness and to the economic future of your family. Even young children can grasp the benefits of education—and the challenges—especially if they are in school themselves. Emphasize that your commitment to school does not lessen your love for them or how much they mean to you.

At first, you may find some resistance to these changes (from both you and your family). But most family members adapt well to a new routine, particularly if you explain why you're in college, how much you need their help, and how important your education is to the family's future. Let them know how grateful and proud you are that they are taking on more work themselves.

Tips . . . For Managing Children and School

If you're a parent, and depending on the ages of your children, you might try some of the following tips.

- If your children are in school, look for opportunities to share in each other's studies. Let them know what you're learning and pay attention to what they are learning. Look for opportunities to make studying a family effort, such as testing each other.

- Keep household chores to a minimum, doing only what's necessary to keep your home comfortable. Put off optional repairs on your home until the end of your term. Ask your children to share responsibilities appropriate for their ages, including feeding themselves snacks or preparing meals.

- Agree on and post a schedule for study hours, chores, and quiet play times in a place where all can see it. Keep a family activity calendar where everyone can see it.

- If major test or assignment deadlines are approaching, consider sending your children to a friend's house for an overnight visit so you can concentrate fully on studying.

- If you have a toddler, create a safe play area in your house so you can focus more on your studying.

Child Care

Many parents who have dropped out of college point to lack of child care as the most important factor. All parents benefit from the peace of mind that comes from knowing their children are safe and well cared for. Find reliable child care as soon as possible if you don't already have it. Have backup arrangements in case your regular child care option is interrupted. You'll find some helpful information in Table 1-4.

Table 1-4
Types of Child Care

In-home care:	Care provided in child's home for major portion of the day by a relative, friend, or paid housekeeper/caregiver. Serves any number of children of all ages.
Advantages:	• Good arrangement for night care. • Minimizes transportation problems. • Good for special care situations such as handicapped children. • May be less costly for three or more children.
Disadvantages:	• May be disrupted if caregiver becomes unavailable. • Less chance for child to be with other children. • May be expensive for less than three children.
Family day care:	Care provided in caregiver's home for major portion of the day by relative, friend, neighbor, or licensed day care provider.
Advantages:	• Family atmosphere, smaller group. • Less costly for one or two children. • Can provide interaction with other children.
Disadvantages:	• Less regulated than day care centers. • Less likely to have special facilities or range of equipment. • More susceptible to change caused by illness, moving, transportation difficulties.
Center-based:	Care provided for the major portion of the day to a group of children in an established setting or facility. Usually serves children from 20 months to 6 years—there are a few infant centers available. Types of programs differ depending on the philosophy of the center.
Advantages:	• Can make long-term arrangements. • More likely to have special facilities and range of equipment. • May have special programs for different child interests or needs.
Disadvantages:	• Will not have family atmosphere of home-based arrangement. • Larger group may not be appropriate for a particular child at a particular time. • Staff turnover may make it more difficult to keep track of who is caring for your child.
Extended day care:	Day care provided in public place (school, recreation center, community center) that serves children after and/or before school hours or when schools are not operating. May also include weekend hours.

(continued)

| Day camps: | Daytime seasonal programs serving children who return home each evening. For children 6–17 years of age; run for one or two weeks or all summer long. |
| Residential camps: | Twenty-four hour programs that run for one or two weeks or all summer long. For children 6–17 years of age. May be special needs or educational focus. |

Adapted from Melissa L. Thomas and Barbara L. Makris, *Child Care Consumer Education: A Curriculum for Working Parents* (Washington, D.C.: Wider Opportunities for Women, Inc., 1983), pp. 2–3. All rights reserved.

Find out what child care services are available. It's possible that your school has an on-site child care program. You also may find information from the following sources.

- Obtain referrals from your student services office, students, instructors, school staff, friends, co-workers, or family.

- The human/social services department in your local area can give you the names and telephone numbers of licensed day care providers and centers closest to your home, work, or school. The department's phone number is usually in the government listings in the White Pages.

- Check your local telephone book's Yellow Pages under the headings "Day Care, Schools, etc." for a list of the centers/schools offering child care in your area.

- You may find advertisements for child care providers in the classified section of your local newspaper under "Babysitting/Child Care Available." Ads also may appear in local supermarkets, laundromats, libraries, or community centers. Parents also may place ads seeking child care.

When selecting a child care arrangement, consider the following issues. The cost of the child care must be within your family budget. You might be eligible for help toward the cost of care through government subsidies, scholarship funds, or sliding fee scales. If you are a working parent, you may be eligible for a child care tax credit. Check with your student services office and your local human/social services department.

It is best if child care is conveniently located close to either home or school or on your commuting route, depending on your schedule. You should consider transportation expenses, also. Find a child care arrangement that operates during hours appropriate for your needs. Some providers offer extended evening and morning hours, weekends and overnight, and before and after school. Consider the demands of work, school, and other obligations when figuring out the child care hours you'll need.

You can learn a lot about family and center-based day care providers during initial phone conversations and visits. Table 1-5 outlines some important questions to ask and things to look for.

Table 1-5
Child Care Providers: What to Look For and What to Ask

Call first and ask . . .

- Is there an opening for my child?
- What hours and days are you open?
- Where are you located?
- How much do you charge?
- When is payment due?
- Do you charge for holidays, absences due to vacations or illness, or late pickups?
- How many children do you care for?
- How much child care experience and education do you have?
- How many adults care for the children?
- What ages do you serve?
- Must a child be toilet trained?

In a home setting . . .

- Are there others living in the home?
- Who and what age are they?
- Who, besides the provider, may be caring for my child?
- Will my child be taken out of the home while in your care?
- Are there pets or smoking in the home?

Visit and look for . . .

- Positive interactions between caregiver and children.
- Children getting lots of attention.
- Children who are happy and comfortable with their caregiver.
- Clean, safe, and healthy indoor and outdoor spaces.
- Safety features such as gates on stairs, caps on electrical outlets, and a locked cabinet for medicine, poisons and cleaning products.
- A variety of toys and learning materials, such as books, puzzles, blocks, and climbing equipment, that your child will find interesting.

Ask the provider . . .

- Can I visit at any time?
- How do you handle discipline?
- What do you do if my child is sick?
- How do you handle an emergency?
- Do you have a back-up caregiver?
- Where do children take naps?
- Do caregivers have up-to-date CPR and First Aid training?
- Do caregivers have training in child care?
- May I see a copy of your license?
- Are you accredited?
- May I have a list of parents (current and former) who have used your care?

Source: Michigan Department of Human Services, "What to Look for in a Child Care Provider," http://michigan.gov/dhs/0,4562,7-124-5529_7143-20990--,00.html.

Finding reliable child care can be a challenge, but it can pay off by giving you much needed peace of mind in knowing that your child is spending time in a safe and stimulating environment.

COMMUNICATING WITH OTHERS

Building and maintaining relationships with friends, family, partners, and school personnel requires effective communication skills. This means clearly expressing yourself while also respecting others.

Expressing Yourself

Be open with people about your thoughts, concerns, and experiences. Of course, you may want to keep some matters private; but letting others in on your feelings makes them feel trusted and more comfortable in sharing their own feelings with you. This is a major step toward a mutually supportive relationship. If you sense that someone needs to talk but is apprehensive, reveal something of yourself and ask what he or she thinks.

Share your plans for school and a career with others as well—with people at work, old friends, classmates, roommates, partners, or parents. Having heard your plans and sensed your commitment to succeed, the people around you will be willing to support you toward your goal. Lisa found that, after bringing her mother to visit her school, her mother offered more help with babysitting, household chores, and emergency rides to school. "She really respected what I was trying to accomplish," she says. "I can't wait until she sees me graduate."

Expressing yourself also means clearly stating your needs and feelings. Sarah worked out clear ground rules with her roommate about how clean to keep their apartment, when men were allowed to visit, and whether smoking was permitted. "I remember the last time I shared an apartment," she says. "For weeks I was angry about how messy everything was, and about the stereo blaring when I was trying to sleep. I kept all my anger to myself, just hoping it would get better." Her new arrangement is much better. As Sarah put it, "We got everything out in the open right away. During the first week, we worked out rules for cleaning, quiet hours, how the bills are divided—we're still coming up with others—and so far, everything's great."

Being clear about your needs is also the key to working well with your professors and school staff. They are there to help you succeed, but it's up to you to ask for help and clearly explain your concerns.

Listening

Effective communication in and out of the classroom means balancing what you say with respect for others. You can show respect for others by listening attentively, even to views different from your own. Show your interest in what someone is saying by maintaining eye contact and otherwise paying attention. Ask questions to make sure that you understand what the speaker means, or let him or her know that you do. If you're the outgoing type in a group discussion, try waiting three to five seconds after someone else has finished speaking so the quieter members of the group can have a chance to speak up.

Dealing with Conflicts

Sometimes you will disagree or argue with other people; that's only natural. The thing to do when these conflicts arise is to deal with them constructively—that is, in a way that helps to improve the situation, not make it worse. Express your feelings clearly and listen to others. Try to empathize with them—put yourself in someone else's position; see the world through their eyes. Empathy doesn't mean feeling sorry for or approving of what someone else is saying. Rather, empathy can usually be expressed by merely saying, for example, "I can see how you would feel so disappointed," or "I can imagine how it hurts." Remember that professors have bad days, that school staff is probably swamped with work, and that everyone has a personal life to be concerned about.

Listen for common ground. It's often easier to get along with others if you concentrate on the things you have in common. Even seemingly minor common experiences, such as being from the same neighborhood or town, or sharing the same career goal, can help get a relationship off to a good start. When all else fails and you're feeling really angry, leave the scene for awhile. Go to your room, take a walk, go to the library. Giving yourself a bit of space can help you see things more clearly and calm your emotions. Section 7 will discuss further strategies for developing effective interpersonal communication skills.

Exercise 1-10 Relating and relationships

In a group, discuss potential problems and solutions regarding the balancing of college, work, family, and friends. Share a concern you have about balancing your life with college. Based on the discussion, and on your own review of this section, list five practical steps you can take to resolve your concern.

1.

2.

3.

4.

5.

ONLINE SOCIAL NETWORKING

Online social networking has become a part of the daily routine for many college students and has greatly changed how students interact. According to some reports, as many as 80% or more of college students belong to a social networking site, such as Facebook, Friendster, Twitter, or Myspace.

These online sites can have real value as a social networking tool, or they can be a distraction, cutting into your study time.

Benefits of online social networking sites for college students:
- Create a positive self-image
- Communicate with friends and professors (many instructors are on these sites)
- Get class notes from a friend if you miss a class
- Contact friends for a ride home or to an event
- Conduct long-distance relationships
- Advertise student organizations, clubs, teams, etc.

President Obama's recent appearance at Facebook headquarters signals the growing importance of social media in the world today. These social networking sites are having quite a global impact.

Online social networking sites can be used to:
- Promote a political campaign or candidate
- Market products and services
- Raise volunteers, supporters and donations
- Garner international support for political uprisings, as seen recently in Libya

Security Dangers of Online Social Networking

Unfortunately, online social networking sites also pose risks to members. Cyber-crime is a growing danger. Identity theft is on the rise with hackers "phishing" (stealing) confidential information from personal accounts. Hackers can also create false profiles in accounts and use them to send spam or viruses.

Personal Risks of Online Social Networking

While "connecting" with friends online has many social benefits as listed above, it can also be used to such an extent that your studies suffer. Spending too much time online can distract you from studying and attending class and can also lead to feelings of isolation. If you mainly "connect" to friends online rather than in person, you aren't able to make eye contact or read body language—the non-verbal cues that are such a large part of communication.

Student dramas dealing with relationships, anger, jealousy, dissing, and dating often go viral with no concern or empathy for the people involved. A University of Michigan study that examined empathy in college students over the past thirty years has reported a big drop in empathy in college students after the year 2000. (*Science Daily,* May 29, 2010) They are now exploring possible causes for this phenomenon, such as exposure to violent media and online social networking. Excessive online social networking can also distract you from important social issues and from getting the most out of your college experience.

More and more employers are checking the online profiles of prospective employees to evaluate their character and personality traits. Make sure that your profile gives a positive image of you.

Some Dangers and Risks of Online Social Networking Sites for College Students:
- Cyber-crime, such as identity theft, spam, and viruses
- Distraction from studying
- Loss of personal contact with friends
- Distraction from important social issues

How to Avoid the Security Dangers and the Social Dangers of Using Social Networking Sites:
- Don't disclose personal information like your full birth date, home address, class schedule, email address, or social plans
- Don't accept friend requests from unknown people
- Utilize the "privacy" settings on your account
- Don't encourage student dramas involving anger, dating, dissing, and jealousy to go viral online
- Avoid excessive use and maintain personal contact with friends
- Be aware that your online profile will follow you into the working world and affect your employment possibilities

THINKING ABOUT SUCCESS

Exercise 1-11 How motivated are you now?

Think for a minute about some of the activities you enjoy most—for example, dating, going to the movies, playing or watching sports, reading, or watching your favorite TV show. On a scale of 1 to 5, how motivated are you to participate in these activities? To illustrate, if you're willing to drop everything or go out of your way to make time for a basketball game or your favorite TV show, you might rate your motivation for that activity a 5. But if you never seem to get around to reading, for example, you might rate your motivation for that activity a 1. Now look at the following list of typical activities and rate your motivation to take part in them.

1.	Regular exercise	1	2	3	4	5
2.	Eating a well-balanced diet	1	2	3	4	5
3.	Recreation, sports, or hobbies	1	2	3	4	5
4.	Relaxation	1	2	3	4	5
5.	Writing a letter to a friend	1	2	3	4	5
6.	Regular and punctual class attendance	1	2	3	4	5
7.	Reading and studying textbook assignments	1	2	3	4	5
8.	Adopting effective learning strategies	1	2	3	4	5
9.	Taking thorough lecture notes	1	2	3	4	5
10.	Getting good grades	1	2	3	4	5
11.	Graduating	1	2	3	4	5
12.	Completing assignments on time	1	2	3	4	5
13.	Learning new computer technology	1	2	3	4	5
14.	Writing reports for class or work	1	2	3	4	5
15.	Working with teams on projects	1	2	3	4	5
16.	Making oral presentations in class or at work	1	2	3	4	5
17.	Staying current in your field	1	2	3	4	5
18.	Developing project ideas for school or work	1	2	3	4	5
19.	Watching television	1	2	3	4	5
20.	Dating (spouse or other)	1	2	3	4	5

Now that you've rated your level of motivation to engage in several personal, school, and work activities, write a brief paragraph discussing what you learned about your motivation. How would you assess your current levels of motivation and in what areas do you want to boost your motivation levels?

There will always be areas in your life where your motivation levels seem low. Low levels of motivation are obviously not permanent. You can boost your motivation levels and boost your success by practicing the strategies outlined in this section. Motivation is perhaps the single greatest factor for college success. It's not always how well you scored on achievement tests like the SAT or ACT but how hard you're willing to work to achieve your college and career goals.

Earlier in this section you looked at the reasons you decided to go to college. Creating a clear vision of how you plan to fulfill those reasons for going to college will help you succeed. Of course, you can't know the future for sure; but you'd be surprised how easy it is to build a pretty clear picture of what you want. After all, you've probably done it many times. Have you ever imagined yourself doing something really well? Alex describes the vision of winning "the big game" that flashed through his mind when he practiced basketball as a kid.

There's probably an image like winning the big game that you've played over and over again in your head, each time adding a new detail to make it feel more real. We may think of these images as silly fantasies. Maybe that's why we usually don't build clear images about school or work. But, in fact, images can help us deal with real challenges—for example, imagine what it would be like to graduate or start your first professional job. Ashalatta has her own vision of graduation day and her new office.

Your Own Visions of Success

Creating images like Alejandro's and Ashalatta's is called **visualization.** As you continue reading this book and gain more experience in school, your vision of personal success will become clearer to you. The more details you can build into your visions, the better. You can almost feel a really vivid vision, just like Alex was able to feel the excitement of winning the big game. Even simple visualizations can be useful when school gets rough. That's because images like these store some very important information, such as what your goals are, how you're going to reach them, and what you imagine success will be like. All this information can be used to increase your motivation to succeed.

> ~Alejandro~
>
> I'm at the free throw line. The game is tied. There's only a second on the clock. The crowd's on its feet. I begin my free throw routine, blocking out all distractions. I dribble twice, then twice more. I shrug my shoulders to relax. My eyes are glued to the hoop. I bend my knees, rise up, extend my arm, release the ball, and follow through. The ball flies in a perfect arc and swisshh, it goes in! The crowd spills onto the floor and carries me off in victory.

Keep your eyes on the prize

A clear vision can help you picture the goals and rewards you're after. Ashalatta's vision of graduation reminds her of the payoff for the hard work she's putting in.

Keep your vision in focus and it will keep you focused. Visualize yourself succeeding in each step toward each goal and your plan. You may not achieve ultimate success immediately, but you will progress toward it. Whether you're in sports, college, or work, success begins in your head. If you're not in the habit of visualizing yourself as a successful person—work on it! This is practice you won't regret.

Take a minute to examine how you see yourself as a student and your goal of graduation. Write a brief paragraph about what improvements you would like to visualize to help you get the most out of college and graduate.

> *~Ashalatta~*
>
> *There I am on stage in cap and gown receiving my degree and a firm handshake. All of my friends are clapping and calling my name. I realize how important they've become to me.*
>
> *All the work has finally paid off. I think back to those late nights during my first term. For hours I'd sit at my desk struggling over those first assignments. I remember the instructors who helped me through, taking time to meet with me.*
>
> *As I return to my seat carrying my diploma, my favorite instructor reaches out to shake my hand. I remember how hard the two of us worked together. The more help I got, the more I wanted to make her proud of me. Now she is. And so am I.*
>
> *Then I see myself at work. I have a beautiful, clean office, diploma on the wall, and the latest computer. I'll never regret the hard work and those late nights struggling over assignments—it has really paid off.*

Although we're encouraging you to use visualization to stay focused in college and graduate, keep practicing visualization during school internships and when you land your first professional job. Jake completed his Associate Degree in Community Behavioral Health Technology. His new job requires him to deliver wellness workshops. Examine how Jake visualizes his successful leadership in a wellness workshop. "I arrive early to the conference center to ensure that everything is in place—my table, the podium, and my overhead projector. I make sure my transparencies are in order. Participants get seated and I welcome them. I see myself explaining each transparency I have prepared. I know what I'm talking about. I think about questions that might be asked and I hear myself confidently addressing each question. The audience is enthused, and they ask a lot of questions—I can tell they're interested. I finish—all went well, and several participants stay to ask me more questions."

This time, develop your career vision. Write a paragraph about your vision of a successful day in your career. Detail it—describe specifically what you would do during such a day. Picture yourself succeeding in whatever activities you include in your description.

A Successful Workday in the Life of

_____

_____
_____
_____
_____
_____
_____
_____
_____

You can get there from here

A clear vision also shows some of the steps and skills necessary to reach your goal—for example, visualizing success in college means more than just graduation. Ashalatta's vision included memories of studying late at night, of asking for help when she had trouble, and of sticking with it even when it seemed impossible. Thinking in terms of smaller steps also gives you smaller goals that you can reach along the way to graduation and your career. Every time you sit down to study, or every time you prioritize your work assignments, you're reaching one of your goals. Knowing that you've reached even small goals helps you feel good about yourself.

Be your own guide

Maybe the best thing about visualization is that you have a chance to see yourself succeeding. A clear vision can become your own instruction manual for being a successful student or a professional employee. When you're down and feeling low, you can stop and review your vision to remind yourself of the goals you're working toward.

Exercise 1-12 Visualizing yourself as a successful person

Imagine a successful day in your college life. Every student seems to have a different idea of a successful day— for example, Mike imagined himself getting up at 6 AM to run four miles before breakfast. "After breakfast, I'd go to my morning classes prepared with questions from the course readings," he adds. "After lunch, I'd work at the college newspaper for most of the afternoon. After dinner, I'd be off to the library for more reading."

Now that you've begun to create a vision of what you want, it's time to learn some practical strategies that can bring your vision to life. You'll learn ways to stay focused on your goals, even when you feel (and you occasionally will) bored, depressed, or discouraged. Everybody has these feelings sometimes. The trick is not to let them come between you and your goals. Let's look at some strategies that will keep you on the road to success.

GOALS AND MOTIVATION IN COLLEGE

Think about what motivated you to further your education. You want a good job, or perhaps a better one than you have now. You want to earn enough money to live comfortably. You want to make your mark on the world. Focusing on goals like these is a great source of motivation. By examining your goals and dreams on a regular basis, you can remind yourself why the struggles you're experiencing in college are worth it. Later in the section, you'll develop a detailed plan that includes your short-term and long-term goals; but, you can begin thinking about them now.

Remember the Small Goals

Graduation is a long-term goal you undoubtedly share with your fellow students. But graduation is really the result of reaching many smaller, short-term goals—for example, maintaining perfect (or nearly perfect) attendance, getting a good grade in math class, and making friends with other students. As a student, you're reaching many small goals every day.

Having short-term goals is a great source of motivation. Each time you set a short-term goal, you give yourself a target to aim for. Each time you reach a short-term goal, you're experiencing success. These small successes give you the confidence and motivation to take on other challenges and continue your march toward graduation and your career.

Exercise 1-13 My short-term goals

List three short-term goals you'd like to achieve in the coming weeks and months, such as improving your class attendance, finding a student organization to join, or improving a study skill. For each goal, include any reasons why reaching the goal will help you succeed in school.

Goal 1

_____
_____
_____
_____
_____

Goal 2

_____
_____
_____
_____
_____

Goal 3

_____
_____
_____
_____
_____

Reaching any goal, even a short-term one, takes planning. Carmen, for example, found out when the computer workshops were offered and made time for them in her schedule. To start creating a plan for reaching any of your short-term goals, ask yourself the following questions:

- **What** do you want to accomplish? Be specific.

- **Where** do you want to do it?

- **When** do you want to do it?

- **How** long do you want to do it?

- **How** often do you want to do it?

Bill's goal plan

Look at Bill's goal plan as an example. Bill wants a degree in business. He is taking five classes, has a part-time job, and wants to play intramural volleyball. He knows he has to plan his life more carefully than ever before if he's going to do all of this and get good grades. His overall plan will include study schedules for each of his classes, his work schedule, and his volleyball schedule. Each of these schedules needs to be planned for carefully. Take the plan for his introduction to business class as an example. (See Bill's goal plan in Figure 1-1.)

Figure 1-1
Bill's Goal Plan

My goal plan is for getting at least a "B" in Introduction to Business. I will:

- Read each section before my instructor discusses it.

- Complete all section exercises after each reading.

- Write down questions to ask in class about the readings and other assignments.

- Review my notes immediately after each class for 5 to 10 minutes.

- Drill and practice each section's terms for one hour each Monday, Thursday, and Sunday, from 4–5 PM (at the library) or 8–9 PM (at home).

Bill's business class requires a lot of time for memorizing terms and definitions. There's no way he'll be able to cram at the end for the final exam, like he's done with some classes in the past. He'll have to keep up with each lesson if he's going to keep up his "B" average.

You'll notice that Bill's goal plan gives him a clear path to follow on his way to succeeding in the business class. His goals are detailed and answer the key questions of where, when, what, how often, and for how long. If he can reach each of these smaller goals, he has an excellent chance at getting at least a "B" in business.

Bill was careful to be realistic about his plan. He fit his goal plan into his real life and his study habits. Setting regular times for studying helps him remember to practice. He built some flexibility into his goals by allowing two times for practicing his terminology. This will help him to meet his study goals, even though his volleyball and work schedules often change.

Like most good goal planners, Bill wrote his goal plan. He also started with the words "I will." By writing his goals and pledging "I will," he made a serious contract with himself to follow the plan. "I even showed my plan to my roommate," Bill says. "I know he'll give me a hard time if I don't stick to it."

This brief look at Bill's goal plan shows how focusing on and accomplishing smaller goals can give you a sense of achievement and can motivate you to take on your larger goals. One way to work towards your small goals is to write them into your lists of daily and weekly tasks. As you complete each task, cross it off the list. Just crossing items off your list can give you a feeling of accomplishment. Another benefit of making lists is that you'll develop a better sense of how much you can accomplish each day; you'll know just how many tasks you can tackle, and chances are you'll tackle them successfully.

When you don't meet one of your goals, review your strategy. Did you give yourself enough time to accomplish it? Maybe your goal was unrealistic. Again, making lists of daily and weekly tasks will help you accomplish what you set out to do.

Take a look at Beth's lists of tasks for tomorrow (Figure 1-2) and for the rest of the week (Figure 1-3).

Figure 1-2
Beth's Task List for Tomorrow

Goals for Monday

- Get up by 7 AM so I can run before class.

- Run around the track for 15 minutes before breakfast.

- Spend one hour in the library looking for ideas for my English project.

- Call Mom and try to patch things up.

- Call the placement office to make an appointment for finding a part-time job.

- Talk to math instructor after class about the next exam.

- Complete readings for tomorrow's classes.

Figure 1-3
Beth's Task List for the Week

Plan for the Week

Tuesday:

- Run for 15 minutes.

- Call tutoring center about finding a math tutor.

- Attend first meeting of Students for the Environment at 6:30 PM.

Wednesday:

- Run for 15 minutes.

- Talk to Ms. Lopez about topic for English project.

- Start reviewing for next math quiz.

(continued)

Figure 1-3
Beth's Task List for the Week (continued)

Thursday:

- Run for 20 minutes.

- Spend one hour reviewing for math quiz.

- Write project outline for English project.

Friday:

- Run for 20 minutes.

- Call Steve to confirm plans for evening.

- Submit English project outline.

Saturday:

- Call Sarah to wish her a happy birthday.

- Stop at several restaurants and ask about job openings.

- Clean room.

Sunday:

- Review job listings in newspaper.

- Review math for two hours.

- Complete readings for Monday's classes.

Exercise 1-14 Listing my goals

Fill in the forms below with your goals for tomorrow and for the rest of the week.

Goals for Tomorrow

Goals for the Week

Monday: _____
_____
_____
_____

Tuesday: _____
_____
_____
_____

Wednesday: _____
_____
_____
_____

Thursday: _____
_____
_____
_____

Friday: _____
_____
_____
_____

Saturday: _____
_____
_____
_____

Sunday: _____
_____
_____
_____

Make Time for Fun

Be sure you plan time for fun and friends; remember that social involvement is important too. Join your classmates for something to eat before or after class, or, if you commute, share rides home. When you're short on time, even a quick cup of coffee with friends from school can be relaxing.

Regular exercise can be fun, too, and staying fit gives you more energy for work as well as play. Many employers prefer fit and healthy employees, because they know such workers are more productive and also help hold down health care costs. So planning time for exercise is good for your health, increases motivation, and improves your job prospects. To make the most of your time, find an exercise partner so you can combine social time with exercise. You'll feel more relaxed, healthy, and productive.

BOOSTING YOUR SELF-ESTEEM TO BOOST COLLEGE SUCCESS

No matter how old you are, self-esteem is probably the single most important characteristic to help you accomplish your goals and get through the struggles and challenges of college. Self-esteem is a confidence in yourself, a self-respect, and a satisfaction with yourself as you work toward your goals—even when you encounter obstacles. When your self-esteem is high, you have a dependable source of motivation to draw from. Take a few minutes to examine your own self-esteem by completing Exercise 1-15.

Exercise 1-15 A look at my self-esteem

Check the statements that describe you.

_____	1.	I accept and appreciate myself for who I am (my looks, feelings, strengths, and weaknesses).
_____	2.	I accept credit and appreciation for what I do.
_____	3.	I take time out to recognize my hard work—pat myself on the back.
_____	4.	I don't allow setbacks to keep me from trying again and again.
_____	5.	I am kind to myself and take care of myself.
_____	6.	I am happy with myself and value myself even when I make mistakes.
_____	7.	I have a healthy admiration for my abilities.
_____	8.	I have a love and respect for myself.
_____	9.	I forgive myself and laugh at my mistakes.
_____	10.	I have confidence in myself.

Now that you've had a chance to examine your self-esteem, what areas of self-esteem do you need to work on?

Together, each of the ten items listed in the self-esteem exercise consists of a love for yourself. This is quite different from being arrogant, conceited, or a perfectionist. Loving, caring and respecting yourself plays an important part in developing the motivation to achieve your goals. High self-esteem lets you remember that you are a worthwhile person, whether or not you succeed at any given task. Self-esteem is especially important now that you're in college, facing lots of new experiences, opportunities, and challenges. Whether your level of self-esteem is low, high, or someplace in between, there are several strategies you can employ to boost your self-esteem as you work toward your educational goals.

Your self-esteem is largely shaped by what you tell yourself—your self-talk. Controlling your self-talk will give you a lot of control over your self-esteem. The concept of self-talk will be a common thread throughout the book. Several sections will encourage you to create positive self-talk to direct and motivate yourself to reach your goals. In addition to positive self-talk, recognizing your past successes and your capabilities is an important way to help you boost your self-esteem.

Creating Positive Self-Talk to Achieve Goals

We all talk to ourselves. Whether you realize it or not, every time you think, you're talking to yourself. Self-talk includes all the thoughts and inner conversations you have with yourself. Self-talk plays a big role in shaping your self-image as a student and, later, as an employee. Your success is tied directly to your self-talk—for example, the conversations you have with yourself leading up to a test can mean the difference between a good grade and disappointment. Your self-talk will dictate how you prepare, how much you prepare, and how anxious you get about the test.

Experts say we engage 10,000 self-talk messages each day and perhaps as much as three-fourths or more of it is negative. Negative self-talk will resemble the following kinds of messages: "I'm not good at math." "I can't remember anything I read." "I'm too fat." "I'm too thin." "I'm not good at sports." "I'm not very smart." These self-talk messages may be casually expressed but may become a serious blow to your self-esteem. Your self-esteem can dramatically affect how well you do in school and your career. That's why it's so important to use your self-talk to respect yourself, appreciate yourself, forgive yourself, and to encourage and motivate yourself. Positive self-talk messages like, "I will get this math," "I have a lot of beauty in me," "I'm glad I'm in college and I'm going to work hard at it," give you a lot more mileage toward achieving your goals.

Remember, what you say to yourself is linked to what you accomplish, as well as how you feel about yourself. If you are engaging in thousands of inner conversations with yourself, what are you telling yourself? Think about your self-talk as you wake up to the alarm clock each morning. What does your morning self-talk motivate you to do? Listen to this morning monologue.

Have you ever had a conversation like this? If you have, it's easy to understand how you could have at least 10,000 conversations with yourself in a day. Notice how this self-talk can motivate you to sleep in. When the self-talk finally shifts to "I've got to get up," this is what happens—you get up (that is, unless you tell yourself to hit the snooze alarm again.) If your self-talk can dictate when you get out of bed, imagine what it can do for you in other areas in your life. Listen to your self-talk. Determine how you will use your self-talk to direct your motivation.

> *(Alarm rings.) "Time to get up already? What time is it? I can't get up. I'll sleep ten more minutes." (Hit the snooze alarm.) "Oh good, ten more minutes. " (Ten minutes later alarm rings.) "I need another ten minutes." (Hit the snooze alarm again.) "Maybe I can skip breakfast and sleep a little later." (Ten minutes later alarm rings.) "I'm still so tired. I've got to get up." ("I'm out of bed.")*

Think of a favorite task that you do well. Try to recall the kinds of conversations you have with yourself. For instance, listen to Jan's self-talk as she sits down to study her Anatomy text.

> *"I love this stuff. People think I'm crazy, but I have to admit it, Anatomy is relevant. In what other course could I learn more interesting and factual material about me? It's fascinating to learn about the structure, plumbing, electricity, and power of my body. I'm learning a zillion terms too—won't that increase my vocabulary. I love this stuff!"*

Jan's self-talk is positive. It reflects her interest and enthusiasm for her Anatomy course. Her self-talk energizes and motivates her to learn. She does a great job convincing herself that this subject is fun. Jan's self-talk may sound ridiculous, but does this sound better?

> *"I hate Anatomy. It's boring and impossible to learn all those terms! When will I ever need all these nitty gritty details anyway?"*

Which conversation would you rather use to motivate yourself? If Jan ever had a fear or dislike for Anatomy, she's had a positive turn-around. If you want to motivate yourself, use positive self-talk to convince yourself of the value and purpose of what you are learning. With repetition, your self-talk becomes part of your repertoire—wouldn't you rather it be positive and motivational?

As you can see, self-talk is a very powerful tool because you tend to believe what you hear all day long. You can create self-talk messages to direct what you want to accomplish or to discourage yourself. Athlétes are constantly evaluating their game and creating self-talk to direct their moves. Naturally, listening to positive self-talk will help you believe in your own capabilities and direct you in a positive path. You may not accomplish everything you tell yourself, but at least you put yourself in progress toward your goals.

Derek was a first-term student in a physical therapy assistant program. His self-talk turned negative when he started having trouble in his math class. "I figured, if I can't even handle an introductory math class, how am I going to handle more advanced classes?" he remembers. "I was really starting to doubt whether I had what it takes to be a good physical therapy assistant." Derek's negative self-talk even made him question his ability to succeed in his major. Tayo, however, had a different attitude. She too had problems with math, but she thought about them in a different way. "Okay, so I'm not a whiz at math yet. I'll just have to work that much harder on it—I'm going to be a great physical therapy assistant!" Tayo knew that her failure in one test didn't mean she would be a failure in math or in her major. Instead, her determined self-talk encouraged her in a positive direction of working harder and seeking help from a tutor. Create self-talk messages that encourage you and discard those that discourage you. The next section will tell you more about how you can develop self-talk to motivate yourself.

Developing Positive Self-Talk for Motivation

Negative self-talk drains your motivation to succeed. By listening to yourself and practicing positive self-talk, you can replace negative thoughts whenever they arise. Developing a habit of positive self-talk will help you face even the toughest challenges in your personal, school, and work life.

For example, if you're battling with the administration over your tuition bill or your student loan check, stop to notice your negative thoughts. Angry thoughts are unlikely to get you the help you need from the administration staff. Believe it, you're much better off with administrators as friends than as enemies. You might think to yourself, "No way am I going to go through this whole process again: filling out the form, getting the signature, returning the form, and then waiting two weeks." In fact, the process isn't all that difficult. What you're really worried about is how you'll get through the next two weeks with so little money.

In this case, your negative thoughts aren't helping you solve your real problem. Notice your thoughts and check them against your real goal: getting money. Now you might say to yourself, "Surely the school doesn't want me to drop out of college just because there's a two-week delay in my loan check. There must be someone who can help me through this." Now you are back on a successful track to getting what you want. The next step is to set up an appointment with a loan counselor, explain your situation, and ask for assistance.

Exercise 1-16 Using positive self-talk

Read the following passages. Notice that the person in each situation is about to adopt negative self-talk. Write down several positive self-talk statements that he or she could use in each situation to keep on a positive track. The first one has been done for you.

1. Daniel just received his grade on a math test. He thinks to himself, "I can't believe it; my second 'D' in a row. I don't know what it is. I study for hours, I pay attention in class, but I still can't get the grades I want." *But that doesn't mean I'm giving up. I'll beat it before it beats me. I'm getting a tutor to help me learn this stuff better.*

2. Jessica has just entered the lunchroom and is looking for a place to sit. She thinks to herself, "Here it is, the fourth week of the term and I still don't really have anyone I want to sit with. It seems like everyone else knows somebody—someone who'll wave and offer an empty chair. It feels a little like I'm invisible."

3. Matt is trying to figure out how he'll get his term paper completed on time. He says to himself, "I know I put off writing this thing far too long. Now it seems like there's no way I'll be able to get it done. I really don't want to mess up the 'B' I have now in the class."

4. Michelle just seems to clash with her boss. "He's driving me up the wall," she thinks to herself. "It seems that whenever I make a comment in a meeting, I get his 'evil eye,' like I offended him or something. And his comments on my proposals seem to be attacks on me personally."

5. Alicia has to give a project presentation in front of her colleagues this afternoon. "I can't remember the last time I spoke in front of a group," she thinks. "I think I have a good presentation to make, but I'm so nervous my hands are sweating just thinking about it."

6. Tyrone has been dieting off and on since he was twelve. He's never been successful at controlling his diet and therefore his weight. He says to himself, "I guess I'm born to be fat and miserable. I'm doomed—I love food and the fatter the better."

Taking control of your thoughts is a great strategy for building motivation for and developing a winning attitude toward college and life in general. It takes some practice, but becoming more aware of your negative self-talk and deciding to use positive self-talk instead will give you more motivation to meet your challenges. Simply stop, notice your negative self-talk, and replace it with positive self-talk.

Recognize Past Successes and Your Capabilities

Another way to boost your self-esteem is to recall past successes. Sometimes when you're faced with a really challenging problem, it's easy to forget that anything has ever gone right, or that you have successfully handled difficult situations in the past. That's when you need to remind yourself and give recognition to past successes and the capabilities you developed. Which do you give more attention to: your frustrations and faults, or your strengths and accomplishments? If you put an excessive amount of energy into noticing your faults while ignoring your strengths, you will be dissatisfied with yourself. Self-dissatisfaction will tear away at your self-esteem. Recognizing your positive self will boost it. You'll continue to have faults and problems to deal with. However, you'll find that *dealing* with them is more positive than *dwelling* on them. Later, this section will introduce you to creative problem solving and decision making strategies to help you deal more positively with problems and find the best solutions for you. Exercise 1-17 will help you give recognition to your strengths by recognizing your past successes and the capabilities you have developed as a result.

Exercise 1-17 Recognizing your past successes and capabilities

In the first column, recall three experiences that you handled successfully and, in the second column, identify the capabilities that you developed as a result of those experiences.

Past Successes	Capabilities
example: *I organized a Boy Scout fund raising campaign and the troop earned money to go on an archeological dig in Mexico.*	*Organization, leadership, and persistence.*
1.	
2.	
3.	

It's easy to forget about past successes when you're dealing with new challenges. Many of your past successes did not come without some failure in the process. In the end you were successful because you stuck it out. Don't forget to use those past successes to remind yourself of your accomplishments and how you got there— these are all a part of your self-esteem. Recognizing your past successes boosts your self-esteem.

DEVELOPING SELF-DISCIPLINE

Self-discipline concerns teaching yourself the positive habits that keep you on a successful track. It's about taking responsibility for your life and making choices that support your goals. You need self-discipline to make it to class on time, to complete your reading or work assignments, and to turn off the TV when you should be preparing for the big test.

Self-discipline starts with taking responsibility for your behavior. You are responsible for your successes and your failures. You're responsible for how you respond to the challenges of college life. Choosing whether to study is up to you. Beginning a major assignment earlier, rather than later, is also your choice. You control the behaviors (your study habits, for example) that determine your success or failure.

Staying on Track

Since you're responsible for your behaviors, you have the power to improve your way of life in school. Self-discipline means deciding to stay awake and pay attention in class, even when you're tired or are feeling a little bored. It means tuning into a class lecture when you feel yourself tuning out. It means asking for help when you need it, even if that makes you feel a little uncomfortable.

As Denis Waitley suggests in *Psychology of Success*, self-discipline is about consciously breaking bad habits. You can break bad habits, such as daydreaming while reading your textbooks or putting off long-term assignments until the last minute. You can use self-discipline to teach yourself new positive habits to replace the habits that hinder your success in school. It takes some time and effort to break habits, especially if they've been with you for a long time. But if you're honest with yourself and focus on your goals, you can make it happen.

Phil is using self-discipline to make better use of his time. "I used to hang out with my friends for a couple of hours after dinner every night instead of studying," he says. "Eventually I realized that I was spending too much time just hanging out waiting for something to happen." Now Phil spends that time in the library. "I take my books with me to the dining hall," he says, "and head straight to the library after dinner. It still feels a little weird, like I might be missing out on the fun. In fact, though, I end up seeing my friends later, anyway. All I really miss out on is the time they waste deciding where to go and what to wear. I still have to resist the temptation to go back to my old ways."

Making It Happen

Here are some steps you can take to use self discipline to teach yourself good habits.

Step 1.	Set your goal.
Step 2.	Identify the bad habit that's hindering your progress toward your goal.
Step 3.	Decide on a positive habit to replace the bad habit.
Step 4.	Visualize success and use positive self-talk.
Step 5.	Keep trying.

Claudia used this process to teach herself to take better class notes. "I knew I needed to improve my notetaking," she said. That was Step 1—setting a goal. "I'd pay attention in class, but two weeks later, when it came time to study, I'd forgotten everything. I realized I was just not concentrating enough on writing down the important points of class lecture." That was Step 2—identifying the bad habit. "I decided I had to start listening for the instructor's major points and write them down immediately." That was Step 3—the good habit. "I said to myself, 'Of course I can take better notes. I usually understand what the instructor is saying; it's just a matter of writing it down.' I'd spend a few minutes before each class visualizing myself actually taking good notes, writing down every important point. I also visualized myself having a great set of notes to study from." That was Step 4—positive self-talk and visualization. "It's taken me a while to bring my vision to life. I occasionally find myself daydreaming or listening but not writing everything down. I just have to snap myself out of it. But my notes have improved." That was Step 5—keep trying until you get it right.

As you can see, self-discipline doesn't really mean doing without the things you want. Instead, it's getting the things out of life you really want. Often this takes hard work, but it's the key to reaching your goals. Focus on changing specific habits one at a time. Soon you'll start seeing real improvements. You'll begin to see how self-discipline leads to greater motivation and a more positive self-image.

Exercise 1-18 Breaking bad habits

Decide on a small change you'd like to make to become a more successful student. Perhaps, like Claudia, you want to improve your notetaking. Maybe you want to increase your study time, to make it to all your classes, or to get along better with people. In the space below, try the five-step process for teaching yourself better habits.

Step 1.   The goal I want to achieve is:

_____

_____

Step 2.   The habit I want to break is:

_____

_____

Step 3.   The good habit I want to adopt is:

_____

_____

Step 4.   Spend a few minutes visualizing putting your new habit to work. Briefly describe your vision:

_____

_____

_____

_____

_____

Step 5.   Keep on trying. Write a brief statement about your commitment to keep trying your new habit. Then take a minute to visualize yourself trying again and again, even if your progress seems slow.

_____

_____

_____

_____

CREATIVE PROBLEM SOLVING AND DECISION MAKING

We all have problems—they're an inherent part of life. You've probably faced a lot of problems that don't have clear-cut or perfect solutions. Do you remember times when your school work piled up—tests to study for, projects and assignments due, and relationships that wanted attention—all at the same time? When your work piles up and deadlines are closing in, you have several problems to solve. How are you going to handle this right now, and how are you going to prevent this from happening again in the future? Complex problems like these seem tough to deal with because there's usually not one perfect solution to the problem.

When you become a creative problem solver, you move from the notion of finding the "right answer" to the understanding that there are many answers. Creative problem solving is not a search for the right answer, but more of a challenge, allowing you to be innovative in finding several solutions to problems—and then deciding on the best solution. It starts with a strong mental effort—thinking clearly, courageously, and confidently.

When you hear phrases like, "that will never work, " or "it's not practical," remember, they are *solution killers*—their intention is to kill your ideas. Henry Ford once said, "Whether you think you can or think you can't—you are right." So don't be limited by don'ts and can'ts. Use a positive approach to create solutions. Problems will always crop up, but with a positive attitude and creative approach, workable solutions will become apparent and confident decisions can be made.

You solve many problems in everyday relationships, in school, and at work. You probably don't even notice a lot of your problem solving, because some of the issues you deal with don't seem much like problems at all. At other times, you're all too aware that you've got a real problem on your hands. Your problem might be to decide what major to pursue, how to say no to your date, or how to prioritize your work assignments. More complex problems take more time to make creative and sound decisions because a rushed decision may mean more grief and take even more time to undo. Do you remember rushed decisions that ended up causing you more grief and problems?

The following strategies and attitudes for creative problem solving and decision making will help you meet the challenges. You will notice that decision making is an element of problem solving. Once learned, you will continue to reap the benefits of creative problem solving and effective decision making strategies in your relationships, in school, and at work.

SIX STRATEGIES FOR CREATIVE PROBLEM SOLVING AND DECISION MAKING

Strategy 1.   Problem Analysis—What exactly is the problem?

Keep in mind that the word *problem* isn't always to be taken in its usual way. *Problem* can refer to any situation or question that needs an answer or solution. The ultimate task of problem analysis is to define or identify the specific problem. Initially, you may have an idea about what your problem is. Rather than accept the problem at face value, analyze it, and get more information about it by asking questions like these:

1. Is this really a problem?
2. What are the effects or the consequences of this problem?
3. What is the cause of this problem?

Answers to these and other relevant questions will help you to more clearly define your problem.

Rashida, a management trainee, has a 9–5 job. She was convinced she could not handle both school and work obligations and initially contemplated dropping out of school. She analyzed her problem further by answering the questions.

1. Is this really a problem?—*Yes, I'm neglecting some responsibilities at work and can't keep up with school assignments. I manage the time I have fairly well.*
2. What are the effects or the consequences of this problem?—*My boss won't be happy with my work performance and I can't get the grades I want and the promotion that will come when I graduate.*
3. What is the cause of this problem?—*I have over-committed to too many classes and I haven't tried to discuss my school plans with my boss.*

To discover the basic issue at hand, it is important to ask yourself relevant questions in order to gather more information and clarify your problem. The questions Rashida asked herself helped her identify her problem. "I over-committed myself to both work and school and I can't solve this problem unless I discuss it with my boss." Before discussing the problem with her boss, she knew she needed a plan. This is where the next strategy comes into play—before you devise a plan, consider the various possible solutions.

Strategy 2.   Possible Solutions—Brainstorm the possibilities.

In this strategy your creativity is unleashed to explore new ideas and solutions. Generate as many possible solutions (even impractical ones) without judging their merit. Don't reject a possibility because you see something wrong with it. Judge solutions only after you have listed the possibilities. For now, allow your ideas to flow freely, expect yourself to be creative, and consider the "impractical." It's better to do something impractical than to do nothing at all. Rashida brainstormed these plans:

a. Quit work.
b. Quit school.
c. Ask my boss if I can work part-time when I'm enrolled in school.
d. Ask my boss if I can continue my full-time job but come in at 10 AM each morning so I can enroll in 8 AM classes on Monday through Friday. My education should be valuable to my boss too.
e. Enroll in only two evening classes so I can fulfill my normal work obligations.
f. Enroll in four classes—ideally two 8 AM classes (M, W, F and T, Th) and two evening classes (Mon. 7–9:45 and Wed. 4–6:45). I'll have to get off work at 3:30 on Wednesdays to attend class.

Now Rashida has some possible solutions from which to make a decision. The next strategy, evaluating the possibilities, is the beginning of a decision making process. After you've identified your problem, created possible solutions, you can evaluate each solution, and make your decision.

Strategy 3.   Evaluate the possibilities.

Review each of the possible solutions. Note answers to the following questions: What are the likely consequences of each possible solution? Which ones work best for you? Why or why not? Which one are you willing to commit to? Here's how Rashida judged her options.

a. Quit work.—*No, I need the income and I want the practical experience.*
b. Quit school.—*No, if I quit school I can't get my promotion.*
c. Ask my boss if I can work part-time when I'm enrolled in school.—*Maybe, this will be my second choice. I can survive but I'll need a school loan with this plan.*
d. Ask my boss if I can continue my full-time job but come in at 10 AM each morning so I can enroll in 8 AM classes on Monday through Friday.—*Yes, this is my first choice. If my boss wants me to get professional training and education bad enough, he might accommodate this plan.*

e. Enroll in only two evening classes so I can fulfill my work obligations.—Maybe, *only if I have to; I'd rather take at least four classes each term so I can complete my degree earlier.*

f. Enroll in four classes—ideally two 8 AM classes (M, W, F and T, Th) and two evening classes (Mon. 7–9:45 and Wed. 4–6:45). I'll have to get off work at 3:30 on Wednesdays to attend class.—*Yes, this would allow me to complete my associate degree in 2 1/2 to 3 years.*

Plans *d* and *f* were Rashida's top preferences. She wondered how she could make her boss see the merit in these choices. She would need to present a specific plan. That's the next strategy—planning.

Strategy 4.   Develop a specific plan.

Making specific plans helps you achieve your goals—it gives you a target to work toward. To develop specific plans, ask yourself the relevant questions: what, where, when, how long, or how often—just as you did in developing goal plans. Rashida's plan looked like this.

1. *Make an appointment with Sue (the boss), Wednesday at 9 AM.*
2. *Discuss the importance of my education and training to me and for the job.*
3. *Ask Sue if I can continue my full-time job but come in at 10 AM each morning so I can enroll in two 8 AM classes on Monday through Friday. I'll also need to get off work at 3:30 PM on Wednesdays to attend evening class.*
4. *Explain to Sue that I want to enroll in a total of four classes—ideally two 8 AM classes and two evening classes (Mon. 7–9:45 and Wed. 4–6:45). I'll have to get off work at 3:30 on Wednesdays to attend class. Explain to Sue that at this rate, 4 classes per term, I could complete my associate degree in 2 1/2 to 3 years.*

Rashida's plan was well thought out and outlined all the specifics. Her boss was actually impressed with her educational goals and plans. She approved the plan with one addition. She asked Rashida to work one Saturday a month as a trade-off for the time she was giving her to attend school. Rashida agreed and was pleased. She could never have believed that her boss would be so supportive and, therefore, never before requested special considerations of this magnitude.

The next strategy will help you put your plan into action. It offers some encouraging attitudes to keep you focused on your plan.

Strategy 5.   Put your plan into action but be flexible, focused, persistent, and committed.

This strategy is basically a set of four attitudes to help you accomplish your plan and stick to it.

Attitude 1. Be Flexible. While it is important to plan, it is also important to plan to learn. In others words, be flexible. Even good plans need to be adjusted as you gain new insights and as the unexpected happens. If you're flexible, you can adjust. Expect to adjust. It's better to adjust your plans than to struggle with plans that won't work. Rashida realized her boss might suggest an alternate plan and she did—working every fourth Saturday—an easy adjustment for Rashida to make.

Attitude 2. Stay focused. Keep your eyes on the prize. Remind yourself of the results and the rewards. Rashida's focus on getting her degree motivated her to make her request.

Attitude 3. Be persistent. Implementing a good plan does not assure perfect results. Expect mistakes. Don't expect a perfect track record—instead expect yourself to get back on track. Persist after each derailment. Remember Robert Schuller's famous statement, "Tough times never last, but tough people do." Stay focused and hang in there!

Attitude 4. Be committed. Commitment is a pledge to follow your plan. It involves applying your self-discipline to stay the course. It's also a matter of choice, not force. Commitment leads to accomplishment. A lack of commitment can cost you personal goals and desires, relationships, and accomplishments.

Strategy 6.   Evaluate the plan.

The final step to solving a problem or making a decision is to evaluate. Did you accomplish what you wanted to? How well did the solution/decision work? More important, if the solution did not work, why? Evaluating is an important strategy because it helps you identify and avoid repeating past mistakes. Better yet, it helps you identify successful strategies to build on.

Rashida was surprised that her boss actually supported her plan. Normally she wouldn't make such an "unrealistic request." She learned to consider the possibilities and act on them.

Exercise 1-19 Using creative problem solving and decision making

Now it's your turn. Think of a problem you'd like to solve. Follow the strategies outlined in the book, and write down what you will do in each strategy.

Strategy 1.   Problem Analysis—What exactly is the problem?

(Analyze it, and get more information about it by asking relevant questions.)

Strategy 2.   Possible Solutions—Brainstorm the possibilities.

Strategy 3.   Evaluate the possibilities.

(Review each of the possible solutions. Note answers to the following questions: What are the likely consequences of each possible solution? Which ones work best for you? Why or why not? Which ones are you willing to commit to?)

Strategy 4.   **Develop a specific plan.**

(To develop specific plans ask yourself the relevant questions: what, where, when, how long, or how often.)

Strategy 5.   **Put your plan into action but be flexible, focused, persistent, and committed.**

(How will you use the four attitudes to help you accomplish your plan and stick to it?)

Attitude 1. Be flexible.

Attitude 2. Stay focused.

Attitude 3. Be persistent.

Attitude 4. Be committed.

Strategy 6.   **Evaluate the plan.**

(After you've implemented your plan, ask yourself the following questions: Did you accomplish what you wanted to? How well did the solution/decision work? More importantly, if the solution did not work, why?)

HIGHLIGHTS

In this section, you've taken important steps toward making the most of your college experience. You've been introduced to many of your fellow students, as well as many facets of your college. You've learned how college success skills connect to become work performance skills. More significantly, you have learned the importance of developing your workforce skills while you prepare for class assignments and projects.

The strategies presented in this section give you a great start toward a successful college experience, offering practical ways to deal with the most common obstacles college students face when they start their course work. Using all these strategies will give you more time and energy for your college efforts, and create a foundation for a truly rewarding college experience.

The rest of the sections of this book build on this foundation. With each section you'll learn many new skills to make your academic and social involvement in college fulfilling and successful. Work with this book, take advantage of all that your college has to offer, and success will follow.

Motivation is what brought you to college. You wanted more education and the opportunities of a career, as well as all the benefits they bring. This section has given you the tools to build the motivation you need to reach these goals and seize the rewards. You've begun to visualize what success in school and work means to you.

Hopefully this section has inspired you to be a goal setter to help you stay on track and persevere. You've also had a chance to examine your self-esteem and realize that high self-esteem means that you are a worthwhile person, whether or not you succeed at any given task. A high self-esteem also helps you work toward your goals because you have more faith in yourself and are more forgiving when you don't succeed immediately. You've explored how self-talk plays a major part in shaping your self-esteem.

Most importantly, this section has explained how self-talk can direct and guide you. Taking more control of what messages you tell yourself will give you more control of your school, work, and personal life. Telling yourself, "I'm going to beat math, it's not going to beat me," gives you a lot more inner strength than, "I have to have a major that doesn't require math—I can't do math." Creating positive self-talk gives you strength and encouragement to pursue the paths you want to follow.

Finally, you've learned a method for creative problem solving and decision making that is useful at school, work, and in your personal life. You will have opportunities at the end of all the remaining sections to practice problem solving so it can become second nature.

As you continue working with this book and the rest of your studies, put the tools from this section to work. With some practice, you'll find yourself using them almost automatically. And as these strategies become habit, so will success.

DISCUSSION QUESTIONS

Note: Read the following discussion questions and activities **before** you read Section 1. This strategy will help you look for answers while you read.

1. What do you most hope to gain from attending college?
2. What obstacles or distractions could keep you from doing your best in college, and how could you overcome them?
3. What initiatives can you take to develop three of the Workforce Skills and Personal Qualities as you pursue your college education?
4. Discuss the advantages of having an associate degree.
5. If you were to graduate with both an associate and a bachelor degree, which two degree programs would you choose?
6. How do you want to get more socially involved in college?
7. How do you want to get more academically involved in college?
8. How can you use the Internet to help you in your courses?
9. What extracurricular activities would you like to get involved in at college?
10. Many students who could benefit from tutoring wait too long before seeking this type of assistance. How could you recognize a need for tutoring and seek the extra assistance in a timely manner?
11. Describe a frustrating encounter with the bureaucracy at your college. How could you better handle such an encounter in the future?
12. Many times it's important to start out early for school to avoid traffic or accident delays. How could you best handle your time if you arrived at school a half hour earlier every day?
13. What are the two most important pieces of information you learned about credit card usage?
14. After viewing the websites for scholarships and student financial aid, list three types of scholarships and/or financial aid programs you may be eligible for.
15. What can you do to be more thrifty with your money while attending college?
16. How can you improve the balance among the various demands on your time and energy, such as school, work, family, friends, and online social networking?
17. If you have children, what solutions have you found that help you make time for study and assignments? What improvements could you make?
18. How does being an effective listener help diffuse conflict?
19. How does visualization help you accomplish your goals? Give an example of how you have used visualization to succeed. In what specific ways and in what courses can you use visualization more to help you in school?
20. Explain the similarities between visualization and planning.
21. How does visualization motivate you?
22. How can you use goals and goal planning to motivate you?
23. Discuss the value of developing short-term goals.
24. How can daily and weekly goal planning help you manage the stress of your busy life?
25. How do you incorporate fun in your day? How can you make your day more enjoyable and, at the same time, improve your learning?
26. Identify the areas in your life in which you are most disciplined. How did you learn to discipline yourself? How can you transfer that ability to be disciplined to other areas in your life where you want to be more disciplined? List the areas of your college life in which you wish to be more disciplined. What specific steps will you take to become more self-disciplined in these areas? (Look at the 5 steps outlined in the section.)
27. How can you build a positive self-image?
28. How does self-discipline improve your self-image?
29. How can visualization and self-talk improve your self-image?

Making Time Work for You

WHAT'S IN IT FOR YOU

College life is a busy life. "I feel like there just aren't enough hours in the day," Janie says, as she rushes across campus eating her lunch. "I had two classes this morning. I don't even have time to sit for lunch. Now I go to my job for the whole afternoon. And tonight I have to read two sections and finish a writing assignment."

How can you manage all of your personal responsibilities as well as study for all of your courses, meet wi' your classmates for group assignments, make it to all of your classes, meet privately with your instructors, c' with the administration, and find tutoring? None of these tasks can be neglected. They are your goals responsibilities. All are part of the balanced life you envision. The key to making this balance a reality in y life is time management—making the most of your time.

In this section you'll explore:

- Your time wasters and the importance of eliminating unnecessary activities
- Tips to manage your time and set priorities
- Methods for creating the best schedule for you
- Tips for beating procrastination
- Tips to help you save time
- The rewards of time management

4. _____

5. _____

6. _____

7. _____

8. _____

9. _____

10. _____

Discuss your results from Exercise 2-5 with a partner in class and write a brief paragraph on what you discovered about yourself.

Of course, it's difficult to say "no" sometimes. You've probably spent hours in front of the TV· thinking occasionally about what you really should be doing. You search the channels for something to watch, finally settling on a sitcom. You think again that you should be studying. "Right after this is over," you say to yourself. When it's over you remember that your favorite show is on in just another half-hour. "It's not worth studying for just a half-hour," you tell yourself. So you watch the next sitcom. When your favorite show is over, you figure that it's really too late to start studying. Sleep is probably more important, anyway.

TV is probably the single biggest waste of time for most students even though, when they stop to think about it, few of the shows are worthwhile. Partying with friends or going shopping may seem a more worthwhile use of your time; but, at times, you still have to say "no" to them. If you stop to think of your goals, your vision of succeeding in college—or your vision of a great job—occasionally saying "no" to an immediate pleasure is really saying "yes" to success. So when friends suddenly call and ask you to go out partying, stop and think about your vision of success. Remember your list of priorities, last week's Time Monitor, and your goal statements. Get into the habit of thinking of your vision, priorities, and goals whenever you're tempted to stray from your studies. These are your sources of strength. You may not always be able to say "no," but you're much more likely to say "yes" to success.

However, living from moment to moment while deciding which task deserves a "yes" and which task deserves a "no" is ridiculous. You'd spend all your time deciding and no time doing. Instead, successful students make these decisions in advance. They use their decisions to make a schedule for their study time, their personal time, and time for all of their high-priority tasks. Scheduling is an essential skill for success in and out of school. Developing effective scheduling skills will also make you a more productive employee.

SCHEDULING

Although you probably found some time wasters you can eliminate, becoming a successful student ultimately means adding many important activities to your daily life. "I'm trying to find enough time for all of my reading," Michael says. "But I have my girlfriend, work, and other things that are important to me." Scheduling gives you the tools to manage your new and busier life without having to sacrifice your most important goals. It helps you get started on new tasks, plan time for important tasks, and remember even minor tasks. Best of all, scheduling helps you make time for fun and relaxation without feeling guilty about other commitments. Your mind is freed from worry about all the tasks you need to complete. You gain control over your time. You march strongly and confidently toward your goals.

Tips . . . For Scheduling Study Time

Now that college is a priority in your life, you'll find the following tips helpful as you think about scheduling study time.

- Study during your "peak" time—when you feel at your best and most alert. Some people function best in the morning, others feel more alert late in the day.

- Use the small blocks of free time between classes or waiting time (at the dentist, on the bus) to study. A lot can be learned in small time periods, and it gives you more free time later.

- Review your notes just before a class that requires you to recite or discuss material so it will be fresh in your mind.

- Review your notes as soon as possible after a lecture course to help retain and better understand the class material.

- As a rule of thumb, you'll need two to three hours of study for every hour of class. Adjust the hours you schedule as you discover how much time you actually need to master each assignment.

- Schedule study breaks and rewards. Five- to 10-minute breaks may be adequate. Select rewards that give you something to look forward to, such as a scoop of ice cream, a soda, or a phone call to a friend.

- Allow adequate time for sleep. Learning is easier when you're rested.

- Start long-term projects early. You'll do better work when you're not racing against a deadline.

Sure it takes time to schedule, but you'll save far more time as a result. As with anything, the first time you schedule may take a lot of time; but it eventually will become routine. And if you think scheduling takes away your flexibility, remember: a disorganized person usually has less time to be flexible with. You can build flexibility into your schedule.

While you're learning to schedule time for work, class, and study, don't forget to make time for fun. Although you may not consciously schedule time for fun, it's a necessary part of your busy life.

Creating the Best Schedule for You

There are several different ways to create a schedule. You may find that one type fits your needs better than others. You'll learn about creating a Master Schedule, a Weekly Schedule, a To Do list, a Long-Term Assignment Schedule, and a Weekly Assignment Schedule. Try them and adapt them to fit your own needs. You don't need to purchase fancy calendars. You can create your own or get a free calendar from a bank. Make your schedule as simple as possible so it's easy to use.

The Master Schedule

The Master Schedule is a schedule of your typical week. It includes all your fixed tasks—activities you do at the same time every week. Fixed activities can include your morning routine, classes, study, work, family demands, eating times, cleaning days, exercise, recreation, and sleep. Think for a moment about which activities are fixed in your life.

Figure 2-1
Lakeisha's Master Schedule

Time	Monday	Tuesday	Wednesday	Thursday	Friday	Saturday	Sunday
7:00	Jog/ breakfast	Jog/ breakfast	Jog/ breakfast	Jog/ breakfast	Jog/ breakfast		
8:00	English 201	Study	English 201	Study	English 201	Breakfast	
9:00		College Math		College Math		Computer Lab	
10:00	Accounting		Accounting		Accounting		Study
11:00		Study		Study		Study	
12:00	Lunch	Lunch	Lunch	Lunch	Lunch		
1:00	Study	Work		Work			Clean
2:00	Sales 105		Sales 105		Sales 105		
3:00							
4:00	Softball				Softball		
5:00							
6:00	Dinner	Dinner	Dinner	Dinner	Dinner		Study
7:00			Study				
8:00	Business Club	Business 101		Business 101			
9:00	Study						
10:00		Study		Study			
11:00	Bed	Bed	Bed	Bed			Bed
12:00							

Master schedules help you arrange your routine activities so that you can better schedule the ever-changing ones, like assignments and appointments. You can draw up your master schedule at the beginning of each school term and at any time your basic routine changes. Look at Lakeisha's Master Schedule in Figure 2-1 as an example. Notice that the shaded areas mark the time that already is committed to regular activities, while the time left blank on her master schedule is available for weekly or day-to-day planning. This is also time that can be scheduled for such activities as long-term assignments.

Master schedules can also help you arrange your routine activities on the job so you can better schedule your ever-changing work assignments and projects. At work your master schedule will help you keep better tabs on all your responsibilities so you can be productive and be punctual with deadlines. Developing the self-discipline now to make the most productive use of your time will become habit. Habit takes time to develop and developing the habit of scheduling is a powerful work skill.

If you work and have regular working hours, a master schedule is best. If you work irregular hours, a master schedule may not be the best choice because your schedule changes too often. Try it to see if it works.

Weekly Schedule

If your schedule changes from week to week, try a weekly schedule. A weekly schedule helps you to organize each week's priorities. To create a weekly schedule, simply make several copies of your master schedule that highlights whatever fixed activities you have. Then, with a different color pen, write in weekly assignments, exams, appointments, study times, recreation, and start times for special projects. At times your fixed activities may be changed or canceled and you can write in other activities over the canceled ones. Note the example in Figure 2-2 of a weekly schedule based on Lakeisha's Master Schedule.

Figure 2-2
Lakeisha's Weekly Schedule

Time	Monday	Tuesday	Wednesday	Thursday	Friday	Saturday	Sunday
7:00	Jog/breakfast	Jog/breakfast	Jog/breakfast	Jog/breakfast	Jog/breakfast		
8:00	English 201	Study	English 201	Study	English 201	Breakfast	
9:00		College Math		College Math		Computer Lab	
10:00	Accounting		Accounting	MATH TEST	Accounting		write proposal
11:00		read for sales		Study		complete draft	for
12:00	Lunch	Lunch	Lunch	Lunch	Lunch	of English	business paper
1:00	acctng problems	Work	review sales	Work	lunch with Sue	paper	Clean
2:00	Sales 105		Sales 105		Sales 105		
3:00						class cookout	
4:00	Softball		study for math		Softball		
5:00			study for math			clean	
6:00	Dinner	Dinner	Dinner	Dinner	Dinner	laundry	read English
7:00	study math	read for sales	read business	read English	start research		read English
8:00	Business Club	Business 101	read business	Business 101	for business		read acctng
9:00	read business		review math		see Julie in play	Sam's party	acctng problems
10:00	read business	acctng problems	review math	read acctng	play		read sales
11:00	Bed	Bed	Bed	Bed	play		Bed
12:00							

Master Schedule

Name: _____

Semester: _____

Time	Sunday	Monday	Tuesday	Wednesday	Thursday	Friday	Saturday
5:00 AM							
6:00 AM							
7:00 AM							
8:00 AM							
9:00 AM							
10:00 AM							
11:00 AM							
12:00 PM							
1:00 PM							
2:00 PM							
3:00 PM							
4:00 PM							
5:00 PM							
6:00 PM							
7:00 PM							
8:00 PM							
9:00 PM							
10:00 PM							
11:00 PM							
12:00 AM							

Class Hours: _____   Study Hours: _____   Extracurricular Hours: _____   Work Hours: _____

Weekly Master Schedule

Name: _____

Semester: _____

Time	Sunday	Monday	Tuesday	Wednesday	Thursday	Friday	Saturday
5:00 AM							
6:00 AM							
7:00 AM							
8:00 AM							
9:00 AM							
10:00 AM							
11:00 AM							
12:00 PM							
1:00 PM							
2:00 PM							
3:00 PM							
4:00 PM							
5:00 PM							
6:00 PM							
7:00 PM							
8:00 PM							
9:00 PM							
10:00 PM							
11:00 PM							
12:00 AM							

Class Hours: _____   Study Hours: _____   Extracurricular Hours: _____   Work Hours: _____

Obviously, you can create a weekly sch___le without a master schedule. You can use a calendar and list the activities and times for each day of the w___ ___ou can also create your own list of all activities for each day in the week. Whether at school or on the job, y___ ___el more in control of a busy schedule if you can glance at all of your week's activities that are written on on___ ___ You may want to schedule several weeks at one time.

Daily Planning: The To Do List

Daily planning is ideal for the person whose sc___ ___is constantly changing and for anyone who wants to get more control over their school, work, or home ___ties. The simplest and fastest way to engage in daily planning is to create a To Do List of the next day's ___riority items that need to be completed before the close of the day. To Do Lists are best completed the e___ ___before so, when morning arrives, you are ready to begin. The To Do List can be maintained in a small ___ ___ok or on index cards. Look at Antonio's To Do List in Figure 2-3.

Figure 2-3
Antonio's To Do List

Oct. 14	To Do Tomorrow
1. Think up questions for English class.	
2. Mail student loan form.	
3. Bring book to class for Judy.	
4. Call tutor to confirm tomorrow's session.	
5. Arrange group study with Kevin.	
6. Ask about format for upcoming math test before class.	
7. Return library books.	
8. Council meeting at 8 PM.	
9. Weight training class at the field house.	

Now make a To Do List of your own. On a piece of paper, write down (in any order) all the tasks you want to accomplish tomorrow. Set priorities for your list by numbering the tasks, in order of importance or from early to late. Combine any tasks that can be completed together, in the same location, or on the way—for example, it may be worth stopping at the library on your way to class to pick up a book for a future assignment, even though picking up the book may not be the highest priority. Then examine your list. Are there any tasks you really can't get to? Scratch them off your list. Once they're off your list, they're off your mind. Finally, make notes on times, phone numbers, or reminders to help you complete the tasks.

Now put this list in your briefcase, handbag, or backpack so you'll have it with you tomorrow. Review your list before bed tonight and again when you wake up in the morning. As you complete each task, cross it off your list. There's something very satisfying about scratching things off a list. If you have any leftover tasks at the end of the day, decide to eliminate them or transfer them to the next day's list.

Scheduling Long-Term Assignments

To show your best work on special projects, term papers, and major exams, you must start working early. By starting early, you'll also avoid the panic of doing all the work at the last minute—which can really take the fun out of learning, as well as hurt your grade. As Will discovered, "I think I sometimes spend more energy panicking at the end than I would have spent by starting earlier." Remember, you want to show your instructor what you know, not just what you managed to cram in at three o'clock in the morning. If you start early you'll feel more in charge, learn more, and enjoy it more.

Scheduling long-term assignments helps you start early and produce your best work. Start by listing the smaller, intermediate steps you can take to reach your goal—for example, let's look at how you could organize the writing of a major paper that you've been assigned to complete by the end of the school term. Note Tonya's term paper schedule in Figure 2-4.

Breaking tasks into smaller parts makes big jobs more manageable. When you organize your time and efforts according to intermediate steps, you feel a sense of relief and satisfaction at the end of each day or each step.

Establishing deadlines for intermediate steps and long-range goals helps you avoid procrastination—putting it off until later. Don't forget to write these intermediate steps on your daily To Do List. You also can write them on a weekly or monthly schedule. Scheduling for long-term assignments allows you to approach each day confidently and also eliminate the "hurry up" feeling when your deadline seems to be closing in on you.

Figure 2-4
Tonya's Term Paper Schedule

Steps to Complete	Dates
1. Think and talk about paper with classmates and instructor.	October 8, 10, 12
2. Gather and read articles and other information on the topic.	October 15, 16, 17
3. Organize materials and outline the topic.	November 1–2
4. Complete the first draft, using a word processor.	November 8–9
5. Have someone read draft.	by November 15
6. Complete and print final draft. Have someone proofread it.	by November 25
7. Submit completed paper to instructor.	December 1

Long-Range Scheduling

Long-range scheduling usually means keeping a running schedule until the end of a school term, semester, or quarter. The ideal schedule format is an inexpensive calendar that allows you to write in all assignments, exams, appointments, trips, and special events. Don't just write down due dates. Rather, write notes reminding you when to begin studying for a test, or write the start dates for each step of a major project. Maria's long-range schedule appears in Figure 2-5.

Figure 2-5
Maria's Long-Range Schedule

September

M	T	W	T	F	S	S
			1 registration/ orientation	**2** orientation/ cookout	**3**	**4**
5 classes begin	**6** meet with advisor	**7**	**8**	**9**	**10** softball game	**11**
12	**13** environmental club (7 pm)	**14**	**15** begin research for business paper topic	**16** begin English essay	**17** softball game/ business paper research	**18** hiking trip
19 start accounting project	**20** math quiz	**21**	**22** submit business paper proposal	**23** English essay due	**24** softball game/ class picnic	**25**
26	**27** environmental club (7 pm)	**28** start chemistry project	**29**	**30**		

October

M	T	W	T	F	S	S
				1 softball game	**2**	
3 accounting quiz	**4** math quiz	**5** submit chem project proposal	**6**	**7** begin English paper	**8** softball game	**8**
10	**11** environmental club (7 pm)	**12**	**13** discuss business paper outline with Wilson	**14**	**15** softball game/ enviromental team meet 6 pm	**16**
17 begin study for accounting midterm	**18** math quiz begin study for math midterm	**19** begin study for chemistry midterm	**20** begin study for business midterm	**21** complete first draft of English paper	**22** softball tournament/ midterm study	**23** softball tournament/ midterm study
24 accounting group 5 pm	**25** study group for midterm 7 pm	**26** study group for chem midterm 7 pm	**27** study group for business midterm 8 pm	**28** complete draft 2 of English paper/ find proofreader	**29** midterm study: accounting/ math	**30** midterm study: chem/ business
31 study math						

November

M	T	W	T	F	S	S
1 *accounting midterm*	2 *math midterm*	3 *chemistry midterm*	4 *business midterm*	5 *English paper due*	6 *team work on environmental fair display 5 pm*	7
8 *pre-registration*	9 *meet with advisor/ environmental club (7 pm)*	10 *complete chemistry project*	11	12	13 *complete environmental fair display*	14
15	16 *math quiz*	17 *present chemistry project*	18 *complete draft 1 of business paper*	19 *begin English paper*	20 *environmental fair (1 pm–6 pm)*	21
22	23 *environmental club (7 pm)*	24	25 *home*	26 *home*	27 *home/begin study for accounting final*	28 *home/begin study for math final*
29	30 *math quiz*					

December

M	T	W	T	F	S	S
		1 *begin study for chemistry final*	2 *begin study for business final/ complete draft 2 of business paper*	3 *complete draft 1 of English paper*	4 *final study accounting/ math*	5 *final study chemistry/ business*
6 *study group for accounting 5 pm*	7 *study group for math 8 pm/ environmental club party (7 pm)*	8 *study group for chemistry 7 pm*	9 *study group business 8 pm/ complete business paper/find reader*	10 *complete draft 2 of English paper/find proofreader*	11 *final study accounting/ math*	12 *final study chemistry/ business*
13 *accounting final*	14 *math final*	15 *chemistry final*	16 *business final/ submit business paper*	17 *English paper due/class party*	18	19
20	21	22	23	24	25	26
27	28	29	30	31		

Figure 2-6
Kevin's Class Assignment Schedule

Subject	Assignment	Estimated Time	Date Due	Time Due
Math	Read chap. pp. 5–26	2 hrs.	Mon. 16th	8:00
English	Write essay	3.5 hrs.	Wed. 18th	10:00
Design	Read chap. 3, pp. 4–30	2 hrs.	Wed. 18th	3:00
Design	Complete project	8 hrs.	Fri. 20th	3:00
Sales	Study for test	6 hrs.	Thur. 19th	2:00
Business	Read article	2.5 hrs.	Tues. 17th	10:00

Weekly Assignment Schedule

Some students prefer to keep each week's course assignments on a separate list. This is especially helpful because it helps you plan enough time for each assignment. Kevin started scheduling assignments last week after he had trouble with a reading assignment. "I sat down to read the section for the next morning's class," he says. "I opened the book and started flipping through the pages to see how long it was. I kept flipping . . . page 80 . . . and flipping . . . page 90 . . . and flipping . . . page 110 . . . and flipping . . . page 134! It was 72 pages long. I didn't finish until 2 AM."

After waking up awfully grumpy the next day, Kevin started creating a Weekly Assignment Schedule. This type of scheduling is a two-step process. The first step is to construct a Class Assignment Schedule. See Kevin's Assignment Schedule in Figure 2-6 for an example. As you complete more assignments you'll get better at estimating how long others will take. Unfamiliar projects often take twice as long as you think, so keep that in mind and double your time estimate.

The second step is to construct the Weekly Assignment Schedule. You convert the Class Assignment Schedule into a plan for the upcoming week. Kevin made one of these as well (see Figure 2-7). If you've completed a master schedule, you can check it to see what times you have available to do assignments. Don't forget some of those small blocks of time between classes or while waiting. When you give study hours top priority, your remaining free hours really will be free.

Figure 2-7
Kevin's Weekly Assignment Schedule

Day	Assignment	Morning	Afternoon	Evening
Sunday	Math: Chap. 5 English: outline			7:00–9:00 9:00–10:00
Monday 1st draft Business: article Sales: review	English:	10:00–11:30	1:00–3:00	 9:30–11:00

Figure 2-7
Kevin's Weekly Assignment Schedule (continued)

Day	Assignment	Morning	Afternoon	Evening
Tuesday	English: final copy		1:00–2:00	
	Design: Part I project		2:00–6:00	
	Design: Chap. 3			7:00–9:00
	Sales: study			9:00–11:00
Wednesday	Design: Part II project			7:30–9:30
	Sales: study			9:30–11:00
Thursday	Design: Part III project	8:00–10:00		
Friday	Design: present project	9:00–10:00		
Saturday				

Sticking to Your Schedule

The final part of managing your time is to stick to the schedules you make. The Tips for Saving Time will help you find more time for your scheduled activities. And the Tips for Beating Procrastination will help you get started—or restarted—so you won't fall behind. Reward yourself whenever you stick to your schedule. It's one of the true marks of success.

Avoiding Procrastination

Sometimes starting assignments, especially long-term assignments, is the hardest part of all. Putting off tasks is known as procrastination. Some people procrastinate so they'll have an excuse for performing poorly on a test or assignment. Other people want to do things so perfectly that they put off assignments and can blame lack of time for not performing better. Procrastination becomes a serious problem if it leaves you with too little time to produce the quality of work you and your instructors expect. Procrastination can become a habit—one that's hard to break—but here are some tips to get you going right away.

Tips . . . For Beating Procrastination

- Focus on the positive. Say to yourself, "I'll feel much better if I start this project now." Or even, "The sooner I get this finished, the sooner I can really relax and have some fun."

- Think of rewards. Plan to reward yourself for taking the first step with a break, a dessert, or a phone call to a friend. Imagine the rewards of completing the assignment, such as getting a good grade or feeling better about yourself as a student.

- Break down the assignment and list the steps for completing it—even just opening a book and reading a few pages. Tackle one of the easier steps right away so you can see some progress toward completion.

(continued)

- Visualize yourself doing the task—typing away at the computer, reading and taking notes, or combing the shelves of the library.

- Go to a quiet place to study where you won't be tempted by distractions, such as friends or TV. Then it'll be just you and the assignment getting acquainted.

Tips . . . For Saving Time

Review the following tips for saving time and try the ones you think might fit your needs. With practice, many of these tips can become habits that will save you a lot of time over the long run.

- Only use the schedules that help you manage your time.

- Set time limits on projects; otherwise, projects seem to run on. Deadlines and time limits help you get finished.

- Be flexible in your scheduling. Expect that there will be some changes and interruptions.

- Study on the run by keeping your notes with you. Use those few minutes between classes and while waiting for class to start to review notes.

- Listen to recorded lectures or tutoring tapes in the car or while you're getting ready for work or school.

- Try reciting information you have to memorize while walking to class.

- Attach index cards with terms or formulas to your mirror.

- If you know you haven't the time for some activity, don't schedule it. Say "no" to requests for which you absolutely have no time.

- Get up 15 minutes earlier each day and you'll feel like you've got a head start.

- Allow 15 minutes extra to get to appointments.

- Prepare for your next morning the evening before. Place items you need for class or work in the car the night before.

- Before your break, take one more opportunity to briefly review underlining, text notes, or class notes.

- When you think you're too tired to study, beat the sleepy feeling by standing up to study, by pacing the floor, or by reading aloud.

- When you reach the end of your study time, write yourself a note so you know where to start next time.

THE REWARDS OF TIME MANAGEMENT

Time management is fun because the rewards are immediate and the results are obvious—you accomplish what you need to do as well as what you want to do. The secret to managing your time is developing habits that help you get more control of your time to live a balanced life of: learning, relaxing, exercising, working, eating, maintaining relationships, fulfilling responsibilities, and other important matters in your life. The more you take control of your time, the more time you have for what really counts. Golda Meir summed up time management best: "I must govern the clock, not be governed by it.

More Rewards of Time Management

The benefits of effective time management can be measured in terms of . . .

1. **Less stress.** You'll feel less anxiety when you get done what's really important—that includes major assignments at school or work, as well as your personal and leisure time. Wasting time causes stress. Look at stress and ways to manage it.

2. **More work done.** When you know what tasks to do first and arrange your time that way, you accomplish more of what really counts.

3. **Better control.** When you manage your time, you spend more time on the things you feel are important. You learn to eliminate your top time wasters to get more time for your top priorities.

4. **Improved quality of life.** Time management also means planning personal time and fun.

5. **Better self-image.** You will like yourself better and so will your family, friends, and boss.

6. **Quicker promotions.** Good time managers are easier to promote. They can be relied on to get the job done quickly and smoothly. When you are organized and working efficiently, it's easier to demonstrate that you are valuable to the organization and more likely to perform.

7. **Better grades!**

Take your time seriously so you have time for the less serious. Time for yourself and for fun are essential to your mental and physical health and make the rest of your time more productive and less stressful. Ken Blanchard once said, "The objective of time management is inner peace."

HIGHLIGHTS

In this section you've explored many different time management tips to help you succeed in school and work. You've probably noticed that time management is really self-management and that it is not simply meeting deadlines and being on time. More important, time management is seeing to it that the way you spend time is the way you want to spend it—to accomplish your goals and priorities.

You've probably uncovered some of your time wasters and taken a good look at ways to reduce or eliminate them to make time for what really counts. Additionally, you've discovered that good planning doesn't rule out flexibility; rather, it gives you more time to be flexible. You've been introduced to several types of scheduling to help you manage your busy life. Select only the schedules that help you organize your time with a schedule that is tailored to your needs and obligations. Hopefully, you can also see the merit of planning for large and small assignments with a schedule that helps you note deadlines as well as the intermediate steps that will help you meet those deadlines.

This section outlines many tips for your consideration to help you set priorities, beat procrastination, and save time. You can put yourself in charge of how you use your time. Time management won't give you more time— just more productive time.

DISCUSSION QUESTIONS

Note: Read the following discussion questions and activities **before** you read Section 2. This strategy will help you look for answers while you read.

1. What is the purpose of time management?
2. How can you save time?
3. List and explain the purpose of each of the different time schedules outlined in the text.
4. Explain the procedure for completing a To Do List as outlined in the text. How can a To Do List reduce stress? List experiences of how using a To Do List has helped you.

Making the Classroom Work for You

WHAT'S IN IT FOR YOU

While you're attending college, you will be studying and learning in many environments, including the lab, library, team assignments, study groups, field experiences, tutoring sessions, and individual study time. Only a part of your total learning time will actually be spent in the classroom; but this time is the basis of your college education. Class time (when your instructor shares his/her expertise and establishes a structure for learning) is what you pay for; the tuition you pay to your school is primarily for the privilege of attending classes. Therefore, it's clear that good classroom skills, as well as developing a variety of learning styles, are essential to your success as a student.

What are good classroom skills? They are the skills that help you get the most out of your class time—from preparation to participation. You'll find that, when you effectively manage your time in the classroom, it will be much easier to manage your study time out of the classroom as well.

In this section you'll explore:

- The many aspects of good class preparation
- The importance of class attendance
- Appropriate classroom etiquette
- Expectations for class participation
- What to expect from your instructors and what they expect of you
- Your preferred learning styles and how to make the most of them
- Your instructors' preferred modes of teaching and how to get the most out of their instruction
- Ways to compensate for learning disorders and difficulties
- Tips to make the most of opportunities for learning outside the classroom
- How to make a comeback when your grades are falling

BEING PREPARED

Exercise 3-1 What are my classroom skills?

This exercise gives you an opportunity to examine your approach to classroom learning. Read each statement. If the statement applies to you, check "Yes." If it doesn't apply to you, check "No."

		Yes	No
1.	I read assignments prior to class time.	_____	_____
2.	I come to class prepared with written questions regarding recent course topics.	_____	_____
3.	I get to class a few minutes early to settle in and review my reading or previous notes, or both.	_____	_____
4.	I miss class only when I am too ill to attend or have an emergency.	_____	_____
5.	I have telephone numbers for one or two classmates who I can call if I miss a class or need assistance on an assignment.	_____	_____
6.	I act courteously and respectfully in class—not engaging in side conversations or disrupting in any way.	_____	_____
7.	I participate in class discussions and ask questions in class.	_____	_____
8.	I thoroughly read each class syllabus to acquaint myself with class policies and assignments.	_____	_____
9.	I complete assignments thoroughly and neatly.	_____	_____
10.	I turn in assignments on time.	_____	_____
11.	I make efforts to be adaptable to the professor's teaching style.	_____	_____
12.	I take advantage of learning opportunities outside the classroom, such as seminars, lectures, guest speakers, the library, professional journals, clubs or organizations, discussions with professionals in my field, or volunteer work related to my field.	_____	_____
13.	When I have difficulty with any course, I seek assistance from school tutors, reliable classmates, learning assistance staff, or my professors.	_____	_____
14.	I talk to my advisor to seek assistance in scheduling and planning my program of studies.	_____	_____
15.	If I get confused during class, I ask questions to get an explanation before I get entirely lost.	_____	_____

If you checked "No" on any of the above statements, these are areas that, with improvement, could help you get more out of your classes.

Your classwork starts long before you take your seat in the classroom. Many students think that being in the classroom is supposed to be a passive experience—that is, they are supposed to sit back silently and listen to the instructor until it's time to leave. Not true! Certainly a large part of your class time will be spent listening to your instructor talk; but you'll be doing this in an active fashion—taking notes, posing questions, offering comments and opinions. You can't take an active part in the classroom, however, unless you've prepared beforehand. You might say your classwork begins before the class does.

Know What the Class Is About

At the beginning of the term, your instructors should give you a **syllabus** for each of your courses. A syllabus is a detailed outline of the material that will be covered in a course and all the papers, quizzes, and so on that will be assigned and when they'll be due. The syllabus is one of your most important tools for being prepared. As soon as you get your copy for each class, read it carefully. You'll get an overview of what the class will cover, and you'll get an idea of how much time you'll need to spend studying and researching assignments for each course. This will help you manage all of your time more effectively. It's a good idea to make an extra copy of each syllabus in case you misplace the first copy. You don't want to fall behind on your readings for class because you can't find your syllabus. You might want to insert or attach a copy of the syllabus for each course inside the front cover of the notebook you keep for each subject, so you can refer to it often.

After you've become familiar with the syllabus, the next step is to follow it. Here's exactly where some students run into trouble. They think that they can get away with attending class without reading the assignments beforehand. Contrary to what these students think, the instructor is not merely going to repeat the contents of the assignment for those who didn't read it. The reading assignment is a "jumping-off place" for the class lecture. In other words, the class lecture or discussion will be based on the reading but will not repeat it word for word. Therefore, if you haven't read the assigned reading before going into class, chances are very good that you won't know what the instructor is talking about.

Not only will your work suffer if you don't prepare for class, but it will soon become apparent to your instructor that you haven't prepared. Many instructors take class preparation and participation into consideration when determining your grade (especially if it's borderline). When you've prepared for class and done the readings, the questions that you ask in class will reflect that. One student found that out the hard way.

~Steven~

I'll admit it. I thought that you read the assignment only if you wanted to know in advance what the instructor was going to say. I really thought he'd just repeat the stuff in the section. After a few accounting classes last year, I noticed the instructor was talking only a little bit about the section, and spending the rest of the class talking about all this other stuff. So I actually went up to him one day and said, "Why aren't you covering the material in the book?" And he looked at me and said, "The material in the text is only the beginning of what you study in class. I can't waste valuable class time repeating what my students are perfectly capable of reading themselves." Boy, did I learn my lesson. I'm glad I learned it before it was too late.

"I was coasting through class, not reading any assignments beforehand. One day I raised my hand to ask a question that was clearly answered in the first paragraph of the reading assignment and it was obvious to everyone and the instructor that I hadn't read the assignment."

Ready to Work

Now that you know about preparing before class, you need to be prepared to work while you're in class. Remember, no aspect of learning in college is passive. Even when sitting in class, listening to a lecture, the successful student takes an active role in his or her education, taking notes, asking questions, analyzing, thinking, and wondering. You've looked at the syllabus and read the class assignment. What else do you need to do to be well prepared?

It isn't enough to merely read an assignment. As you read, you naturally will develop questions in your mind about what you're reading. These questions are important. Jot down any questions or comments you have about the assignment and be prepared to share them in class. Perhaps you didn't understand a few passages, or maybe you don't see how this material fits in with the rest of the course. Your instructor won't know that you're concerned about these issues unless you're ready to bring them up in class. Remember, too, that the questions you ask in class benefit your classmates as well. They may have been intending to ask the same questions themselves, or perhaps you've brought up a point they hadn't thought of. So don't feel inhibited about coming to class loaded with questions, comments, and observations; it's an important part of the learning process. "I write questions as I read the assignment," says Alicia. "Then during class I cross off the questions that the instructor answers during the course of the lecture. Any questions that I haven't crossed off by the end of class, I ask during the question-and-answer period. That way I don't waste time asking questions that would have been covered anyway."

Be sure to bring all the necessary materials to class. This includes your text, syllabus, notebook, pens, pencil and eraser, and anything else you might need. In a lab situation, make sure you have all the materials you need to complete a procedure or to properly perform an experiment.

Prepare yourself for class as well. All the notebooks and texts in the world won't be much help if you're tired and underfed. Some students are notorious for getting up at the last minute and coming into the classroom clutching a cup of coffee, trying to wake up. How much do you think these students are getting out of their classes? Remember, attending classes is the privilege you're paying for. "My lab partner last year was always coming in late to classes after partying all night," remembers Nicole. "Once she actually fell asleep during an anatomy lab. Needless to say, her grades were terrible, and she wasn't a favorite with the faculty."

THE IMPORTANCE OF CLASS ATTENDANCE

~Roberto~

I'll admit it, I spent most of the first day of classes at the coffeehouse, talking with some friends. I figured that, on the very first day of classes, most of the instructors would just sort of introduce themselves and then let the class out early. I didn't think they'd do any work. Well, my psychology class was assigned a one-page paper due on the second class. I walked into the second class without a paper—not even knowing there was an assignment, because I hadn't looked at the syllabus—and got a zero. Well, it taught me a lesson; I never made that mistake again. And do you know what? I noticed that a lot of my friends who were skipping that first day of class had some problems, too. You don't see the really successful students sitting around campus when they're supposed to be in class.

College classes are your opportunity to learn directly from instructors who are skilled and experienced in their area and who are devoted to helping you learn. Rarely will you get such an opportunity.

That's the great thing about college—it's an environment totally devoted to you and to your education. Now that you've got this opportunity, don't waste it.

As you can tell from Roberto's experience, the first day of class is just as important as any other. Your instructors may choose to devote the first class to distributing and reviewing your course syllabus. This is a great opportunity to ask questions about future assignments, course requirements, and the amount of out-of-class work you'll be expected to do. You'll learn what your instructors' individual policies are regarding lateness, absences, paper formats, and deadline extensions. Your instructors may discuss how your grade will be determined. The first day of class can be a treasure trove of information.

Every class after the first is important as well. Instructors have a lot of information to give you and only a certain number of class hours in which to give it, so every minute counts. Even if you've memorized the syllabus and do all your assignments, you still need to attend *every* class. Sometimes the syllabus changes; your instructor may add or delete assignments or change the due date of some. Also, many instructors, despite their best intentions, find themselves falling behind in the course and may double up assignments to get the class back on track. Pop quizzes are not listed on the syllabus; if you miss one, your grade will be zero.

You may think that the importance of regular class attendance is obvious. It may sound ridiculous, but a major cause of failure among college students is poor class attendance. Students who miss most of their classes also miss tests, assignments, and opportunities to learn. In the end, they're only cheating themselves. Students who attend class *most* of the time, but not always, may regret it when their attendance record brings down a borderline grade. Be aware that the student with a good attendance record, whose grade is between a "C+" and a "B-" will almost always get the higher grade. His fellow student, with the same numerical average and a poor attendance record, will probably earn the "C+."

Get There Early

Go to every class—*on time*. As with any appointment, it's a good idea to be on time or even a bit early. Class is your appointment with your instructor and fellow classmates. Show your respect by not making them wait for you. There are many advantages to arriving early to class. First of all, if you plan to arrive early, chances are that any unforeseen delays won't make you late for class. If you take into account possible traffic jams, faulty alarm clocks, last minute phone calls, and other interruptions, you'll manage to arrive on time.

Arriving early allows you to prepare yourself for class—to find the best seat, get your text open to the right section, review your notes from the previous class, even take a few moments to discuss a question or problem with your instructor. You might discuss the homework assignment with classmates, or just take a quiet moment for yourself before you start to work.

When You Miss a Class

Even with the best intentions, there will be days when you cannot attend class. Try to make these days as few as possible. No one expects you to attend classes if you've got a fever of 102; on the other hand, a mild head cold or a case of the "blahs" shouldn't keep you away from class. Instructors appreciate it when students make the effort to attend class despite obstacles; they make the effort, too. If, because of illness or an emergency, you absolutely cannot attend class, let your instructor know. A phone call or note is not only courteous, it lets the instructor know that you take your responsibilities as a student seriously. Likewise, it's a good idea to let your instructor know if, for some reason, your essay or homework assignment will be late because you cannot hand it in yourself. Even better, ask a friend or classmate to deliver your assignment for you; responsible behavior and commitment to success make a big impression on any instructor.

~Jessie~

I had a terrible cold and a fever of 102. I hadn't missed a class all year, but I couldn't go when I felt so miserable. I was nervous, though, because my instructors always seemed to be really annoyed with people who missed a class. So I left her a note saying that I was sick and couldn't attend class the rest of the week. The day class was scheduled, I called the instructor at her office to make sure she'd gotten the note (I was really nervous). She was so nice—she asked me how I was feeling and said she'd send a classmate over with the handouts and assignments I'd missed. Well, it turns out she doesn't have anything against students being absent when they have to be; it's just that so few of them ever bother to let her know. It gives the impression that they just don't care. She appreciated the fact that I'd let her know, and she even extended the deadline for my next paper by a week, so I could get back on my feet.

When you've been absent, don't ask your instructor if you "missed anything." It is your responsibility to find out what you missed. Call a classmate to find out about assignments, class discussion, missed notes, and handouts. Always ask your classmates first. If for some reason your classmates can't give you all the information you need about the missed class (an unlikely occurrence), only then should you ask your instructor.

Why not ask the instructor? you might ask. It is the instructor's responsibility to hold class as scheduled, not to repeat what went on in class for individuals who missed that day. Remember, you're not that instructor's only student; you're not even the only student who missed class. Look at it this way: suppose an instructor has 120 students in four classes, and five students from each class missed one day. If each of these twenty students came up to the instructor individually to ask what material they missed, that instructor would spend as much time teaching out of class as in class. Make an effort to acquaint yourself with your classmates; find one or two with whom you can exchange phone numbers. That way you each have a reliable network of fellow students you can depend on for missed notes, handouts, and any other information.

> **~Selena~**
>
> I asked my biology professor for some of the notes I missed one day. She looked up at me with this really tired expression and said, "Do you know you're the tenth student to ask me that this afternoon?" I felt awful. I mean, it's not her fault I missed class. My roommate's in the same class, so now I ask her for the notes I miss.

CLASSROOM ETIQUETTE

Learning effectively in the classroom includes behaving in a way that is respectful of your instructors and your fellow students. Your instructor is there to teach, and your classmates are there to learn (like you); let them do their jobs. You may not think so, but small things like turning in papers late, whispering to the person sitting next to you, not raising your hand when you have a question, and coming late to class are disruptions that can keep other people from working effectively. Review the following tips on classroom etiquette so you can work more effectively with others.

> **~Ray~**
>
> In my algebra class, there are three students who whisper constantly in the back row. They sit so far back that the instructor can't really hear them, but those of us who sit near them can. I always want to say to them, "If you want to talk so much, why don't you go to the lounge and let the rest of us stay focused on the instructor's explanations." One of these days I just might do it, too!

Tips . . . For Being Courteous in the Classroom

- Resist the temptation to chat with your fellow students once class has begun. If you have something important to talk about, write a note to remind yourself to talk about it after class.

- If you have a comment, question, or observation to make in class, raise your hand and wait to be recognized before you speak. In some smaller, more informal classes, instructors may dispense with this rule and let everyone speak when they like. Unless your instructor states that this is the case, though, raise your hand. Don't interrupt your instructor or another student who's talking; raise your hand. You'll get your chance to speak.

- This may seem obvious, but eating, drinking, smoking, and loud gum chewing are out of place in the classroom. Not only that, they're certainly not activities that help you concentrate on what's going on in class. "I know one girl who always brought her lunch to chemistry class." says Emily. "One day she spilled her cup of soup all over the experiment she was doing in lab—there was chicken and noodles everywhere! I'll tell you, she never brought a crumb of food into class again."

- Turn in neat and carefully completed assignments. Your instructors have to read many other essays besides yours; they shouldn't have to spend all their time trying to read your handwriting. Ming helped one of her instructors hand back papers last semester. "You wouldn't believe the number of papers that never got handed back or even graded because they were such a mess. You couldn't even read the names on some of them; others had no cover page. I remember one that was written in pencil! Students don't seem to realize that their written work reflects *them*."

(continued)

- Take the responsibility to turn off your cell phone before entering the classroom. It is rude to let a phone distract the class, and intentional efforts must be made to turn off cell phones. If you have a personal emergency and need to be available by phone, explain your situation to your professor, and leave the classroom if you receive a call.

- Turn off all sounds and alarms from your laptops, PDAs, watches, etc.

- Refrain from distracting behaviors in the classroom such as using laptops to surf the Web or check email.

- Address your instructor in a respectful manner. "Hey Mack, what's up?" is okay for your friends, but not appropriate for your instructor. If you're unsure how to address your instructor, call him or her by Ms., Mrs., Mr., Dr., Professor, or ask his/her preference.

- Arrive early for class. Plan for those unforeseen circumstances, traffic jams, or friends who need a favor, by leaving home or your dorm early. While some teachers are lax about tardiness, it is disruptive to the lecture or other activities when all heads turn to watch your entrance. If your schedule just won't allow you to get to this class on time, drop it and take one that is convenient for you.

- Remain in the classroom for the duration of the class. If you must depart early due to unavoidable circumstances, inform your instructor before class. Avoid scheduling your job, appointments, or activities during your class period.

- If you plan to ask your instructors to bend the rules for you, like permission to hand in a late paper or to make other special arrangements, do so in private, not in front of the class. No instructor can respond fairly to a special request with the whole class awaiting the response.

- When you participate in a class debate or discussion, you often will have opinions that differ from those of your classmates. Learn to argue and discuss the class material in a serious, respectful manner. Academic arguments should never become shouting matches. State your opinion and offer facts to back it up. Often you'll find that you agree with your classmates on more points than you'd thought at first; the rest of the time, learn to disagree without being disagreeable. "Some people seem to think debates are shouting matches," grumbles Jorge. "And it never fails—the people who shout the most are always the ones who've done the least work. They just try to cover it up by being loud."

- If the instructor is speaking too fast or too softly for you to understand, raise your hand and let her know, in a polite and tactful way. "Excuse me, Mrs. LaVoie, could you speak a little more loudly? It's hard to hear you from this row, and I don't want to miss what you're saying" is the right way to make such a request. Shouting, "Hey, we can't hear back here, y'know" is not.

- If you are part of a network of classmates who fill in each other on missed classes, be sure your notes are clear and concise, and let your friends know they can call on you for help. They'll return the favor one day.

- Avoid dominating classroom discussion or interrupting the teacher or a classmate with some point you want to make. This type of student not only annoys the instructor, but also irritates the other students.

- Help maintain the cleanliness and appearance of the classroom. After class, discard all trash.

- Review your course syllabi for each professor's specific class policies.

CLASS PARTICIPATION

You attend every class, and you make sure you get there five minutes early. You don't whisper to your neighbor or otherwise cause disruptions in class. Is this enough to guarantee success? No—an important element is missing. To get the very most out of your class time, you have to be an active participant. This means you take an active interest in the lesson, pay careful attention, and offer your own input when appropriate. You have read earlier that many instructors consider your attendance record when determining your grade. Almost every instructor will factor in your level of class participation when deciding your grade. Even instructors who lecture to hundreds of students a day tend to remember those individuals who occasionally ask a question or volunteer an opinion.

~Nina~

I couldn't believe it when I got a "C+" in my psychology class last year. I got "Bs" on all the papers I handed in. I asked my instructor about my grade and he said that, even though I wrote well, he couldn't tell that I did anything else well because I never opened my mouth in class. In fact, he said, sometimes he had to look around the room to see if I was even there. It turns out class participation counted for 30 percent of the grade in that class. I found out later that it said so on the syllabus; but to tell you the truth, I hadn't read it that carefully.

Class participation shows your instructors that you take an active interest in your education and in the topics they are teaching. Becoming an active participant also helps you get the most out of every class. If you have questions about the material being taught, the best time to ask is right away—when you're getting acquainted with the material for the first time.

Some students feel shy about speaking up in class. They feel that their questions are "dumb," or that the other students will resent their speaking out and taking the instructor's attention. You will probably find that most of your fellow students actually appreciate your asking a question or bringing up a complex issue. Some of them may have been meaning to ask that question themselves. Even if the other students do seem to have more of a handle on the material, remember there is no one in the class who is such an expert on the material that they can't benefit from hearing further explanations. "I've had classmates come up to me after class and say, 'I'm glad you brought that up!'" says Michael. "I'd rather feel a little awkward about asking a question in class than sit there the night before an exam wishing I had."

Read the following list of suggestions to learn ways in which you can become a more active learner in the classroom.

Tips . . . For Participating in the Classroom

- Come to class prepared. Again, this may seem like an obvious element of student success, but many students fail to make the connection between being prepared and getting good grades. Don't make that mistake. You can't make the most of each class if you aren't prepared when you walk in. Do the readings and homework; write any questions you have about these assignments and bring them to class.

- Ask questions. That list of questions won't do you any good unless you use it. If you have questions about the material being presented in class, raise your hand, or write the question and ask at the end of class. It is a rare instructor who ends class time without allowing a few minutes to review and to field questions about the class.

- Volunteer. If your instructor needs a volunteer to role-play a situation, demonstrate a procedure, or summarize a reading passage, offer your services. Tariq became such an enthusiastic classroom volunteer that one of his instructors offered him a part-time job as a research assistant.

(continued)(continued)

- Take an active role in group activities and group discussions. You can get a lot out of talking with your fellow students, and you'll find that many students appreciate a classmate who's willing to lead a group discussion. Don't be shy. No one's asking you to teach the class. You might just read the instructions for a group activity or write experiment results on the blackboard.

- Be an active listener. This may just be the most important factor in becoming a good class participant. Active listening means paying attention to the speaker. You stay "tuned in" to the discussion even when you disagree with the speaker, or when one of your least favorite topics is being discussed. Active listeners expect class to be interesting, so they're interested. Listen for the main points of a lecture. Paying attention means you won't miss it when the instructor clarifies for you the information that will be required on the upcoming test.

- Resist the temptation to "tune out" or daydream when the pace gets slow. Sit at the front of the class, if possible; you'll feel more involved, and you won't have to strain to see what's written on the blackboard. Sit straight in your seat and focus on the instructor. Are there any other questions you could be posing to yourself about the material?

- If you're *really* having trouble concentrating, quietly excuse yourself, get a sip of water, stretch a little, and get some fresh air—then get back to class. This shouldn't take more than a minute, and you shouldn't make a habit of it. However, it's better to miss a minute or two of class and come back refreshed and alert than to waste much more valuable class time staring out the window, daydreaming, and otherwise missing what's going on.

CLASSROOM EXPECTATIONS: YOURS AND YOUR INSTRUCTOR'S

College classes are a team effort. You, your classmates, and your instructors work together to achieve your goals. Your instructor's goal is to teach effectively. Your goal, and that of your classmates, is to learn. It's important that all members of the team do their parts; each member of the team has expectations of the other. In other words, there are expectations you have of your instructors and expectations they have of you. When you're clear on what these expectations are; your chances for success in the classroom are that much greater.

Your Expectations

What can you expect in the classroom from your instructor? First and foremost, you can expect classes to be held as scheduled and on time. If an instructor is going to be late or has to cancel a class, you can expect to be informed in advance. If your instructor is held up at the last minute and is late for class, students generally are expected to allow a 10–15 minute grace period before concluding that the instructor is not going to show up at all. Responsible instructors will seldom, if ever, be late.

You can expect that your instructor will give you a syllabus or course outline at the beginning of the semester and let you know about any other texts or additional materials you will need to obtain for the class. You also can expect that your instructor will explain information and assignments in a clear and logical manner. After all, if the class doesn't understand what's being taught, the instructor isn't getting his/her job done.

You can expect a free exchange of ideas in the classroom. College instructors traditionally have what is called "academic freedom," which means that they can raise sometimes controversial issues without fear of jeopardizing their jobs. The classroom is a forum in which to exchange and learn about new ideas. While you certainly are responsible for understanding the material presented to you, you are under no obligation to *agree* with everything you're taught. In fact, one of your instructors' expectations will be that you learn to evaluate issues for yourself and to establish and be able to defend your own views.

You also can expect that your instructors will make the time to answer any questions or concerns you have about your work in class, to grade your papers and tests, and to provide appropriate feedback when necessary. If you get back a corrected test or paper that you feel does not offer enough feedback, speak to your instructor. Correcting papers is an extremely time- consuming process, and instructors cannot always devote the time to each individual essay or test that they'd like. Let them know if you need more of their comments. Your professors also should let you know how you're progressing in class and in those areas in which you need to improve to achieve greater success.

Naturally, over the course of your college studies, there will be some instructors you prefer more than others. Sometimes an instructor and a student just don't "click." However, successful students know that this is no reason to put any less effort into the class or the teacher-student relationship, just as you would have to with your boss in a professional job. Personality conflicts should not affect your work in class. Let your instructor know you're trying and are working hard; he or she will appreciate your commitment, and you in turn may find that your instructor is much nicer than you'd thought.

Your Instructor's Expectations

Now that you're in college, you are expected to take a more active role in your education. Unlike high school, a college education is not required; you don't have to go to college unless you want to. Because college is your choice, however, it is up to you to make the most of it. Your instructors are there to help, instruct, and guide you; but they are not ultimately responsible for your learning. Your instructors expect you to act like an adult who is in charge of his or her own education.

To this end, your instructors will expect that you show up to class on time, ready to work. They expect that you will hand in assignments neatly and on time and that you will let them know if you are having trouble with the assignment. You must take the initiative; it is not your instructors' job to make sure all your questions are answered and your problems solved. That's your job— they're here to make it easier.

> **~Latifah~**
>
> In high school, my teachers always reminded us about essays and assignments that were due soon. In college, instructors give you an assignment and may never say anything about it till the day it's due—four weeks later! It took me a while to get used to that and start reminding myself about due dates.

Your instructors expect that you will come prepared for class, and, while you're in their classroom, to behave courteously and respectfully to everyone. They expect you to participate in class, ask questions, and make the most of the classroom learning environment. When both your expectations and those of your instructors are fulfilled, the classroom can be a dynamic and exciting learning environment.

The Connection Between Class and Work Expectations

Your instructor will expect you to treat class time as you would time spent on your job. It's almost as if your instructor is your employer. Your instructor is very aware of how you manage yourself, whether you and your assignments arrive on time, the quality of your participation, and the efforts you put into your assignments. Managing your work habits in the classroom gives your instructor a picture of how conscientious you will be on the job. She is also the person that may write a letter of reference to a prospective employer. Treat your instructor with respect, give your assignments the most professional look you can, be a class contributor, and be punctual. Would any employer expect less?

ADAPTING TO THE CLASSROOM:
YOUR LEARNING STYLE AND INSTRUCTORS' TEACHING MODES

There are many different styles of learning, and not everyone learns well the same way. Whether they're aware of it or not, most people have a preferred learning style. Learning styles refer to the way you receive, store, and retrieve information. Some people learn best by reading. Others learn more effectively through writing, listening, speaking, visualizing, or manipulating (which is the term for "hands-on" or "learn by doing" activities). These are the main learning styles; chances are good that you prefer one or two more than the others. When you know what your preferred style of learning is, you can adapt yourself better to the classroom and learn more effectively outside of class. When you know your learning strengths and how to take advantage of them, as well as your weaknesses and how to compensate for them, you've taken another big step toward student success.

Likewise, you'll find that instructors have their preferred methods of teaching and, therefore, will teach to some learning styles more effectively than to others. A lecturer teaches best to students who learn best by listening. A teacher who regularly illustrates lessons on the blackboard or with overhead transparencies is a good match for the visual learner. An instructor who engages the class in group discussions appeals more to the listening and the speaking types of learner. A class that involves laboratory experiences, such as typing, film-making, or chemistry, is a good learning environment for the manipulating-type learner. Good instructors will involve your class in learning activities that require you to use and develop a variety of learning styles. You also want to be able to use a variety of learning styles, depending on the demands of the particular task you're engaged in and the surroundings in which you want to work. You may not be able to change your instructor's teaching mode, but you can develop your less preferred learning styles, as well as take advantage of your strongest learning style.

Learning Styles

There are formal learning-style assessments, probably available through your school's learning center or counseling center. You can informally examine your own learning styles with the following learning styles checklist.

Exercise 3-2 Your preferred learning styles

Use the following learning styles checklist to examine some of your own learning-style preferences. Read the following six groups of questions and place a check next to the statements that best describe you. After you have checked off your answers, total the number of checks you have in each group. The group or groups with the most check marks indicate your learning-style preferences.

Reading

_____1.   I enjoy reading and make the time to do it often.

_____2.   I'd rather read the instructions for a project than use a trial-and-error method.

_____3.   I remember material better when I've read it than when I've just heard it talked about.

_____4.   I read fairly quickly and retain a lot of what I read.

_____5.   I'd rather read a report than listen to it.

_____   Total checks

Writing

_____1.   I like to keep track of my schedule and appointments by writing them down.

_____2.   I like to write notes to myself—questions, comments—as I read.

_____3.   I take good notes when I'm in a lecture class.

_____4.   I enjoy writing reports and essays; it's easier to organize my thoughts on paper.

_____5.   I make fewer mistakes when I write reports than when I give oral presentations.

_____   Total checks

Listening (Auditory)

_____1.   I'd rather have someone tell me how to do something than read the instructions myself.

_____2.   I usually remember what I hear.

_____3.   I'd rather read aloud than silently.

_____4.   Reciting material helps me to remember it better.

_____5.   I'd rather listen to the news on the radio than read the newspaper.

_____   Total checks

Speaking

_____1.   I need to discuss things to understand them.

_____2.   I would rather participate in a group discussion than listen to a lecture.

_____3.   Explaining things to others helps me understand them better myself.

_____4.   I'd rather talk about my work with instructors than read their notes on my written work.

_____5.   I'd rather give a speech than write a report.

_____   Total checks

Visualizing

_____1.   I like to picture things in my mind when I read.

_____2.   I'd rather follow a diagram to construct something than read the written instructions.

_____3.   I can more easily remember things if I picture them in my mind.

_____4.   I follow the lesson better when instructors use outlines and draw illustrations on the board as they lecture.

_____5.   I like to draw pictures and diagrams to help me understand material.

_____   Total checks

Manipulating

_____1.   I prefer a trial-and-error method to reading instructions.

_____2.   I get impatient just listening and taking notes—I want to *do* something.

_____3.   I prefer a lab class to a lecture.

_____4.   I understand material best when I have the opportunity to apply it.

_____5.   I find it difficult to sit still while I study; I need to move around and to take frequent breaks.

_____   Total checks

Record below the total number of checks in each group. Circle the learning style(s) in which you have three or more checks. Having three or more checks in a group indicates a strong learning-style preference.

_____*Reading* (learn best by reading printed words).

_____*Writing* (learn best by expressing yourself in written form).

_____*Listening/auditory* (learn best by hearing).

_____*Speaking* (learn best by expressing yourself aloud, either alone or in group work).

_____*Visualizing* (learn best by picturing information).

_____*Manipulating* (learn best by doing/practicing what you are studying).

How did you score on the learning styles checklist? Did you know that you had one or more preferred styles of learning? You may have known before you took the test; or perhaps this is all new information to you. Now that you know more about your preferences, you can make them work more effectively for you. You use a combination of several learning styles as you study, attend class, and complete assignments. Now you can try to think of ways in which to study in your preferred style more often and to take advantage of the way you learn best. Also, you might begin to think of ways you can strengthen other learning styles. You may find that, if you're having trouble in some classes, the problem is not that you don't understand the material but that your instructor teaches in a way that is not compatible with your strongest learning style. The more learning styles you master, the more ways you have to learn. Just as exercise builds muscle, exercising your less preferred learning styles will strengthen them and make you a stronger, more flexible learner.

Tips . . . For Making the Most of Your Preferred Learning Style

*   If your preferred style of learning is *reading*, you're in luck. You'll do more reading than anything else in college. Keep your texts with you in a lecture so you can refer to the written word. Reading the written instructions to lab work and other projects will help you when diagrams or demonstrations don't make sense. Keep reading; this is one skill you cannot develop too highly. In Section 4, you'll have a chance to develop reading strategies to help you learn and concentrate while you read.

*   If your preferred style of learning is *writing*, you should be able to incorporate this skill into every aspect of your college learning. Take notes during lectures and other classes. When your instructor explains or illustrates a procedure or experiment, you may find it helpful to write down the information as though it were a lecture. Write as much as you can and work on improving your writing style; like reading, writing is one of the most valuable skills you can apply to any subject.

(continued)

- If your preferred style of learning is *listening,* you probably excel in lecture classes. If you have trouble with written material or diagrams, ask your instructor or a classmate to explain the information again. You probably have a good memory for what you hear, so chances are you don't need to have spoken instructions repeated to you. You might benefit from having a study partner read aloud from the text if you're having trouble understanding what you read. Jason regularly tapes lectures so he can hear them again when he studies. "I hear things the second time I didn't quite catch the first time," he says.

- If your preferred style of learning is *speaking,* you might do well to join a study group in which you can discuss the class material with friends and classmates. When you review your notes and texts for a test, read them out loud to yourself. Take advantage of any opportunity you have to give an oral report in place of, or in addition to, a written one.

- If your preferred style of learning is *visualizing,* it may help to create your own study aids by drawing diagrams and charts of important information. It doesn't matter how well you draw; the important thing is that you have a visual learning tool. Just the act of creating charts and the like can be as helpful as referring to them later.

- If your preferred style of learning is *manipulating,* you probably do best in lab situations and group activities. An excellent way to take advantage of this learning style is to volunteer to do extra-credit projects for class. You might build a model or replica, conduct an experiment, or investigate a new method. You might even be asked to give a demonstration to the class. Ask your instructor for ideas on taking a more hands-on approach to your studies. Julie decided to create blueprints for her dream house in her advanced computer-aided drafting and design class.

Since teachers do not always structure learning around the way you may learn best, you'll want to master as many learning styles as possible. For as many people who grew up "hating to read," there are probably an equal amount who "hate to write." While it may have been possible to escape using all learning styles in high school, once you're in college and even on the job, being proficient in all areas is generally an expectation. The best way to develop proficiency is to plunge right in and work on self-improvement—do more reading, writing, listening and so on. Consider taking extra classes or workshops to strengthen areas that need it. Every learning style you strengthen will boost your self-esteem as well as your performance.

Your Instructor's Teaching Mode

Just as your learning style affects how you master your studies, so does your instructor's teaching style. Different teaching styles are compatible with different learning styles. The most common modes of teaching include lecturing, visual presentation, group collaboration, and manipulating (hands-on). Your teachers will also engage you in learning outside the classroom by giving you the following types of assignments: reading your text or handouts, writing papers, and preparing projects and presentations. Although these are indirect modes/approaches to teaching, they are structured by your teacher to give you additional and application learning experiences. Many of the writing and project assignments will simulate actual work experiences— make the most of them. When your teacher allows you to choose a project, select a project that will help you develop your professional skills.

Most of your instructors will use a combination of these modes to present information in an exciting and challenging way. Being aware of your instructor's mode of teaching can help you study and prepare for classes and exams more effectively, because you have a good idea of how the material will be presented. Your course syllabus, assignments, handouts, and exams can give you hints about your instructor's teaching mode. Of course, the biggest hint is in going to class. You can also informally assess your instructor's teaching mode by completing the questionnaire that follows. You may never have thought about analyzing your instructors and their styles of teaching before; many students find this exercise to be extremely helpful to their work in class—a real eye-opener.

Exercise 3-3 Your instructor's teaching mode

What's the most challenging class you're taking this term? Think about that class and its instructor as you review the following teaching mode checklist. For each of the six main teaching modes—lecturing/speaking, visual presentation, group collaboration, manipulating (hands-on), reading, and writing—estimate the percentage of time your instructor uses each. For example, you may put down: <u>50%</u> reading, <u>25%</u> lecturing, <u>15%</u> writing, <u>5%</u> visual, <u>5%</u> group collaboration, and <u>0%</u> manipulating (hands-on). The modes with the highest percentages indicate your instructor's teaching preferences.

Name of Class: _____

_____%   ***Lecturing:*** My instructor uses lectures to deliver course information or gives oral instructions on most assignments, or both.

_____%   ***Visual presentation:*** My instructor uses visual aids and materials to present information (overhead projector, videos, charts); outlines lectures on the board or with transparencies; illustrates and diagrams appropriate material.

_____%   ***Group collaboration:*** My instructor gives us problems to solve in groups, engages us in small group discussions, and organizes class projects.

_____%   ***Manipulating:*** My instructor lets us learn by doing—engaging us in application activities, projects, experiments, or constructing most things we're learning about.

_____%   ***Reading:*** My instructor gives a text or handout reading assignment on a regular basis.

_____%   ***Writing:*** My instructor frequently gives writing assignments.

Next, rank your instructor's preferred modes of teaching (from the most to least favored) in the left column and your preferred learning styles (from the most to least favored) in the right column.

My Instructor's Teaching Modes	My Learning Styles
1st _____	1st _____
2nd _____	2nd _____
3rd _____	3rd _____
4th _____	4th _____
5th _____	5th _____
6th _____	6th _____

To which of your learning styles does this instructor teach most often?

_____

Do you and your instructor's preferred learning/teaching styles match up well in this class? Why or why not? If they're not compatible, what might you do to make them more so?

_____
_____
_____
_____

When your instructor's teaching mode does not appeal to your preferred learning style, you probably will have to work harder to pay more attention and keep up your interest. It's interesting to note that, the older you are, the better able you are to adapt your preferred learning style to different teaching modes.

Tips . . . For Getting the Most Out of Your Instructor's Teaching Mode

- If your instructor prefers to lecture, you can get the most out of it by preparing written questions to pose to your instructor during class. He or she will welcome the chance to discuss a topic more fully. Take detailed notes and be a careful listener; good lecturers and active listeners make an effective learning team.

- If your instructor prefers to use visual presentations, try sitting at the front of the class so you don't miss anything. If you need glasses, be sure to wear them.

- If your instructor prefers to encourage group collaboration, prepare (reading, studying, developing questions, and notetaking) thoroughly prior to your group work. The more actively you contribute, the more you and your group will learn. Take notes on group discussions; your instructor may develop an essay or test question from a point brought up in a group discussion.

- If your instructor prefers to involve the class in a lot of manipulating (hands-on) activities, you can learn more by taking careful notes on procedures you might have to perform in class. Ask your instructor if there is a time when the lab or workshop is free so you can practice on your own.

- If your instructor gives you regular reading assignments, make every effort to read your assignments thoroughly before she covers the material in class. It's important to use an effective reading strategy to help you learn as you read. (Read ahead in Section 4 so you can adopt some effective "reading to learn" strategies now.) If you only engage in superficial reading and don't learn as you read, it may seem that the teacher is teaching too fast—they expect that you have already read and studied the reading assignment.

- If your instructor gives you frequent writing assignments, give it your best professional effort. Write clear and concisely, make sure it's error free, and make it neat—word process it. Have someone whose English and writing skills you trust proofread it for you. Writing assignments are designed for you to engage yourself in your learning and to apply what you are learning. (Section 7 will give you some effective writing strategies.)

COMPENSATING FOR LEARNING DISORDERS AND DIFFICULTIES

Today a lot more is known about learning disabilities such as Attention Deficit Disorder (ADD) and other learning challenges faced by those with physical disabilities. Educators and counselors know more about how to compensate for learning disabilities and difficulties so everyone has a greater opportunity for education and career training. Learning assistance and disability programs have helped many students develop new strategies to read, concentrate, and learn better. Additionally, services are available to physically challenged students to assist them in overcoming barriers to learning. Don't let disabilities and difficulties keep you from your education goals—seek the appropriate assistance to support your education and, ultimately, your career goals.

Learning Assistance

Learning assistance services are often available through colleges and community or state agencies for students with learning difficulties and other disabilities. Students who need learning assistance may find some of the following services available:

- textbooks on audio tapes
- supplemental instruction on video
- note takers (for those with visual impairments)
- test readers
- learning skills workshops
- tutoring

Too often students don't know where to get the appropriate assistance. At Morgan State University, students with disabilities, including learning disabilities, are encouraged to contact Student Accessibility Support Services (SASS) located in 318 McKeldin Center, 443-885-3946. Your state's department of education and/or college board offices may also be able to assist or direct you. Finally, call the National Center for Learning Disabilities for referral and resources 888-575-7373.

Attention Deficit Disorder (ADD)

Almost everyone has trouble concentrating, but for some people it's a problem that can interfere with their success in school. If you are overwhelmed by an inability to concentrate, talk to a counselor at your school or in your community. If they suspect you have a learning disorder, or perhaps Attention Deficit Disorder (ADD), they can help you receive testing as well as learning assistance. Currently, there are a growing number of adults diagnosed with Attention Deficit Disorder (ADD) and probably many more who have not been diagnosed. Another type of ADD is attention deficit hyperactivity disorder (ADHD). It is often depicted as a restless hyperactivity that seriously disrupts your ability to concentrate. You don't have to be hyperactive to have ADD, nor does hyperactivity alone qualify you for the diagnosis. ADD was once considered a childhood disorder that disappeared before adulthood. It is now recognized as a lifelong condition which has its onset in childhood.

Many college and community counselors are specifically trained to assist students who have learning difficulties and disabilities. With education and assistance, people diagnosed with ADD can succeed in college. Adult college students with ADD typically report being unable to organize and complete assignments, having poor study habits, having difficulty concentrating on textbook material, being restless, having a low stress tolerance, and a sense of under-achievement. People close to those with ADD often become frustrated and can't understand how someone can be so disorganized and leave so many projects unfinished. ADD people may have their difficulties, but they also have a certain giftedness—imagination, intuitiveness, and energy—which often promotes high productivity.

An evaluation for ADD is the first step to helping you get in charge of your life. Check with your school's counseling department, student support services, or local counseling service for evaluation and/or learning assistance. A next important step is to educate yourself, your instructors, those you live with, and those you work with, about ADD. The more you and they know, the more tolerance and understanding will exist. Additionally, therapy can help ADD individuals and their families gain more insight, cope, make behavior adjustments, and communicate acceptance. Medication can also be a great deal of help too, but it is not the sole solution. Note the following suggestions made by people with ADD for gaining control over their lives.

Tips . . . For Managing Attention Deficit Disorder

- Get a "coach"—someone to help you get organized, stay on task, encourage you; someone to be in your corner.

- Try to get rid of negativity—use encouragement.

- Give yourself permission to be yourself.

- Forgive yourself and get back on track again . . . forgive yourself again.

- Use structure—make lists, use post-it-notes to write reminders, and keep a notepad with you.

- Read with a pen in hand for underlining and margin notes.

- Take time to "let yourself go!"

- Let yourself waste some time without guilt.

- Take time-outs to calm down.

- Be with people like you and who appreciate you.

- Start projects. Starting is at least half the battle.

- Exercise vigorously and regularly to work off excess energy and thus soothe and calm your body.

- Let successful moments last and linger.

- Learn to anticipate consequences of behavior so you can avoid unrewarding behavior.

- Embrace and thrive on challenges as long as you realize they won't all work out.

- Prioritize.

- Break bigger projects into smaller steps.

- Realize that it is okay to do more than one thing at a time—ADD'ers get things done this way.

- Make time between activities to gather your thoughts.

ACTIVE LEARNING BEYOND THE CLASSROOM

You know that your education extends beyond the classroom. Outside the classroom there are many opportunities to apply what you're learning in class and to learn even more. Some of your instructors will include work outside the class as part of your coursework; your major may require an internship or field experience. Even if outside learning opportunities are not a part of your instructor's teaching plan, or a requirement of your major, it's still an excellent idea to enhance your classroom experience with knowledge gained outside of school. Here are ways you can be more active in learning outside the classroom; ask your instructor or advisor for more ideas.

Tips . . . For Learning Outside the Classroom

- Talk to professionals who work in the field you are preparing to enter. You'll learn more about the nature of the work involved and whether this is really the field for you. Professionals can suggest additional courses to take and ways to get additional experience while you're still in school. Professional people appreciate your interest in their work; when you graduate, these individuals can be valuable networking sources as you look for a job.

- Join a club, society, or other campus organization for students who share the same program of studies.

- Read journals in the occupational field you plan to enter. Libraries like to order professional journals that coincide with the programs of study that their school offers. Even if you have no particular profession in mind just yet, you can still do extra reading. Read about a topic mentioned in one of your classes that seems interesting. Browse through the school library and take out any books that catch your eye. The more you read, the more you'll be able to relate the new information you're learning in class to information you read on your own. Learning to make connections between old and new material is an important skill in college.

- If your school has a cooperative education program, find out how it works and how you might benefit from it. Cooperative education programs usually help students to be placed in jobs that relate to their major.

- Visit your instructors outside of class. Talk to them about aspects of classwork that you're especially interested in, or ask them questions. The more your instructors get to know you, the more they can help you.

- Enroll in elective courses that will strengthen some of your weaker skills. If writing is not your strongest skill, enroll in some additional writing courses that you otherwise would not be required to take. If giving oral reports is a problem for you, take a public speaking elective.

- What types of paid or volunteer work experience could you get involved in while in school?

  _____

  _____

  _____

  _____

  _____

  _____

Active learning outside the classroom helps you apply what you're learning in the classroom to other activities. It's not only involvement in these types of learning experiences that make you an active student, it's your desire to learn more. Taking an active role in your education in and out of the classroom makes you a more successful student and helps you better prepare for your profession.

MAKING A COMEBACK WHEN YOU NEED TO

Throughout this section you've learned ways to use the classroom environment to your best advantage. You've also started to think of ways to increase your learning outside the classroom. Naturally, none of these tips and strategies you're reading about will work unless you use them. Unfortunately, some students in their first terms of school do just that—they read information but don't apply it and use it. Some of these students fail a course, some a term, and others drop out of school altogether. It's as if their vision of success dropped out of sight. Hopefully, you will begin using the information in this book right away. But what if, like Jamie, you've tried

> **~Jamie~**
>
> *I just blew off the whole first semester. My grade point average was barely a 1.0. I had a hard time getting adjusted to college; I was seriously thinking of quitting. I mean, why bother? It seemed like I wasn't any good at any of the subjects. My parents insisted I speak to my advisor before making any big decisions. I'm so glad I did. She helped me get back on track. So I had a bad first semester. Why throw away my college plans just because of that? I decided that, even if I'd made some mistakes in the past, I wasn't going to make things worse by making a bigger mistake.*

to "coast" through your first term and now are suffering the consequences? In other words, how do you make a comeback when you need to?

Suppose you buy a car and after four months it begins to develop engine trouble. Do you get rid of it? Not likely. You still need the transportation; otherwise, you wouldn't have bought it in the first place. You've made an investment in the car, one you can't lightly throw away, just because some problems have developed. Instead, you need to diagnose the problem and, if you're unable to do that yourself, find a reliable mechanic who can, and get it fixed. Once you get the car fixed, you can drive it for miles, good as new. Likewise, you started school because you knew it was an important goal for you, one that's necessary to the future you envision for yourself. If you're running into trouble at the outset, you still have no reason to throw away your whole college career. Instead of giving up on your vision of success, get the problem diagnosed and work at the changes needed to fix it. Make a comeback!

How do you get yourself back on the track to success? First, evaluate your efforts. Nine times out of 10, if you're having trouble with schoolwork it's because you're not *doing* all of it. Are you reading all your assignments? Are you taking notes and being an active listener in class? Do you complete all assignments as directed and hand them in on time? Are you attending *every* class? Are you studying, reading, and preparing assignments in advance? Those projects and study sessions that are crammed in at the last minute might get the assignment completed, but they aren't helping you learn.

Discuss your progress (or lack of it) with your instructor. Own up to your faults or lack of effort; don't blame these on other circumstances. No instructor wants to hear, "I've been too busy" or "I'm under a lot of stress, I can't do all this work." *Everyone* has a lot of work to do in college, and everyone feels stress. The student who says, "I've made some mistakes this term, but I really want to improve. What suggestions do you have for me?" will almost certainly get help from instructors. Let your teachers know you've made a new commitment to your education—and then show that commitment, in and out of class. It may be a cliché, but it's true—actions speak louder than words.

If you've been making an effort and your grades still aren't up to par, you may need extra tutoring in a specific subject or skill. See your instructor or advisor for help. Tutoring in different subjects is available in almost every school. Take advantage of the facilities at your school.

If your grades begin to slip, get extra help immediately. Get the problem under control before it starts to seriously affect your grade point average. If you don't understand why you got a question wrong on an exam or a poor grade on an essay, ask your instructor right away. Don't wait until the next exam or essay—it may be too late.

Sometimes personal problems can cause difficulties in the classroom. When you are focused on things that are worrying you, it's hard to concentrate on what you should be learning. If this is your situation, talk to someone about the problem. Instructors, advisors, campus counselors, friends, family members, roommates, physicians, clergy members—all are people you can turn to in a crisis. Make an effort to keep personal problems under control so they don't interfere with your education; if your education suffers as a result of the problem, then you have two problems. Help is out there for any difficulty you might have, but finding and using the help is up to you. Think of it as a further investment in your future, a way of protecting the investment you've made in your education.

Making a comeback will mean making changes in how you function as a student. Since we are creatures of habit, change isn't always comfortable—at least, not at first. It might mean giving up some hours at work, less TV or socializing; it might involve investigating new study methods to replace those that aren't effective. It means saying good-bye to those things that don't work.

Getting back on track will involve adopting new study strategies, setting new priorities, and getting help where you need it. Remember, every change begins with an ending (giving up something) and ends with a beginning (trying something new). Remember the investment you're making in attending college. Like a car, your education is a means of transportation. Where will your education take you?

HIGHLIGHTS

In this section, you've explored several strategies to increase your ability in the classroom environment. You know about the importance of preparation and of going into class having done the homework and ready to learn more. It shouldn't be a surprise to know that your instructor can quickly assess the quality of your preparation for class. More importantly, you'll feel sharper and in control when you are prepared. In the classroom, you know how to behave in a way that makes learning easier for you and your classmates. The success habits you are developing now will also pay off in your career.

You've become aware, perhaps for the first time, of your own preferred learning styles and how to make the most of them. You examined instructors' different modes of teaching and how to adapt yourself to each. You also have some ideas now about using your learning skills outside the classroom. And, in the event that you have not started your college career by making the best use of your abilities, you've got some tips on making a comeback and getting back on track, with your vision of success clearly in mind.

Finally, you might ask, "If most of my learning takes place outside of the classroom, why worry about attendance?" This is a good question with several responses. First, it is your instructor's responsibility to use class time to provide clarity to difficult assignments and material, to bring additional information to class beyond your text, and to develop learning experiences and assignments that help you better understand and apply what you are learning. Secondly, your instructor will provide feedback on papers and assignments for further learning. Your learning experience encompasses a blend of learning through reading, writing, critical thinking, discussing, listening to expertise, exploring, and group collaboration—a blend of in and out of the classroom experiences.

DISCUSSION QUESTIONS

Note: Read the following discussion questions and activities **before** you read Section 3. This strategy will help you look for answers while you read.

1. Discuss your usual class preparation. Explain your strengths and weaknesses. Are there differences in the amount of preparation you do for each of your classes? Why? What will you do to better prepare for classes needing more of your attention?
2. How does an instructor recognize that you haven't prepared enough for class?
3. Review each of your course syllabi and make a list of all exams, written assignments, and projects due for all your classes this term. List them in order of the due date. Why is this a useful exercise?
4. What do you usually do when you don't understand concepts or problems from your homework assignment? How can you learn the most from such a situation? Explain.
5. How can missing your first day of class impact the outcome of the course? The section states that you need to attend every class. Why? How can attendance affect your grade?
6. List eight reasons for arriving to class early.
7. Discuss the responsibilities of the student and the instructor when you miss a class.
8. Discuss instances in which a lack of classroom etiquette was displayed.

9. List eight tips for being courteous in class.

10. How can you become more of an active participant in class? Of the seven tips outlined in the section on class participation, which do you feel you can learn from most? Explain. In what ways would you like to improve your class participation?

11. Compare the expectations an instructor may have of you as a student with those an employer may have of you.

12. List and explain the five top expectations an instructor should have of students.

13. How do high school and college expectations differ? How do students' expectations differ? How do instructors' expectations differ?

14. What did you discover about your learning style preferences? How will you strengthen your less preferred learning styles? How can you use your preferred learning styles to make the most out of college?

15. What teaching modes do your instructors seem to prefer?

16. Of the six tips this section identified for learning outside the classroom, explain which ones most appeal to you. Of the six tips listed or other ideas you have, what outside learning activities would you be willing to engage in?

17. List any of your present courses that you might need tutoring in. What tutoring services are available to you?

18. If you're having difficulty in any of your courses, what action will you take to turn the situation around?

19. How are the section's Tips for Managing Attention Deficit Disorder useful even if you are not affected by ADD?

20. How do classroom expectations compare to actual job expectations?

Improving Your Memory and Learning Skills

WHAT'S IN IT FOR YOU

You need the best learning strategies to make the most of your college experience. As Tomás discovered, most college learning takes place outside the classroom through reading and studying. "I spend much more time studying for my classes than I ever spend in class," he says. Good study skills help you feel more in control. "I have so much reading, and there's always a test coming up. I have to make each study session count or else I'll fall behind." This section will lead you straight to the best learning strategies so you can make the most of college learning.

In this section you'll explore:

- How to improve your concentration and memory
- Techniques to help you learn while you read your assignments
- Strategies for reading math and science
- Self-talk that helps you take charge of your learning

LEARNING HOW TO LEARN

Learning in college is a matter of improving your learning skills and taking advantage of the skills you already have. Together with a positive attitude, you can become a more successful learner. Try the following exercises to figure out how you learn now.

Exercise 4-1 Finding your learning strengths

How true are the following statements for you? Circle the appropriate number on a scale from 1 to 5, 1 meaning never true, 5 meaning always true.

1.	I enjoy studying and learning.	1	2	3	4	5
2.	I can concentrate on reading for long periods.	1	2	3	4	5
3.	I remember details that I read.	1	2	3	4	5
4.	I remember details that I hear in class discussions.	1	2	3	4	5
5.	I remember details that I hear in class lectures.	1	2	3	4	5
6.	I am able to find the main points in a textbook reading.	1	2	3	4	5
7.	I am able to summarize a reading in a single paragraph. (Try it now with one of your recent reading assignments.)	1	2	3	4	5
8.	I take comprehensive notes on all important points in a reading.	1	2	3	4	5
9.	I am able to make sense of math readings.	1	2	3	4	5
10.	I am able to make sense of readings in science.	1	2	3	4	5

You probably found that you have some strengths as well as some areas on which you'd like to work. This section will help you improve your rating on these skills. If you're concerned about your math, reading, or writing abilities, there are probably additional services available at your school. Notice the statements you rated highly; these are your learning strengths. For example, Susan uses good notetaking to remember class discussions. "I've always taken good notes during lectures, but I'd start daydreaming during discussions," she says. After the first exam, she discovered that she was missing important points that were raised during discussions. "Now, even after the instructor stops her formal lecture, I still listen for key points and write them down."

Use positive self-talk to improve your attitude. For example, positive thoughts can help you start studying. Often the biggest obstacle to effective studying is simply not starting. Think of studying as your most important link to a successful future. Remember that the sacrifice and self- discipline necessary for successful studying are also necessary for success in the working world. Use your self-talk to build a clear vision of yourself as constantly learning, progressing, and succeeding. Include in your vision the study strategies you're about to learn. Use this vision to motivate yourself to make the most of your studying.

Exercise 4-2 Using positive self-talk

Write down a negative thought you've been having recently about studying for an upcoming test or an assignment. Replace the negative thought with one that will help you reach your goal.

_____

_____

_____

IMPROVING YOUR CONCENTRATION

You can study best when you can concentrate—that is, focus all of your attention on what you're doing. You can maximize your concentration by minimizing distractions—anything that draws your attention away from your studying. Distractions may be internal, such as worries, stress, and daydreaming, as well as external, such as too much noise, other people, and an uncomfortable room temperature. Noticing distractions is the first step in eliminating them.

Eliminating External Distractions

External distractions are those things around you that disrupt your concentration while studying. Perhaps you're studying with bad lighting, too much heat, other people running around, or the TV blaring in the background. It may take very little effort to create a study area where you can concentrate.

You want your study area to be pleasant and convenient, yet free of distractions. If you happen to be at home, explain to your family that you need quiet time for studying. Tell them, for example, that you need to be left alone between 8 and 10 PM. Use the tips from Section 2 on time management to reduce the number of distractions in your home. On class nights, arrange to study at the college library or another quiet place before returning to all of the distractions of home. "I just decided to make class nights study nights as well," says Lauren. "I'd get out of class and head straight for the library to start the assigned readings. It gave me a jump on the next week's work and made my time on campus more productive." It may also be easier on your family if they know they can plan to be without you on specific nights and can expect your help on other nights.

If you're sharing an apartment, you'll have to either agree with roommates on quiet study times or find another place to study—such as a friend's unoccupied room, the library, or an empty classroom. You may find that you can get a lot of studying done during the day in your dorm room, while your friends are in class and there are fewer temptations to socialize. Often there are isolated areas in libraries where friends are less likely to run into you. Plan to meet friends after you study, instead of trying to mix studying with social time. Don't tell anyone where you're studying if you really want to get work done. After weeks of dutifully going to the library after dinner every night, yet spending most of his time socializing nonetheless, David finally found a quiet corner in the library where nobody seemed to find him. "I used that spot for the rest of the year," David said. Wherever the location, if you're distracted, find another place. You'll be able to ignore some distractions, but you'll make better use of your study time if you eliminate distractions altogether.

Tips . . . For Creating a Good Study Environment

- Go through the following checklist to create a study environment made for concentration.

- Keep the room temperature comfortable—better cool than too hot. A hot room makes you uncomfortable and sleepy.

- Keep such supplies as a dictionary, calendar, note cards, notebooks, paper, pens, sharpened pencils, erasers, scissors, and clips within easy reach so you won't waste time searching for them.

- Study in a comfortable chair at a table or desk.

- Sit straight for better concentration and so you can study longer and more comfortably. Some people actually stand and read when they find themselves feeling drowsy.

- Make sure you have plenty of good, bright light.

- Make sure your study area has adequate ventilation. Lack of circulating air can make you sleepy.

Noise is one of the most common and serious distractions. Eliminate such background noise as television, conversation, and music. If necessary, spend a few dollars on earphones so others can watch TV or listen to music. You may believe that the "right" music doesn't interfere with your studying, but eliminate it to make the most of your study time. Focus on studying when you study, and, when you're finished, reward yourself with music.

Do everything you can to prepare your study area for maximum concentration.

Eliminating Internal Distractions

You can greatly increase your concentration by eliminating internal distractions, such as test anxiety, financial worries, daydreams, forgetfulness, and disappointment. Some techniques, such as those listed below, can help.

Tips . . . For Eliminating Internal Distractions

- Use positive self-talk, which is probably your most powerful tool for overcoming internal distractions. For example, while studying the night before an exam, replace worries about the exam with positive thoughts about your studying, such as "I just need to do my best" or "I bet I can learn this if I go over it again."

- Make notes to yourself. Keep a note pad beside you so you can write down reminders to yourself when various concerns pop into your mind. Promise yourself you will deal with these concerns after you've finished studying. Even writing your worries down helps to diminish them somewhat.

- Set realistic study goals. Use the time management skills in Section 2 to clarify goals, set priorities, and make deadlines. Set the start and finish times for your study sessions. Knowing what you have to do and how much time you have will give structure to your study time and improve your concentration. You'll study more efficiently.

- If you're losing your concentration, study more often but for shorter periods of time.

- Remember to take frequent short study breaks. Walk around the room, have a glass of water, get a breath of fresh air. You'll be refreshed for the next round of studying.

- Plan rewards. Reward yourself with a phone call to a friend, a hot cup of coffee, a cold drink, or your favorite TV program after you've completed your allotted study time. Human beings work best with positive reinforcement.

- Establish a regular routine of eating, sleeping, and exercise. Your ability to concentrate depends on adequate sleep, decent nutrition, and the increase in well-being that comes with exercise.

- Bring interest in the material and a sense of purpose to the task. It's easy to let yourself get bored and use that as an excuse for not concentrating and not learning. Try to bring a sense of purpose to your learning, "Why is it important or how will I use this information or why should I get interested?" Studying with purpose and a greater sense of interest will help you stay focused to improve your concentration.

Exercise 4-3 My greatest distractions

What distracts you most often when you're trying to study? Are the distractions internal or external? What can you do to minimize your greatest distraction(s)?

Distractions	**Plan to Minimize Distractions**

IMPROVING YOUR MEMORY

Your studying will be more effective if you can remember more of what you learn. Joy, for example, was frustrated during exams even after studying for hours. "I'd know the answer but simply couldn't remember the details. It was like having the answer on the tip of my tongue." With some practice, the memory strategies in this section will pay off right away.

Exercise 4-4 How is your memory now?

Respond to the following items about you and your memory.

1. What do you forget the most? (Names of people you meet, directions, phone numbers, math formulas, vocabulary, theories in psychology or sociology, foreign languages, favorite subjects.)

2. What do you always remember? Perhaps you have a good memory for faces, or you can drive somewhere on your own because you remember how you got there the last time. Do you remember material from your favorite subjects?

3. What techniques do you use to remember something important?

_____
_____
_____
_____
_____
_____

How Your Memory Works

Improving memory is really about helping your brain store information. As information enters your brain it passes into your *short-term memory*. For instance, your short-term memory allows you to remember a telephone number just long enough to make a call. If you don't rehearse the number again and again, you forget it. Even 20 seconds later you'd have to look up the number again. Or, if someone interrupts you, you'll forget the number because new information quickly forces out older information. However, if you repeat the number enough times, perhaps writing it several times, the number gets stored in long-term memory. So long as you use the number occasionally, you never need to look it up again. Long-term memory has nearly unlimited storage capacity. It contains thousands of facts, details, impressions, and experiences that you've accumulated throughout your life. You might remember the name of your first grade teacher or the phone number of your old house.

The strategies below are designed to help you send more information you're studying into long-term memory. Without memory strategies, most students begin to forget a reading assignment or a lecture right away—up to 50 percent after 24 hours. People forget about 90 percent within a week's time if the information is not used. But information gets stored in long-term memory when you spend time studying it, repeating it, organizing it, thinking and writing about it, and using it.

Six Memory Techniques

1. Understanding

Just as memory is essential for understanding, understanding the material you're studying will help you remember it. You can test your understanding of material by trying to explain it to someone else. Conversations with classmates outside of class are great for testing and improving your understanding of class material. You can also test your understanding by writing summaries of lectures and of reading assignments. If you can explain the material in your own words, you're understanding it and rehearsing it at the same time. Think for a moment about something you're good at and how you would explain it to someone else.

If you don't understand what you are studying, you won't be able to learn it. Ask your instructor or other classmates to help you understand difficult material. Better yet, struggle with it yourself. Try drawing or diagramming what you understand until you piece it together. For example, if you were reading about how electric generators work, try drawing, phrase by phrase, what you are reading until you end up with an illustration. The process of illustrating allows you to "struggle" with technical and difficult information until you can make some sense of it and eventually understand it. Illustrating will help you "write" the information into your long-term memory to make it more permanent.

2. Association

Association is connecting new information with something you already know—for example, reading about a new computer technology is easy if you've been using computers for many years. Much of your college coursework will deal with familiar subjects. You'll find yourself recalling earlier experiences with the subject in and out of your formal education. You may be familiar with business terms, such as *investment*, the *New York Stock Exchange*, and *deficit* because you frequently hear them on television or read them in newspapers and magazines. At other times, you may feel completely lost when reading or listening to new information. That's because you aren't able to associate the information with what you already know.

If you don't understand something during a lecture or in your readings, ask fellow students or the instructor for help. In some cases the gap between what you're learning and what you already know is too great. That's not surprising, considering how different everyone's educational background is. That's why most colleges offer tutoring services or review courses in math, English, the sciences, and other subjects. These classes are often the best way to stay on a successful track in college. Rather than getting frustrated—and wasting time and money—identify the gaps in your knowledge and take steps to fill them. That's what education is all about.

A familiar association technique is **mnemonics** (pronounced: *ne-mon-ics*). Although the name itself may be unfamiliar, you'll recognize some of the techniques. Mnemonics make use of easily remembered phrases, rhymes, words, or acronyms to aid in memory. Mnemonics are often used because some material cannot be logically connected to prior learning or it may be difficult to organize in any other meaningful fashion. Mnemonics help you organize material in sometimes silly ways. Usually, the more outrageous, the better. Mnemonic devices take only a small amount of time to master, but they are effective because they grab your attention and demand your concentration. They can even make you laugh during an exam.

Creating mnemonics

- **Rhymes.** Do you remember this mnemonic rule and rhyme for spelling?

> i before e
> except after c
> or when sounded like a
> as in neighbor or weigh

- **Funny phrases.** If you were trying to remember the order of the nine planets from the sun (**M**ercury, **V**enus, **E**arth, **M**ars, **J**upiter, **S**aturn, **U**ranus, **N**eptune, and **P**luto), you could make up a phrase using the first letter of each planet as the first letter of each word in your phrase. Here's one possibility: **M**y **v**ery **e**ager **m**other **j**umped **s**traight **u**p; **n**ever **p**lopped. If you can remember this silly sentence, you will be able to jot down the first letter of each word to remind you of the name of each planet. A more common example is the phrase **E**very **G**ood **B**oy **D**oes **F**ine used by piano students to remember the lines on the treble clef. You have to memorize the mnemonic for it to be useful. Once you have learned the material, you may not need the mnemonic but may remember it for life.

- **Acronyms.** Acronyms (words formed from the first letter of each word in a group of words) are common mnemonics. The acronym **HOMES** is used to remember the five Great Lakes (**H**uron, **O**ntario, **M**ichigan, **E**rie, **S**uperior). Piano students use the acronym **FACE** to remember the spaces on the treble clef.

- **Key words.** You can easily make up your own mnemonics to remember a list of sentences by picking out a key word from each sentence. Use the first letters of the key words to make a sentence. Memorize the sentence and you'll have a mental outline of the material you're trying to remember. Look at this outline of the oxygen cycle:

1. <u>O</u>xygen is in the air.

2. Oxygen is breathed in by <u>a</u>nimals.

3. It is breathed out as <u>c</u>arbon dioxide.

4. Carbon dioxide is absorbed by <u>p</u>lants, which combine it with water to make food.

5. Plants release the surplus _oxygen_ into the air.

To remember the key word and order for each sentence, use the first letter from each of the italicized words to make a mnemonic. For example, "Only animals can play outside."

Exercise 4-5 Creating your own mnemonic

Using one of your current assignments, create a mnemonic to remember important information, such as a list of names, concepts, or places.

3. Recitation and Recall

Recitation is repeating aloud information you're trying to memorize until you can recall it perfectly. It's as if you were wearing a path in your brain to where the information is stored in your long-term memory. When the path is well worn, recalling the information becomes almost automatic. You can recite important sections of a reading or your notes. You're rewarded each time you correctly recite a section. If you make a mistake, just try again until you get it.

Reciting material aloud with drama and energy will improve your recall of the information more than reciting the information silently; so, you'll probably feel less awkward if you're in a private area. If you're sitting at the library or in a classroom surrounded by people, you can recite silently or by writing.

Remember that reciting information is not the same as understanding it. Remembering a passage from a textbook will be of little use to you on a test if you don't know what it means. So recitation always works best when used with the understanding technique described earlier.

If you can recall information, you know it. Recalling information means being able to state information from memory alone—without the use of cues or prompts. Don't confuse recall with recognition. When you recognize material, you realize that it is familiar but you don't know it "by heart" as you would in recall. Recognition is superficial learning. Recall is solid knowing. If you only prepare to the point of recognition in a multiple choice test, the test will appear to be tricky. Multiple choice tests require a strong recall for specific detail. You will learn more about test taking and the importance of recall in Section 5.

4. Organizing Information

Organizing the information you're trying to remember helps both memory and understanding. This technique is called **meaningful organization.** Look for sensible patterns and for order to the many concepts and ideas you're learning. As you organize information and learn how the material fits together, you may uncover new meaning to the material, and you'll further wear the pathway to the information in your long-term memory. Four techniques for organizing information are categorizing, charting, chunking, and mapping.

Categorizing. You can create categories for items you're trying to remember—for example, notice how the following list of 16 words is divided into four categories in Table 4-1. Remembering four categories and the four items belonging in each category is easier than remembering a single list of sixteen items.

> **candy canes, wheat roll, banana, ribbon, caramel, coffee, napkins, carrot sticks, juice, milk, tissue, candy bar, soda, paper cup, orange, licorice**

Table 4-1

Candy	Drinks	Paper Products	Health Foods
candy canes	coffee	ribbon	wheat roll
caramel	juice	napkins	banana
candy bar	milk	tissue	carrot sticks
licorice	soda	paper cup	orange

Charting. You'll find that some lecture notes and reading assignments can be understood and remembered by using meaningful organization. In fact, the process of organizing the information promotes more learning. To illustrate, if you are taking a chemistry course and you need to understand three different scales for measuring temperatures, you can develop a chart, such as Table 4-2, to organize them for easier comparison and learning. The process of determining the organization promotes learning.

Table 4-2

Scale	Water Freezing Point	Water Boiling Point	Normal Body Temperature
Fahrenheit	32 F	212 F	98.6 F
Celsius	0 C	100 C	37 C
Kelvin	273 K	373 K	310 K

If you're in a class that requires you to know a variety of theories, try organizing them into a chart. You might first list the name of each theory, then the name of the person who formulated each theory, and finally the characteristics of each theory.

Chunking. Chunking is commonly done with numbers. A series of numbers, like 7, 0, 1, 3, 9, 7, 4, 6, 4, 8, is a lot more difficult to learn than (701) 397-4648. Chunking phone numbers like this makes it possible to carry around dozens of phone numbers in your memory. Try chunking other numbers you have to learn and recite them with a rhythm the same way you recite a phone number.

Mapping. Mapping is a graphic way to display relationships among concepts and ideas. Constructing a map of related ideas improves both understanding and recall. To construct maps, enclose pieces of information in circles, squares, or other formats and draw lines or arrows to display how the information is related. Look at Figure 4-1, which maps the sources of student motivation.

Figure 4-1
Example of Mapping Technique

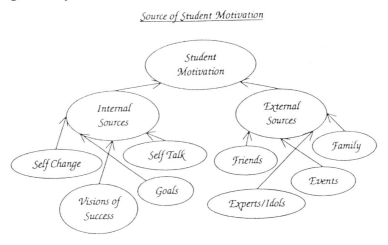

There are numerous methods to organize information for more thorough learning. It may take a little more time to organize the information, but it will improve your understanding and recall. Pick a study problem and try one or two of these organization techniques to help you master the information. Which one do you find most useful?

5. Visualization

Do you remember more when you read, hear, or see a picture? Studies have shown that although people learn in all three ways, more people remember better with a picture. You can make a mental picture (mental visualization) of what you need to remember—what you read, your notes, or lectures. One way to use this technique is to change important words you're trying to remember into mental images. Then, when you recall the images, you'll also recall the words. Avoid spending a lot of time trying to create logical pictures—the corny ones are usually easier to remember. Research has shown that we remember more things we laugh about. Visualization is also a popular technique suggested by memory experts to remember people's names. Just as an old photo helps you remember what you liked at age eight, mental visualization is a powerful tool to help you remember better and longer.

A good way to use the visualization technique is to visualize a picture in which the objects you are trying to learn are in some active interaction with each other. The more action you picture, the easier it will be to recall. For example, to learn the paired words pig-fur, picture a pig sauntering across a stage modeling a fur coat. Remember to make the picture as active as possible so the memory will stick with you.

Exercise 4-6 Does visualization work for you?

To test how visualization can work for you, first try the next exercise using only recitation. Memorize the following words in pairs, a pair being two words directly across from each other. You'll then be provided with one word from each pair, and you'll have to provide the matching word. For example, if you have this pair of words, dog—computer, repeat to yourself: dog—computer, dog—computer. Give yourself one minute to learn the pairs of words in the following table.

Column One		Column Two	
nose	table	ice	jig
run	cookie	clip	book
heart	bear	chair	iron
pen	tire	heat	mail
fence	window	sun	street
rainbow	tree	desk	carrot

Now cover the table and give yourself 45 seconds to write the missing word from each pair in the spaces provided.

street _____	table _____
run _____	bear _____
ice _____	chair _____
book _____	carrot _____
window _____	mail _____
pen _____	tree _____

Now count the number you got correct. _____(out of 12)

With the next columns of new words, visualize the objects in each pair interacting with each other. The more action you picture, the easier it will be to recall—for example, remember the pair of words, nose and table. Imagine a big nose walking across the table top and sneezing. Make the pictures as active as possible so the images will stick in your mind.

Now, just as in the last example, give yourself one minute to learn the pairs in the next table, using visualization.

Column One		Column Two	
elephant	garage	hair	water
face	tornado	lips	orangutan
tulip	hill	turkey	ladder
lightning	rope	sink	cat
pizza	jet	moon	hat
horse	mirror	shower	ant

Now cover the table and give yourself 45 seconds to fill in the missing word for each pair below.

ant _____	face _____
jet _____	lips _____
garage _____	hair _____
sink_____	lightning _____
ladder_____	hat _____
mirror_____	hill _____

Now count the number you got correct. _____(out of 12)

Which memory technique worked the best for you, recitation or visualization? If you had good results with visualization, try using it to remember concepts from your reading and notes, especially when preparing for a test. Visualization also is effective for remembering a process, a procedure, or a system.

For example, in a health technology class, you may be studying the digestive system and need to remember the "food route"—from the pharynx, esophagus, stomach, small intestine, to the large intestine. The following example illustrates how mental visualization could be used to remember the digestive system.

6. Test Yourself

> *First the pharynx serves as a passageway for both the digestive system and the respiratory system. So for the first step, picture your food marching from your mouth to the pharynx. There a **pharaoh** (reminds you of **pharynx**) stands with a sword directing the food to go down the right path—the digestive tract. The next picture frame might be the food marching through the esophagus, where **Easy Gus** (**esophagus**) is pushing the food down his long slide to **St. Mac** in the **stomach**. Create the rest of the picture frames yourself. Remember that this technique requires mental visualization that helps you remember, not pictures that make perfect sense.*

Test and retest yourself prior to the exam and you'll have a better idea of what you already know and of what still needs work. Take every opportunity you can to prepare questions for your own practice tests. Write down the questions your instructor asks in class and take note of the points emphasized during lectures. Make up questions as you read texts and review your notes. Pay attention to the types of questions used on your first exam to give you ideas to compose your own practice questions.

GETTING MORE OUT OF YOUR READING

Have you ever finished reading a section of an assignment only to chastise yourself for not remembering a thing you've just read?

You are probably reading more since starting college than ever before. Reading skills are essential

> **~Kenny~**
>
> *Nothing about college surprised me more than the amount of reading. I never had to read that much, and generally I just can't concentrate that well. Sometimes I'd finish reading a section of an assignment and couldn't remember a thing I'd read. Once I learned ways to stay focused, learn, and remember what I read, I became a stronger reader.*

for handling and making the most of your school reading load and will continue to be important on the job. This section outlines reading strategies designed to strengthen your concentration, comprehension, and recall. If you try to read your textbooks in the same way you read books for entertainment, you won't likely remember what you need for the test or for the job. When you have a lot of classes and other demands to juggle, you'll want to make the most of your study-reading time by determining what's important. You'll add muscle to your reading by using a method that helps you concentrate, learn, and remember what you read. One such reading method is SQ3R, which was designed by Francis Robinson in 1941 for the military to help soldiers in training learn and retain what they were reading.[1] The reading method is still popular today. SQ3R takes more time initially, but in the long run you learn to identify what is important and use strategies to retain that information.

How to Use SQ3R, a Study-Reading Method

S = Survey—Take 5 to 10 minutes to briefly survey your reading assignment to get an overview of what you will be reading. Look at the introduction, objectives, headings, graphics (illustrations, charts, maps, diagrams, pictures), summary, study questions, terms, and the other end of the section activities. This step orients you to the section, helps you gather the information necessary to focus on the section and formulate questions for yourself as you read the section. Now that you have surveyed the entire section to build a framework of mental structures for understanding the section, it's time to begin the reading process. The next step, "question," and the next two steps, "read" and "recite," are repeated as you read the entire section.

Q = Question—Before you read each section, scan it to see if any questions stand out. For example, "How does SQ3R help you retain what you read?" Write down your question on the left third of a piece of paper as shown in Figure 4-1. Boldface headings and lists of information can be converted to questions.

R = Read—After your survey and questions, you are ready to begin reading your assignment one section at a time. You have built mental structures to help you learn and remember and now reading fills in the information around those mental structures. As you read a section, look for the answers to your questions and jot them down, in your own words, on the right two-thirds of your piece of paper. Try to separate the details from the main ideas. Use the details to help you understand the main ideas but don't expect yourself to memorize every detail. Some texts will have a lot of dense and complicated information and you will need to read more slowly—and that's okay.

R = Recite—Reciting material is done at the end of each section. Look at the question(s) you wrote on your paper, cover the answers with a piece of paper, and see if you can recite the answers to the questions from memory. If you can't remember the answers, look at your answer or reread that section of the book to help you recall the answer. Reciting material as you go helps your mind to concentrate and learn as you read.

Use these three steps—question, read, and recite, until you complete your entire section.

---

[1] Francis P. Robinson, *Effective Study,* 4th ed. (New York: Harper & Row, 1970). All rights reserved.

R = Review—Once you've finished reading the entire section, go back over all your questions. Cover the answers to the questions you've written down and see if you can still recite them. If you can't recite some answers, spend a little more time on those. We learn through repetition and the review step gives you another opportunity for repetition of the material to place it more permanently in your mind for better access when you need it.

Figure 4-2
Example of SQ3R

1)	What are the five steps to SQ3R?	Survey, question, read, recite, and review
2)	How does SQ3R help you retain what you read?	It helps you concentrate, learn, and remember what you read by setting up a framework/orientation to the material, developing questions about the major points, searching for answers, and learning the answers.
3)	Explain each of the five steps.	Now it's your turn to answer.

SQ3R seems to be the grandfather of other study-reading strategies such as PRQRT, which is explained next. As you read and learn about PRQRT, look for the similarities and the differences in the two reading methods.

How to Use PRQRT, Another Study-Reading Method

Step 1—Preview

Previewing simply means taking a quick overview of a reading assignment. Allow yourself 5 to 10 minutes to explore the following items: title, pictures and captions, introduction, learning objectives, the first sentence of each section, bold print and headings, graphs, listings and tables of content, summary and final paragraphs, and activities and questions at the end of the section. Your entire preview should be brief.

Previewing improves comprehension in several ways. It gives you "the big picture" of what you're about to read. It helps you build a map that guides you to major points and shows you how they fit together as a whole. It also provides clues about what's important in the reading.

Previewing before you start reading helps you determine why you are reading the material. It actually enhances your sense of purpose in reading. When you know why you are reading an assignment, you will read more actively.

Some texts have questions at the end of each section that refer to the reading. Whether or not your instructor assigns these questions, review them and keep them in mind. When you begin reading, you can search for and underline the answers. Knowing the answers to these questions will help you prepare for tests and you will learn better when you're actively searching for answers.

Step 2—Read, Question, and Recite

The read, question, and recite strategies are used together to create an active and effective reading method.

First, **read** one section of your assignment without underlining. However, during this initial reading, place a light check in the margin next to major points. Remember to be selective—you want to mark only the most important points.

Second, go back to each point you checked and develop a **question** that is answered by the point you checked. Then write a brief but clear form of the question in the outside margin and underline the answer in the text. Underline sparingly—key words only—to reduce what you'll need to review later. Examine the sample in Figure 4-3.

Third, after you have completed reading the section, cover the text and **recite** (from memory) the answers to the questions. If your answers are wrong, review and recite again. Mark areas with which you're having difficulty for your next review.

Use only a brief amount of time to write questions—keep them simple. Instead of writing a complete sentence: "What is an icon?" you could simply put "icon" in the margin and underline the definition in the text. Don't forget to search for answers to questions that may be asked at the end of the section. If appropriate, include these questions in your margins.

As you read, you may come across words and phrases you don't understand. Often new words are introduced in *italic* or in **boldface**. Most authors define terms common to the subject at least once. You may need to look up definitions in a dictionary to understand what you're reading. It's better to take the time to look up words than to waste the time reading what you don't understand. Keep your dictionary close at hand to save time. This is an excellent way to build your vocabulary. When you find the definition, you may want to record it in one of three ways: (1) circle the word in your text and briefly note the definition as close to the word as possible, (2) keep a running list of terms and definitions, or (3) use flash cards to write terms on one side and definitions on the other side.

Figure 4-3
Example of PRQRT

Muscle Memory

Muscle memory <u>occurs when a certain muscle movement is changed from a conscious action to an automatic response,</u> requiring no thought. Top performance athletes spend thousands of practice hours ingraining in their minds certain motor skills. They work on the technical aspect of a motor skill until it becomes unnecessary for them to think about it. This special "knowing," allows them to perform at the highest levels during competition.

Muscle memory

You may have been told during a sports competition, "Don't try so hard." The coach is giving the message to rely on your muscle memory. Tension and doubt trigger biochemical changes that interrupt muscle memory. The pressure and anxiety of trying too hard has several adverse effects. <u>Physically, it increases heart rate, blood pressure, muscle tension, and the flow of perspiration. Psychologically, it can cause sensations of panic, confusion, and a feeling of fatigue.</u>

How do pressure and anxiety affect muscle memory?

Muscle memory is <u>produced by repetition</u> much the same way learning is achieved by repetition. <u>Both develop and become automatic with practice. Both can be inhibited due to stress caused by negative self-talk,</u> which we communicate to ourselves in the form of self-doubt and worry. Both muscle memory and learning are enhanced <u>with practice or repetition and positive self-talk.</u>

How are muscle memory and learning alike?

How can you enhance muscle memory and learning?

You may be able to grasp the meaning of unfamiliar words by referring to the context—how the words are used in a sentence or paragraph. The following sentence is an example: My father is a very **assertive** man because he can *comfortably express his views in a respectful manner*.

The term *assertive* is explained later in the sentence. If you still don't understand the meaning, look it up. Whenever you encounter a new word, spend a minute rehearsing it so you can understand it each time it appears in the future.

In addition to looking up definitions, there are several other ways you can better understand what you're reading. You can always ask a dependable classmate, your instructor, or a tutor to explain difficult material. You also might try stopping and slowly rereading until the meaning sinks in. Visualize or draw the material if possible. Or try saying it in your own words or writing a summary. Use any of these techniques to clear up confusion right away, rather than getting frustrated. You'll feel more positive and in control when you take the time to work through points that seem confusing.

The read, question, recite process helps you to reduce your study material to major points and develop questions for exam preparation. It takes a little more time, but you'll learn more and will prepare more thoroughly for tests and discussion.

Step 3—Test

Test yourself after you finish the entire reading assignment. Recite the answers to your margin questions and recite all related definitions. The test strategy should take 10 to 20 minutes—twice as long as the preview. Use this testing strategy on a regular or daily basis until you can easily recite the material. Self-testing will begin the process of making the material a permanent part of your memory.

This reading system of preview, read, question, recite, and test (PRQRT) will improve your comprehension and recall of course material. It will reduce the need for cramming and marathon study sessions before an exam. If you cram for an exam, you'll quickly forget the material you studied. Cramming not only causes problems on the current exam but causes even more serious problems for future exams. You may be surprised at the number of exams throughout college and your career that keep "asking" you about the same information. These exams may include midterm and final exams, competency tests, national certification exams, and job-related exams. Reading offers you a chance to gain life-long knowledge. Learning while you read saves time.

Exercise 4-7 Using PRQRT

Try using the PRQRT method to read the following selection, entitled *Eat More Fiber*.

EAT MORE FIBER

Why is a healthy diet usually expressed in negative terms? Eat less fat, reduce cholesterol, cut back on red meat, eggs, and simple sugars. A more positive slant to promoting a healthy diet is to eat more fiber. A diet high in fiber may protect against a variety of cancers, heart disease, diabetes, and intestinal problems.

High fiber foods include whole grains, fruits, vegetables, and legumes (beans and lentils). All types of fiber have two things in common: they are found only in plant foods and they are resistant to human digestive enzymes (that is, they pass through the digestive track without being completely broken down).

Fiber is broken down into two types—soluble and insoluble. Insoluble fiber is like a sponge—it absorbs many times its weight in water, swelling up within the intestine. Insoluble fiber is found mainly in whole grains, on the outside of seeds, fruits, legumes, and other foods. Insoluble fiber is often lost when the outer material is peeled, processed, or removed. Insoluble fiber helps promote more efficient elimination by producing a larger and softer stool that the digestive system can pass quickly and easily. It also helps to alleviate diverticulosis—when food gets trapped in small intestinal pouches (diverticula) which become inflamed. Additionally, it is thought to play a role in colon cancer protection.

Soluble fiber is found in fruits, vegetables, seeds, brown rice, barley, oats, and oat bran. It helps to produce a softer stool but does less to help the passage of food; rather, it works chemically to prevent or reduce the absorption of certain substances into the bloodstream. Soluble fiber also appears to lower LDL (bad) cholesterol levels and retard the entry of glucose into the bloodstream, an especially important factor for diabetics.

Eating large amounts of fiber in a short time can result in intestinal gas, bloating, and cramps. Usually this isn't serious and subsides once the body adjusts to the fiber increase. Add fiber-rich foods gradually to your diet. Be sure to drink plenty of liquids to aid in proper bowel function. The Food and Drug Administration (FDA) recommended dietary allowance (RDA) of fiber is 20 to 30 grams per day. Adding fiber to your diet is a positive move toward disease prevention and weight loss (because you have less room for other food), and most high fiber foods are also high in complex carbohydrates, your best energy source.

As you can see, the SQ3R and PRQRT reading methods and the many other strategies provided in this section will help with just about any reading assignment.

When to Use SQ3R or PRQRT

No study-reading method is useful 100 percent of the time for all subjects. Different study methods work best in different situations. Both SQ3R and PRQRT are excellent techniques to use with textbooks that provide a lot of information and require you to learn the material in depth such as biology, psychology, and sociology. Both methods are probably less useful with math textbooks or other textbooks that focus on problem solving. When reading math textbooks, focus your energy on solving mathematical problems given in the text. The next section will discuss strategies to help you read and succeed in math. SQ3R and PRQRT may also be less useful in reading beginning foreign language texts, which focus on vocabulary, verb tense, and sentence construction. As you read and use the many learning, reading, and memory techniques outlined in this section, you will learn which help you most.

Also note that if your professor is not reviewing much of the textbook material in class, it is probably well worth your time to read the sections using the SQ3R method. If your professor uses the textbook as a supplement or reference to class lectures, you will need to balance the amount of time reading the sections, solving problems, reviewing notes, and completing homework assignments. Look for clues as to what your professor expects you to study most.

Now that you've learned a couple of power study-reading methods, plan to start reading your assignments early. If while reading, you find some material that you don't understand, jot down a question to ask your teacher or tutor the next day. Both SQ3R and PRQRT take time and should not be used the night before a test. Using either method will put muscle in your reading and help you learn and remember what you read.

Reading and Studying Math

More people complain about trouble with math than any other subject. Often it is because they have not mastered some essential foundational skills. You may have trouble with college-level math if you didn't master—or have forgotten—these basic skills. Across the nation, almost 60 percent of all college students are enrolled in developmental/remedial or transitional math courses to prepare for college-level math. In many colleges, up to half of these students are not succeeding, and math becomes the leading cause of failure and dropout in college. The majority of all college programs normally require math at some level. When students feel they "can't do math," they are limiting themselves from many careers and generally from the highest paying ones. In math, as in most of life's endeavors, the difference between success and failure is often only a matter of inches—a little more serious effort and effective study/learning strategies. If math is difficult for you, consider using some of the following tips to help you succeed in math or to "beat math before it beats you." Put an asterisk by the tips you need to adopt.

Tips . . . For Math Success

- Attend all classes and take full class notes. Research has shown that successful students don't miss class and usually take notes on what is discussed. Failing students take few meaningful notes and often miss class. Remember, missing even one class can put you behind in the course by at least two classes. Do you know why?

- If you need more help, ask your instructor how you can get a tutor or if you can sit in on another section. By hearing a difficult concept explained a second time, you may understand it much better.

- Be determined to complete all assigned problems, always read the section before going to your math class, and work the practice problems in your reading assignments. This will give you a much better understanding of what is being discussed in class. When students fail to study and spend enough time with math outside of the classroom, they'll think the instructor is "going too fast" during class simply because the material is still too unfamiliar.

- Organize your notes into one 3-ring binder notebook devoted only to math. Use the first half for class notes and the second half for homework. While in class try to connect what you learned on your own to what the instructor is teaching.

- In your notes, write the main points, steps to solve problems, definitions, formulas, examples, solutions, or proofs. Review your notes as soon as possible after class, study/recite them up to eight hours later, and then plan regular reviews so the information you have learned will become more permanent.

- Discipline yourself to keep up with your homework and the class. If you allow yourself to fall behind, the entire course will likely become a real struggle for you. Study math at least 2 hours a day, 5 days a week and you won't regret it.

- While you are studying, write questions about any difficult math problems. Never avoid asking a question out of fear of looking stupid. Do not allow a question to go unanswered. **Get help fast** from your instructor, classmate, or a tutor. Don't settle for a fuzzy understanding.

- Know and understand your math terminology. Use 3" x 5" review cards to study math's own unique vocabulary. Carry these cards with you everywhere and review them at odd moments throughout the day and you won't even feel like you're studying.

- Never attempt to memorize a formula (or rule, proof, or procedure) until you have attempted to understand it first. This understanding will help you recreate a formula (or procedure, etc.) if your recall falters in any way.

- If math is your most difficult subject, make it a priority to study it first when you're most alert and fresh. It will go better for you and you will recall more.

- Use your mistakes to learn. Analyze mistakes on tests and assignments. Did you follow the wrong procedure, read the directions incorrectly, or did you make a careless mistake?

Math Anxiety

Many people believe they are math anxious when they are really test anxious or poor math test-takers. Once they deal with these problems, they can be very successful in math. Do you understand the math you are learning, or maybe even like it, but you don't do well on math tests? Do you find that there are tests in other subjects on which you go blank or feel anxious? If your answer to these questions is yes, you will want to work to manage test anxiety in math or other subjects. In the section on test taking, you will learn more about how to conquer test anxiety. It is important to learn how to manage, but not necessarily eliminate, the anxiety you feel during tests. Some anxiety keeps you on your toes and makes you more alert so you can function at your best. Too much anxiety can immobilize you. When you're intentional about having a positive attitude toward math and your ability to do math, you will mobilize yourself and reduce your anxiety. By using positive math affirmations and eliminating all negative math self-talk, you can develop a positive attitude and increased enthusiasm for math and manage math test anxiety. Challenge your negative self-talk and tell yourself: "I can succeed in math." "I am learning more math each day." "Math helps me to get to where I want to go." "I will do word problems." Let your positive self-talk direct you. Be relentless with your positive self-talk until you are where you want to be. Also tell yourself to be patient—LEARNING MATH TAKES TIME. Read the following Tips for Conquering Math Test Anxiety and try them.

Tips . . . For Conquering Math Test Anxiety

- Think positively. Approach your math classes and assignments with the confidence that, with the help of your instructor, other students, tutors, and your own commitment, you'll master any math skills you need.

- Improve your study skills. The techniques suggested in this section will help you learn more while studying math—the more you learn, the more confidence you'll have. People in your math tutoring center are also familiar with your anxiety and will have a program to help you improve your skills. Often, simply being more organized about your studying will increase your confidence.

- Use relaxation techniques, such as stretching and deep, slow breathing when you feel anxious during study sessions or tests.

- When you sit down for exams, write any formulas or other information you've memorized as soon as the test session begins. Then you can relax, knowing that you have important information already written down.

- If math anxiety still bothers you, talk to your instructor and to people in the math department or your college's counseling center. You'll probably find whatever assistance you need.

Adopting Strategies to Put Muscle into Your Math Reading

Slow down! This is the first thing you need to tell yourself when you read your math textbook. For most of us, SPEED KILLS when it comes to reading math textbooks. To learn math as you read, you will need to stop and practice problems so you can apply what you read. You'll also need to stop to learn new math vocabulary and symbols. Math has its own language and every word and symbol counts. Words like "power" and "factor" will have very specific meanings in math. If you are uncertain about the meaning of a term, look it up or ask someone to explain it. If you keep on reading without stopping to learn your math terms, you will get lost. Likewise, it is important to read from the beginning to the end of a section because each page assumes you have mastered the previous pages. Remind yourself that it is important to understand each sentence before you go on. Reread as many times as necessary to master a math concept or procedure. When possible make drawings of problems so you can visualize and understand them better. Spend time to understand diagrams and other kinds of illustrative material in your textbook. Cover your text and recite, review, and practice anything you want to become a permanent part of your memory. All these strategies will put more muscle into your math reading and you will get more out of class. Learning math takes extra time for everyone but failure takes more time in the long run.

Examine the following math reading about fractions. Notice that seven terms are used in the paragraph. The bold print terms are defined in the paragraph. The terms in parentheses were discussed in an earlier section of a math text, and therefore not in bold type in this reading.

> **Fractions**
> *A fraction is an expression that represents the (quotient) of two numbers. For example, the fraction 5/7 is the equivalent of the quotient 5 ÷ 7. In fractions, the (dividend) is called the **numerator** and the (divisor) is called the denominator. If the numerator is less than the **denominator,** the fraction is said to be a **proper** fraction. If the numerator is greater than the denominator, the fraction is said to be an **improper** fraction.*

Wow! To read that paragraph, you have to slow your pace and be sure you understand the explanation of each term being introduced. There are also three terms (quotient, dividend, and divisor) that should be familiar to you based on previous learning about division. If you have forgotten the definitions of these words, as many have, you may need to look them up so you clearly understand what you are reading. Consider writing their definitions in the text.

Reading and learning math requires a slower pace of reading and a higher level of concentration for everyone. Not only will you need to slow down and reread, but you will need to stop to experiment with sample problems. When reading math, keep a pad of paper and a pencil in hand to stop and practice. Just as discipline and practice help athletes master their sports, disciplined daily practice is the key to developing your math ability.

When reading and practicing math problems, ask yourself these questions:

- What am I being asked to find?

- What information am I being given?

- What procedure(s) should I use?

After you know the answers to these questions, use the following steps to complete the problem.

- Always follow step by step. If you skip a step, you may not be able to go back and find where you made a mistake.

- If possible, estimate answers before you compute.

- Work neatly. Especially when working with decimals, it's important to keep numbers lined up and in the right place.

- Decide if the answer makes sense.

- Proofread to check for careless mistakes. Whether you are completing homework or a test, include time to check for mistakes, such as not reducing to the lowest common denominator, wrong signs, or computation errors. Try to determine what type of errors you commonly make so that as you complete homework and tests, you will watch for these mistakes.

- Check your answer by working backward. With equations, always plug in your answer for the unknown variable to see if it works.

- Practice another example—create your own problem.

Notice that, in the following example, the solution is worked out step by step. The answer is plugged in to show that it works. Think about how the answer makes sense.

Sara earns $30,000 per year in Boulder, Colorado and pays $___ s $150 more than twice the amount Henri pays earning th_____ Henri pay in taxes?

$$2x + 150 = 3,000$$
$$2x = 3,000 - 150$$
$$2x = 2,850$$
$$x = \frac{2,850}{2}$$
$$x = 1,425$$

Check: $2 \times 1,425 + 150 = 3,$
$2,850 + 150 = 3$
$3,000 = 3$

You'll need to understand and me_____ formula_____ng your math facts and formulas will help you complete _____, it's also important to know how and when to apply the___

Always read mathematics with gr_____, take a moment to practice it. Practicing will put the skill into long-term r_____ you're having trouble with a problem, identify what you are confused about so you can discuss _____ your _____ ion as it arises so you don't fall behind. When you get a _____ on your homework, help_____ others will reinforce your own learning. Math skills tend to _____ you don't get the basic skills, you won't get the advanced ones. Get help as soon as _____ get worse. If you read to understand and practice to memorize, then whe_____ review.

Reading in Science and Technica___

When you understand your science a_____ curiosity and motivation grow even more. A healthy curiosity is a step to building _____

Science is a system for explaining the natural world in an orderly manner. It is all about observation, gathering information, making hypotheses (educated guesses), and testing them. Remember that the study of science constantly changes as new discoveries are made. Developing questions about what you read will encourage you to learn and to read more.

As in math, the reading of science or of any technical material will require that you slow your reading rate. As you read, you will want to look up terms you don't know and then rehearse them—perhaps write them on flash cards for practice. Knowing the terminology of the field is basic to understanding what you read.

In addition, you'll want to follow these suggestions:

- Science textbooks frequently describe procedures. To better learn and understand these procedures, write them in a step-by-step outline. Practice them either in your mind or in real life, if possible. This will also prepare you for exams.

- Systems and processes are also commonly explained in science texts. One practical way to grasp a system or process is to draw a diagram of it. You'll often understand systems better with diagrams than with words.

- Organizing information into charts helps to show the relationships between ideas. Examine Table 4-3, where a chart is used to organize and learn information from a reading assignment on clouds and weather forecasting.

Table 4-3

Cloud Type	Description	Weather
Cirrus	Thin, feather-like, delicate	Usually appear in dry weather, but often mean a storm is on the way.
Cumulus	Large, puffy, flat bottoms, domed tops like cauliflower.	When bright and white, bring fair weather; when thick, heavy, and dark, bring rain, thunder, and lightning.
Stratus	Thick layers of clouds; resembles blanket, flat and often gray.	Frequently bring drizzling rain or fine snow. Fog is a stratus cloud.

Reading Graphics

You'll encounter many graphs, tables, and illustrations in your textbooks and other coursework. Among the most common are the following:

- **Bar graphs.** Bar graphs show the relationship between two variables, such as how the quantity of something changes over time (see Figure 4-4).

Figure 4-4
Bar Graph

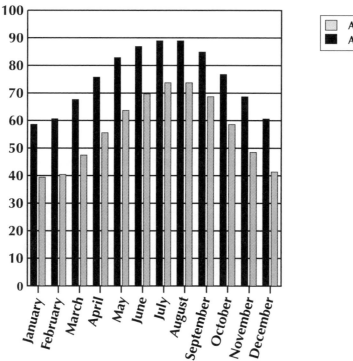

Average Daily Temperatures for Hilton Head Island, SC

Legend: Average Low Temperature / Average High Temperature

- **Line graphs.** Line graphs also show the relationship between two variables (see Figure 4-5).

Figure 4-5
Line Graph

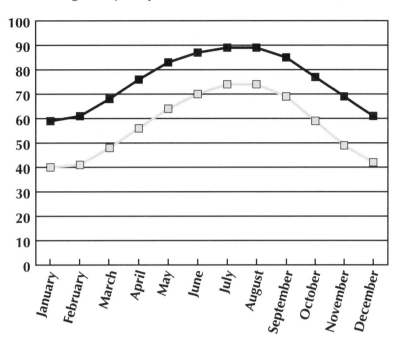

Average Daily Temperatures for Hilton Head Island, SC

- Circle or pie graphs. Pie graphs display the parts of a whole and the relative size or importance of the parts (see Figure 4-6).

Figure 4-6
Circle or Pie Graph

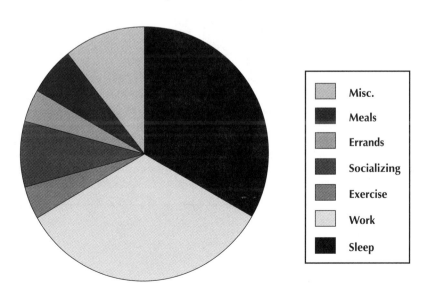

Time Spent on Daily Activities

- **Tables.** Tables organize information or data into columns or rows so the information is easier to digest (see Figure 4-7).

Figure 4-7
Table

10 Leading Causes of Death in the United States, 1900 and 2010
(in Death Rates per 100,000 Population)

Causes of Death	Death Rates Per 100,000 Population	% of All Deaths
		1900*
1. Pneumonia	191.9	12.5
2. Consumption (Tuberculosis)	190.5	12.5
3. Heart Disease	134.0	8.3
4. Diarrheal Diseases	85.1	5.6
5. Diseases of the Kidneys	83.7	5.5
6. All Accidents	72.3	4.7
7. Apoplexy (Stroke)	66.6	4.3
8. Cancer	60.0	3.9
9. Old Age	54.0	3.5
10. Bronchitis	48.3	3.2
		2010
1. Diseases of Heart	597.6	24.2
2. Malignant Neoplasms (Cancer)	574.7	23.3
3. Chronic Lower Respiratory Diseases	138.0	5.6
4. Cerebrovascular Diseases	129.4	5.2
5. Accidents	120.8	4.9
6. Alzheimer's Disease	83.5	3.4
7. Diabetes	69.1	2.8
8. Nephritis, Nephrotic Syndrome, Nephrosis	50.5	2.0
9. Influenza and Pneumonia	50.1	2.0
10. Suicide	38.4	1.6

* These data are limited to the registration area that included 10 registration states and all cities having at least 8,000 inhabitants. In 1900 this composed 38 percent of the entire population of the continental United States. Since accidents were not reported in the 1900 census, this rate was taken from Lerner (1970).

Sources: *Abstract of the Twelfth Census of the United States, 1900.* Table 93. Washington, DC: U.S. Government Printing Office, 1902, and "Deaths: Leading Causes for 2010," by Melonie Heron, Ph.D., Division of Vital Statistics, *National Vital Statistics Reports* 62 (6), December 20, 2013. Centers for Disease Control and Prevention, National Center for Health Statistics, National Vital Statistics System.

- **Illustrations.** Illustrations may be drawings or diagrams that describe an item, an idea, or a process (see Figure 4-8).

Figure 4-8
Illustration

Common Chemical Symbols

A chemical symbol is a letter or a pair of letters which stands for a chemical element as illustrated below.

	Atoms joined together	Formula	Name
	2 oxygen atoms	O	oxygen
	2 hydrogen + 1 oxygen atom	H^2O	water
	1 carbon atom	CO^2	carbon dioxide

Tips . . . For Reading Graphs, Tables, or Illustrations

When reading graphs, tables, or illustrations, take note of the following:

- Read the title of the graph, table, or illustration. Usually, the title describes the main point of the graphic.

- Read headings and labels to understand the components of the graphic. Note the units of measure, such as time, percentages, and dollars.

- Read any additional text, such as footnotes. You'll often find additional information about the information presented and its source.

- Try to draw a conclusion from the graphic. Is there an identifiable trend—for example, do you see the same trend in a line graph that the author does? Do you see other interesting trends?

CHALLENGING YOUR OWN STUDY TRAPS

You've learned some excellent power strategies for studying. They will help you learn more and learn it better. Having great strategies is not always enough. You still need to motivate yourself to use them. Your self-talk will be the most important motivational factor in learning. It directs you to study or not to study and how to study. How does your self-talk influence your study and learning? Figure 4-9 lists examples of self-talk study traps and how to challenge them.

Figure 4-9
Self-Talk Study Traps

---

1. "I have so much to do, I don't know where to begin."

Take control. Make a list of things you have to do. Break tasks down into manageable parts—what part(s) can you do now? Prioritize. Schedule your time realistically and don't forget to schedule breaks. Start studying early. What other ways can you take more control of your study? Tell yourself, "I'll handle this!"

2. "This stuff is so boring, I can't even stay awake."

Attack it! Don't let this be an excuse for not giving it your best effort. Put more life into your learning by being active in your learning. Decide why this material is important to you. Take good notes. Tell yourself, "Only boring people get bored."

3. "I guess I know it."

Don't guess. Instead of guessing, test yourself—see what you do and do not know.

4. "Cramming before a test helps keep it fresh in my mind."

Space your study. Recall increases as study time gets spread out over time. Tell yourself to "keep up the pace."

5. "I'm just lazy."

What an excuse for not getting started! What impact does this type of self-talk have on you? Instead of telling yourself you're lazy, tell yourself what you want to get done and how you'll do it.

Exercise 4-8 How does your self-talk direct your study?

Examine some of your own self-talk and how it directs your study. List five self-talk statements you have expressed recently concerning your study. Explain the impact.

THE 60 HOUR RULE

Many students who do not do well in classes need to have a job or want to have a job. Students can either take a full load of courses and work a few hours or work 20 to 40 hours and take a lighter load of courses. Landis in his book, *Studying Engineering: A Road Map to a Rewarding Career*, states, "If you must work while going to school, how can you achieve a reasonable balance between the two? A way to manage your study and work loads is to follow the '60 Hour Rule' developed by Dr. Mulinazzi, a professor of civil engineering at the University of Kansas." The 60 Hour Rule assumes that a person can be productive for 60 hours a week for the length of a semester. Take 60, subtract the hours working at a job, and then divide the remainder by 3. The result is the number of credit hours a student should take in a semester.

Source: Landis, R. (2000). *Studying Engineering: A Road Map to a Rewarding Career*. Discovery Press.

HIGHLIGHTS

Becoming a skilled learner is within your grasp. The techniques and strategies for improving your concentration, memory, and reading in conjunction with the use of positive self-talk will give you greater control over your learning. You've explored ways to improve your concentration by eliminating external and internal distractions. You've practiced the following six techniques to improve your memory and, therefore, your learning: understanding through writing and conversations, association with the use of mnemonics, recitation and recall, organizing information with maps and charts, visualization, and self-testing.

You've seen how a reading method can improve recall and comprehension. Using SQ3R and PRQRT strategies help you to identify important information and to anticipate possible test questions. These reading methods are slower, but they will help you select material to learn as you read—this means no rereading sections because, "I can't remember anything I read," which is even more time consuming. Both SQ3R and PRQRT let you read and learn materials immediately and set up quick reviews in your text to help you prepare for future tests.

Finally, you've examined how self-talk is perhaps the most important factor in learning. Self-talk guides your determination as well as the direction you take with your study. Your self-talk can help you avoid study or motivate you to study. It can direct how you will study and how much you will study. "I just don't feel like studying." "I will use PRQRT to read my psychology section before I watch TV." These two self-talk messages will produce very different results.

These strategies are tools you need for success in college. Practicing them now will pay off with improved performance in and out of the classroom.

DISCUSSION QUESTIONS

Note: Read the following discussion questions and activities **before** you read Section 4. This strategy will help you look for answers while you read.

1. Describe and evaluate your study environment. Discuss any ways you might need to improve it.
2. How is PRQRT a combination of memory techniques? (Be sure to address each part of this reading strategy.) SQ3R?
3. Why do many fail to learn what they read in text assignments?
4. Discuss the advantages and disadvantages of both SQ3R and PRQRT. How would you evaluate the usefulness of these reading methods?
5. Explain the difference between the *recite* and *test* strategies in PRQRT.
6. What are the similarities and differences between SQ3R and PRQRT?
7. Discuss your weaknesses and strengths in math. What memory techniques and reading strategies might help you overcome your weaknesses and further boost your strengths? Explain.
8. What is a key emphasis in studying science? Explain.
9. What self-talk study traps have you been using? How can you overcome them? How important do you think your self-talk is in directing your motivation to study and learn?

Listening, Notetaking, and Test Taking Skills

WHAT'S IN IT FOR YOU

Now that you've learned effective ways to prepare before class, it's important to also develop your skills as an active listener and a good notetaker when you're in class. These two skills are so valuable because they are the only way to remember the quantity of material that your instructors will present. Being an active listener will not only be a valuable skill for school and work but in your personal life as well. In this section you will also learn a notetaking format in which you prepare self-tests as you take notes.

Test taking is an important part of your college studies. Your test grades help your instructors determine how much of the course material you've learned. Tests don't measure how smart you are; they are simply tools that evaluate the progress you've made in your studies. Test preparation is like running a marathon; the more you train, the better your chances for success. You can take any test with confidence if you train properly for it. For many, testing will continue to be important in getting a job, certification, job placement, and promotion. This section offers tips and strategies that successful students use to "ace" tests.

In this section you'll explore:

- How well you listen in the classroom
- Tips to develop your active listening skills
- Notetaking tips and formats
- How to prepare for tests
- Test taking strategies for objective tests
- How to master essay questions
- Test anxiety and how to overcome it

LISTENING ACTIVELY

Active listeners come to class with an interest in the material. They have questions and thoughts about their reading assignments. When they get to class, they sit in front, and once class begins they are attentive—they don't read or talk until appropriate. Active listeners are this way because they have decided to get excited about what they are learning.

Take a moment to assess how well you are already practicing active listening in class.

Exercise 5-1 Listening Inventory

Indicate how well you listen in the classroom:

	Yes	Sometimes	No
1. Do you come with interest and a positive attitude that says "I want to learn"?	_____	_____	_____
2. Are you open to listening to and trying to understand ideas even if they are very different or opposed to your beliefs?	_____	_____	_____
3. Are you able to concentrate on what the speaker is saying?	_____	_____	_____
4. Are you able to block out external distractions such as worry, noises, or preparing your own response?	_____	_____	_____
5. Do you remember the main points made by the instructor?	_____	_____	_____
6. Do you find yourself listening carefully to the content of the instructor's message?	_____	_____	_____
7. Are you able to hear, understand, and grasp the intent of what is said?	_____	_____	_____
8. Do you pay attention to and understand the instructor's body language?	_____	_____	_____
9. Do you come prepared—reading assignments completed, questions ready to ask?	_____	_____	_____
10. Are you attentive, alert, focused on the present?	_____	_____	_____

The items you answered "no" or "sometimes" to are areas to improve on. Read the following list of suggestions to learn ways in which you can become a more active listener in the classroom.

Tips . . . For Active Listening in the Classroom

- Listen to the content of the message—the words, figures, ideas, details, and logic the instructor conveys. Words only comprise a small portion of what is communicated, but those words are the core of the message. Ask for clarification if you do not understand the content of what is being communicated.

- Listen to the intent of the message. The more you understand the background of an instructor or a speaker—her bias, position, track record—the better you'll be able to understand the intent of her message. Listening for the intent requires balancing the content, the nonverbal communication, and the speaker's background or position. When you listen for the intent, you are listening to "why" she says something rather than what is said.

- Observe and assess the instructor's nonverbal communication. Nonverbal communication is a combination of body language and tone of voice. It is "how" the words are spoken, which will communicate much more than the actual words.

- Be determined to stay focused and attentive. Active listeners want to listen and use self-talk that encourages their desire to listen and learn. Take notes—that will keep you attentive. Listen for clues to tests.

- Communicate your interest in what the instructor is teaching. Sit up front, ask questions, lean slightly forward, and maintain eye contact. Don't be tempted to work on homework or talk to your classmates—your instructor will definitely notice this.

- Be open to the message even when it's something you are opposed to. Postpone judgment so you can listen and make an effort to understand. Understanding does not mean that you have to accept what is being said. Wait for your instructor to finish her explanation before you formulate your comment or question.

- Come to class prepared. Read and study assignments and prepare questions. Work to resolve worries and distractions before you get to class so you can put a high level of energy into listening. Active listening requires lots of energy.

Active listening is not only a fundamental skill for school success but career success as well. At work you will be resolving problems, giving and receiving directions, participating in meetings, serving and receiving service. These activities involve active listening as well as talking. Effective communication requires active listening—it is the foundation of good communication.

Being an active listener is also the first step to taking good notes. The act of taking notes, in fact, makes you a better listener. You have to concentrate more when you're taking notes. The next part of this section will introduce you to notetaking strategies.

TAKING NOTES

Notetaking is important for two reasons: the process of thinking and writing while listening helps push information into long-term memory; you preserve the major points of the lecture in writing so you can review them later.

Good notetaking is a skill that you develop as a student but carry to the workplace. Much of your life will be spent taking notes of meetings, conferences, and phone conversations, as well as of your own thoughts. For now, notetaking will keep you active and alert in class and help you to keep an accurate account of lectures.

Effective notetaking is a three-step process: listening, thinking, and writing. The first step, listening, means more than hearing. As discussed earlier, active listening is the key to getting the most out of lectures. An active listener is interested, wants to listen, wants to learn, and maintains a positive attitude. This means being determined to pay attention in spite of distractions. Active listening leads directly to the second step in the notetaking process: thinking. You must think about the meaning of what is being said so you can select the most important information to remember. And finally, once you've listened and thought about the meaning of what's being said, you must complete the third step: writing down the most important information so you'll be able to review it later.

This may seem like a lot to do in the midst of a lecture, but in fact there is time. Your instructor probably speaks at a rate of 100 to 150 words per minute. You can think at a rate of 400 words per minute—so you have time to complete the listen-think-write process. Remember, good notes save you hours of work later.

Your preparation before class will help you take better notes, too. You can prepare by completing all written and reading assignments and reviewing and testing yourself on previous notes. This will give you the basic background for most lectures. As Jason realized, "My notetaking was much easier when I wasn't confused every few minutes by a new term or phrase. By completing the assigned readings, I often could predict what my instructor was about to say."

The most beneficial notes are those that are study-ready. This means that your notes are written for use in rehearsal and in self-testing. When you learn to write study-ready notes, you'll save the time you might have spent reorganizing your notes or writing separate study tests.

The following notetaking strategies will help you construct study-ready notes:

- Complete all readings and other assignments before class.

- Use a three-ring or loose-leaf notebook. This type of notebook will allow you to place handouts or additional notes in the proper sequence. It also will allow you to replace notes that you may have rewritten or reorganized. Sometimes you may want to pull a few notes from your notebook to study. You can't do any of these with a spiral notebook. Use 8-1/2" x 11" inch paper and write on only one side.

- Leave plenty of margin space for additional comments or study clues. Skip a space to separate notes on new ideas. Tightly packed notes are difficult to study. Leave space for missed ideas and later ask a classmate or your instructor to help you fill in the gaps. You also may want to allow space for items you would like to clarify or expand on later.

- Use the top margin to note assignments, course, date, and the page number of your notes, as in the example below. This will help you find the notes from specific lectures more easily.

Course: Social Science	*Assignment: <u>Read chap 12</u>*
Date: May 2, 2015	*<u>complete all chap ques</u>*
Page: 1	*Due: <u>May 6</u>*

- Record definitions of technical terms exactly as given.

- Note the points your instructor stressed by placing a star or asterisk (*) in the margin next to the items emphasized. These items may appear in your exams. Here are some of the following ways your instructor verbally cues you on important points.

  - . . . a major point . . .

  - . . . pay special attention to . . .

  - . . . note this . . .

  - . . . an important reason . . .

  - . . . don't forget . . .

  - . . . a chief cause . . .

  - . . . what do you think is the reason for this?

  - . . . this will probably be on the test . . .

  - Repeated statements.

  - Numbered lists.

  - The instructor's voice slows down.

- Copy the diagrams and drawings your instructor writes on the board.

- Record your instructor's examples. These usually clarify more complex points, and if you don't record them, you may forget them.

- Take notes during group discussions. Group problem-solving questions often show up as essay questions on tests.

- Take notes throughout class. Don't stop taking notes 10 minutes before you're dismissed. Your instructor may make her most important point right before the end of class.

- Use abbreviations and symbols that you can easily remember. These are particularly helpful when your instructor moves at a fast pace. Some of the most common ones are listed in Table 5-1.

Table 5-1
Common Abbreviations and Symbols

Abbreviation	Meaning	Abbreviation	Meaning
i.e.	that is	=	the same as
e.g.	for example	≠	not the same as
dept.	department	>	greater than
info	information	<	less than
imp or *	important	w/	with
betw	between	w/o	without
incl	including	x	example
ques	question	&	and
subj	subject	NY	New York
decrg	decreasing	vs.	against
chap	chapter	...	therefore

- To speed notetaking further, leave out unimportant words, such as "a" and "the" from your notes. Write phrases or names in full the first time they come up and use initials thereafter—for example, if your behavioral health technology instructor discusses the Mini Mental Exam, write it in full the first time; from then on write MME.

- Notice how your instructor has organized her lecture material. If she has not consistently used headings in organization, develop some of your own headings to help you further learn and organize the material.

- Review your notes as soon as possible after class to begin to solidify them in your mind. To "lock-in" material, briefly review all notes between exams on a daily basis.

Notetaking Formats

An effective notetaking format also will help you to prepare study-ready notes. Notes taken in paragraph form are difficult to study. Two effective formats are the **outline format** and the **column format.** Note how both enable you to test yourself when preparing for an exam.

Outline format

The outline format is a system of taking notes using numbers, letters, indents, and bullets (•) to highlight important information and how the important points relate to one another. Notice in the example in Figure 5-1 that each main point is recorded at the left margin and its supporting points are indented and written below. You may develop your own system of numbering and bullets, but the basic structure is the same. While you prepare for a test, you can quiz yourself on terms, definitions, and explanations by covering the information above or below each major point with a piece of paper.

Figure 5-1
Outline Format for Notetaking

Course: *Sociology of Aging*   Assignment: <u>*Read chap 6*</u>
Date: *Dec. 5, 2014*   <u>*complete all chap ques*</u>
Page: *1*   Due: <u>*Dec. 7*</u>

I.   ELDER ABUSE
> *A. <u>Physical Abuse</u>—infliction of physical pain, confining, and/or restraining against a*
> *person's will*
> *B. <u>Psychological Abuse</u>—infliction of mental anguish such as name-calling, threatening,*
> *frightening, and/or humiliating*

II. ELDER NEGLECT
> *A. <u>Passive</u>—unintentional failure to fulfill a caretaking responsibility (often inability)*
> *B. <u>Active</u>—intentional failure to perform a caretaking responsibility*

III. FINANCIAL ABUSE OR EXPLOITATION
> *A. The misuse of an older person's money or property by a person in a position of trust*

IV. SOME WARNING SIGNALS OF ABUSE
> *A. Physical Signs*
> > *1. Recurring or unexplained injuries, such as bruises, cuts, or burns*
> > *2. Combination of new and old injuries*
> > *3. Injuries without underlying diseases*
> > *4. Dehydration or malnutrition*
> > *5. Injuries in areas usually covered by clothing*
>
> *B. Social-Psychological Signs*
> > *1. Depression or withdrawal*
> > *2. Hesitation to talk openly*
> > *3. Fearfulness of caregivers or helping professionals*
> > *4. Confusing or contradictory statements by competent elder*
> > *5. Resignation or denial*
>
> *C. Signs of Denied Civil Rights*
> > *1. Unwarranted social isolation*
> > *2. Signs of physical restraint*
> > *3. Inability to talk with older person in absence of caregiver*
> > *4. Unwarranted schedule of imposed activities*
>
> *D. Signs of Medical Neglect*
> > *1. Non-treatment of medical problems*
> > *2. Over-sedation*
> > *3. Presence of bed sores*

Figure 5-1
Outline Format for Notetaking (continued)

     E. *Signs of Neglect*
        1. *Changes in reasoning ability*
        2. *Abuse of alcohol or drugs*
        3. *Decline in characteristics of self and/or home*

     F. *Financial Signs*
        1. *Unjustified control of competent adult's finances by another person*
        2. *Refusal of needed services*
        3. *Lack of knowledge about financial matters*
        4. *Refusal to make financial decisions or pay bills without consulting another*

Column format

Another effective format is an adaptation of the Cornell method developed by Dr. Walter Pauk of Cornell University, and the T-notes system developed by Archie Davis of Illinois Central College and Elvis Clark of Mineral Area College and several other notetaking methods that have developed over the years. It uses a column system, so the terms, main ideas, and illustrations placed in the left column are separated from their definitions, details, and labels recorded in the right column. Since the right column usually contains more information, draw a vertical line from the top margin to the bottom of the page, allowing one-third of your paper for the left column and two-thirds for the right column.

You can use a sheet of paper to cover either column and test yourself on the information in the opposite column. Examine Figure 5-2 as an example of terms and definitions in the column format.

Figure 5-3 shows how main ideas are recorded in the column format. Notice that one term and definition was recorded in between the two main ideas.

Figure 5-2
Column Format for Notetaking: Terms and Definitions

Course: Human Behavior *Date: May 2, 2015* *Page: 1*	*Assignment: Read chap 12* *complete all chap ques* *Due: May 6*
Ethnocentrism	*view that one's culture is superior to others*
Prejudice	*an opinion or learning opposed to anything without just grounds or sufficient knowledge*

Figure 5-3
Column Format for Notetaking: Main Ideas

Course: *Human Relationship Skills* Date: *April 29, 2015* Page: *4*	Assignment: <u>*Read chap 9*</u> <u>*complete ques 9–18*</u> Due: <u>*May 4*</u>
3 behavior/communication styles	*1. Nonassertive* *2. Aggressive* *3. Assertive*
Assertive Communication	*Express thoughts, feelings, beliefs, in direct, honest, & appropriate ways that respect rights of others*
Tips for assertive communication	*1. Use "I" statements to show ownership of feelings* *2. Body lang.—should be consistent w/verbal message* *3. Maintain eye contact* *4. Use moderate tone of voice*

Figure 5-4 shows how drawings, illustrations, or diagrams are recorded in the column format.

Test and recite words the same way here. You cover either column and recite. In much the same manner, you can place math formulas with numbered parts on the left and corresponding explanations on the right. Science classes make frequent uses of drawings, such as cell structure or anatomy. These can be numbered and placed in the left column and labeled in the right column.

Some notetaking systems recommend that you leave at least an inch and a half at the bottom of each page to write a summary. This exercise helps you clarify and condense notes. You'll strengthen your memory in the process, too.

Figure 5-4
Column Format Notetaking: Drawings, Illustrations, and Diagrams

Course: *Medical Terminology* Date: *April 6, 2015* Page: *1*		Assignment: <u>*Read chap 5*</u> <u>*& prepare for quiz*</u> Quiz: <u>*April 7*</u>
		1. Muscle *2. Bursa* *3. Tendon* *4. Ligament* *5. Cartilage*

Notetaking, like any other skill, will improve rapidly with practice. You'll soon be able to create a set of accurate, well-organized notes—one of the most useful tools for success in school, which will continue to be useful on your job.

PREPARING FOR TESTS

As stated earlier, the most important factor in successfully taking tests and relieving test anxiety is good preparation. It's important that you begin to study for a test as soon as possible, and that you manage your time effectively so you can prepare. You learned about time management in Section 2; go back and review that information when you set up your study schedule. Once you've made the time, how do you make the most of it? Your study schedule might look like the one in Table 5-2.

Table 5-2
Sample Study Schedule

Date	What to Study (Goal)	Time	Check When Completed
Mon., Jan. 25	Review psych notes Chap. 5–7. Complete math problems. Develop psych study sheets from text. Read nutrition assignment. Test self on psych text questions.	3–4 PM 7–8 PM 8–9 PM 9–10 PM 10–11 PM	
Tues., Jan. 26	Test self on psych text questions. Develop psych study sheets from notes. Test self on psych notes Chap. 5–7. Write rough draft—nutrition paper.	3–4 PM 7–8 PM 8–9 PM 9–10 PM	
Thurs., Jan. 28	Recite psych study sheets. Complete math problems. Test self on psych study sheets. Continue rough draft—nutrition paper.	7–8 PM 8–9 PM 9–10 PM 10–11 PM	
Sat., Jan. 30	Recite psych study sheets. Complete math problems. Test self on psych study sheets. Continue rough draft—nutrition paper.	9–10 AM 10–11 AM 11–12 noon 12–1 PM	
Sun., Jan. 31	Test self on psych notes Chap. 5–7. Recite psych study sheets.	7–8 PM 9–10 PM	
Mon., Feb. 1	Psych exam	10 AM	

Getting Started

The first step to your best test performance is reading your texts and taking good notes in class. Good reading and notetaking strategies will get you on your way.

When you have a good grasp of the material, you'll want to focus on certain topics to study for your exam. Your instructors can be very helpful here; they may provide suggestions or study guides that narrow your study material for you. Sometimes instructors provide review sessions as well. Meet with your instructor before class or, better yet, during office hours to discuss an upcoming exam. Ask, "What advice or instructions do you have as I prepare to study for this exam?" If the instructor doesn't help you narrow the focus of your study, ask a more specific question: "Are there any areas in particular that you would encourage me to focus on?" If your instructor has not told you what kinds of questions to expect, ask whether the test will be essay, short answer, multiple choice, true-false, or some other format. Most instructors will be happy to help you prepare, if you convince them that you're interested in learning more and performing better, not just studying less. Remember to be polite and display genuine interest and concern—a considerate approach will take you far.

Prepare Study Materials

After deciding what material should be emphasized in your test preparation, you may want to develop some study materials. Study sheets are an excellent way to review material. Study sheets allow you to test yourself. They are set up according to the column method of notetaking described in this section. In this method, the left side of the sheet usually contains terms, questions, main ideas, and illustrations; and the right side contains definitions, answers, details, and illustration labels. You can test yourself on the material by covering one column or the other.

Some information, such as formulas, facts, terms, and definitions, can best be studied using flash cards. Index cards make great flash cards. Write terms, questions, and formulas on one side; on the other side write definitions, answers, and explanations. Flash cards are very helpful when you have to study on the run. You can carry them with you and test yourself on the material whenever you find yourself with a few spare moments.

Rehearse Your Performance

Once your study sheets and flash cards are ready, you're ready for regular practice tests until the big day. There are two basic ways to test yourself: reciting and writing. Both methods help you put information into your long-term memory. Recite your notes again and again until you can do so from memory. Written practice tests are important when you'll be expected to present charts or provide thorough explanations, such as on essay tests. In these instances you may want to do more writing than reciting. Taking your own practice tests is an excellent way to see what you know and what you don't.

How to Predict Test Questions

Predicting test questions will help narrow down your study materials and keep your test preparation focused. Keep your own test bank—develop a separate notebook to note likely test questions. Note possible questions after each lecture. Listen carefully to cues your instructor gives during class and asterisk (*) those he or she emphasizes. Your instructor may repeat important points, slow down his or her speech, write them on the board, or even say, "This will be on the test." Try to put yourself into the instructor's mind and think about what kind of questions he or she would ask. Ask your instructor what type of questions will be on the test and follow the strategies recommended in the next few pages for specific test styles. Quiz questions also have a way of appearing on final exams. If you are geared toward predicting test questions, you'll be more alert as you read assignments and as you listen to lectures.

Making It a Group Effort

Working with a study group can be an excellent addition to studying alone. Study groups compare notes, divide class readings and teach the material, predict test questions, explain difficult concepts, rehearse material, and drill. In study groups, students help not only themselves but each other. Ask your instructor and other students about joining a study group on campus. If there isn't one that's right for you, your instructor or student advisor might be willing to help you set one up yourself.

When forming a study group, look for classmates who take good notes, turn in assignments on time, participate in class, and make good grades. A good size for a study group is four to six students. When you have all the members of your group, establish a regular time and place to meet. Most important, set an agenda for your meeting and stick to it. Remember that groups need goals and plans just as individuals do.

Cramming—Your Last Resort

Cramming at the last minute is not much fun. It's what some students resort to when they have neglected to keep up with regular study reviews. Regular reviews solidify material in your brain. Each time you review/repeat information, your neurons (brain cells) make connections and the more you repeat the material, the thicker the connections between neurons. It's like making a new path through a thick field of grass. The more you walk on the same path, the easier it gets to walk through the field because the path becomes wider and worn. The more you repeat or use information you are trying to learn, the more you wear that path in your brain and access to that information becomes a lot easier—often automatic. Cramming just doesn't allow you to retain information very long—you just don't develop that well-worn path of neural connections, and it will be very difficult to access crammed information several days later or again at final exam time. Cramming is still time-consuming, stressful, and cheats you from learning and solidifying material in your brain. Most students would rather not cram—it usually happens when they're trying to make the best of a bad situation. Cramming may help you get by temporarily so you can do better next time. If you have to cram, the following tips may help you.

Tips . . . For Last Resort Cramming

- Be selective. You can't study it all. Decide what may be the most important material in the course and do your best to repeat and process that material as thoroughly as possible. Consider some of the following text items for cramming: summaries (some books concisely review the major points in each section in the summary), topic sentences, tables, charts, end-of-the-section questions and vocabulary lists, and last paragraphs in each section (new heading) of your section readings.

- Make a time plan. After you decide what to study, determine how much time you have and how much time you can allow for each set of material. Follow your time plan—it will help you to work faster and will mentally allow you to see that there is an end in sight.

- Plan brief breaks. Give yourself a few minutes to stretch, get an energizing snack, and a mental rest. Scheduling a brief break may actually make you work faster because you'll want to complete a specific amount of material and will be less apt to waste time.

- Use your positive self-talk to guide and encourage you. Choose your self-talk carefully. Avoid self-talk that punishes you. Instead, select self-talk that guides your time plan: "I'm going to study this for twenty minutes and move to the next section." "I'll be done with all my sections in two hours—I can do this." "I'm surprised at how fast I'm going." "I'm going to get this whole section learned by break time." "This is a temporary situation; next time I will study and review after each class."

Down the Home Stretch

Should you review the day before the test? Yes. Take an hour or so to review any material you're still not sure of. Work a few example problems or practice essay writing. But don't overdo it. If you've been managing your study time well up to now, you've done enough studying. You want to relax a bit the day before so you're well rested for the test. You might want to spend some time the day before engaged in a sports activity so your body is refreshed and revitalized on the day of the test. Remember, exercise helps relieve tension. After a good night's sleep, you're ready to do your best. Now you're relaxed and prepared, but are you ready for the test? You can use a number of strategies to help you do your best on different kinds of tests.

TAKING OBJECTIVE TESTS

There are several different kinds of objective tests. The kind of test on which you will have to work depends on the kind of information your instructor wants from you. If you are familiar with the basic kinds of tests, you will have an important tool to help you do your best. Objective tests generally are composed of four types of questions: true-false, multiple choice, matching, and fill- in-the-blank. Tests that are made up of these kinds of questions are called "objective" tests because, when they are designed properly, each question has only one correct answer; this makes the test easier to grade objectively and fairly.

Whichever kind of test you have, be sure to read the instructions very carefully. Some instructors might add a "twist" to the instruction or have you perform several tasks in answering each question. Look at the following directions.

> *Read through the statements in the following list. Cross out the statements that are true. Circle those that are false and rewrite them to make true statements.*

A student who wasn't careful about reading directions might forget to rewrite the false statements. Or he might look down the list of statements and ignore the directions, figuring he just needs to label the statements "T" or "F." That student might fail the exam simply because he didn't take a few moments to thoroughly look over the test. Even if you are familiar with a particular type of test, double-check the instructions.

True-False Questions

True and False questions may be used less often in college. However, it is very helpful to understand true and false test taking strategies simply because multiple choice exams, perhaps one of the most popular types of exams, are basically a series of true and false questions. Multiple choice questions are either asking you to look for a true or false option—*Which of the following options is false?* Or *Which of the following options is correct/true?* When you read the following true-false test taking tips, think about how they relate to multiple choice tests.

When your instructors give you tests that include true-false questions, they may want you to engage in higher levels of thinking that go beyond your memory of basic facts.

Some true-false statements test you on the basic facts. Consider this one.

 F   *A pronoun is a word used in place of one or more nouns.*

If you know your material, simple statements like the one above are easy to answer. However, few true-false questions are set up to be that easy. The following true-false question would test your ability to apply your knowledge.

 F   *In the sentence, "Whose notes did you borrow?" "whose" is an interrogative pronoun.*

Much of the challenge of the true-false format lies in the wording of the statements. Beware of three frequent wording styles that often appear in true-false statements: **modifiers, negatives,** and **strings of items.**

Modifiers

Modifiers are words that describe. They can provide clues about whether a statement is true or false. Modifiers that leave no room for variance are called *absolute* modifiers. Absolute modifiers include:

no	none
never	every
each	nobody
no one	only
all	always
at no time	entirely
everybody	

Absolute modifiers imply that a statement is true without exception. Therefore, they tend to appear in false statements, as in the following examples.

T   **All** dogs chase cats.

T   **All** diseases of the nervous system have an effect on every system in the body.

Occasionally, absolute modifiers will appear in a true statement.

 F   **All** spiders have eight legs.

 F   **No** human being can live without water.

Modifiers that leave some room for variance are called *qualifying* modifiers. They include:

usually	seldom	many	possibly
might	perhaps	quite	hardly
most	ordinarily	may	generally
some	often	few	probably
frequently	sometimes	likely	commonly

The absolute modifiers in the previous examples have been changed to qualifiers and now the statements are true.

 F   **Many** dogs chase cats.

T   F   Diseases of the nervous system have an effect on **most** other systems of the body.

Exercise 5-2 Analyzing the use of modifiers in tests

Use one of your old tests (or ask your teacher for a sample test) which contains true-false or multiple choice questions. Underline the absolute modifiers and circle the qualifying modifiers. If you were using a true-false set of questions, how many statements containing qualifying modifiers were true?

_____

If you were using multiple choice questions, how many options containing qualifying modifiers were the correct option? _____

What other discoveries have you made after analyzing your old test?

_____

_____

_____

_____

Negatives

Negatives also will change a basic statement. Pay attention to negative words in a statement, such as, *false, never, not* and *cannot,* as well as to negative prefixes, such as dis-, il-, un-, non-, im-, ir-, and in-. When you read true-false questions, it is a good idea to circle each negative.

T (F)　　　*Today angioplasty is considered to be an (in)significant procedure in correcting cardiovascular diseases.*

(T) F　　　*The three sides of a scalene triangle are (not) equal in length.*

Watch out as well for statements that contain more than one negative (remember that a double negative equals a positive).

T F　　　*It is (not) (un)common for people to catch a cold even in the warm summer months.*

(T) F　　　*Edgar Allen Poe is (not) (in)frequently referred to as the father of the modern detective story.*

If you find several negatives in a sentence, cross them out *in pairs*. If there is a negative left, the entire statement is negative. If no negatives are left, the overall statement is positive because the negatives have canceled out.

Exercise 5-3 Noticing the negatives in tests

Take the same test you analyzed in Exercise 5-2 and this time draw a box around the negatives used in the true-false statements or the multiple choice statements and options. List any trends you discovered about the test writer's use of negatives.

_____

_____

_____

Did you make any other discoveries about negatives and their effect on the test or test answers?

_____

_____

_____

Strings of items

Some instructors will include a series or string of items in a true-false statement. A statement is not true unless it is true for every item listed. It only takes one false item in a string to make the whole statement false. Mark each item in the string true or false when you analyze the question below.

　　　　　　　　　　　　　　　T　　T　F　T　T　T
T (F)　　　*Sources of vitamin E include vegetable oils, wheat germ, chicken, corn, nuts, seeds,*
　　　　　T　T　　T
　　　　　olives, asparagus, and spinach.

T (*F*)   *Presidents Lincoln, Garfield, Kennedy, and Carter were all elected in years ending in "0."*

Some true-false questions may contain two statements connected by a conjunction, such as because, so, therefore, thus, or consequently. If the entire statement is false, the fallacy most often will occur in the second part of the sentence.

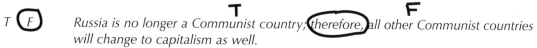

T (*F*)   *Russia is no longer a Communist country; therefore, all other Communist countries will change to capitalism as well.*

Note that, in the above example, the absolute qualifier *all* was an additional clue that the statement was false. If you know that a statement cannot be proved, chances are it is false.

If you have no idea whether a statement is true or false, it is a good idea to guess anyway—you have a 50 percent chance of getting it right. Make the best guess you can, based on what you know.

Multiple Choice Questions

Multiple choice questions are the most commonly used test format in college; they require very careful reading and analysis because you have to choose not just a correct answer but the best answer.

Multiple choice tests have unfortunately been coined "multiple guess" tests. This notion is misleading and implies that it's okay to study less for this type of test. However, college level multiple choice questions actually require more thorough study—studying and knowing detail. Many errors on multiple choice tests are due to inadequate test preparation—studying only to the point of **recognition.** If you only recognize information, that means it simply looks familiar—you know it looks familiar but you really haven't learned it. Multiple choice tests usually require **recall.** When you can recall information, you've learned it. You can access the detailed information from your mind because you have used learning strategies to solidify it in your brain—you know the material. Knowing your material makes it a lot easier to know what's true and what's not. When you only learn to the point of recognition, you are more likely to think the questions are "tricky."

Prepare for multiple choice tests by learning and knowing detail; be able to know the difference between true and false statements. Remember, multiple choice questions are a set of true-false questions. You can use the true-false test strategies to analyze your multiple choice options. An effective strategy is to identify each option as either true or false—**a true/false analysis.** The following multiple choice question is asking for a false statement. Circle the word "false" to remind you that you are looking for the false statement, then use the true/false analysis to identify each option as either true or false. Using multiple choice analysis strategies like these will help you answer the questions more accurately and will give you more confidence in test taking.

____*d*____   1. Which of the following statements is (false) concerning the use of caffeine?
      a. Caffeine can temporarily step up your heartbeat. **T**
      b. Caffeine can increase stomach acid secretion. **T**
      c. Caffeine can ward off drowsiness. **T**
      d. Caffeine has been directly linked to some kinds of cancer. **F**

Tips . . . For Answering Multiple Choice Questions

Here are some other tips for answering multiple choice questions:

- Often the longest or most specific option will be the correct one. Instructors tend to write more detail in the correct option to ensure that it is clear and accurate.

- As with true-false questions, qualifying modifiers are used more often than absolute modifiers in the correct option.

- Eliminate options that contain silly remarks or words that you would not be expected to know. Sometimes an instructor will throw in a couple of nonsense answers because she knows that when you know the material, you will recognize inappropriate responses.

- The best answer should be a grammatically correct extension of the question. If you're in doubt about the grammar of the question, ask your instructor. Sometimes instructors make errors in compiling their test questions.

- Look for exception words such as *but* and *except*. Exception words can change the meaning of the statement, so it's important to be aware of them. You may want to circle exception words so that you are alert to them. Exception words give you a definite clue to the type of answer you are looking for. "All of the following are true but . . ." obviously tells you to look for a false option.

Exercise 5-4 Applying true-false and multiple choice test taking strategies

Complete the following multiple choice test using these techniques: 1) Circle negative words, prefixes, and exception (*but* or *except*) words for each question and appropriate options. 2) Use a T/F analysis on each option.

MULTIPLE CHOICE QUESTIONS

Directions: Select the ONE option that best completes each of the numbered statements.

1. Which of the following is false concerning test anxiety?

    a. Common symptoms of test anxiety include nervousness, a queasy stomach, sweaty palms, headaches, poor concentration, confusion, and sleeplessness.
    b. The most important thing you can do to relieve test anxiety is to be prepared for the test.
    c. Visualization is generally ineffective for combating test anxiety.
    d. Physical preparation including eating, resting, and exercising can help relieve test anxiety.
    e. Positive self-talk can help relieve test anxiety.

2. Test preparation, as explained in your text, involves all but which of the following?

    a. Reading your texts and taking good notes in class.
    b. Asking your instructors about the types of questions that will be on the test.
    c. Preparation of study materials.
    d. Rehearsing.
    e. Avoiding giving yourself practice tests; they're too time-consuming to be worthwhile.

3. On the day before the test you should

    a. reserve most of the day for study and self-testing.
    b. engage in a physical activity and get in some relaxation.
    c. take an hour or so and review.
    d. a and b
    e. b and c

4. Objective tests

    a. are essay and short answer tests.
    b. include multiple choice, true/false, matching, and fill-in-the-blank questions.
    c. are more difficult to grade fairly.
    d. usually have several answers.
    e. all of the above.

5. Multiple choice questions

    a. usually have true and false options.
    b. require careful reading and analysis of the question and the options.
    c. may include more than one correct option, requiring you to select the best option.
    d. may use absolute or qualifying modifiers.
    e. all of the above.

6. Which of the following tips for answering essay questions is incorrect?

    a. Outline your response in a logical manner.
    b. Always state your opinion; your instructors don't expect you to stick to the facts.
    c. State supportive evidence for each point.
    d. Identify important points.
    e. Write concisely.

After completing the multiple choice exam, list at least five test taking strategies you could use to complete the test.

1. _____

2. _____

3. _____

4. _____

5. _____

Multiple Choice answers: 1. c, 2. e, 3. e, 4. b, 5. e, 6. b

Matching Questions

Matching questions usually consist of two lists. Each item in the first list has to match an item in the second list. Count the items in each column; if there are extra items in the answer column, you know you'll have some unused answers. Read both lists carefully to familiarize yourself with them. Next, begin matching items on the left to those on the right. Avoid the temptation to select the first item that appears to match. Scan the entire list so you make the best choice. If you have identified two or more possible matches, write the number of the item to be matched by each of the possible matches in the second list.

Each time you find a match, write the answer in the appropriate blank and cross out the option so you can clearly see it's been used. The more answers you find, the easier it will be to make decisions about the remaining unmarked items. You shouldn't guess on this kind of test until you have completed all the items you're sure of. The following example highlights these suggestions.

Directions: Match the food items in the left column with their low-fat substitutes.

e	1.	butter	a.	~~Grape-Nuts Cereal~~	~~6~~	5
f	2.	hamburger	b.	~~water chestnuts~~		
g	3.	eggs	c.	~~chicken, turkey, fish~~		
d	4.	sour cream	d.	~~nonfat yogurt or cottage cheese~~		
a	5.	nuts	e.	~~Butter Buds~~		
h	6.	potato chips	f.	~~ground chicken or turkey~~		
i	7.	fried foods	g.	~~Egg Beaters or egg whites~~		
b	8.	avocados	h.	~~pretzels, plain popcorn~~	6	
c	9.	red meat	i.	~~baked, broiled~~		

Matching tests often are used to test terms and definitions, names, and facts. They are more difficult if the items are similar and hard to distinguish. If this is the case, studying to know the small distinctions is important. Avoid relying on recognition. Test yourself on terms, names, and facts to prepare for matching questions.

Fill-in-the-Blank Questions

This type of question requires you to write the appropriate answer in a blank to create a true statement. When you answer fill-in-the-blank questions, read each question carefully before you answer because it can contain many clues. Write an answer that will complete the statement in a grammatically correct fashion. Check your answers to make sure they are logical ones. For example, if the statement is missing a noun, have you completed it with a noun? It pays to reread your answer to make sure it makes sense.

The borders of Utah, Arizona, New Mexico, and *Colorado* meet at Four Corners.

It is important to read and *analyze* each question before you answer it.

ESSAY TESTS

Another kind of test involves writing essays or short answers in response to more open-ended questions. Essay tests are often the preferred test among college instructors. These tests require an extended piece of writing that combines an understanding of the facts, logic, and analytical and organizational abilities. Essay questions present many challenges, but they're also an opportunity to show off what you know.

Instructors use different approaches to grading essay tests, so it's a good idea to ask your instructors what they look for when correcting essays. Essay questions are commonly graded on the following criteria:

- Factual accuracy
- Reasoning ability
- Organization
- Completeness
- Clarity of thought
- Mechanics (spelling and grammar)

Sometimes an instructor will give you essay questions in advance, which will help you narrow your studying considerably. Most of the time, however, you'll have to prepare for essay tests without knowing the questions ahead of time. Practice with essay questions of your own. Write about:

- Questions at the end of the section
- Questions your instructor asked in class
- Questions you may have written in the margin of your text
- Questions raised by other students and discussed in class
- Details from your notes (If you are using the column system of notetaking, you could base an essay question on information from the left-hand column)

Answering the Questions

As with any test, read through the questions before you start to write. Answer the easier questions first. Plan your answer before you begin. It's very helpful to jot a brief outline of your response on the back of your essay booklet. You may want to keep the following suggestions in mind:

Tips . . . For Answering Essay Questions

- Take a minute to preview all the questions and jot down any notes, mnemonics, or outlines that will help you develop your responses.

- Use the margins to jot down formulas, charts, or steps that you will be using. This will free your mind so you can better focus on developing your responses.

- Be clear about what is being asked. How many questions are asked? Check to see if you answered what was asked.

- Outline your response in a logical sequence.

- Identify important points.

- State only one main idea per paragraph.

- Stick to the facts unless you're specifically asked for an opinion.

- State evidence to support each point you make.

- Write concisely; make each word count.

- Proofread your answers. Do they make sense? Did you answer the question completely? Do you have an adequate conclusion?

- Keep an eye on the clock. Know how much time you can devote to answering each question.

When you understand the wording used in essay questions, you'll be able to write the best kind of response. You'll avoid the common error of responding to something that wasn't asked simply because you misunderstood the wording of the question. Table 5-3 lists and explains many of the terms commonly used in essay questions.

Table 5-3
Common Terms Used in Essay Questions

Term	Explanation
Analyze	Break topic into small parts and discuss each part.
Apply	Show how something works.
Compare	Discuss similarities.
Contrast	Discuss differences.
Criticize/evaluate	Discuss pros and cons, costs and benefits, the good and the bad.
Define	Give the meaning.
Describe	State the details and particulars.
Discuss	State main points, facts, and details.
Enumerate/list	Write a list of main points. Number the points.
Evaluate	Give your and/or an expert's opinion or judgment. Include evidence to support the evaluation.
Explain	Make an idea clear. Show logically how a concept is developed.
Illustrate	Give an example.
Interpret	State the meaning in simpler terms; state your analysis of the topic.
Justify	Present evidence to support the topic.
Outline	List a short overview of points.
Prove	Support with facts (especially facts from the text and lecture).
Relate	Show connections.

Table 5-3
Common Terms Used in Essay Questions (continued)

Term	Explanation
Solve	Come up with a solution.
State	Present main points.
Summarize	Give an overview of main points.
Support	Back up a statement with facts or proof.
Trace	Describe an event from beginning to end.

Exercise 5-5 Analyzing two essay test question responses

Examine the two take home essay responses to the following question: *What health recommendations would you make to improve the quality of one's cardiovascular system, gastrointestinal system, cholesterol levels, muscle, and skeletal systems? Address as many angles as possible.*

List five weaknesses in the way the first student responded to this essay question.

1. _____

2. _____

3. _____

4. _____

5. _____

List five strengths in the way the second student responded to this essay question.

1. _____

2. _____

3. _____

4. _____

5. _____

What advice would you give to the writer of the first essay response? Include advice on both preparation for the essay test and answering the questions.

_____

_____

_____

_____

_____

_____

First Student's Essay Response

(1.) Diet and exercise are major factors for maintaining health in the body. Eating provides the body with the nutrition it needs to function. It also gives it energy so that all the organs and systems perform well and stay healthy. Exercising keeps everything flowing and in shape. Smoking is another thing that should not be done. Smoking affects the lungs and the heart causing disease in both. It also has been shown to cause cancer.

Second Student's Essay Response

1. What health recommendations would you make to improve the quality of one's (1) Cardiovascular system, (2) Gastrointestinal system, (3) Cholesterol levels, (4) Muscle, and (5) Skeletal system? Address as many angles as possible.

(1) Cardiovascular system
  As we grow older, the heart must work harder to accomplish less.

  A. *Exercise—with the advice of a physician*
      Exercise reduces the chances of high blood pressure (hypertension) which in turn can cause damage to kidneys, heart or eyes. High blood pressure at rest is high if it measures greater than 140/90. Exercising to keep weight down will also decrease high blood pressure and enable you to get around better so you can exercise to keep healthy.

      Exercise will also lower cholesterol. Cholesterol which is termed "HDL" is the "good cholesterol" which clears out the LDL ("lousy cholesterol") from the system. LDL is decreased when doing aerobic exercise three times a week for 30 minutes per session.

      Another reason to exercise is to decrease atherosclerosis, which is the build-up inside the walls of the blood vessels which occurs in those individuals who do not do enough exercise.

  B. *Don't smoke! Smoking affects the cardiovascular system in many ways:*
      1. Causes high blood pressure
      2. Lack of oxygen to the heart makes the heart work overtime and can cause a heart attack.
      3. Atherosclerosis—Smoking causes a build-up inside the walls of the blood vessels and the accumulation of plaque in the arteries.
      4. Smoking increases LDL (Low Density Lipoproteins) and decreases HDL which cleans out the "lousy cholesterol."

  C. *Good Nutrition*
      Good nutrition involves less salt. Salt causes high blood pressure resulting in stroke or heart attack. Good nutrition also means eating foods low in cholesterol or without cholesterol to reduce the chance of heart attack. Eat soluble fiber such as beans, oats, fruits and vegetables. Use polyunsaturated monounsaturated fats to increase HDL and lower cholesterol. Good nutrition also makes you stronger and helps you feel better about yourself so you can exercise and have a cardiovascular system free of cholesterol and chronic condition. Good nutrition will help you maintain your expected weight.

D. Medical Checkup
    Have a good checkup from your doctor to make sure blood pressure and cholesterol levels are good.

    Medication prescribed by your doctor will help reduce blood pressure and lower the chance of heart attack or stroke.

E. Reduce Stress
    Avoid stress by exercising regularly and manage time for yourself whether recreation or family time.

(2) Gastrointestinal system
    Digestion involves many organs. As we grow older, the muscles of our digestive system work slower. Constipation is very common and many people use laxatives to take care of the problem. Because they are addictive, laxatives may work against the digestive system. Therefore, proper nutrition high in fiber and less medication can take care of constipation in a natural way. Plenty of water and exercise will also help. Loss of appetite can be the cause of depression and certain medication prescribed by a physician along with exercise can help fight against this form of adult psychopathology. Eat smart: less fat, protein and carbohydrates. Avoiding stress may also prevent some constipation.

(3) Cholesterol Levels
    I would make it a point to lower the cholesterol level. Cholesterol is a white, waxy, fat-like substance which is manufactured in your body primarily by the liver. No type of cholesterol you eat is good for you. To decrease the risk of heart attack because of high levels of blood cholesterol, avoid foods which are high in cholesterol, like liver, eggs, beef, and chicken with skin. Exercises like brisk walking, biking, swimming, and jogging increase the good cholesterol in the body. Avoid foods high in saturated fat, like palm oil or coconut oil. Avoid smoking.

(4) Muscles
    Do appropriate regular exercise to maintain strong muscles and flexible joints. Aerobic exercise, swimming, jogging, biking—all these activities help maintain muscle tone which enhances good motor performance in older individuals. This in turn makes them more coordinated in tasks requiring muscular work. Being physically healthy and having good muscle tone, a person can avoid depression because they are likely to be active and independent.

(5) Skeletal System
    I would make every effort to improve the quality of the skeletal system. Conditions affecting the skeletal system are arthritis—inflammation of a joint and osteoarthritis—degenerative joint disease. There are no cures for these different conditions. The recommended treatment to alleviate pain and to maintain the mobility and strength of the afflicted joints would be to see a physician who could prescribe anti-inflammatory drugs over the counter (e.g. aspirin and cortisone derivatives). Heat and cold applied as directed may help elevate the severe pain which can accompany these conditions. Mild exercise such as swimming, arts and crafts, less weight-bearing activities, and stretching exercises can help keep joints from becoming so stiff and can hold off the agonizing effect on older or younger adults. Also, those who are more restricted or bed-disabled could be encouraged to keep as active as possible by doing stretching activities in bed or in a chair. Exercises like this can help them not to have joints stiffen up as much. Another advantage is that such exercises help keep up good mental attitudes that contribute to feeling useful and not succumbing to a housebound lifestyle.

    Osteoporosis is a silent, progressive disease characterized by a loss of bone mass and increased porosity, and possibility of bone fractures which affects four times as many women as men. Health recommendations to improve the quality of the skeletal system and to prevent this slow, debilitating disease include the following. First of all, don't smoke. Hormone replacement in postmenopausal women or calitonin for those who cannot take estrogen would be one factor. Calcium supplements *or calcium-rich foods to strengthen the bones is a good idea. Weight-bearing exercise, like walking, cycling, cross-country skiing, racquet sports and weight/strength training helps to keep the skeletal system strong and prevent disease or accident; keep regular checkups with your physician.*

Conclusion

In conclusion to each topic discussed, eating smart, not smoking, lowering stress and, more important, exercise, all will help persons of all ages live a healthier and more productive life.

Short Answer Questions

Most of the strategies outlined for essay questions hold true for short answer questions. The main differences between the two are length and format. The key to answering short answer questions is to be concise. Whereas essay questions usually ask you about several ideas, short answer questions usually ask you to discuss only one. Don't stray from the point that really answers the question. Figure out how much time you need to spend on each short answer; spend that much time and no more. You don't want to waste time writing a lengthy response to a question that is not worth that many points on the exam.

Just When You Think It's Safe to Leave

A frequent question asked of instructors is, "Can we leave when we're finished with the test?" What's the hurry? Take the full time allowed for a test. If you finish early, quickly check to see that you have written the answers the way you intended. It's not likely you'll regret checking your answers, but you might regret it if you don't.

When you've completed your final checks, and if you are permitted to leave, do so quietly. Respect your fellow students; remember, they're still working. Get a soda, get some fresh air—relax. You've earned some recreation time.

Preparing for Final Exams

You can take the headache out of studying for final exams by deciding to prepare for your final when your class starts. Often your course syllabus will tell you a little about your final exam. Most final exams are comprehensive—covering material from the entire course. With this in mind you have more motivation to retain all the information as you go through the course. On the first day of class, find out what styles of questions will be used on the final. Keep all your study guides and test banks for your final exam review. Review periodically. Don't forget to schedule in fun, relaxation, and some exercise during your final exam week. If you've studied regularly, your mind will continue to prepare itself even when you're relaxing.

Getting Feedback

Remember, your grade is only one source of feedback regarding your progress in school. It can, however, offer some valuable information. When your instructor returns your graded exam, look at both the positive and the negative comments. Figure out what you did well and on what you need to work. What questions did you answer correctly? On what material were you weak? Consider talking to your instructor to get additional advice on how to improve. Use your grades as another tool for learning.

OVERCOMING TEST ANXIETY

Test taking is probably not anyone's favorite activity, but many students become much more anxious about the whole process than they need to be. Many students think their success or failure on a test is the same as their success or failure as a person. This is simply not so. Tests are just one tool for evaluating how much information you've absorbed in a particular course. Tests are not foolproof, and they're not always accurate in determining how much you know. *Tests are not a measure of your intelligence!* Tests are just *one* way to evaluate your success in school.

Some anxiety before and during tests is normal—it can even be motivating. It's a sign that you're taking your job as a student seriously and that you care about performing well. Too much anxiety, however, can hurt your chances of doing your best. Some of the common symptoms of test anxiety are nervousness, worry, fear, irritability, queasy stomach, sweaty palms, headaches, poor concentration, confusion, shortness of breath, and sleeplessness. If you've ever suffered from any of these symptoms before or during a test, several strategies can help relieve your anxiety. Adequate preparation, positive self-talk, visualization, and relaxation exercises all can help you relax and do your best.

Be Prepared

The first and most important thing you can do to help relieve test anxiety is to be prepared for the test. Nothing will make you more nervous than to walk into the test room knowing that you haven't studied. Start reviewing material for the test several weeks in advance. Plan daily reviews. When your brain is engaged in daily review sessions, the material has time to gel. A lot of learning will take place during these quick reviews. Make short review sessions a part of your daily study routine. The best quick review times are just before and after class. Don't just review new material from the most recent class—conduct quick reviews on all the material that will be on your next test.

Being prepared for a test also means being physically prepared—well-fed and well-rested. Don't try to study until all hours the night before; get plenty of sleep. When you wake up, be sure to eat a good breakfast. You need plenty of fuel to work at your best. To maintain a high level of energy and mental alertness, begin early to adopt healthful habits of eating properly, exercising, and sleeping adequately. Brian's final preparation is walking over to his test. He says, "I'm so wound up before an exam I need to get rid of my excess energy. By the time I sit down, I'm ready for mental work." It's a good idea to arrive early for the test so you can take a few minutes to prepare yourself mentally.

Positive Self-Talk

The best way to prepare yourself mentally for a test and relieve your anxiety is to practice positive self-talk. Test anxiety often is related to negative self-talk. In the days before an exam, perhaps you've noticed yourself saying, "I just can't learn this"; "I hate this class"; "I just know I'll flunk this test." This kind of negative self-talk becomes a habit, and, for some students, it becomes a greater obstacle to a good test performance than the test itself. Rather than struggling to learn the material for a test, these students end up struggling with their negative self-talk.

Start replacing your negative self-talk with some positive phrases. "I can learn this" and "I know I'll do well on the test" are just two examples of encouraging statements you can say to yourself before an exam. Make positive self-talk a habit—in time, it will change your attitude about tests.

Be sure to keep encouraging yourself during the test. Choose calming and encouraging self-talk to maintain a positive attitude throughout the test. Look over the test to find questions you can answer easily. "I used to try the hard ones first," says Matt. "Then I'd run out of time to answer the questions I knew. Now I answer the easy ones first and feel like I got something accomplished. Then I don't feel so nervous about the rest of the test." You, too, will feel more confident handling the difficult part of a test if you know you've already answered some questions successfully.

Visualization

Picture yourself succeeding. In the weeks before the test, take a few moments before you start to study and visualize yourself taking the test—confident and calm. Visualize yourself answering the questions easily, with plenty of time to go back and check your work. Imagine leaving the testing room feeling great, knowing you did your best. Include in your vision a reward for completing the test. For example, Alyssa makes a date with herself for a cup of coffee at the sandwich shop or to go to a movie. She says, "When I'm in the middle of taking the test and feeling like I'll never make it, I imagine that soon I'll be out of that room and doing something I enjoy. Sometimes it's the only thing that gets me through." Picture the terrific grade on your test when the instructor hands it back to you. What will you do to celebrate your success?

Like positive self-talk, visualization is a tool that goes to work on your subconscious mind. Make visualization a habit, and it will help to relieve your feelings of test anxiety.

Relaxation

So you're sitting there, test in hand. Your head hurts, your palms are sweaty, your mind is racing, you feel sick to your stomach, and you're in a panic. What you need to do is relax. Try some of the following tips.

Tips . . . For Combating Test Anxiety

The more tense you are, the less you'll be able to concentrate and do your best work on the test. When you're in the grip of test anxiety, try the following strategies.

- Breathe! Some people start to hyperventilate (breathe too quickly) when they're nervous. Other people forget to breathe enough. Before you begin to work on a test, close your eyes for a moment and take a few slow, deep breaths to relax. Do this whenever you reach a test question that seems especially difficult. It only takes a few seconds and helps keep you calm and focused on your work.

- Visualize. Repeat the visualizations you used when you were studying for the test. Picture yourself answering each question correctly and completing your work ahead of time so you can double-check your answers.

- Before you even pick up your pen, take a few minutes to read over the entire test. As Karen discovered, "Once I know what questions I'll be facing, I feel more relaxed. It's not knowing that makes me a wreck." The suspense of the unknown is the real cause of anxiety, not the test itself.

- Note how many questions you have to answer. Are there essay questions? Read them and estimate how much time you'll need to answer each one. (Occasionally, tests will give suggested answer times for each question.) Take your time in previewing the test—it's an important step in doing your best work. Chances are, by the time you pick up your pen to write, you'll be feeling a lot calmer and more confident.

- Take a moment to relax your body. Stretch your arms over your head or do a few neck rolls. Relieving some of your physical tension can help you concentrate better. Take a short break to look out the window or shut your eyes for a minute if you feel tired.

- Gently but persuasively get yourself to stop any negative self-talk messages. When you notice your thoughts are racing or your mind is cluttered with worry and self-doubt, it's time to use self-talk to create specifically worded phrases of positive self-direction. Give yourself specific directions about what you want to do and what you will accomplish on your exam. "I will answer as many questions as I can." "I know a lot of this stuff." "Let the clock tick on—I'll get done." "Boy, I answered that question well." Don't forget to feed yourself regular encouragement and praise throughout your exams—you'll be less anxious when your self-talk is friendly and encouraging.

(continued)

- Get physical! Of course you can't do this in the classroom, but when you engage in regular aerobic exercise like running, brisk walking, bicycling, jumping on a trampoline, roller blading, swimming, playing basketball or something that elevates your heart rate and keeps it elevated, you will substantially reduce your body tension. Exercise in the evening or morning before an exam. If you already engage in regular aerobic exercise, you already appreciate the benefits. If you're just beginning, be patient with yourself while you build your endurance.

- If these techniques don't seem to be working for you, go to your college's counseling center. Your college counselors can assist you in solving your problems and finding solutions to get you back on track.

TEST-TAKING HINTS
John Wheatland

What are some words that you associate with taking a test?

Pressure ——————➤ Tension

and

Tension makes you forget

hence

Reducing tension is the key!

SPLASH DOWN METHOD

1. Do **not** look at your test paper.
2. On the back of your paper write down all the terms, formulas, facts, etc. that you know.
3. Read the instructions and write your name on the paper.
4. Read each question. Answer *first* the ones you know *best* and are worth the *most*.

TEST-TAKING STRATEGY

1. Splashdown
2. Read directions (listen)
3. Skim exam
4. Notice weights assigned to each question
5. Plan time for completing exam
6. Review and check all work

Keep corrected tests for review & studying!!!

WHAT ARE THESE?

- ROYGBIV
- Every Good Boy Does Fine
- My Very Educated Mother Just Served Used Nine Pies

They are called **mnemonics** and they help you remember facts, information, and things.

- USE THEM!
- MAKE THEM UP!

EMOTIONAL AND PHYSICAL PREPARATION FOR A TEST

What are the two pieces of equipment that must perform well on test day?
- Mind (Brain)
- eBody

VALUE OF SLEEP

Students who do *not* get enough sleep *fail* even when they know the material!!!

CASE STUDY
- Economics class—17 students
- One week of preparation: studying, quizzed, reading, and 8 hrs sleep night before exam.
- Students felt confident taking exam

RESULTS (1)
- Class average: 89.2%
- 2 people got 100%
- No one under 'C'

RESULTS (2)
- Class average: 75.4%
- No one got 100%
- Five (5) 'D's

Party to celebrate
- Refreshments, swimming, volleyball, etc.
- Everyone up until 3 am
- Slept until 6 am
- Retook test 7 am
    - ⇨ Questions in different sequence
    - ⇨ Different color paper

GET ENOUGH SLEEP!

When the body is *not functioning*, the brain *compensates*:

- Sleepy—get enough sleep
- Stomach—eat breakfast . . . and lunch
- Bathroom—go, go, go
- Illness—stay well
    - ⇨ Healthy diet
    - ⇨ Exercise regularly
    - ⇨ Get plenty of sleep

HIGHLIGHTS

In this section you've learned how a three-step notetaking system—using active listening, thinking, and writing, can help you understand and retain what you've learned in class. You've also discovered that active listening requires an attitude of wanting to listen and learn and that just the act of taking notes will help you improve your ability to concentrate. This section outlined tips to help you improve your active listening. Practicing active listening now will definitely help you improve your attentiveness and concentration for future classes and your future career.

Two formats for notetaking, the outline and column formats, were introduced. The column format helps you create self-tests for later test preparation, while you take notes. Notetaking sometimes seems impossible—the teacher may seem to be going too fast or you may think you're writing too slowly. However, with a little practice you can quickly sharpen your listening and notetaking skills.

In this section you have also examined important skills for preparing for tests. You've been encouraged to prepare yourself mentally and physically through positive self-talk, visualization, and relaxation. You were also introduced to strategies to prepare and use study materials. And you've explored valuable tips for handling the most common kinds of tests.

The key to performing at your peak in any test situation is preparation—the earlier you start the better. If you know your material and know what kind of test you'll be taking, you're that much more ahead of the game. This, in turn, will help to relieve the common feeling of test anxiety. Take your time, do your best, and you'll be able to see tests not as something to be nervous about, but as valuable tools that will help you learn and accomplish more in college.

DISCUSSION QUESTIONS

Note: Read the following discussion questions and activities **before** you read Section 5. This strategy will help you look for answers while you read.

1. How is active listening important in notetaking?
2. Give five examples of the importance of active listening in your future job.
3. List five reasons you may have difficulty paying attention and staying focused during a lecture.
4. Explain the three-step process to effective notetaking.
5. What are the advantages of using a three-ring binder for notetaking?
6. Why does poor class preparation make notetaking more difficult?
7. Which of the two notetaking systems explained in the section do you prefer to use? Which seems to help you study or prepare for tests best? Explain.
8. Discuss the best ways you have found to use your notes to prepare for exams.
9. List and explain the purpose of each of the four strategies discussed in the section for overcoming test anxiety.
10. How can negative self-talk impact test performance before and during the test? Has negative self-talk ever worsened your test preparation? Give a couple examples. Has it ever worsened your test performance? Give an example.
11. What kind of self-talk do you want to use as you prepare for an exam? Write a brief self-talk script on how you will prepare for the next exam for your most difficult class.
12. Evaluate how you manage your time for study and test preparation for each class you're enrolled in this term.
13. What questions can you ask your instructors about their examinations so that your test preparation will be more on track? (Be tactful.)
14. Describe two ways of developing study materials for test preparation.
15. Discuss the type of test questions you prefer and why.
16. How can you rehearse for tests?
17. How can a study group benefit your test preparation?
18. What kinds of study activities do you think a study group should do?
19. In terms of test preparation, what do you usually do the day before the test? Is there anything about your "day before" routine that you would like to change? How?
20. Is there anything about your test preparation you would like to change?
21. Describe the most unusual exam you have taken. Don't forget to describe the directions.
22. What type(s) of test questions do you find to be the most difficult and why?
23. Write a true/false question that tests your ability to apply knowledge.
24. Explain absolute and qualifying modifiers. Give an example of each. Discuss their impact on true/false questions.
25. Discuss negatives (pairs of negatives too) and their impact on true/false questions. What can you do to be more attentive to negatives in true/false questions?
26. Explain strings of items and tips for handling them.
27. Write five tips for taking multiple choice tests.

28. Explain why knowing strategies for taking true/false tests helps you on multiple choice tests.
29. Write five tips for taking matching tests. What can make this kind of an exam question more difficult? How can you best prepare to handle the more difficult matching questions?
30. Write five tips for completing fill-in-the-bank questions.
31. Consider the last essay questions you had. What criteria do you think your instructor used to grade them?
32. Discuss the three most useful tips for answering essay questions.
33. What is meant by getting feedback after a test?
34. What is the most difficult aspect of test preparation for you? Why? What can you do to overcome the difficulty?
35. How can you prepare yourself mentally and physically for a test?
36. List three ways in which multiple choice tests can be one of the most difficult tests to prepare for.

Learning to Think Critically

WHAT'S IN IT FOR YOU

Critical thinking is one of the most important skills you'll learn in college. Both your professors and your employers want you to be a critical thinker. Professors want you to thoughtfully question the experts. Employers will give you assignments with little direction and expect you to "think it through." Beyond college and work, your critical thinking skills will help you think about and analyze situations better. You'll learn to avoid hasty judgments and gain confidence in your own ability to think.

In Section 1, you read about the SCANS report (the U.S. Department of Labor survey of necessary skills for the workplace). The SCANS report listed thinking skills (another way of saying critical thinking) as one of those sets of skills. In Section 1, you also focused on two types of critical thinking skills: creative problem solving and decision making. In this section you'll become familiar with the qualities of a critical thinker and some guidelines for thinking and reading critically.

In this section you'll explore:

- What critical thinking is and why it's so important for school and work
- The process and tools of critical thinking
- Basic guidelines for becoming a critical thinker
- How to become a critical reader
- How to think critically about the media

WHAT IS CRITICAL THINKING?

Humorists have defined critical thinking as "the art of thinking about your thinking while you're thinking in order to make your thinking better." There is some merit to this silly definition because, as you will see, critical thinking does involve several ways of thinking. Essentially, critical thinking means evaluating ideas, and this section will provide you with tools to do that. Critical thinking is very important to many aspects of your life. When you have to evaluate the stress in your life and ways to manage it, or determine what kind of person you would like to share your life with, or find the best course of action in dealing with a work problem, using a critical thinking process will help you understand, analyze, and evaluate each situation.

The Importance of Critical Thinking to Your Professional and Personal Life

In your profession, it's not enough to have a lot of information—you'll need to evaluate it and apply it to your work. Maybe you know a lot about computer programming, but it takes critical thinking to assess the needs of your company and adapt a computer program to fit their needs. Even in your personal life you'll need to evaluate your own behavior. Maybe you know a lot about health, but it takes critical thinking to evaluate your health habits and needs and then apply the appropriate plan to get the desired results. It's one thing to complain about being overweight or out of shape and another thing to take a reasonable action to fix the situation for a healthful lifestyle.

Critical thinkers learn to think for themselves and develop their own views based on logic, reasoning, questioning, and information-gathering. They reserve judgment until they learn more about the facts. Critical thinkers evaluate what they hear and read, and they are also open to evaluating their own ideas. In essence, critical thinkers enjoy the freedom of not being bound by everybody else's views and judgments because they are actively developing their own while learning and growing in the process. This means questioning their own views, discovering sometimes that their own views are inaccurate, and adopting new views based on the new evidence. Even attitudes can be critically evaluated. If you tell yourself that you aren't beautiful, that too needs to be critically evaluated.

> **~Sung Lee~**
>
> I couldn't understand why I got such disappointing grades on the reaction papers I wrote for my gerontology course. I understood the articles I was reading and thought I had summarized them well. But still I wasn't making the grade, so I spoke to the instructor. He said that he wanted me to do more than just summarize and repeat what the authors had said. Did I think the authors were making a good point? Did I agree with them? Why or why not? The instructor said he didn't want me to report, he wanted me to think. I finally learned that they were two different things.

Uncritical thinkers form views casually without much, if any, evaluation. They treat opinions as if they were facts, may readily accept views from an "authority," and welcome others' wisdom when it supports their own views. Watch what the uncritical thinker does when someone opposes his view. He gets defensive and may state his opinion even more forcefully. To avoid this mindset, realize that it is you that chooses your own opinions, and you can change them. It takes courage to admit your mistakes and change your mind when you are confronted with truths. Critical thinking helps you evaluate your own self-talk and attitudes to help you enhance your mental health and well-being.

WHAT QUALITIES DO CRITICAL THINKERS POSSESS?

Examine some of the qualities of a critical thinker in Exercise 6-1. As you read each quality, evaluate yourself—check the ones you need to improve on.

Exercise 6-1 Qualities of a critical thinker

_____ I look beyond the usual way of doing things and look for new approaches.

_____ I generate many possibilities rather than settling for a few familiar ideas.

_____ I postpone judgment until the facts are learned.

_____ I recognize the limits of my own knowledge.

_____ I have patience to allow confusion and unsettled questions to exist until I gain a deeper understanding.

_____ I am willing to gather the information necessary to better understand the problem at hand.

_____ I am willing to evaluate/analyze the information gathered.

_____ I am willing to examine viewpoints opposite my own or to put myself in another's place to genuinely understand him or her.

_____ I am able to identify and solve unstructured problems.

If you need to improve on any of the qualities of critical thinking, this section will help you do that. You'll also learn that critical thinking can be fun. You get to examine, question, reflect on what you are learning, and expand on the possibilities. Critical thinking will help you evaluate the personal side of your life too. You are constantly faced with problems to examine, solutions to devise, and then you have to think about why you were or were not successful, and learn from your failures and successes.

It's not much different on the job either. Your ability to think critically on the job will help you examine problems and design solutions. Many job assignments that you receive will come with minimal directions—that's where your critical thinking skills are required. Do you ever remember getting upset with an instructor because she "didn't give you enough direction on how to complete an assignment"? Yet this is exactly the situation you'll be faced with on the job. You will get assignments and problems to solve with very little, if any, direction. Your boss wants you to solve these problems from ground zero. For example, your boss may assign you the task of purchasing a computer and software for inventory, accounting, and billing. If you have minimal knowledge about types of computers or software, this will be a challenge but not an impossibility. Critical thinking skills will help you to find the best way to accomplish this task. It's these kinds of job challenges that make you realize the practicality of the qualities of a critical thinker. There are many situations in your professional and personal life that don't require intense critical thinking. However, for those situations that need a more thoughtful and logical approach, your ability to think critically can help you avoid the unpleasantness and disappointment that comes from poor thinking and hasty decisions.

Exercise 6-2 Putting into practice the qualities of a critical thinker

Go back and read the Qualities of a Critical Thinker. Select any four of the qualities of a critical thinker and explain how they are important to one of the following three tasks: (1) the task of purchasing a computer and software, or (2) the task of selecting and completing a project for one of your classes, or (3) planning a week-long vacation.

Task:

1. _____

2. _____

3. _____

4. _____

As you can see, a critical thinker is an active thinker. The critical thinker analyzes many aspects of a problem (or situation) before reaching a solution (or viewpoint) and explores possibilities before making a decision (or conclusion). Many of life's activities don't require such active thinking. However, you will face personal, school, and work challenges where possessing critical thinking qualities will give you the self-confidence to tackle and solve these challenges.

THE PROCESS AND TOOLS FOR CRITICAL THINKING

The basic process of a critical thinker begins with gathering information, then analyzing it, and finally drawing conclusions from it. The critical thinker will gather enough information to make a sound judgment. This doesn't mean they don't make mistakes. You probably use a critical thinking process for planning many events in your life; for example, preparing for a job interview. Getting prepared for a job interview requires gathering a lot of information. Where is the job interview taking place, how long does it take to get there, what is the best route, what should I wear, what questions will

~Jennifer~

I'm a Communications Major. My instructor gave us a list of contemporary books to select from and develop both a professional workshop and professional publication on the book. I chose the book, Communicating with Alzheimer's Patients. Other than reading the book, I didn't know where to start on this project. My instructor gave me a few suggestions and encouraged me to brainstorm. She explained to me that this project was a problem solving assignment and that she wanted me to use my critical thinking skills to develop the project. So I reluctantly sat down and tried to "storm" out my ideas. I asked my roommate, too. We actually came up with oodles of ideas, and the further I got into my project, the more I came up with ideas. I developed my workshop, wrote a small booklet to go along with it, and presented them. I really feel proud of what I finally accomplished. You couldn't have told me in the beginning that it would have worked out so well. I was certain that the task was too overwhelming. Now I can put on my resume that I can develop, design, and present workshops, and produce workshop learning materials.

they ask, how should I answer the questions, what questions do I have for them, and what do I know about the organization? Just examine one question: What questions will they ask? This requires you to brainstorm the many possible questions, consider possible answers for each, and determine what would be the most appropriate responses. Isn't this process one you would use for thinking through many work, school, or personal situations?

Tools for Critical Thinking

Let's examine some specific tools you can use in the critical thinking process to gather information, analyze it, and draw conclusions. You can use the following critical thinking tools to write a report for class, investigate a situation at work, or examine a problem in your own life. As you read through each of the tools, think about how you already use some of them.

1. **Tools for gathering information**

    *   Ask others for their viewpoints.
    *   Brainstorm the possibilities.
    *   Read a variety of viewpoints on the subject.
    *   Conduct a survey.
    *   Observe and record your observations.

2. **Tools for analyzing the information or data**

    *   Compare positions and views. What are the differences and similarities?
    *   Examine the pros and cons of your brainstorming. Use a plus (P), minus (M), and interesting (I) evaluation system to evaluate each idea.
    *   As you read other viewpoints, read with a questioning attitude and look for answers. Try to distinguish fact from opinion. Detect biases or prejudices, yours and the authors. Look for more on this in a later section.
    *   Interpret your findings. What do your statistics mean? Explain the data.

3. **Tools for drawing conclusions and reassessing**

    *   Draw reasonable conclusions based on your comparisons and data analysis.
    *   Apply (try out) your decision/conclusion.
    *   Evaluate. How well does your conclusion hold up? How well is your decision working?
    *   Reassess as new information becomes available.
    *   Make modifications as necessary.
    *   Keep reassessing and adjust as necessary.

Exercise 6-3 will let you try out some of the tools for the critical thinking process.

Exercise 6-3 Putting your critical thinking tools to work

Your employer wants you to determine what type of work clothing is best for the sales persons in her sports store. List and explain what critical thinking tools for 1) gathering information, 2) analyzing, and 3) drawing your conclusion, you would use to think through this issue.

1. Gathering information _____

    _____

    _____

    _____

    _____

2. Analyzing information _____

    _____

    _____

    _____

    _____

3. Drawing a conclusion _____

    _____

    _____

    _____

    _____

Basic Guidelines for Critical Thinking

You can learn to think critically just as you learn to master any other skill. Critical thinkers use many of the following guidelines in their daily lives. As you read each guideline, think about school, work, or personal areas in your life where you can put them to use.

> ***Accept and learn to appreciate that diversity of opinions exists.*** Your opinions exist in the company of many other opinions. Make a genuine effort to see things from other people's point of view and what experiences helped them form their view. For example, what are the positions of the democratic and republican parties; why and how did they evolve?
>
> ***Ask questions to learn more and to clarify.*** Ask for examples. Ask what the person means. What is the source? What are the specific objections? What are the benefits? What is the purpose? Using questions is one of the most essential tools of critical thinking because it's used for gathering information and developing a better understanding for an issue.
>
> ***Learn to live with uncertainty.*** Some issues cannot be clearly defined or understood immediately. Do you ever feel confused about class projects before you get started? Allow yourself some uncertainty or some confusion—it's part of the process. When the project is complete, the uncertainty and confusion also diminish. Work projects may initially seem unclear—just remind yourself that when you're "in process," uncertainty is a normal part of the process.
>
> (continued)

Avoid making inaccurate generalizations or stereotypes. When you hear yourself making a sweeping statement such as, "men are insensitive," or "women are too emotional," question and challenge this kind of thinking. Rethink such generalizations.

Challenge conventional wisdom. When you fall into the trap of doing things the way they're always done, you leave little room for creativity. If we always allowed ourselves to be slaves to conventional wisdom, we wouldn't even have computers or clean water. What areas of conventional wisdom would you like to rethink?

Evaluate your opinions as well as the expert's opinion. When you're open to examining your own opinions, you're open to discovering new and better ways of doing things or confirming that your ideas really do work. Be careful of the notion that the experts should know; they may be following conventional wisdom. Be open to new and stronger ideas.

Allow yourself to disagree with others. Even the experts disagree with each other. New ideas can evolve from constructive disagreement.

Don't allow yourself to be overcome by solution killers. When you're on the job and a co-worker says, "That will never work," don't let it kill your ideas. Now is the time to assert yourself and say, "Before we trash this idea, I want to explore it further." Many "breakthrough ideas" go through the chopping block first.

Use brainstorming to jump-start ideas. When you allow yourself to come up with limitless ideas without prejudging them, you jump-start one idea off another. One idea generates another, which leads to something else, and you never know when you're going to strike gold.

Be focused but flexible. Remain focused on goals because goals serve as guidelines, but balance this with flexibility so that you are open to discovery and better ways of doing things.

Be aware of what you know and what you don't know. It's important to gather more information when you really don't know the answers. Your openness to seek new information will only increase your knowledge base.

Withhold judgment until the evidence convinces you. Don't feel pushed to make hasty decisions when you haven't got the information you need or haven't had time to examine it.

Be imaginative and practical. Keep a balance between what you know will work and clever brainstorms. A balance of practicality and imagination will keep each side in check.

You have no doubt realized that using the guidelines for critical thinking will make you more creative. It's just this freeing creativity that helps you clarify the unclear and from that leads you into directions you may not have considered. In Exercise 6-4, you'll get a chance to examine how the guidelines for creative thinking can help you in school.

Exercise 6-4 Putting the guidelines for critical thinking to work

Review the guidelines for critical thinking. Select five guidelines and explain how you can use them to improve your learning in school.

1. _____

2. _____

3. _____

4. _____

5. _____

DEVELOPING CRITICAL READING SKILLS

Critical reading skills are important to your growth and learning in college. You'll be reading more than you probably ever have before, and the material you read will become more complex as you progress in your education. You'll also find that your professors will often want you to do more than simply absorb information. They'll want you to discuss, challenge, argue, and develop your own opinions. The disagreements you have with an author's opinion can make excellent topics for writing assignments. Essay questions frequently require you to critically address reading topics. Critically reading work documents like directions, instructional manuals, plans, and proposals will help you learn your job better and make more creative improvements.

Questioning: The Tool of Critical Reading

Critical readers use many of the basic guidelines for critical thinking, especially questioning. Questioning is at the heart of critical reading. Critical readers ask themselves whether they agree or disagree with the author. They understand that the nature of reading involves seeing things temporarily from the author's perspective. This does not mean they accept everything they read; on the contrary, they investigate and challenge it. Critical readers read actively, looking for the major points, supporting ideas, biases, and other sides to an issue—they are reading with a purpose. In college, critical readers write comments and questions in the margin and bring them to class to discuss. When you read critically, you push yourself to new levels of understanding. You know your material better because you thought about it, questioned it, and assessed it—you involved yourself in it.

Before you begin reading, orient yourself to the book or section. Skim through the preface, table of contents, section introduction and summary, subtitles, graphs, pictures and captions—just as you did in Section 4 with the PRQRT reading to learn method. When you're oriented to the material prior to reading, you will read with more purpose and expectation because you're aware of the structure of the reading—you have a general idea of where it starts and where it is going.

The most important tool in critical reading is to maintain a questioning attitude. What does the author mean, what is her major point, what kind of background does the author have, what are my opinions on this material, what do other authorities say? A questioning attitude keeps you active and alert while reading. As you read, probe for answers to questions and, if you own the book, make note of your questions in the margins and underline any answers you find in the reading. The following critical thinking questions will help you probe your reading.

Ten Critical Thinking Questions to Probe Your Reading

1. **What's the author's opinion?** You can ask this question on the different issues posed throughout your reading. Try to make predictions on what the author's opinion is by observing what he/she **implies,** or suggests indirectly. Does the author back his/her view with **fact,** which can be substantiated, or **opinion,** his/her personal judgment which cannot be verified?

2. **What's the author's purpose?** Just as you have a reason for reading, the author has a reason for writing. She/he may simply want to deliver information, or persuade you, or share an experience. As you read, ask yourself, "Why does the author want me to read this?"

3. **What's the author's mode of discourse?** A great clue to the author's purpose is in his/her **mode of discourse.** A mode of discourse is a general style of delivering information, and there are four basic types. **Narrative** discourse tells a story—it details a sequence of events. **Descriptive** discourse describes something. **Persuasive** discourse is a piece of writing that tries to argue a point or to otherwise persuade you to a certain way of thinking. **Expository** discourse explains something; the mode of discourse of this book is expository.

4. **Is the author objective or biased?** Does the author make objective statements—expressing facts without distortions of personal feelings or prejudices? Or does he/she appear openly biased—one-sided in favor of a certain group or position? Does he/she use language that is neutral and reasonable or exaggerated and emotional? Is his/her language vague or precise? Does he/she disguise a bias? Does the author stand to gain anything by influencing my opinion? Is the author employed by an organization that would benefit from expressing a particular view? An article on gun control written by the leader of the National Rifle Association is bound to be biased.

5. **Does the author provide support for his/her views and statements?** Is the author's argument strong and supported by the facts? Try this exercise for evaluating an author's argument: write a sentence at the top of a piece of paper that summarizes the author's main argument. Then draw a line down the paper, dividing it into two columns. In one column, list all the facts and arguments the author uses that support his/her argument. In the other column, list those points in the argument that are not supported. A strong piece of writing should give you little to write in the second column.

6. **What are the author's credentials?** What is the author's background? Is he/she an expert or does he/she have significant work experience in the area? Has he/she written previous books on the topic?

7. **How good are the author's sources?** Where do the author's sources come from? Are they reliable? Are they recent, if being recent is important to the material? Does the author use more **primary** or secondary sources? A primary source is a direct source of information; it comes from someone who was actually at the scene. An autobiography is a primary source. So is a first-hand account of a criminal trial, written by someone who watched the proceedings. A **secondary** source is one step removed—it is information taken from a primary source. A biography based on someone's memoirs is a secondary source (the memoirs being the first); a magazine review of a movie is a secondary source (the movie script would be the primary source).

8. **What's the other side of this issue?** You can identify opposing views of an issue by calling on your previous knowledge or seeking other viewpoints. For example, if you read a health magazine that discourages you from taking vitamin supplements and instead encourages you to eat a nutritionally balanced diet with variety, think about what you know about vitamins or look to another source. Maybe your physician encouraged you to take vitamin supplements as insurance. You do not have to solve this issue, but you can at least raise the issue. It may urge you to ask other experts or read more about what other nutrition and health authorities say. The more you read on a topic from different sources, the more you'll learn and can compare.

9. **What is the author's thought pattern?** An author will organize the main thoughts and ideas of a piece in certain definite patterns. In an article discussing two different study methods, for example, the author might make use of a *comparison and contrast* pattern. An article on a new dental technology might include *definitions* of new terms. Refer to Table 6-1 to review common thought patterns and questions to ask as you read.

10. **Ask questions of yourself as well.** What are my views on this subject? How would I evaluate the author's opinions or viewpoints? Based on my experience, does it sound true or not? Do I agree or disagree with the statement(s)? What are my biases? How does the information relate to what I already know? Making connections to what you already know is how you construct knowledge. Essentially, that's what knowledge is: a series of connections between old and new information.

<u>Table 6-1</u>

Common Thought Patterns		
Thought Pattern	**What to Look for**	**Questions to Ask**
Definition	Meaning of word or concept.	Is the definition complete?
Comparison and contrast	Similarities and differences between two or more things.	Are there additional similarities or differences?
Classification	Items grouped into categories.	Would these items fit better in different categories?
Cause and effect	Reasons and results.	What else could explain both the cause and the effect?
Example	Explanation by example, with such phrases as "for example" or "for instance."	What examples would challenge the author's point?
Sequence	Numbered items, such as first, second, third or events arranged according to time.	Could items be added or removed from the sequence? Could the sequence be ordered differently?
Process	Phases of how something is accomplished or created, such as a four-stage production process.	Can the process be changed?

CRITICAL THINKING: YOU AND THE MEDIA

You are surrounded by the media. Wherever you go, you are bombarded with messages from radio and television. Magazines, newspapers, and tabloids are at the checkout lines of almost every market. Even the telephone is a source of prerecorded messages telling you that you may have won a prize or encouraging you to buy something. The media is full of news, information, and entertainment; a lot of the time it is filled with advertisements, each trying to disguise itself as one of those things. Advertising is the means by which people try to get you to purchase their goods and services. There's nothing wrong with advertising (except perhaps that there's so much of it); but, unfortunately, many people don't think critically about it the way they would any other kind of information they receive. Critical thinking about the media is an important skill to learn because it will enable you to separate the hype from the facts, the fantasy from the reality.

The same critical thinking tools that you applied to problem solving, decision making, and reading can be applied to the media messages you encounter every day. The following tips and strategies will help you think critically about the media.

Exercise 6-5 Thinking critically about the news

With a small group of four to six students, select a prominent news story. Each member of the group should select a different newspaper or magazine article, editorial, or notes of a newscast covering the story. As a group, discuss the following questions about the articles you've collected.

1. How do the various media's coverage differ on the story?

2. In what ways are they similar?

3. Which stories give a fairer picture of the event? Explain.

4. Did any of the various media attempt to sensationalize the story? Explain.

5. What emotional response are the various media trying to arouse in you?

Tips . . . For Thinking Critically About the Media

- The most important thing to remember about the media is something you learned when you studied critical reading. Do you remember the section that talked about author bias? It was suggested that you ask yourself, "Does the author stand to gain anything by influencing my opinion?" The important thing to remember about advertising is that *all* of it is biased—that is, every advertiser has something to gain by influencing your opinion. Everyone is trying to sell you something. Therefore, advertisers will present information in a way that they think will make you want to buy their products.

- Watch out for the difference between fact and opinion. Remember, anything that can be proved or verified is a fact. "Cleans 20 percent more dishes than Brand X" is a statement that can be proved or disproved; "Makes you feel clean and confident" is not.

- Learn to be aware of editorial viewpoints in newspapers and magazines. Try this exercise: choose a prominent news story on which to focus. Then collect several different newspapers, news magazines, and other sources that cover the story. Read each article about the story. How do they differ? In what ways are they similar? You will find that, even when the facts in each story are basically the same, the overall tone of each story can vary dramatically. (You might want to focus on a recent election as the topic for your research.)

(continued)

- What emotional response is the advertiser trying to get from you? Flip through some magazines and focus on the ads. Which are funny? Are there any that make you feel angry, happy, annoyed? Some ads are provocative so you will remember the ad when it comes time to buy. Others try to get you to associate good feelings with their ad so you will then associate good feelings with the use of their product. Still others might try to make you feel that, by using their product, you will be joining a very select and exclusive club. An example of this is ice cream manufacturers who give sophisticated, foreign-sounding names to their product so you will think it's an expensive European import. It's expensive, all right, but it's not an import!

- Watch television commercials with a sharp eye. Because commercials are on TV, they can dramatize their pitch to viewers. How realistic are the ads? Ask yourself, "Do people in real life ever act like that?" Have you ever seen a housewife hated by her family because she used the wrong cake mix? Have you ever seen anyone get a job because he changed aftershaves? Or anyone get a new boyfriend because of a great new eyeshadow? Remember that most commercials are exaggerations; no one product you could ever buy could improve your life the way products seem to on television.

HIGHLIGHTS

This section has introduced you to a variety of new thinking skills. You've examined guidelines and tools for thinking and reading critically. You know that critical thinking is essentially evaluating ideas, thinking for yourself, and active thinking—asking questions about the information before you accept it. The result of critical thinking is learning more, understanding more, and remembering it longer, which is obviously useful for college, as well as in your work and personal life. Critical thinking helps you think harder about issues and helps you stay more flexible because you realize that many issues have no single answer. Critical thinking is truly a valuable tool that's worth all your efforts to master.

DISCUSSION QUESTIONS

Note: Read the following discussion questions and activities **before** you read Section 6. This strategy will help you look for answers while you read.

1. What is critical thinking and why is it important in your college, career, and personal life?
2. What is the three-step process of critical thinking? Discuss the importance of each.
3. What is probably the most essential tool of critical thinking and why?
4. What is the importance of the following basic guideline: accept and learn to appreciate that diversity of opinions exist?
5. Explain the following statement from the section: "Do you ever feel confused about class projects before you get started? Allow yourself some uncertainty or some confusion—it's part of the process."
6. What generalizations or stereotypes are you familiar with that seem to be generally accepted by many in our society? List as many as you can. (Example: Women are emotional or men are insensitive.) Explain why you think each generalization or stereotype is accepted.
7. What was meant by the sentence, "When you're a critical reader, you participate in an inner dialogue with the writer"?
8. Discuss the importance of reading with a purpose.
9. Why make predictions while you read?
10. How does critical reading make you learn more while you read?
11. What are some tips for thinking critically about the media?

Presenting Your Best Work

WHAT'S IN IT FOR YOU

An important part of your learning experience in school is presenting your new found knowledge to your instructors and fellow students in the form of written essays and oral reports. Writing and speaking skills are necessary for success in school and in virtually any career you may pursue afterward. College is probably the best opportunity you'll ever have to work on improving your presentation skills. You'll be assigned essays, reports, and research papers. You'll give oral reports, talks, and presentations. Many instructors consider your writing and speaking skills when determining your overall grade. The presentation skills you develop will be valuable assets at work.

In this section you'll explore:

- The basics of effective writing strategies and how to write
- How to write a well-organized research paper
- Strategies for overcoming the fear of public speaking
- Tips for making interesting, well-organized oral presentations

THE BASIC STEPS TO EFFECTIVE WRITING

Whether you're writing a one-page essay or a 10-page report, any piece of writing is easier if you take the process step by step. There are five main steps to good writing: choosing a topic, prewriting, organizing, preparing a rough draft, and revising.

Step 1: Choosing a Topic for a Writing Assignment

Whether you get a list of topics to choose from or the topic is determined by you, the topic you choose can influence how successful your writing will be. Your best writing will come when you have a topic you are genuinely interested in and one that you believe is important to learn more about. Examine the following tips for choosing a topic.

~Toyin~

I knew I'd be doing a lot of reading in college, but I had no idea I'd have to write about everything I read. I didn't know where to begin, and I got some pretty low grades on my first papers. Then I signed up for an elective on effective writing. Wow! What a difference. Once I learned how to organize my thoughts on paper, it seemed like I could write about almost anything. I feel I have a really valuable tool that works for all my classes and work. And last week my English instructor asked if I could help tutor some of the other students in essay writing.

Tips . . . For Choosing a Writing Topic

- **Select a topic that interests you,** something you want to know more about, or something that you know well and want to inform others about. If you get assigned a topic that you just don't seem interested in, think about it—what aspects of that topic can you get interested in?

- **Instead of racking your brain to find the right topic, think in terms of ideas.** Ideas are statements or opinions about a topic. For example, Erin wanted to write about the topic downhill skiing. Here are two of Erin's ideas about skiing: (1) Skiing is a great lifetime sport with no age limits, and (2) Learning effective turning and stopping techniques takes the fear out of skiing. These two ideas should give Erin a lot more to think about, especially about arguments to support her ideas.

- **Brainstorming.** Brainstorming is letting your brain take off and think of any topic idea at all, no matter how silly or impossible it might seem at the time. Let the ideas flow freely without critiquing them. Try brainstorming with others; sometimes ideas flow faster in groups.

- **Write about ideas from your journal.** Keeping a journal allows you to make daily written entries about your life, issues, thoughts, feelings, aspirations. Your journal is an idea book.

- **Write about your environment.** How is it beautiful, unique, or disgusting? What can you compare it to? How can it be improved? Why is it serene or why is it disturbing? What other questions might you have about your environment?

- **Write about local, national, or world events.** What's amusing, shocking, unusual, happy, memorable, terrifying? What's your reaction? What changes would you like to see? What can make these changes take place?

(continued)

- Write about people (family, friends, someone you admire). What do you find intriguing about the people you know? What behaviors have you observed? What have you learned about relating to people who are different from you?

- Write about what you want to do with your life. What career do you want to pursue? What hobbies or sports do you want to develop? How do you want to contribute to society?

One of the most common problems with topic selection is choosing a topic that is too broad. You can tell if your topic is too broad if you don't know where to start, you don't know where to stop, or the topic is overwhelming. Tara wanted to write on the topic of exercise. "I wanted to begin with the benefits of exercise but I realized that would depend on what type of exercise I was writing about. So I narrowed it down to aerobic exercise and that helped me know where to start."

Step 2: Prewriting

Once you have your topic in mind, it's time to generate details for your paper. This is the step where people often find that their ideas get "locked up." Prewriting strategies help you unlock your ideas. Prewriting helps you produce a lot of possible details that you could include in your topic. The following list outlines five different strategies to unlock your mind and generate details for your topic.

Prewriting strategies

Brainstorming. Brainstorming works for prewriting too. Write words and phrases only. There's no need to worry about sentence structure now. Give yourself a 10 to 20 minute time limit. Ideas have a way of popping in and out of your mind all day long. Carry an idea notebook with you to jot down ideas, small bits of wisdom, or quotes that you come across throughout your day. There have probably been many times when an idea came into your mind and, even with your best intentions, you forgot it.

> *~Harper~*
>
> *I'd always have some great ideas for writing topics, but I'd scribble them in the back of an old notebook and never find them again. Then I bought a package of those stick-on memo pads—in neon colors! I jot down my ideas and stick them on my books, my desk, everything. My roommate says my ideas are taking up the whole room.*

Some people find it easier to use a tape recorder to capture their thoughts; they play the tape back and record their ideas. Maybe you can find a friend to brainstorm with and write down your ideas. Your friend can ask you to state your ideas more clearly. If your ideas flow faster when you talk about them, take advantage of it. Whether using an idea notebook, index cards, a tape recorder, or your own system, be sure to keep track of the results of your brainstorming.

Freewriting. Freewriting allows you to write with what some call "reckless abandonment." This means nonstop writing. You write whatever comes to mind about your topic. Give yourself a 10 to 20 minute time limit. This stage of writing can be a lot of fun alone, with a partner, or in a group.

Questioning. Write any questions that come to mind about your topic. The more questions you write, the more ideas you generate. While you are creating questions, you may come up with answers. Write those down too.

Branching. Branching begins on a clean sheet of paper. You write your topic in the middle of the paper, put a circle around it, and branch out with new ideas. As you think of related ideas, write them surrounding the circle. Draw lines that connect related ideas. Keep branching out with new ideas. Figure 7-1 is an example of Erin's branching process.

Figure 7-1
Sample of Branching

Exercise 7-1 Choosing a topic and prewriting

Your instructor asks you to write a persuasive essay on one of your leisure interests and persuade others to try it. On a separate sheet of paper, use any two of the eight Tips for Choosing a Topic for a Writing Assignment, and select your topic.

List the advantages of each of the topic selection methods you used.

In the space provided, use two of the prewriting strategies to develop details for your paper.

Step 3: Organizing

After you've generated details and ideas for your paper, review and evaluate your list. Cross off those items you're not interested in or that shouldn't be developed for your paper. If you think an idea is really great, put an exclamation point (!) next to it and begin thinking about how you might develop this idea as a major point in your paper.

Next, try to determine a logical sequence. Sometimes numbering ideas from your prewriting lists can help you develop a sequence that will guide your writing. When you have listed your ideas in a logical order, you're ready to form an outline. An **outline** lists the main points of your paper and a few notes about what you'll say about each, in the order they will appear. Your outline should include the three main parts of a paper: the introduction, body, and conclusion.

Introduction. An introduction presents your paper's theme (or argument), purpose, and scope (the range of issues you will cover). Let the reader know exactly what you're going to say, *in the order you're going to say it.* This is a very important point. Your readers will usually be your instructors, and the introduction is a great place to show them how well organized your thoughts and opinions are. Organization is almost always an important factor in determining your grade.

Body. The body of your essay is where all the main points are covered. This is where you argue, persuade, analyze, and describe. Remember that the body of your paper must follow the order of topics you stated in your introduction.

Conclusion. The conclusion of your paper is just that—it sums up the main points argued in the paper. A conclusion is generally no longer than a paragraph, but it can be longer if you are summing up a particularly long essay. In your conclusion, you should tell the reader how your discussion of the topic (body) fulfilled the purpose of the paper (stated in the introduction). Take a look at Jan's outline in Figure 7-2.

Jan is enrolled in an associate degree program in Community Behavioral Health Technology. She developed the following outline for a paper assigned in her Behavioral Health Technology II course. Notice how she has clearly outlined the introduction, body, and conclusion.

Figure 7-2
Example Outline

Eight Principles to Help Clients Set Goals and Achieve Them

I. *Introduction*

   A. *A life-long philosophy to help clients set goals and stick to them*

   B. *Principles for successful goal setting*
      1. *Involvement*
      2. *Focus on present*
      3. *Develop plan of action*
      4. *Get a commitment*
      5. *Check on your client's progress at each session*
      6. *How to help clients if they don't do what they planned*
      7. *Have clients create new and positive self-talk*
      8. *Don't give up on your clients*

II. *Body*

    A. *Involvement*
        1. *How to begin to help your client*
        2. *Positive relationships motivate people to change their behavior*

    B. *Focus on present and future*
        1. *You can't change your past but you can plan changes for your future*
        2. *Put energy into planning*
        3. *Ask "what" questions*

    C. *Develop a plan of action*
        1. *Be specific*
        2. *Help client develop smaller steps to accomplish goals*
        3. *Who else can support your client?*

    D. *Get a commitment*
        1. *Hear your client say: "I will . . ."*
        2. *Make a written commitment*
        3. *Ask "what if" questions to check commitment*
        4. *Have client chart progress*

    E. *Check on your client's progress at each meeting*
        1. *Ask your client how his/her plan is progressing*
        2. *Make modifications if necessary*
        3. *Use "what" questions to encourage clients to evaluate their plan and progress*

    F. *How to help clients if they don't do what they planned*
        1. *Always forgive*
        2. *Don't ask "why" they failed*

    G. *Have clients create new and positive self-talk*
        1. *Help client become aware of old negative self-talk messages that keep them from achieving their goals*
        2. *Help client replace negative self-talk with new positive self-talk*
        3. *Positive self-talk will counteract previous brainwashing messages of self-doubt, inability, or dislike*

    H. *Don't give up on your clients*
        1. *Obtain another commitment to client's plan*
        2. *Help patient find ways to modify the old plan*
        3. *Develop a new plan*

III. *Conclusion*

    A. *The eight strategies are simple but effective*
    B. *Encourage your clients to incorporate strategies into many aspects of their lives*
    C. *The end result of successful goal setting is*
        1. *Goal achievement*
        2. *More self-esteem*
        3. *More self-respect*
        4. *More personal power*

Exercise 7-2 Organizing your prewriting ideas

Go back to the Exercise 7-1 prewriting activities. (1) Select the prewriting strategy that you thought was most effective in developing details and ideas for your persuasive paper. (2) Cross off those items that you're not interested in or that shouldn't be developed for your paper. (3) Place an exclamation point (!) next to items that you think are really great ideas. (4) Next, try to determine a logical sequence by numbering items from your prewriting list. (5) Based on your sequence of items, develop a brief outline of points for your introduction, body and conclusion.

Introduction:

Body:

Conclusion:

Step 4: Writing a Rough Draft

The next step is to write a rough draft of your paper, using your outline as a guide. Write a topic sentence for each idea in the outline and use that sentence to lead off each paragraph. Be sure to stick to only one main idea in each paragraph. For this draft, don't worry about spelling and grammar. Now is the time to write with energy and abandon. Revising and polishing will be the next step.

Think about what your readers need to know. Generally, it is a good idea to pretend your reader knows nothing about the topic (even if your instructor does). Don't assume your reader has the same knowledge about a certain point you do; you don't want to omit any valuable information. What details, descriptions, and examples can make your topic come alive? Put them in. Try to capture your reader's interest even as you educate him/her.

If you get stuck while writing, give yourself a break. Writing is hard work, and sometimes your mind just needs a rest. Frustrations often disappear and your ideas resume their flow when you allow yourself some time to relax and clear your head. Likewise, once you've written your rough draft, it's helpful to leave it alone for a day before you begin your revisions. "When I get writer's block," says Anita, "I go out and take a long walk. Exercising my body seems to exercise my mind—by the time I come back to my desk, I'm full of new ideas."

Whether you're starting your outline or your rough draft, just start writing. Starting is the important thing. Procrastination just creates anxiety, which only gets worse as your deadline approaches. If you put off an assignment too long, you won't have the time to do a good job on it, and that's really something to be anxious about. Remember, at this stage you're not aiming for perfection. Just write. You'll find that during revisions your paper will change a lot. That's fine. Get rid of those ideas that didn't work; rearrange your outline. The best ideas will stay and form the basis of a strong and well-thought-out essay.

Step 5: Revising

When your paper is in the basic shape you want it to be in, it's time to fine-tune it. Check the logic and clarity of the arguments in your paper. Make sure that the theme or argument is clearly stated in the introduction, and that each section of your paper contains evidence to back up your argument. Make sure that each paragraph has a topic sentence and following sentences that support it. Cut out any unnecessary words or sentences. Get rid of entire sections if they don't enhance your essay.

Evaluate your essay for grammar, sentence structure, and clarity of thought. Correct errors and reword sentences that don't sound right. Get a friend to proofread your paper. Sometimes a second pair of eyes can spot errors that you missed. Read your paper out loud to someone and ask for a reaction. Is your argument persuasive? Is it interesting? "I always ask my best friend to read my final draft," says Ethan. "He's honest with me and tells me if there are any mistakes. Of course, he's an English major so he spots them right away."

Be sure to make the final draft of your paper as clean and neat as possible. Most instructors will ask for typewritten papers. Be sure to include a cover sheet and staple the sheets together. Many instructors will consider the appearance of your paper as well as its contents.

Look at Jan's essay paper which she constructed from the outline in Figure 7-2. Note how closely she has followed her outline.

Figure 7-3
Sample Essay

<u>Eight Strategies to Help Clients Set Goals and Achieve Them</u>

submitted by Jan Moss
May 1, 2015
for: Behavioral Health Technology II

If you help your clients develop strategies for goal setting and achievement, they will gain more control of their lives and therefore more self-esteem. Clint Eastwood was interviewed about his movie "Absolute Power." He said this about setting goals: "For yourself, figure out what you want out of life, then set your goals and maintain them as long as is biologically possible. Respect your efforts, respect yourself. Self-respect leads to self-discipline. When you have both firmly under your belt, that's real power." This paper will outline eight strategies to help you help your clients figure what they want out of life, set goals, and maintain them. The goal setting strategies include: how to begin involvement with your client, the importance of focusing on the present, how to develop a specific plan of action, getting a commitment orally and in writing, monitoring progress, how to help clients get back on track, developing positive self-talk, and the importance of not giving up on your clients.

The first strategy is involvement. This is a professional, yet warm and friendly involvement. A genuine interest should be reflected in your demeanor toward your clients. The best tool to develop a positive working relationship is active listening—listening attentively and reflecting (paraphrasing) to your clients what you understand from their conversations. If your clients can develop a positive working relationship with you, they feel more accountable to you and are more motivated to change their behavior.

The second strategy is to help your clients focus on present and future plans; not on why past plans failed. Your clients can't change their past, but they can plan changes for their future. Encourage your clients to put more energy into planning and less into making excuses or complaints.

To help your clients develop plans, ask "what" questions. "What" questions encourage your clients to think about what they want to accomplish and how. For example, ask, "What kind of plan would you like to make?" "What do you want to accomplish?" "What will make your plan work?" Avoid asking "why" their plans failed. Asking "why" is basically asking your clients to give you excuses. Asking "what" forces your clients to think and evaluate for themselves what they want to accomplish and develop plans to do it.

The next strategy involves developing a specific plan of action: what, where, when, and how long. When you help your clients develop specific plans, it gives them a target to aim for. For example, if your client sets an exercise goal and his plan is to take a brisk walk on Monday through Saturday, at 7 PM, in his neighborhood for forty-five minutes, when 7 PM rolls around, he knows this is the established time for exercise. He knows what the plan is and how long he intends to walk. Consider advising your client to select alternate times, perhaps 7 or 9 PM, just in case of conflicts. If your client wants to accomplish too much too fast, encourage him to plan smaller steps to accomplish his goals. Small steps will promote small successes as he progresses toward this long-term goal. It's better that he is successful walking for twenty minutes than to feel like he failed at the goal of forty-five minutes.

After your clients have developed a plan of action, it's important to get a commitment. You want to hear your clients say: "I will do it" as well as having them sign an informal written contract. Getting your clients to make a commitment, both orally and in writing, will promote accountability. Perhaps you can also ask your clients who else would be supportive in their plans (another person besides you), to be accountable to. It may also be important to check your clients' level of commitment. Ask "what if" questions to check commitment: "What if . . . , will you still do it?" "What would keep you from doing it?" "If something interrupts your plan, will you reschedule it?" Encourage your clients to chart their progress. A free bank calendar may be all they need to quickly chart their progress. Seeing their progress in writing is very reinforcing.

Check on your clients' progress at each meeting. Ask them how their plans are progressing. Assist them in making modifications in their plans if necessary. You don't want your clients to try to stay with a plan that is doomed to failure or may in some other way be inappropriate. Again, use "what" questions to encourage clients to evaluate their plan and progress. "Is WHAT you are doing working out?" "WHAT would make your plan work better?" "WHAT times are better for you?"

If you discover that your clients are not working on the plan they committed to, it is important to maintain a forgiving attitude and encourage them to forgive themselves. Forgiveness allows people to continue and refocus on their plan. Again, don't ask "why" they failed or "why" they didn't do as planned. Asking "why" is asking for excuses! Ask, "What can you do next time to accomplish your plan?" This statement gets them to evaluate, plan, and focus on accomplishment, not on their failure.

Another strategy to help your clients toward goal accomplishment to help them create new and positive self-talk that directs and encourages them to reach their goals. Help your clients become aware of their old negative self-talk messages that keep them from achieving their goals. Ask them to think of new self-talk that can replace the old. For example, replace: "I don't have time to walk!" with "I'll find time to walk!" Have your clients write down the new positive self-talk messages. You may even encourage them to post their new self-talk messages in a place where they can be reminded by them. Positive self-talk messages will counteract previous brainwashing messages of self-doubt, inability, or dislike.

Finally, don't give up on your clients. Instead, obtain another commitment to their plan, help clients find ways to modify the old plan, or develop a new plan. Help them persist.

These basic eight strategies are simple but effective in helping clients to establish and accomplish goals. Encourage your clients to view the goal setting strategies as a philosophy that they can incorporate into many aspects of their lives. As your clients successfully establish realistic goals and strategies to accomplish them, the end result is greater goal achievement, more self-esteem, more self-respect and, therefore, more personal power.

Practice, Practice, Practice

Writing is an important skill for college and career success. It's a skill you'll want to master. The best way to master writing—or any other skill, for that matter—is to practice. Just write. Keeping a journal is an excellent way to practice writing, as are the In Your Own Words exercises in this book. If there is not enough room in the text to write all your thoughts in those journal exercises, take a blank notebook and continue to write. Carrying around a small notebook will encourage you to write when the mood strikes. Ideas for journal writing are limitless. You can write about topics that interest you in your classes (this also can help you remember class discussions). Special events, new ideas, future plans, wishes, and goals also make good journal writing material. You might be surprised to see how writing down your wishes, goals, and dreams can help make them happen.

Many of the tips you have learned about writing for college can be applied to work. When you're assigned a project at work, start right away. Project development requires prewriting, organizing, drafts, and final copies, just as writing for college does. Developing quality projects at work also requires taking a break from writing. Taking a break from writing tasks gives you time to refresh yourself and time for ideas to formulate and gel. Practicing the basic steps to effective writing while you're in college will help you feel more confident on your job.

THE RESEARCH PAPER

A common writing assignment in college is the research paper. A well-written research paper makes you an expert—a knowledgeable person on a topic in which you are interested. As with any writing assignment, research papers are best completed in a step-by-step manner. The following steps will help make any research paper a manageable project:

- Know the ropes.

- Choose a topic.

- Gather information.

- Construct an outline.

- Write a rough draft.

- Revise and polish.

Know the Ropes

The most important thing to do when writing any paper is to find out what the instructor wants. You don't want to run into trouble at the start because you're not clear on what the assignment is. The following issues should be clear in your mind when you set out to start work on your paper. In fact, you'll learn a lot about these issues by writing them down, and they'll be there so you can refer to them as you develop your paper.

- How long should the paper be? Many instructors will give you an estimate, like 8 to 10 pages. Some students think they will earn extra points by writing a paper twice as long as recommended. This doesn't work. Instructors know how much information they want from you. Also, if you ignore the guidelines for paper length, your instructor might get the idea that you don't follow directions very well.

- What topics are allowed? Essays are usually in answer to a specific question. For a research paper, you will generally be allowed to choose your own topic, as long as it pertains to the course. To be on the safe side, get your instructor's OK before starting work on your topic.

- What other parts of the paper require approval? Some instructors insist on approving topics, outlines, even rough drafts, before you continue with the project.

- Are there any required elements to include, such as a bibliography, table of contents, footnotes, or abstract (i.e., a brief summary)? Find out which style your instructor prefers for each of these components.

- How will the paper be graded? What aspects of the paper are most important? Some instructors may expect a broad coverage of different perspectives on a topic; others may prefer a critical analysis of a narrow range of perspectives. Some instructors will take off points for poor grammar and spelling; others will overlook a few minor mistakes.

- When is your paper due? What are the penalties for being late? Many instructors have strict penalties for being late; some may even consider a paper late if it is not submitted at the beginning of class on the day it is due. If, due to unforeseen circumstances, you must hand a paper in late, have the courtesy to let your instructor know beforehand. No one likes excuses at the last minute. If you must submit a paper late, at least know ahead of time what it's going to cost you; changing minor errors may not be worth a late penalty.

Choose a Topic

If you're not assigned a topic, you'll have to choose your own. Talk to your instructor about possible options. Ask your friends for ideas. Start with a general topic and then narrow it down. Again, a common mistake is not narrowing the focus of the paper; students end up writing about such broad topics as "health" or "nutrition"—topics that certainly can't be covered in one short paper. When students choose a topic that is too broad, they often become overwhelmed by the sheer amount of information they find.

The next step in shaping your topic is developing a thesis statement—the major argument or theme on which your whole paper is based. It's not enough to have a topic; you must have a point of view about it. Clearly state this argument, preferably in one sentence, so it can help guide the development of your paper. For instance, suppose the topic of your paper for business class was computers in American small businesses. Your thesis statement would state your opinion: "American small businesses have used computers to increase productivity." Or, perhaps, "American small business has failed to take full advantage of computers." The rest of your paper would be devoted to proving your statement.

SEARCHING AND RESEARCHING VIA THE WEB

As you undoubtedly know, the information on the World Wide Web is growing each second and search tools were designed to help you quickly sift and sort through this mammoth amount of information. Locating webpages that contain information you want would be an overwhelming task without some sort of index or directory. Search tools are websites that maintain indexes or directories of other websites, allowing you to search for sites that contain information that may be of interest to you. Search tools can be grouped into three main categories: web directories, search engines, and metasearch engines. Thankfully, these search tools are free to you because they generally sell advertising space on their websites to generate income to pay for the service.

Web Directories

A web directory is a directory on the Web that specializes in linking to other websites and categorizing those links by topic area. Staff editors routinely review and organize new websites into subject-based search directories. Search directories aid your research because they categorize and subcategorize websites so your search for information is conducted only in the selected category of information. You simply select (click on) a category related to the information you are searching. Web directories are excellent for browsing through collections of sites on a related topic, much like browsing through a library shelf. Example web directories and their addresses are listed below. There are many more—search the Web for a current listing of Web directories.

Web Directories	Address
Open Directory Project	www.dmoz.org
Yahoo! Directory	dir.yahoo.com
Librarians' Index to the Internet	www.lii.org

Exercise 7-3 Using a web directory

1. Go to Yahoo! Directory http://dir.yahoo.com and use the next step to access information on the topic of "clean humor."

2. Search for "Clean Humor" by clicking on "Humor," which is listed under the "Entertainment" category. Keep searching, experimenting, and clicking on the humor related categories and subcategories until you can find a list of clean jokes. Write your favorite shortest clean joke on the following lines.

_____

_____

_____

_____

_____

Search Engines

Search engines are computer programs that look through databases or collections of information in an attempt to index and locate desired information by seeking keyword(s) typed in by the user. Since hundreds of new pages are created each day, it is impossible to catalog every new page on the Web. You can use the query box to enter keyword(s) (a description of the information you want to find), and the search engine will search only the keyword(s) matches in the directories' database for the information you requested. A search engine will also offer its own search tips or advanced search options to give you more efficiency and control over your searches. Because search engines use automated computer programs to index websites, they can contain links to billions of webpages, making them the most comprehensive source of search results. However, a weakness of the search engine is its ability to return so many results that you may need to sort through lots of results to find what is useful to you. Example search engines and their addresses are listed below. There are many more—search the Web for a current listing of search engines.

Search Engines	Address
Google	http://www.google.com
Yahoo!	http://www.yahoo.com
Bing (was MSN Search)	http://www.bing.com
Ask	http://www.ask.com

Exercise 7-4 Exploring search engines

1. Use all four of the previous listed search engines to ask: What are the health effects of excessive sitting?

2. What similarities and what differences did you find?

_____

_____

_____

_____

_____

Metasearch Engines

A metasearch engine submits your query to several other search engines and returns a summary of the results. Therefore, the search results you receive are a combined result of multiple searches. No two metasearch engines are alike. Some only search the most popular search engines while others also search lesser-known engines, newsgroups, and other databases. They also differ in how results are presented. Examples of metasearch engines and their addresses are listed below. There are many more—search the Web for a current listing of metasearch engines.

Metasearch Engines	Address
Vivisimo	http://vivisimo.com
MetaCrawler	http://www.metacrawler.com
Dogpile	http://www.dogpile.com
Ixquick	http://www.ixquick.com

Tips . . . For Searching the Web

- Use more than on search engine because they can each give you different results.

- Really learn how to use your search engine. Most search engines have a wide variety of advanced search options, tools, and services that are available, so search for them and try them so you will be equipped for more productive searches. Having this search knowledge will help you in school, on the job, and in your personal life.

- Get to know the basics of common web search terms. Use the Web to search for the following to make your searches more productive:

  - "Basic dictionary of Web search terms"—use these six words or rephrase them to conduct a search
  - Boolean search techniques help you conduct effective searches, based on the rules of computer database searching, and will cut many unrelated documents. Boolean logic (named after English mathematician George Boole) is a term used to describe logical operations that allow you to combine words and phrases into search statements to retrieve documents from searchable databases. Boolean logic consists of three search operators: OR, AND, and NOT.

    AND—Basic Boolean Search Operator—Using **AND** narrows your search by combining words. It will retrieve documents that use both the search words you specify, as follows:

    > stress AND self-talk

    OR—Basic Boolean Search Operator—Using **OR** broadens your search to include results that contain either of the words you type in. **OR** is a good tool to use when there are several common spellings or synonyms of a word, as in this example of synonymous words:

    > conservative OR republican

    NOT—Basic Boolean Search Operators—Using **NOT** will narrow a search by excluding specified search words. **NOT** retrieves documents that contain one, but not the other, of the search words you enter, as in this example:

    > Florida NOT travel

    Not all search engines and directories support Boolean search techniques. Consult the FAQ's (Frequently Asked Questions) on a search engine or directory's home page to learn if it will support these techniques.

  - Use the add and subtract symbols in your search

    Minus—Use the "-" sign to find pages that have one search word on them, if you need the search engine to exclude other words often associated with that search word. For example, searching nutrition-weight loss, tells the search engine that you only want pages that contain nutrition and not weight loss.
    Plus—Use the "+" sign if you have words that must be returned in all your search results. Place the plus sign in front of the word that you need included, such as, learning+brain. Your search results will give you items that have both words included.

(continued)

- – Use quotation marks around keywords or phrases to tell the search engine to only return pages that include these search words exactly in the order you typed them. If no results are found, most search engines will give you a list of results without quotes.

- Try rephrasing your query.

- Use the correct spelling, but . . . if you misspell a word, most search engines will ask you, "Did you mean...." and then correct your spelling for you.

- Use a Metasearch engine to get many search engines to provide you with results. (Several metasearch engines were listed prior to these tips.)

- Expand your web search to other countries in the world—go international.

- Ask an expert for help. You'll find experts on the Web, at your school, or maybe your computer savvy classmate.

Like the rest of technology, your Internet search tools are upgraded often. New websites will be reviewed and placed in the directories. Also, websites become outdated and can disappear quickly. Search engines will be improved and advertising will change constantly. If only we could keep updated as fast as technology!

Exercise 7-5 Using the add and subtract search technique

1. Use the add and subtract search technique to learn about brain-based learning. For example, type learning+brain in the search box.

2. Select a website article and write below the most interesting finding you learned about brain-based learning.

USING THE WEB FOR CLASS RESEARCH

Internet resources provide a gold mine of information, but it's not always factual or accurate. Experts caution that anyone can create and author a website and no laws govern its integrity. For example, according to health experts, Web information about weight loss is probably inaccurate or misleading more than half the time. With credibility issues like this in mind, read the following tips and questions to help you evaluate Internet information.

Tips . . . For Evaluating Information on the Web

- **Author credibility**—Who is the author and what are his credentials? Is the author an expert in the field? What evidence is there that the author is qualified to publish on this topic? What degree(s) does the author hold and in what fields? Is the author's work associated with and/or sanctioned by a credible organization or corporation? Does the author have other published writings? Has the author listed his credentials: years of experience, license or certification, job title, degrees, sponsoring organization, or other credentials for the purposes of allowing website users to determine his credibility?

- **Sponsoring organization**—Where does this information come from? Note that the last few characters in an email address usually indicate the type of organization or country to which the person belongs. For example if an email address ends in **.edu**, it is an educational organization, if it ends in **.gov**, it is a government organization, **.org** most often implies a nonprofit organization, **.mil**, for the military, **.net** for network, and **.com** for a commercial organization. Australia will use **.au** at the end, Canada—**.ca**, Italy—**.it**, Japan—**.jp**, and the United Kingdom—**.uk**. These address clues give you a partial idea. Check further to see if the document is on the author's personal website or if it is only part of the organization's official website.

- **Accurate information and data**—Most reliable Internet data can be tracked to the original sources such as the Census Bureau, The Bureau of Labor Statistics, or the Federal Administration on Aging. Does the author reference the data he uses? Is the information stated as a fact or a point of view? Does the author use data to support a controversial issue, political view or ideology? Does it appear that the author has neglected other important details or data? Is the author an authority on the information reported? Is it consistent with other authoritative reports? Is the data recent? Does the author provide proof? Is the information provided as a public service? Is it free from bias? Why is the author providing the information? How thorough is the information?

- When possible, check the online information against other sources.

- Don't give in to temptations to use the Internet as your sole resource. Always use other sources in addition to the Internet for your research. Webpage authoring software has made it easy for almost anyone to create a website. Many contain personal opinions, philosophies, and ideas, without editorial safeguards to ensure the accuracy and objectivity of the content.

- Question what you read. Keeping in mind some of the previous questions and some of your own will help you evaluate the reliability of many of the websites you are using for your research.

Style for Citing Online Information

Ask your instructor how she/he wants you to cite online information. Also refer to a current writing style manual to see examples of online citation. This text will give an example of the American Psychological Association (APA) style of citation. APA asks you to list the author's name (if known), date of the website information (if known), title of the page or article, name of website, the URL for the page you are referencing, and the date you accessed this page.

> Author's last name (if known), first initial. (Date published). Full title of work. *Name of website (in italics)*. [Retrieved] Date, [from] URL of website
>
> **Example:**
>
> Mayo Clinic staff. (2011, May 28). Positive thinking: Reduce stress by eliminating negative self-talk. *Mayo Clinic*. Retrieved February 12, 2012, from http://www.mayoclinic.com/health/positive-thinking/SR00009

Gather Information

Your instructor may offer suggestions regarding research sources. Your school library will offer a wealth of information. If you've used your library a lot, you already may know where to start. If you're uncertain about how to use all of the library's resources and services, ask if there are any scheduled orientation sessions. If none are scheduled, ask a librarian for help. Librarians are trained professionals who are there to help you. So instead of wasting valuable time looking for resources, ask the librarian for directions.

You'll want to use the library's card catalog system (most are computerized) to locate materials on your topic. You can locate books on your topic by the subject, author, or book title. If your library does not have the book you need, it may be available through the **Inter-Library Loan System,** a program that allows libraries throughout the United States and many other countries to share their resources. It may take several weeks to receive books through inter-library loans, another reason to start your research early.

You can locate magazine or journal articles by checking a general index to magazine articles, such as *The Reader's Guide to Periodical Literature*, or specialized indexes like the *New York Times Index* or the *Consumer Index*. Your library will not likely have all the magazines in the Reader's Guide, so from there you may have to use an "in-house" guide to see which magazines your library has. Magazines may be located with the bound periodicals or on microfilm or microfiche. Ask a librarian for help in using the microfilm or microfiche machines. If you need to use a resource that cannot be taken from the library, most libraries have copy machines so you can make copies of your most important information.

Information also may come from pamphlets, bookstores, interviews with experts, and even TV documentaries. There may be experts on your topic at your school or in the local community. Call local organizations, such as advocacy groups, government public affairs offices, unions, and professional associations. Even a brief phone conversation with an expert can yield interesting leads for further research. Try to find the most updated resources for your paper. This does not mean that you should avoid older resources, but the most valuable older resources will be mentioned even in the most recent works. So, it still makes sense to start with the most recent works. Collect more resources than you'll need, since you're likely to eliminate some of them by the time you're finished. Some instructors require a minimum number of resources.

Select Information from Your Resources

List each resource on a separate large-size index card (you can do this on a computer, too). Include the author, title, publisher, date and place of publication, and your evaluation of the resource. Keep careful track of the resources you review. If you're careful about noting your sources, you'll avoid the hassle of going back over all your books to find where you located a particular quote or fact.

Now that you have your resources, you'll want to skim them to locate information for your paper. Read your resources for major and supporting points, quotes, and key ideas. Briefly note these on the back side of the index card (or within your computer format) with page numbers. Accurate quotations with correct page numbers are essential for footnotes. It's generally best to use a separate index card for each idea you record. That way you can sort your note cards in the order that you'll present the ideas.

<u>**Figure 7-4**</u>
Basic Elements of a Research Paper Outline

I.   Introduction
    A. Thesis statement—the main point of your paper.
    B. Points that will back up your statement:
        1. First point.
        2. Second point.
        3. Third point.

II. Body
    A. First (strongest point)—topic sentence:
        1. Supporting detail.
        2. Supporting detail.
        3. Supporting detail.
    B. Second (next strongest point)—topic sentence:
        1. Supporting detail.
        2. Supporting detail.
        3. Supporting detail.
    C. Third point—topic sentence:
        1. Supporting detail.
        2. Supporting detail.
        3. Supporting detail.

III. Conclusion
    A. Restate thesis and summarize evidence.
    B. Concluding statement.

Construct an Outline

The actual writing of your paper will be much easier if you're working from a complete outline. A complete outline should contain every point you plan to make in your paper. You may want to include the elements suggested in Figure 7-4. Notice how these elements are applied to a topic in Figure 7-5.

Figure 7-5
Sample Research Paper Outline

Computers in Modern Manufacturing

I.   Introduction
    A.   Computers are an essential part of modern manufacturing.
    B.   Computers play the following critical roles in manufacturing:
        1.   Manage corporate information.
        2.   Assist in product design.
        3.   Assist in manufacturing process.

II. Body
    A.   Computers allow corporations efficient use of critical information:
        1.   Computer networking promotes sharing of ideas and information between workers.
        2.   Computer access to national and global sales and distribution information aids just-in-time and custom manufacturing.
        3.   Computers help work teams monitor manufacturing quality.
    B.   Computers assist product design (Computer-Aided Design):
        1.   Computers help compile consumer satisfaction information.
        2.   Computers make it possible to test products before they are built.
        3.   Computers reduce cost of design improvements.
    C.   Computers assist in manufacturing process (Computer-Aided Manufacturing):
        1.   Computers monitor quality of manufacturing process.
        2.   Computers help workers manage complex manufacturing.
        3.   Computers are necessary to run manufacturing robots.

III. Conclusion
    A.   Computers are essential for modern manufacturing, assisting information management, product design, and product manufacturing.
    B.   Global competitiveness may well depend on how well workers and management can make use of computer potential.

Write Rough Draft(s)

Actually, you probably will write at least a couple of drafts of your paper. **Drafts** are the transition from outline to complete paper. Once you have your outline complete, you need to connect your ideas with complete sentences and paragraphs. Write **transition sentences,** which help the reader move from one idea to the next. Transition sentences contain such words as *therefore, thus, then, because,* and *as a result of.* Let your reader know how your ideas are connected to one another. Remember to discuss each point of your paper in the same order you introduced it. After reading your introduction, your reader should know exactly what you're going to discuss and how. At any given point in the paper, the reader should know what information has been discussed and what is still to come. Save the draft of your conclusion until last; you may still make some minor changes in the body of the paper that will need to be reflected in the conclusion.

Be sure to document your sources, even when your paper is still in draft form—you don't want to run the risk of forgetting to do so later. Also, keep in mind that **plagiarism,** intentional or not, is a very serious offense, one that many schools punish with course failure and, occasionally, expulsion. Plagiarism is taking other people's work and presenting it as your own. You're required to give credit to the people and the sources whose words and ideas you use by providing accurate footnotes and references. Be aware of this especially when incorporating other people's opinions into your work. You must make it clear what ideas in your paper are your own and which belong to someone else.

Also, know that copying from the dictionary or any other reference work is plagiarism, even if no author's name appears on the cover of the book. You may incorporate facts in your paper, of course, because facts belong to no one; but using someone else's description of fact, word for word, is stealing. Be aware of your school's guidelines. When in doubt, give credit or consult with your instructor. The cost of being lazy about footnotes and sources is far too high.

Using someone else's ideas word for word should be footnoted and treated as a **direct quote.** To illustrate, Alexa correctly quoted the following passage from a newspaper article about computers in college education:

> *Computers are changing the way learning in college takes place. In a recent* Washington Post *article, Brook A. Masters observed, "What college students need now is someone to guide and motivate them as they obtain information."* [1]

Notice in the last example that Alexa properly introduced the reader to the author before offering the quote, as is appropriate when using direct quotes. She then footnoted the quotation. She could have elected to use a more extensive quotation, such as the following:

> *Computers are changing the way learning in college takes place. In a recent* Washington Post *article, Brook A. Masters observed:*
>
> > *Educators say the most basic change wrought by technology is in the professor's role. Professors primarily have been a source of knowledge, standing in front of the class and imparting what they know. But computer databases and networks are absorbing that task. What college students need now is someone to guide and motivate them as they obtain information.* [2]

Notice in the last example that Alexa indented the longer quotation, leaving out the quotation marks. Indent any quotation that is five or more lines long. Notice also that she still introduced the quote and footnoted it.

Another alternative is to restate the author's ideas in your own words, or **paraphrase.** Alexa paraphrases the last quote in the following example:

> *Computer technology is introducing new challenges and opportunities for college teaching. Computer databases and networks are rapidly replacing the professor's traditional role in the classroom as the source of knowledge. Educators argue that professors now must figure out how to help students make use of all the information they can find using computers.* [37]

Notice that, since the words in the last example were Alexa's, she left out quotation marks and an introduction to her source. However, since the ideas were not hers, she still footnoted the source from which they came. Footnoting is equally important in each of these examples—leaving out the footnote in any of these examples would have been plagiarism.

There are many styles to footnoting, listing resources, and writing a bibliography page. Your professor may recommend a specific style, such as the American Psychological Association (APA) style or the Modern Language Association (MLA) style. Check with your professor on this.

---

[1] Brook A. Masters, "Professors Turn to High Tech to Reach the Next Generation," *The Washington Post*, September 26, 1993, p. A6.
[2] ibid
[3] ibid

Revise and Polish

Evaluate your paper for grammar, sentence structure, spelling, and clarity. Your instructor may want your paper to conform to a particular style manual for research writing, so check with your instructor before writing your final draft. Reword passages that sound awkward or unclear. Consult a thesaurus if you want to improve your argument with stronger or more precise wording.

Make sure you have given credit to your sources. Have you placed quotation marks around quotes, or set off any quoted material that's five lines or more? Have you footnoted each quote or referenced item and used the proper style consistently?

Your final copy should be typed on white, 8-1/2" x 11" paper, on one side only. Most instructors prefer double-spaced papers, because they're easier to read and leave enough room for corrections and comments. Leave at least 1" margins all around. Create a title page that includes the paper title, your name, the course name and section number, your instructor's name, and the date.

MAKING PRESENTATIONS

Oral presentations are becoming a more common assignment in college. Both at school and work, they are an important way of presenting your ideas to others. After college, you will find that many careers require strong speaking and presentation skills. Presenting your ideas to your boss, fellow workers, potential clients, community meetings, and professional organizations are just some of the situations in which you want to present your best work to an audience. Just as with writing, careful research and plenty of work go into an effective presentation. However, presentations add the challenge of performing live in front of an audience. Therefore, careful preparation and plenty of practice also are essential.

During your college work, you may encounter different kinds of presentations. "I remember being part of a skit simulating a business meeting," Raul recalls. Mary remembers presenting the findings of a research paper. Terrence participated in a panel discussion. Luiz and three other students presented a stress management workshop. The variety of possibilities for presentations is endless. But the basics of preparation and presentation are similar for them all.

Tips . . . For Preparing a Presentation

- Prepare as seriously as you would for a writing assignment. Do the necessary research, including documenting any resources. It's true that you won't be able to present as much information as you would in a long writing assignment, but the information you present should be just as good. You'll have to be prepared to answer questions from your instructor or other students on the spot.

- Less is more. Most people try to present too much information. It's more effective to present one point in depth than to cover several inadequately. Be as clear as you can. Unlike the readers of your written reports, the listeners of an oral presentation don't have the opportunity to go back and reread information. You have to make sure they understand it the first time.

- Make sure your presentation, like your papers, is organized. Every presentation should have a definite beginning, middle, and end. Time-honored advice on speech-making went, "Tell 'em what you're going to say, say it, tell 'em what you said, then sit down!"

- Prepare an outline, notecards, visual displays, and anything else you need well in advance. You'll need them to practice with.

(continued)

- Consider ways to get the audience involved—for example, consider a quick survey or a short quiz about your topic before you begin and tell the class that the answers will come in your presentation.

- Rehearse. Practice giving your presentation to a couple of friends and ask them for feedback. Make sure your presentation fits comfortably into the time allowed for it. Be sure that any demonstrations you're planning actually will work where you'll be doing them. Will everyone be able to see? Will you need an outlet, an extension cord, a VCR, a large table, and so on? The more comfortable you feel about your report, the more relaxed you'll be when you give it.

After completing your preparations, you'll face the second set of challenges—the actual presentation. Many people are quite anxious about speaking in public—even if it's just in front of a few classmates.

Making effective oral presentations, like any other skill, can be learned. And like test anxiety, fears about public speaking can be overcome. You might even find that you enjoy it. Your school may offer classes in public speaking, perhaps in the English or fine arts departments. This is a great opportunity if you can find it. You'll get expert advice, and all of your fellow students will be struggling—and having fun—right along with you. You also may have opportunities to make oral presentations in other classes.

Tips . . . For Making Presentations

- Know that it's OK to be nervous. There's probably no one in the world who doesn't get a few butterflies in the stomach at the thought of speaking in front of a group. In his book *Psychology of Success,* Dr. Denis Waitley points out that feeling a little nervous before a performance or important task is good—it shows that you're keyed up and motivated to do a good job. When the "butterflies" turn to "moths," however, they can make things difficult. Keep in mind that every audience, no matter how big or small, wants you to do well. They're rooting for you. Catch your instructor's eye or that of a friendly classmate before you begin to speak. Know that you've got their support.

- Check your self-talk. When you think about speaking in front of a group, do you say to yourself, "I can't stand it" or "I'll just die if I have to present my paper in front of the class"? Rest assured that most people have made presentations to a class and survived. Some positive self-talk can help boost your confidence. Try telling yourself, "I'm gonna knock them out with this speech!" "I know I can do a great job!" Make positive self-talk a habit and you'll be amazed at the results.

- Make clear distinctions between ideas by pausing. Let the audience know what you're going to discuss next. You want the audience to follow your train of thought as easily as possible. Many people, when they're nervous, try to rush through their report. If you feel yourself rushing, pause. Take a couple of deep breaths and pick up where you left off. No one will notice a slight pause in the middle of an interesting talk. They'll be wondering what you're going to say next.

- Convey your interest, energy, and enthusiasm for the topic. Enthusiasm is contagious. Concentrate on the aspects of your topic that you're most eager to share with others.

(continued)

- Speak in a conversational, friendly manner. Don't use jargon or other complex words without first explaining them to your audience.

- Use visual aids. People love to look at things, and you may feel more relaxed if you know the audience isn't focused directly on you the whole time. Visual aids don't have to be charts or diagrams. Use photos, replicas, models. Elena had to give a presentation to her nutrition class about complex carbohydrates. She served an enormous platter of fruit, raw vegetables, and rolls to the class, and then began to talk. "Everyone enjoyed my talk, too," she remembers. "They said, 'Next time, do a report on chocolate!'"

Group presentations present their own challenges. Most of the previous suggestions also are crucial for group presentations. Panel discussions usually involve several students presenting their own work on topics that relate to the work of other members of the panel. One member should assume the role of panel chairperson and briefly introduce the members of the panel and the topics they'll discuss. The chair should offer a paragraph summary of how the presentations seem to be related to one another—something the audience can look for as the panel progresses. For every panel member to have enough time for his or her presentation, one member should assume the role of timekeeper and signal to the presenters when their time is running out. At the conclusion of the presentations, the chair can offer the audience an opportunity to ask questions of the panel.

Group presentations, such as skits, demonstrations, and experiments, often involve additional challenges that require their own planning and preparation. Make sure that you begin planning early so you'll have time to pursue creative ideas for your presentation. Consider ways that different members of the group can take advantage of their unique talents. If one student has good handwriting or is able to draw neat illustrations, take advantage of that talent. If another member is good with technology, consider making a video or computer presentation. Get everyone involved. Practice your presentation as a group until it runs smoothly. Working with a group, especially if you're demonstrating something, often can be complicated. Practicing is the only way of figuring what can go wrong before it's too late.

HIGHLIGHTS

In this section you've explored another major step on the road to college and career success. You've become acquainted with and practiced the basics of presenting your best work in both written and oral presentations.

You've begun to develop your skills as a writer by learning a step-by-step approach to writing essays, research papers, and reports. You've been encouraged to keep a journal to improve your writing skills and to use a computer to make the task of writing faster and easier. Most important, you've become aware of the importance of strong writing skills for college and career success.

You've also explored some tips on presenting your ideas to a live audience. You've examined ways to deal with the public-speaking anxiety that so many people have, as well as the ways to make your presentations lively, fun, and informative. Like writing, strong oral presentation skills are tools that will take you far.

DISCUSSION QUESTIONS

Note: Read the following discussion questions and activities **before** you read Section 7. This strategy will help you look for answers while you read.

1. Explain the importance of each of the five steps to good writing.
2. Is brainstorming more effective on an individual basis or with a group? Explain.
3. What are the benefits of an "idea notebook"?
4. Brainstorm a list of jobs you might find interesting.
5. Explain the components of organizing a paper.
6. What advice did the author give on topic sentences and writing a rough draft?
7. List what you think are the top five tips for writing rough drafts.
8. What two suggestions does the text give on taking a break while writing?
9. Why is "just starting" important when writing?
10. List five tips for revising.
11. Discuss five benefits of keeping a journal.
12. Concisely explain the six steps outlined in the text on research paper writing.
13. Write a brief summary on "Knowing the Ropes" to research paper writing.
14. What should you consider about turning in late papers?
15. What is a thesis statement? List five pointers on writing one.
16. Discuss other resources you can use for a research paper other than printed resources found in your school library.
17. List and discuss your favorite websites that you use to help you with course work, e.g., dictionaries, encyclopedias, study skills, libraries.
18. What is the difference between a web directory and a search engine?
19. What is the difference between the Web and the Internet?
20. What does double quotation marks placed around keywords or phrases do to a search? At what instances would you not use double quotation marks placed around keywords or phrases?
21. Explain the use of Boolean search operators.
22. What is a metasearch engine?
23. Discuss the major sources of bias that you have noted while researching on the Web.
24. Are you ever tempted to use the Web as your sole resource? Why?
25. Explain plagiarism and the use of facts and opinions in your own writing.
26. Explain the different formats used for quoting brief remarks, quotations five or more lines long, and paraphrasing another author's idea.
27. What styles of footnoting have you used? Which do you prefer and why?
28. Concisely state six tips for preparing a presentation.
29. What do you think are the top three features of a terrific speech? Explain.
30. Concisely state six tips for making presentations.

SECTION 8

Sharing Your World

231

WHAT'S IN IT FOR YOU

College is a new environment and a new experience. You're working and spending time with lots of different people. This section will tell you more about getting along with people in college and work. You'll learn about some of the negative attitudes so common today that prevent people from getting along as well as they could, and how you can recognize these attitudes in yourself. To try and make the world a better place, it's best to examine ourselves first. There are many negatives in life you can't change, though, such as crime. This section will teach you ways to avoid and protect yourself from crime. In short, this is a section on both sharing your world and protecting it.

In this section you'll explore:

- The advantage of our diverse world
- Ways to overcome stereotypes, prejudice, and discrimination
- Tips for understanding and relating to students with diverse backgrounds
- The significance of body language
- Effective listening skills
- How to communicate assertively
- Strategies for dealing with sexual harassment
- How to protect yourself from crime
- Tips to protect yourself from rape and date rape

TAKING ADVANTAGE OF OUR DIVERSE WORLD

The world is a mixture of people of different ethnicities, backgrounds, abilities, and faiths. In addition to all the other challenges you're facing now, you're being exposed to a much more diverse community of people than you have ever experienced before. You're sharing a good part of your life with students from different backgrounds, nationalities, religions, and cultures. This new diversity is hard for some students to get used to. They have always gone to school and to work with people "just like them." The fact is, despite all the differences you'll discover between yourself and others, students from all over have a lot in common. For example, your fellow students all enrolled in school to build a solid foundation for their future.

It's easier for everyone to achieve their educational goals when they don't have to deal with prejudice and discrimination; unfortunately, almost everyone does have to deal with them in one form or another.

College is the ideal environment in which to get to know people from other cultures. College is, after all, a learning experience, and learning is not confined to the classroom. Think of the entire school environment as your classroom, where every person has something to teach you. Using this opportunity to develop good relationships with others will prepare you for working in a diverse workplace.

America is one of the most culturally diverse nations on earth. People of African, Asian, Latino, Arabic, European, and Native American ancestry enrich schools in America. Your college experience may be the first opportunity you have to mingle with people from a variety of other countries or other races. But diversity is not just about getting to know people from other lands. It's about getting to know people who are different from you in many ways—students with physical challenges, those who are older than you, those from a different religious or economic background. It's human nature to prefer things that are familiar; people feel comfortable with others from their own background. But no matter where you go or what you do in life, you'll always be in contact with others who are different, and it's essential to learn how to respect those differences. Remember, to other people you are the one who seems different.

> ~Clara~
> **(an exchange student from Ethiopia)**
>
> *When I arrived on campus, I was excited, but it didn't take me long to see that I would have to learn to like new foods, get used to a different way of thinking, and adopt new ways to relate to people. It was hard to make friends at first because people avoided me. I looked different from most people and I wore clothes from my country. But that didn't mean I didn't want to be treated like everyone else. Now I have friends I hang out with, but it really took a long time to meet people who liked me for who I am.*

AVOIDING STEREOTYPES, PREJUDICE, AND DISCRIMINATION

Stereotyping means just what Terri said—attributing the perceived characteristics of a category of people to every individual within that category, leaving no room for the specific qualities within each person. Therefore, because of the stereotyped notion that all tall people can play basketball, Terri's friends assume that she must, too. Other stereotyped notions include the ideas that people of Latino heritage all have fiery tempers, that all Asians are good at math, that women are crybabies, that men are insensitive, that Jews are cheap, that Irish people drink too much, and so on.

> ~Terri~
>
> *I get really fed up sometimes when I go to school and someone asks me to play basketball and is shocked when I say "no thanks." I really don't like many sports. Plus, the last time I tried to play basketball, I stepped on people's feet, tripped, and never hit the hoop. But people assume that, because I'm 6'4", I must love to play basketball and should be really good at it. I'm supposed to be "a natural." Well, maybe a lot of tall people play well, but I don't. I'm an individual, and I wish people would treat me like one, instead of assuming that just because I'm tall, I should play basketball because they need a tall center.*

Where do stereotypes come from? It's hard to say. In some cases they are an exaggeration of a cultural characteristic—for example, in Japan, learning is very highly regarded. Students in Japan usually go to school much longer hours than those in the United States. And whereas in this country students are encouraged to be very creative and freethinking, Japanese schools tend to stress the exacting disciplines of science and math. Students who grew up in Japan, therefore, tend to be strong in these subjects, because they receive a lot of instruction in them. When you exaggerate this idea, however, you get the notion that "all Asians are good at math." Anyone whose last name sounds Asian is supposed to be a whiz at anything involving numbers, even if they've gone to the same classes you have and have been taught the same way you have since kindergarten.

Exercise 8-1 Stereotypes

Are there any common stereotypes about your religious or cultural heritage? What are they? How do you think people got these ideas? How do these stereotypes make you feel?

Since it's hard to know where and how all stereotypes begin, a lot of people don't even question them. They just "know" that group is lazy, that group is mean, and these people are stupid. As you can see, many stereotypes are very negative and simplistic. People end up disliking others based on stereotypical ideas that aren't even true. So-called hate crimes continue to be in the news. College students have had racial slurs and other hateful phrases spray-painted on their dormitory doors. Others literally have been attacked and beaten on the street because some people didn't like who and what they were. Less harsh, but still painful, is exclusion—being left out because you're from the wrong group.

Prejudice is "pre-judgment." It's judging a person based on what you *think* you know about them or the group of people they come from. Prejudice generally refers to *negative* assumptions and judgments about people. It's letting stereotypes do the thinking for you—and that's not thinking at all. Prejudice is also based on ignorance, assuming the worst about someone you know little or nothing about. It's assuming your new lab partner is less intelligent than you are, because she's a female. It's treating a blind or deaf person like a child, because you think all people with disabilities are "slow." It's assuming that the new person in your study group is a drug dealer, because he comes from a particular part of town. Notice that in all these instances you don't actually know anything about the person, you have a *preconceived notion* about them in your mind, and you're assuming your idea is right.

How do you feel when people assume things about you? For instance, suppose you overheard someone say that you must be really stuck-up and think you're better than your friends, because you decided to enroll in college? Would this be a fair statement? How would this comment make you feel?

Prejudice and Discrimination

Discrimination is action based on prejudice; it is the unequal treatment of members of a group. Discrimination usually occurs against the members of "minority" groups, when members of the "majority" deny privileges to members of another group. Discrimination can be as subtle as avoiding eye contact to excluding others from participation in activities. Exclusion can be as subtle as "forgetting" to issue invitations to members of a certain group, or as blatant as slurs and warnings scrawled on the walls of a house. An

> ~*Paolo*~
>
> *I decided to go to summer school to get ahead. I thought I'd try apartment living for the summer. I called about a few apartments that were advertised and finally I found one that was available. The landlord told me how to get there over the phone. I arrived within 10 minutes, and the landlord was outside the building like he said he'd be. He asked me in a rather unfriendly voice, "What do you want?" I explained that I was the person who had called to see the apartment. He told me it was already rented. I told him that I had just called, and he yelled, "It's already rented!" It was obvious that he didn't know I was black when he first heard my voice on the phone, and if he had, he wouldn't have asked me to see the place.*

infamous example of this kind of treatment is the burning of crosses on the yards of black people who have moved into a predominantly white neighborhood. People who discriminate against others usually justify their actions which makes them feel that their actions are proper.

Exercise 8-2 My own experience

Have you ever been the victim of discrimination? What happened?

Relating to Students with Diverse Backgrounds

Prejudice, intolerance, and discrimination are too much a part of all our lives. To make the very most of college, learn to accept and respect other cultures and other people. It can only make your life richer, and getting to know people from a diversity of backgrounds is one of the best educations you can ever receive. What can you do to make the most of the diversity of your school, and to combat prejudice and discrimination wherever you see it?

Put yourself in the shoes of these people. How would you feel in their situation?

- Anne stood outside a school basketball court watching some guys shoot hoops. They knew her but did not ask her to join in, even though they knew she had been captain of the state's championship girls' basketball team. "You can't keep up with us guys," they said. Anne knew she could but wasn't given a chance to play.

- After class finished, a couple of students were recruiting others to play volleyball. Jon loved to play, but he wasn't asked. Because he was in a wheelchair, his classmates either didn't think of asking him or didn't think he'd be able to play. Even if they did invite him, would they be willing to accommodate him? Do they know to what degree he needs assistance?

- The biology instructor asked everyone to choose partners for a lab experiment. No one would choose Mai, the new Vietnamese student, as a partner, so the instructor finally assigned her to work with someone.

- Mark's psychology class was discussing homosexuality. A lot of the students were voicing derogatory comments and saying other prejudicial things about gays. Mark wondered what the class would think if they knew that he was gay.

- Sam wanted to join a study group but, because he had dyslexia, a reading disability, he was afraid to ask if he could join. He thought the other students might get impatient with him.

- During a class discussion in sociology, the topic of welfare families was brought up. Several students made remarks to the effect that they thought people on welfare were lazy, trying to get something for nothing. Liza didn't know what to say. Her family was on welfare after her dad left her mom with four kids and no money. Liza knew how hard her mother worked to make the best life she could for her kids. She knew that most people on welfare really want to work and get out of the system. But she didn't know how her classmates would respond if she spoke up.

- Some of the students in Fatima's carpool make jokes and put-downs when they drive by the mosque downtown on the way to school. Fatima is a Muslim and feels resentful of the remarks made about her religion and heritage.

- Jason found it very hard to make friends when he enrolled in school. Two years before, he'd been in a bad accident that had given him burns over 40 percent of his body. His classmates wouldn't even make eye contact with him.

College is a much more rewarding experience for everyone when they can focus on their studies and not on the negative attitudes of others. Prejudice and discrimination are problems that have plagued mankind for centuries, but you can do your bit to bring down the walls of prejudice wherever you see them.

Many companies have realized the importance of effective work relationships in improving work satisfaction, team work, productivity, and in opening world markets. Companies often involve their employees in culture diversity training to reduce prejudice and discrimination and to improve work relationships. Language and culture courses are often taught to employees to prepare them to enter world markets. We are fast beginning to see that our market is the world.

> **~Tayo~**
>
> I finally got so fed up I had to say something. I take the bus to class with three friends. Two of them kept making nasty remarks under their breath about my friend Beth, because she weighs almost 250 pounds. It's really painful for Beth to hear people comment on her appearance like that. So one day, after she got off at her stop, I turned to my other friends and said, "Look, maybe you don't mean any real harm by it, but I don't want to hear you two insulting Beth anymore. I'm her friend and it hurts to hear you talk about her like that." They couldn't believe I spoke up. I wasn't nasty about it, I just said what was on my mind. I'm sure they still call Beth names behind her back, but they never do it now when I'm around. I'm glad I said something. A real friend speaks up.

Tips . . . For Eliminating Prejudice and Discrimination and Improving Relationships

- Learn to recognize prejudicial attitudes in yourself. In what stereotypes do you believe? Where did you learn them? Make an effort to treat people as individuals and get to know them on that basis. Would you want to be thought in terms of a stereotype of some cultural or social group? Keep in mind the Golden Rule: *Do unto others as you would have them do unto you.*

- Look for the best in others.

- Practice inclusion. Make an effort to reach out to people. A popular saying goes, "If you're not part of the solution, you're part of the problem." How can you be part of the solution and fight prejudice? Reach out to others. Invite a disabled friend to join in your softball game; that wheelchair might be hiding a mean pitching arm. Even if she chooses not to play, she'll appreciate being asked; everyone wants to feel like they belong.

- Be the person who asks the new student to be your lab partner or asks him out for a soda after class.

- When you hear your friends or other people making racial remarks or other put-downs, speak up. Let them know you're offended by that kind of talk. It takes courage sometimes to speak up and voice your feelings, but it's worth it. Many times you'll find that someone else wanted to speak up as you did, but didn't have the nerve.

- Learn more about other people. Read books, go to cultural fairs, talk to people. Make friends with people from different backgrounds and ask them questions.

(continued)

- Get involved. The more kinds of people you're exposed to, the more you'll learn about them. Remember, prejudice is based in ignorance; some prejudiced people hate others they've never even met. Many campuses now have student organizations devoted to reducing discrimination and hate crimes and to increasing tolerance and respect for others. If there is a group like this in your school, join it. If not, why not start one?

- Be kind, remembering how fragile the human spirit is.

What else can you do to reduce or eliminate prejudice?

COMMUNICATING

While large groups of people often don't get along because of ignorance, individuals are frequently kept apart because of a lack of communication. Good communication skills are vital in your career, college, and life. These skills help people get along better and allow you to express yourself effectively when things are not going along so well. Communication is a two-way street, an ebb and flow of information between two or more people. Therefore, you need to master two specific skills—listening and speaking. When you listen effectively, you truly understand what the other person is saying. When you can speak effectively, you can let others know exactly what you think and how you feel, in a way that gets the point across without offending. Good communicators avoid the problems that arise from misunderstandings. How good a communicator are you?

> **~Ray~**
>
> *My girlfriend and I get along well most of the time. Sometimes we argue, though. The funny thing is, it seems like we never argue about the big stuff—it almost always turns out that one of us didn't understand the other. We had a fight once and didn't speak for three days, because she thought I was picking her up to go to the movies and I thought we were meeting there. Each of us thought we'd been stood up. Sometimes we just don't communicate.*

When you listen effectively, you truly understand what the other person is saying. This section will introduce you to **reflective listening** to help you gain the skills to become a more effective listener. When you speak effectively, you can let others know exactly what you think and how you feel, in a way that gets the point across without offending. This type of communication is called **assertive communication.** Skills to help you become more assertive will also be introduced in this section.

Good communicators avoid problems that arise from misunderstandings. When you become more assertive and a better listener you will have fewer misunderstandings. Complete Exercise 8-3 to assess your listening effectiveness.

Exercise 8-3 Listening skills assessment

Effective listening is probably the foundation for good relationships and good communication between people. How are your listening skills? Complete the following assessment to become more aware of ways that you may want to improve your listening skills.

Directions: Circle the number that best indicates the frequency of your involvement in each of the twenty statements below. Be honest; your answer should represent what you actually do, not what you wish you would do.

Use the following scale:

1-Never   2-Usually Never   3-Sometimes   4-Almost Always   5-Always

1.	Do you refrain from moralizing and preaching?	1	2	3	4	5
2.	Do you encourage others to talk?	1	2	3	4	5
3.	Do you refrain from giving advice until you understand the whole story and advice is requested?	1	2	3	4	5
4.	Do you listen equally well whether the person is a man or woman, young or old, or someone who is not your friend?	1	2	3	4	5
5.	Do you try to put yourself in the other person's shoes when listening rather than to make judgments from your own point of view?	1	2	3	4	5
6.	When someone is speaking, do you remove all distractions out of sight and mind and give them your undivided attention?	1	2	3	4	5
7.	Do you look at the person speaking, occasionally smiling or nodding your head?	1	2	3	4	5
8.	Do you let the other person finish before you speak?	1	2	3	4	5
9.	Do you try to understand, beyond the actual words, what message is being conveyed?	1	2	3	4	5
10.	If the speaker hesitates, do you encourage him or her to go on?	1	2	3	4	5
11.	Do you restate an idea and ask if you have the proper understanding?	1	2	3	4	5
12.	Do you really want to listen to people?	1	2	3	4	5
13.	Do you listen even though you can anticipate what is going to be said?	1	2	3	4	5
14.	Do you ask questions in order to have an idea explained more fully?	1	2	3	4	5
15.	Do you ask for clarification of words and terms with which you are unfamiliar?	1	2	3	4	5
16.	Do you refrain from making immediate evaluation of communicated ideas and wait until the whole problem has been disclosed?	1	2	3	4	5
17.	Are you genuinely interested in people?	1	2	3	4	5
18.	Do you allow people to express their emotions freely, such as anger, hurt, frustration, sadness?	1	2	3	4	5
19.	Do you avoid confrontation until the problem is understood and a favorable rapport is developed?	1	2	3	4	5
20.	Do you try to help people solve their own problems?	1	2	3	4	5

SUBTOTALS _____

TOTAL (sum of the subtotals) _____

LISTENING RATING: **SCORING:** Divide the total by 20. Round your answer to the nearest whole number. (Examples: 3.4 = 3, 3.5 = 4) Use the following scale to identify your listening level:

5 = Actively listens

4 = Usually listens

3 = Occasionally listens

2 = Seldom listens

1 = Never listens

(Total) _____ /20 = _____ (Score)

Score rounded to nearest whole number:

After completing the listening assessment, what did you discover about your own listening skills?

REFLECTIVE LISTENING

In Section 5, you learned about active listening—listening effectively and attentively in class to understand and absorb as much of the material as you can. When communicating with others, you can also use **reflective listening,** an active form of listening which communicates that you understand what the speaker has said. For example, note the following student statement and instructor response:

Student Statement

"I can't stand Mr. Mames, my math instructor. He treats me like I'm an idiot every time I ask him for help."

Instructor Response

"He really makes you feel stupid."

The instructor was actively engaged in listening and reflected to the student what she understood. Reflective listening also communicates respect for the speaker. The instructor's response did not address whether or not she agreed with the student's evaluation, just that she genuinely understood. Too many of us just *hear* when people talk. Have you ever been in a conversation where you were paying only half-attention? Suddenly you realize you don't know what they've been talking about for the last few minutes.

Perhaps you're too eager to speak to really listen to the other person. A famous writer once noted that, for most people, the opposite of speaking isn't listening, it's waiting. Waiting for their turn to speak, that is. Reflective listeners not only listen to what's being spoken, they're paying attention to what's being said without words. That is, they pay attention to other people's body language. Gestures can tell you a lot.

Paraphrasing

Reflective listeners also communicate their understanding and attention by an attentive body posture, nodding their head, commenting, or paraphrasing what someone else has said. When you paraphrase (i.e., repeat a statement in your own words), you really let someone know that you've been paying attention and know the message he's trying to get across—you are reflecting. Paraphrasing allows you to communicate your understanding without commenting or giving judgment on what's being said.

Paraphrasing is a good communication technique to use when you know you should be responding to someone but you're not quite sure how. A lot of people have a problem deciding how to respond in a conversation. "I would just sit across the table and nod my head when my friend was telling me about her breakup," says Rhonda. "My neck was getting sore!" Kevin has the same problem. "I want my friends to feel like they can confide in me, but when they do, all I can think of to say is 'uh-huh, uh-huh.' I feel like I should be saying or doing something, but I don't know what."

Paraphrasing can be helpful in many situations. You can use it to clarify an assignment from your instructor: "So you want us to complete our rough draft by *this* Friday?" "You mean the paper has to be on one of those three topics?" Effective paraphrasing is specific and brief. In an argument, paraphrasing helps you keep clear about who's said what, without letting emotions distort what's been said. Look at the following examples of paraphrasing.

With a friend

Vanessa:	"So he said he had to deduct a grade because the paper was more than three days late. That was so unfair, I just walked right out of the classroom."
You:	"You walked out because you were really upset, huh?"

With an instructor

Mr. Juarez:	"Because next week is a vacation week, all papers have to be handed in Friday by five o'clock. No exceptions."
You:	"This Friday by five. No exceptions."

In an argument

Cathy:	"I am so furious with you! You never pick your stuff up off the floor or do anything to keep the room clean."
You:	"You're angry with me because you think I don't help out enough."

Did you notice that, regardless of the viewpoint, the example responses only paraphrased the content of the message? Even if the active listener disagrees with the stated viewpoint, judgment is reserved. It really doesn't hurt to withhold your opinion at this point. How do you think each individual feels when someone simply communicates understanding? The person may have been expecting an argument. Don't you feel more at ease talking with someone who really listens to your argument, instead of immediately jumping into her own?

Exercise 8-4 Paraphrasing

How are your paraphrasing skills? Check them by writing a response that paraphrases each of the statements below. Remember that effective paraphrasing reserves judgment, even when you're responding to an upsetting or controversial statement.

Statement 1:	"I really can't stand that instructor. Imagine giving us an assignment over the long weekend! I know she only gave me that "D+" because she doesn't like me."

Your paraphrase:

_____
_____
_____
_____
_____
_____
_____
_____
_____
_____

Statement 2:   "I really like my classes, but I'm not doing as well as I could. Maybe I'm not cut out for college. I seem to have lost my self-confidence."

Your paraphrase:

_____

_____

_____

_____

_____

_____

Try paraphrasing the next time someone brings a problem to you—even if it's a problem he/she has with you.

READING BODY LANGUAGE

Reflective listening involves paying attention to both the spoken and the unspoken message. Sometimes body language confirms the message being spoken. Other times it's saying something quite different—and that's a message in itself. Reading people's unspoken messages takes practice, but, because so much of body language is instinctive and universal, you can learn it fairly quickly. How do you move when you're expressing different emotions? If you roll your eyes, shrug your shoulders, smile, or frown, what are you communicating?

~Kirsten~

Tony, in my study group, kept asking me for my notes because he skipped a few classes. He always has a great excuse. One day I forgot them on purpose. We were sitting in the lounge with our group and I was really perturbed with him. He asked me what was wrong. I said, "Nothing." He didn't buy that. He told me he could tell that I was upset—it was written all over me. I guess I looked as perturbed as I felt. I wasn't smiling and my arms and legs were crossed tightly—I looked mad. So we talked and I told him that I didn't think he was contributing much to the group any more. He promised not to miss classes any more. I'm glad he pushed me to talk because now the group's doing better and so is Tony.

Tips . . . For Reading Body Language

• Is the person you're talking to making eye contact? When people are upset or don't want to be in a particular situation, they tend to avoid eye contact. Other people have difficulty looking others in the eye because they feel shy or nervous.

• Does the person to whom you're talking seem tense or stiff? When people are upset, they often knit their brows together or clench their hands in a way that expresses their inner tension.

• Does the person to whom you're talking fidget a lot? Tapping fingers, twirling hair, and other gestures can indicate nervousness.

• Does the person to whom you're talking sit back in her chair or lean forward? When people are very involved in a conversation, they tend to lean in toward the people they're talking to. Leaning back in a chair can signal that a person feels removed from the conversation or is feeling very relaxed.

Many books are available on the fascinating subject of body language. Your school or community library should have a couple of them. You'll be surprised what body language can tell you.

Reflective listeners respond to both spoken and unspoken messages being communicated. Sometimes what is being communicated is emotion. It may seem difficult to choose the right words when someone makes an emotional statement, but in addition to paraphrasing, you can also state how they seem to be feeling—"You're really frustrated." You'll find that people appreciate your understanding ear. Most people aren't looking for advice, just a "sounding board" for their ideas and emotions. Keep listening reflectively and with empathy, in a nonjudgmental way, whether you're listening to an instructor give an assignment or to a friend who's crying on your shoulder. To be nonjudgmental means to avoid giving advice, evaluating the rightness or wrongness of views, or arguing your point of view. It means that you accept the rights of others to see things the way they do. This does *not* mean that you must agree with them; rather, you simply let them express their views.

Remember the basic points of being an attentive listener: give people your undivided attention—put aside the book, turn off the television, radio, or stereo—when someone is speaking to you. You really can't give your full attention to two things at once. Make eye contact; this action says "I'm listening to you now."

Eye contact and an "open" posture communicate that you are listening attentively. An open posture means that you are facing and leaning toward the person; in this way, you communicate interest and attentiveness. Be sure also to respond to others in a clear, moderate tone of voice. Harsh, loud tones won't get your point across any faster.

Exercise 8-5 Practicing reflective listening

Purpose: to develop skills in listening, paraphrasing, and observing nonverbal communication.

Directions: Choose a classmate or partner. Starting with the first sentence, one partner should finish the statement; the other partner responds with reflective listening/paraphrasing and, when necessary, stating the feeling (as noticed in the other's body language). Then, switch roles.

1. My biggest worry about school is _____ ,
    because _____ .

2. The problem that disturbs me most in this world is _____ ,
    and I think we could resolve this problem by _____ .

3. Discrimination against _____
    can be overcome by _____ .

4. I want to learn more about _____

5. Equal rights for women is not only a woman's issue; it is a man's issue, because
    _____ .

6. I believe that discrimination exists in America, because _____
    _____ .

How would you rate your reflective listening skills? Did you ever feel awkward? How does your partner rate his or her active listening skills? How did he or she feel?

BEING ASSERTIVE

The other side of effective communication is speaking assertively. At times you will want to express your point of view to others. Communicating your thoughts and feelings in an assertive way means standing up for yourself and being direct while still respecting others. Whether you're telling a date what you want or do not want to do, expressing your views in class, presenting a persuasive speech, or discussing issues with co-workers, being able to express yourself assertively will make you a strong communicator. How are your assertiveness skills? Complete the following assessment to become more aware of ways that you may want to become more assertive.

Exercise 8-6 Assertiveness skills assessment

Directions: Circle the number that best indicates how you would generally respond to each of the following situations. Be honest; your answer should represent what you actually do, not what you wish you would do. Use the following scale:

1-Never 2-Usually Never 3-Sometimes 4-Almost Always 5-Always

1.	If I am upset with friends/parents/roommates, I directly express these feelings to them.	1	2	3	4	5
2.	I can readily say "no" to friends' requests for help when I am overextended.	1	2	3	4	5
3.	If someone's cigarette smoke is bothering me, I would readily ask them to stop.	1	2	3	4	5
4.	I can confidently invite someone of the opposite sex out on a date. (If married, respond as if single.)	1	2	3	4	5
5.	I am able to confidently tell my date/spouse how I feel about things he/she does that irritate me.	1	2	3	4	5
6.	I will readily ask my roommate/spouse to share household responsibilities.	1	2	3	4	5
7.	If my dinner in a restaurant was not prepared as ordered, I would readily request that it be corrected.	1	2	3	4	5
8.	I can confidently change my mind when appropriate.	1	2	3	4	5
9.	I can confidently ask others for assistance.	1	2	3	4	5
10.	I readily ask questions in class.	1	2	3	4	5
11.	I can easily communicate with most persons regardless of their status.	1	2	3	4	5
12.	I can confidently return a defective piece of merchandise.	1	2	3	4	5
13.	I can confidently request a raise or a promotion.	1	2	3	4	5
14.	If my boss made, in my opinion, an unfair request, I would express my feelings to him/her about this.	1	2	3	4	5

15. If someone behind me was constantly talking during a lecture,
    I would confidently ask them to stop. 1   2   3   4   5

16. I maintain eye contact during conversations. 1   2   3   4   5

17. I can confidently offer my opinion in a class group discussion. 1   2   3   4   5

18. I can confidently initiate conversations in most situations. 1   2   3   4   5

19. I graciously accept compliments. 1   2   3   4   5

20. When someone cuts in line in front of me, I can appropriately
    confront the situation. 1   2   3   4   5

SUBTOTALS _____

TOTAL (sum of the subtotals) _____

5 = Always Assertive
4 = Usually Assertive
3 = Occasionally Assertive
2 = Seldom Assertive
1 = Never Assertive

(Total) _____ /20 = _____ (Score)

Score rounded to nearest whole number:

After completing the assertiveness assessment, what did you discover about your own assertiveness skills?

Qualities of an Assertive Communicator

When things aren't clear, assertive communicators will ask questions. They know that they can't speak knowledgeably about topics they know little about. Many people fall into the trap of trying to discuss things they don't know about; they're afraid to ask questions, afraid it will make them look "dumb." Asking questions helps you get a better understanding of a situation so that when you assert yourself it is based on a clear understanding. In addition to asking questions, assertive communicators also use active listening. It shows that they are paying attention and they're interested in learning more before they express their views.

Being assertive doesn't mean you're right all the time. One of the qualities of an effective communicator is being able to say, "I was wrong about that" and "I'm beginning to see your point" and "I never looked at it that way before." Changing your mind is a sign of active thinking. Assertive communicators know that the point of conversation is to exchange ideas, not to win a debate. Therefore, they feel confident enough to admit when they're wrong, and they don't need to press the point when others don't agree with them.

Tips . . . For Assertive Communication

- Use "I" statements to show ownership of your views—for example: "I believe that . . . ." or "I get frustrated about . . ." Not "You frustrate me." Assertive communicators own their own feelings; they don't blame others for how they feel.

- Make eye contact when you speak to people; it shows you're paying attention.

- Speak in a moderate tone of voice. Shouting doesn't make your point any quicker, but it displays a lack of confidence in yourself and your ideas.

- Listen before you speak. Effective communicators like to listen before they join in the conversation. The more you listen, the more you know. The more you know, the more you can contribute.

- Don't interrupt others. Let them finish speaking before you start.

- Learn to make requests and share your feelings without becoming angry or accusing. "Could you please turn the stereo down? I need to study this section" is more effective than shouting, "Turn that down now! Can't you see I'm trying to study?"

- Think before you speak. Consider how to phrase what you want to say. Consider your beliefs, feelings, and needs as well as others'. Thinking before you speak will help you express yourself more appropriately. Assertive communicators are thoughtful communicators.

When you're assertive you will be more confident about expressing your concerns and wishes in difficult situations. An assertive statement is firm while being respectful. In the following sections you will read about dealing with sexual harassment and date rape. Your ability to assert yourself is a primary form of protection against both of these violations of your person.

Other Communication Styles

The best way of expressing yourself is in an assertive way. Communicating assertively, like anything else, is a skill that must be learned. People who haven't learned this skill generally communicate in one of two other ways; they tend to be either nonassertive or aggressive. Both styles are considered to be ineffective and can negatively affect human relationships. These three styles—assertive, nonassertive, and aggressive—are referred to as both communication and behavior styles, because they are ways of speaking and acting. You can assert yourself in both the way you speak and the way you behave.

Nonassertive individuals are usually timid and allow others to violate their rights by failing to express their honest feelings and thoughts. They tend to permit others to "walk all over" them. Nonassertive communicators want to please others and avoid conflict. When you're afraid to express your views, you're nonassertive. Sometimes fears, real or imagined, are factors in keeping you quiet. A nonassertive person will keep silent or speak timidly instead of running the risk of upsetting others or risking their displeasure. "I have trouble telling my roommate when her stereo's up too loud," says Michelle. "She was blasting her music last week when I was studying for a test and it took me an hour to work up the courage to ask her to turn it down."

The opposite type of communication style is **aggressiveness.** People who are aggressive often feel as insecure as nonassertive people, but they express these feelings by responding in ways that do not show respect for others—they often "put down" others to make their point. Aggressive people tend to shout or speak harshly and to get impatient. While nonassertive people think so much about others that they find it hard to express themselves at all, aggressive people think about themselves first and, therefore, don't think much about the feelings of others.

In contrast, individuals who are **assertive** will stand up for their personal views and express their thoughts, feelings, and beliefs in direct, honest, and appropriate ways that show respect for others. Assertiveness is effective because you can consider others and still get your point across.

DEALING WITH SEXUAL HARASSMENT

Most women experience sexual harassment in the form of unwelcome sexual advances, requests for sexual favors, and other forms of unwanted verbal and physical conduct of a sexual nature. The conduct can be as blatant as grabbing or touching, or as subtle as hints and suggestions. Pervasive displays of nude or pornographic pictures at the workplace also have been ruled as harassment. The harassment can be carried out in forms of demanding sexual favors for grades or promotion, or to maintain employment. Or it can be an environment that is so infused with unwelcome sexual conduct that it creates an intimidating or hostile atmosphere.

> **~Johanna~**
>
> *I'd read about sexual harassment before, but I was really shocked when it happened to me. The boss at my old job made a lot of rude remarks and suggestions. I was so shocked I hardly knew what to do.*

As you might suspect, more women file charges of sexual harassment than men. The evidence also shows that women are more frequently exposed to sexual harassment than men. Studies have shown that sexual harassment is more about power than sex, and about the harasser's feelings of insecurity.

If you are harassed sexually at school, report it first to a school counselor. This person can guide you to your school's procedures for complying with sexual harassment laws. Your local Office for Civil Rights and the Equal Employment Opportunity Commission also can guide you in the proper procedures for taking action against sexual harassment.

Sexual harassment is unacceptable conduct and should not be tolerated. It builds barriers between men and women. Both sexes need to be more aware of sexual harassment. Both need to assert themselves when they are offended by inappropriate conduct at school, at work, and in other areas of life. Both men and women need to expect respect from each other and to speak up when they see sexual harassment occurring.

PROTECTING YOURSELF FROM CRIME

We expect others to respect our rights and our human dignity. We expect others will follow the Golden Rule. These are worthy expectations, but unfortunately not everyone uses these principles to guide their lives. Many people think of crime as something that happens to "somebody else." Amy was shocked and frightened by her attack—her friend "seemed" nice, and she wasn't on the alert for potential danger. No one deserves to be the victim of crime. Everyone, however, should try to actively protect themselves against it.

> **~Amy~**
>
> *A bunch of my friends and I were out drinking. I ended up going with a guy friend to his car to drink some more and talk. He started kissing me and I was shocked about how quickly he was getting to the point of sexual intercourse. It happened so quickly I didn't have time to respond. I told him several times to stop but he wouldn't. I know I shouldn't have been in this position, but I didn't think it would turn out this way. He apologized later and said that he would never do this to anyone but that he was just so drunk.*

As you start your college career, you are taking responsibility for your life in many new ways. Keeping yourself safe should be one of your top priorities. Doing what you can to protect yourself on and off campus is your responsibility. This section will look at ways you can take an active role in protecting yourself from crime, including robbery, assault, and rape.

Being Active in Your Personal Safety

How safe is it where you live and go to school? Have you ever been mugged, robbed, or assaulted? Do you know others who have been victims of crime? The best time to take precautions against crime is *before* you're a victim of it. Don't wait until crime hits you before you decide to act. When you're busy with school, you may get lazy in other areas like self-protection. But when you are a victim of crime, the trauma involved is much more time-consuming than the precautions that might have prevented it. Some of the self-protection measures discussed in this section may seem incredibly obvious, but it's just because they are obvious that many people neglect them. On school campuses, too, students tend to be lulled into a false sense of security. You feel safe because you're familiar with the campus and the people there. That's just the feeling that criminals count on; they hope you won't be concerned about crime, because then you won't take basic precautions and will be a more likely victim for crime.

Colleges are not free of crime. A lot of students are on their own for the first time, making their own judgments and decisions. Initially, some students take greater risks and leave themselves more vulnerable to assault. In addition, there are students, and even outsiders, who take advantage of the school environment and of the trust that students want to have in each other.

Being active in your own personal safety means being aware of crime and taking rational measures to protect yourself from it. One effective measure is taking a self-defense class. Even one class is likely to teach you new ideas and self-defense techniques. Does your school offer self-defense courses? If not, why not ask for one? Get a group of students together to request a self-defense course being added to the curriculum.

As you're reading about the following safety precautions, assess your own environment at school, home, and work. How can you take a more active role in your own self-protection? You cannot anticipate every criminal activity, but you can make yourself less vulnerable. Even a person well trained in self-defense may fall victim. Knowing and planning how to protect yourself may deter the burglar or attacker who might be around you.

Safety Where You Live

How safe are your living quarters? Forty to 50 percent of criminal attacks take place in a person's own living quarters. Know your home well. Know where your exits are, as well as phones, light switches, hiding places, and objects you could use to protect yourself.

If you were going to break into someone's quarters, how would you do it? Try to put yourself in the shoes of a criminal. What are the most logical places of entry? Make sure doors and windows are secure, with sturdy locks. Have emergency numbers written by the phone—fire department, police, ambulance. Who would you call in an emergency? Does your locality have a "911" emergency system that can link you to all emergency services? Most communities do—find out about yours.

What devices do you have to protect yourself? Where are they located? If you live with your family or roommates, do you have a plan for what to do in an emergency? The more prepared you are for a possible attack or burglary, the more you take away the element of surprise and panic. You'll feel more confident, not more paranoid.

If you live in a dorm, the dorm should be locked during the night. Don't ever prop open a door to a dorm; this leaves every resident vulnerable to attack. Cooperate and keep everyone more secure by locking doors to common areas. If you lose your room key or a card key that allows you to enter your locked dorm, report it to the residence hall director immediately.

STRATEGIES FOR COLLEGE SUCCESS

Make sure you have an extra set of keys available. Put them in a safe place. *Don't* put them under the doormat or on top of the door frame. Burglars know all about those hiding places.

Lock all your doors and windows whether you're home or not. If you're going to be out at night, leave a light on. You may want to leave a TV or radio playing as well, to give more of an impression that someone is home. Keep your curtains closed, especially at night. Have you ever walked on a campus or through a neighborhood at night and noticed all the people, very clearly, in their rooms and houses? Sometimes you don't realize how much you are advertising when your curtains are open.

Safety over the phone. Have you ever had phone calls where the caller asked you information, like "Do you live alone?" "Do both you and your husband work outside the home?" "Do you have pets?" "Do you own a _____ ?" "We will be mailing you a gift certificate, but first can we confirm your phone number and address?" The telephone is one of the easiest ways for someone to gain valuable information about you, whether you're single, what you own, what your credit card or bank account numbers are, and so on. Then there are the crank and obscene callers. Review the following suggestions for taking precautions when using the telephone.

Tips . . . For Phone Safety

- Don't welcome burglars by phone. Never provide your name, phone number, address, account numbers, or other helpful information to telephone solicitors, contest callers, wrong numbers, and others whom you have no grounds for trusting.

- If someone calls you to ask about your account or service problems, ask for the caller's name, business, and number and tell the caller you will call back. Then look up the phone number of that business. Is it the same phone number given you? It could be another extension, but if the numbers are different, call the business and speak to someone in charge. If the call was a hoax, call the police.

- Never disclose that you are alone, that you are going on vacation, or when you are at work.

- If you are a female living alone, you may want to list your phone number with only your initials or with a man's name (John and Linda Henderson).

- Don't keep your phone off the hook; you may miss an emergency call—maybe from a neighbor who is alerting you.

- If you have phone trouble, report it right away and request or demand immediate attention.

- Hang up on obscene callers; they're calling in hopes that you'll react to them. Report crank or obscene calls to the police, to your residence hall director, and to the telephone company. If complaints stack up, they may try to trap the caller.

- Purchase a caller ID machine or service.

You can use the phone to investigate people who come to your door. After checking their ID, you might call their place of business before you allow them in. Be sure to keep a chain on the door when you answer it. Look through the peephole of the door if you have one. If you don't have a peephole, you might want to get one. If anyone comes to your door needing help, offer to make a phone call for them, rather than letting them into your home. If you live in a dorm and see someone suspicious or unfamiliar in the halls, call your residence hall director.

248 ◆ SECTION 8

If you lose keys to your apartment or home, change your locks. A locksmith can alter your locks without you having to purchase new ones. Don't attach any personal identification to your keys because, if they get into the hands of the wrong people, you could lead a potential intruder straight to your living quarters. Keep your house and car keys on detachable rings.

Basically, you want to advertise as little about yourself as possible—otherwise you make yourself more vulnerable to crime. Avoid placing your name on your door and mailboxes. Don't ever leave a message on an answering machine saying you've gone on vacation or away for the weekend. The less you reveal about yourself, the less criminals can find out about you. You can share information with friends and family, but try not to share information about yourself with the world at large if you can avoid it.

Safety in Other Buildings

How safety conscious are you when you're in different buildings, labs, and rooms at school or work, especially at night? Do you know where all the exits are? Do you know where there are doors you can safely lock yourself behind? Do you know where the nearest available phone is? Are your emergency numbers available to you when you're away from home? Do you ever work late and alone in a lab? Do you have buddies who look out for you? Being away from home doesn't mean you should relax your self-protection. Attackers look for people who are off guard and easily intimidated.

What would you do if you were attacked on an elevator? Check elevators before getting in and stand near the control panel. If you're uneasy about getting on an elevator with someone, wait for the next elevator. If this makes you uncomfortable, simply pretend you forgot something or are waiting for someone. Remember, a little embarrassment is preferable to feeling panicked when you're in an enclosed space with someone you don't trust.

Think about self-protection wherever you are. Being mentally prepared will give you an edge. When you watch actors escape a crime on TV, remember, a planned script was written for them—they knew exactly what they would do. In real life, the more thought you give to self-protection, the less vulnerable you will be.

Safety on Foot

Do you take the safest route to your destination? When at all possible, avoid dark or deserted areas and plan routes that are well lighted and busy. If you have to walk through a dark and deserted area, you may want to consider walking in the middle of the street. If you're approached and need help, screaming "help" may not get as much attention nowadays as yelling "FIRE!"

If you walk routinely, you may want to vary your route. Get to know what buildings, businesses, and restaurants are open. Minimize packages you're carrying so you can be alert and able to react when you have to. Bring change and money for emergencies—for phone calls and cab or bus fares. If you suspect you're being followed, cross the street and head for the nearest populated and well-lighted area. If you're really scared, run to the nearest home or business to call for help. If you're being followed by someone in a car, immediately reverse your direction and make an effort to note the license number. And, of course, never hitchhike.

Be attentive to your surroundings. Are there people behind you or in front of you? Communicate the message that you know where you're going. Walk quickly and purposefully—you will look stronger and less easily intimidated. Trust your instincts; if you feel uncomfortable in a place, leave. You may feel safer, and become less of a target, if you walk with a companion—human or dog. If you're walking for exercise, you might want to not only vary your route but consider varying your schedule, too. Be careful when walking with headphones; they make your walk more pleasant but can make you less aware of your surroundings.

Avoid carrying large sums of money; carry only as much as you need. Don't "flash your cash" either. Write down the account numbers of your credit cards, so if they are stolen you can report their exact numbers immediately. Carry wallets, purses, packs, and briefcases close to you. If you're mugged for belongings, it's safer to give up your purse than get hurt, and the mugger may have a weapon. Then call the police immediately.

Some people carry personal protection devices such as canes, walking sticks, and pepper spray to momentarily stun an attacker so they can flee from the scene. You could carry devices that would draw attention to yourself, like a shriek alarm or a police whistle. Ask your local police for information on legal self-protection devices and alarms.

Safety on the Road

People used to think of their cars as being extremely safe places; but, with the rise of carjacking crimes, this is not as true as it used to be. The most important thing to remember is always to drive with your car doors locked. Roll down the windows only as much as you have to. Should anyone attempt to carjack your car, *get out and let them take the car.* An automobile is not worth risking your life for.

Regular car maintenance can make you safer. Make sure you've got plenty of gas in the tank, and take your car for regularly scheduled tune-ups. You don't want to be stuck on the side of a lonely stretch of highway because you didn't bother to check the oil level in your car. Keep emergency supplies in your car—flares, jumper cables, matches, candles, blankets, or water. If your car breaks down, especially in a remote area, leave your hood up, tie a white cloth to your door or antenna, and stay locked in your car unless you're safe enough and close enough to get help yourself. When someone offers assistance, roll down the window only enough to request that the person phone for help.

Tips . . . For Car Safety

- Drive with enough money in your wallet for gas or to make an emergency phone call.

- Park in well-lighted spots. At a shopping center, try to park under one of the large outdoor lights, near the stores.

- When you come back to your car, have the keys in hand so you're not fumbling for them as you stand next to the car. Likewise, have your house keys ready when you come back to your house.

- If you ever suspect that you're being followed, don't drive home. Drive to the nearest police station, fire station, hospital emergency room, open gas station, or another well-lighted business or residence. Try to get the car's license number and description, if possible. If there are no safe areas nearby, repeatedly honk your horn, turn on your emergency flashers—anything to draw the attention of the police or others who can be of help.

Safety on Public Transportation

Make safety your priority when you're using public transportation as well. Use the best-lighted and most frequently used stops, if possible. Wait with others until your bus or subway train arrives. Can you find a companion that's going the same route? Choose seats near the bus driver or in a subway car near the conductor. After a hectic day at school, this may seem like an excellent time to take a nap, but stay alert. Watch out if you're sitting near the exit door—an attacker can reach in and grab a purse or jewelry. If you're verbally or physically harassed, attract attention by screaming or talking loudly and firmly. That police whistle or shriek alarm may work here, too. When you arrive at your destination, be alert about who gets off with you. If you feel uneasy, walk directly to a place where there are other people.

If You're the Victim of Crime

Most crimes are crimes of opportunity—that is, someone takes advantage of the fact that windows were left open, car doors unlocked, or someone was walking alone in an isolated location; the crimes were not thought out beforehand.

If you're the victim of a crime—any crime—call the police immediately, identifying yourself and your location. If you arrive home and it appears that someone has entered, don't go in; call the police, campus security, or your residence hall director, or all three.

UNDERSTANDING RAPE AND DATE RAPE

Rape is a crime of violence, not sex. It is emotionally devastating not only to the victim but to the victim's family and close friends, as well as to society in general. Rape is forced sexual intercourse where physical force, threats, and fear are used to overpower and control the victim. If it is against your will, it is against the law. Rape is a felony. Date rape in particular has received a lot of media attention in recent years.

Surveys reveal that nearly 85 to 90 percent of rape victims know their assailant and about half occur on a date.[1] One out of every six American women has been the victim of an attempted or completed rape.[2] And, 10 percent of sexual assault victims are male, raped by other males.[3]

Rape can be the most difficult crime to deal with and to recover from. Society still tends to make the victim feel as though she were to blame in some way. A victim sometimes is thought to have been "asking for it" because she dressed or behaved in a provocative way. The fact is, rape is a crime of violence, not sex. Rapists are not attracted to their victims in a sexual sense; they are attracted to them as people who seem weak and can be dominated by force. Victims feel the effect of the attack for a long time. Not only is the memory of the attack painful, as well as any physical injuries, but victims also have to deal with family, friends, and acquaintances who may not know how to respond.

If You're a Victim of Rape

If you are a victim of rape, whether by a stranger or someone you know, report the crime at once. Call the police or the emergency number "911." Alternatively, call your community rape hotline; hotline numbers usually are located in the front of your telephone book under Community Service Numbers. Members of the hotline will inform you of your options, explain legal processes, and provide counseling and assistance through the medical exam to court proceedings, and after.

If you call the police, they will want to know your name, address, and age, the location of the rape, a description of the assailant, and the events that occurred before and during the assault. They will expect that you will be emotionally upset after the attack. You will be asked to have a medical exam to gather evidence of the rape and to take tests for sexually transmitted diseases for your own sake. They will ask you not to bathe, douche, or change clothes so they can gather as much evidence as possible.

A rape crisis center should be able to continue to help you by providing counseling for you and members of your family or your support system. As with any trauma, there are emotional scars; but healing is possible using your own resources and the help of your family, friends, and others. Remember that you are not at fault—the perpetrator is. You did not "ask for it"; you are the victim of a crime, not the guilty party. There are complicated, painful feelings involved following rape; get the assistance of a rape crisis center or another counselor to help get you through the experience. Help is out there.

---

[1]Sexual Assault on Campus" from the National Institute of Justice, http://www.nij.gov/nij/topics/crime/rape-sexual-violence/campus/measuring.htm, March 2014.

[2]"Who Are the Victims?" Rape, Abuse & Incest National Network, http://www.rainn.org/get-information/statistics/sexual-assault-victims, March 2014.

[3]Ibid.

Keeping Yourself Safe from Rape

In general, make your personal safety a top priority. Review the suggestions given earlier in this section for maintaining personal safety on campus, at home, and on the road. Since so many rape victims know their attackers, it makes sense to know the ways in which you can stop a situation from getting dangerous. Review the following tips to avoid date rape.

Tips . . . For Avoiding Date Rape

- Try to know as much as possible about a date before you go out. Get acquainted with him before your date, if possible. If he's in school with you, chat between classes or over lunch.

- When you go out on a date, know your sexual intentions. Know what you want to do and what you don't want to do.

- When you're just getting acquainted with someone, try to arrange dates in public places or other places where you'll be surrounded by others. Avoid spending time alone with someone in his room, his car, or another isolated place if you don't know him very well.

- Be aware that, while wearing revealing clothes or flirting is certainly not wrong, it can be misunderstood or misinterpreted. Be clear about your true intentions so you can avoid unpleasant misunderstandings.

- Use your assertive communication skills to give clear messages to your date. Don't allow yourself to be bullied or belittled because you don't want to have sex with someone. Communicate your intentions clearly. If you say no, say it firmly. A mature person will not take your refusal as a rejection of him. If your date doesn't want to accept your answer, don't argue or belabor the point. End the date.

- Watch out for the date who encourages you to drink or use other drugs. Know your limits. Drinking too much or getting high will make you less alert to your date's messages and hamper your ability to assert (or even defend) yourself. Reports reveal that 55 percent of rape victims and 75 percent of rapists were drinking before the attack.

- Remember that no one has the right to demand sex from you just because they have spent money on a date. You're not obligated to have sex with anyone for any reason.

Note: Although these suggestions are obviously directed toward female students, male students will want to read them as well; you might want to share this section of the text with a sister or female friend.

Source: *How to Avoid Date Rape,* http://outreach.org/2011/06/05/how-to-avoid-date-rape

HIGHLIGHTS

In this section you've explored more about the diverse world you're a part of, now that you're in college. You've begun to explore the differences, as well as the similarities, of the different people with whom you study, work, and have fun. In the process, you've also examined some of the negative attitudes that keep people from appreciating others' differences, and you have considered your own feelings about them.

You've begun to consider the feelings and perspectives of students who have experienced prejudice and discrimination, and you've been shown some ways to help get rid of these attitudes. One of the ways you've been introduced to is reflective listening in which you listen attentively and paraphrase what the speaker has said to show you understand. A second way is assertive communication in which you express your thoughts and feelings in a way that shows respect for yourself and the others around you.

You've also started to become aware of the importance of personal safety on and off campus. You examined ways to deal with sexual harassment and how to avoid other crimes, including rape.

In short, you've started to learn how to keep your world safe, even as you begin to share it with others.

DISCUSSION QUESTIONS

Note: Read the following discussion questions and activities **before** you read Section 8. This strategy will help you look for answers while you read.

1. What is meant by "culturally diverse"?
2. What are the advantages of living in a culturally diverse environment?
3. Explain the difference between stereotyping and discrimination.
4. List five examples of a) stereotyping and b) discrimination. (Do not use the examples in the text.)
5. What prejudicial attitudes have been directed at you? How do you feel about them?
6. Explain the difference between prejudice and discrimination.
7. Why do you think prejudice exists? List and discuss as many reasons as you can.
8. What prejudices do you see in yourself? How can you overcome them?
9. Explain the difference between reflective listening and assertive communication. (Make sure you explain when you use each type of communication and why.)
10. Explain the difference between assertive, nonassertive, and aggressive styles of communication, and give an example of each. Why might a person choose to be nonassertive or aggressive at times?
11. Explain why assertive communication is a thoughtful form of communication.
12. List six qualities of an assertive communicator.
13. Give an example of how you would assert yourself to prevent (a) sexual harassment and (b) date rape. (What would you say?)
14. What is sexual harassment? Give a range of examples.
15. What steps can you take now to enhance your personal safety (a) where you live (on the phone, too), (b) at school and in buildings, c) on foot, and d) on the road?
16. How can you better protect yourself from rape? List as many prevention strategies as you can.
17. What procedures should you follow if you or someone close to you was a victim of rape?
18. How does racism show itself on your campus/at your school?
19. How is college a laboratory for developing effective human relationship skills across cultures?
20. What can you do to build better relationships with people from other cultures and other races on campus?
21. How can active listening build better relationships?
22. How does critical thinking help you to be more assertive?
23. How can you use assertive communication to deal with sexual harassment?

Career Exploration

WHAT'S IN IT FOR YOU

Planning for your career is a journey whether you just finished high school, you're starting a new career, or you're a bit undecided and taking your basic and general education courses. By enrolling in college you've made an important decision to learn the skills and knowledge required for a new career and to earn a degree or other credentials required to obtain a new job. To stay on course, keep reminding yourself of your college and career goals, so when it gets tough you can be determined to stay focused.

Forecasters say tomorrow's jobs will have upgraded educational standards. The U.S. Department of Labor's study on work and workers of the 21st century has projected a shortage of qualified entrants into the workforce. On the positive side, this means there will be more jobs for those who meet the qualifications. There's no sugar-coating it—school can be rigorous, but it's also very rewarding. It's an investment in yourself and your future. Dig in and stay with it—your education is your ticket.

As you begin to study this section, you may or may not already have a clear idea about the career direction you want to follow. If you're not clear about ideas for a future job, this section will help you examine your workplace values, interests, and skills, and investigate and narrow your career choices and opportunities. Even if you have chosen your future profession, the self-assessment exercises in this section will help you learn more about yourself and your abilities, and that kind of knowledge is an asset in any career. You'll also learn valuable job-search strategies that you can begin to use even before graduation. Get ready to explore your options.

In this section you'll explore:

- Your values, interests, occupational personality type, and skills, and how they relate to your career choices.
- Career options based on your self-assessments.
- Job search strategies.
- How to market yourself for a job through resumes, portfolios, cover letters, and job applications.
- Online strategies for networking and job applications.
- How to make the most of the job interview.

KNOW YOURSELF

The basis of successful career planning is knowing yourself. It's this self-knowledge that guides you toward a career that suits your personality. Satisfying careers are generally those compatible with your values, interests, personality type, and skills. You will get a chance to assess each of these characteristics and how they relate to your occupational choices. Also, most colleges have a career services office which will offer a variety of in-depth self-assessments to help you learn more about your values, interests, skills, and related occupational fields. Additionally, career services offices have professional staff to help you understand the results and make career plans.

First, though, a word of caution about assessments. The assessment exercises in this section should serve only as indicators of your personal characteristics. You can make these quizzes and exercises more reliable by making your best attempt to answer them without bias (i.e., slanting your responses according to how you would like them to be, instead of the way you actually are); looking up all words with definitions you are unsure of; and, if you have a particular occupation in mind, trying not to respond in a way that you think a person in that field should respond.

ASSESSING YOUR WORKPLACE VALUES

Why do some people choose to be teachers, others to be chemical operators, police officers, presidents, truck drivers, veterinarians, or writers? One answer is values. Your **values** indicate what you consider important, worthy, or meaningful. You use your values as standards or principles to live by—even to choose jobs. Your values often are unidentified; nevertheless, they are powerful forces that guide and influence your decisions throughout your life. You rely on your values to make decisions; but when you are unclear about what your values are, decision making becomes more difficult and perhaps confused.

Identifying your values will help you take control of your decisions, whether they're about college or career or something else. This section will help you identify the values you hold that need to be satisfied in your work environment if you're going to be happy in your career. If you've ever had a job with which you were unhappy, chances are it did not satisfy some of your important values. Once you have become aware of your values, you can make better decisions about your career direction. The exercise below will help you identify values you prefer in your job/workplace.

Exercise 9-1 My workplace values

1. Read each of the workplace values listed below. If some are missing that you feel are important to you, add them to this list. Then check the values that you would like to be satisfied in your future career. Be honest with yourself to get the best results.

2. Next rank the checked values in order of importance to you, from 1–10, with 1 being the most important value. Write the numbers right next to the check marks.

Exercise 9-1 My work values (continued)

_____	opportunity for work family life balance	_____	being an expert
_____	opportunities for supervision/leadership	_____	flexible work structure
_____	helping or caring for others	_____	glamour, prestige, social status
_____	learning/professional development	_____	managing projects
_____	teaching or training	_____	dealing with the public
_____	working outdoors	_____	influencing others
_____	developing new ideas	_____	taking risks
_____	making adequate money	_____	job security and stability
_____	strong financial compensation	_____	family security
_____	prestige and status	_____	control
_____	responsibility	_____	recognition, respect
_____	routine, predictable work projects	_____	variety, changing tasks
_____	adventure and excitement	_____	working independently
_____	competition	_____	self-employment
_____	challenges, high demand environment	_____	low pressure environment
_____	making decisions, having power to decide	_____	physical activity
_____	precision work	_____	sedentary (nonphysical)
_____	close guidance/supervision	_____	having challenging work
_____	equal opportunity	_____	having regular hours
_____	team work, work groups	_____	improving society
_____	integrity and truth	_____	using cutting edge technology
_____	high moral standards	_____	using intellect/knowledge
_____	spirituality	_____	working with nature
_____	feeling like you belong	_____	contributing to society
_____	organization, structure	_____	working with your hands
_____	using creativity; being innovative	_____	other
_____	traveling	_____	other
_____	opportunity for advancement	_____	other
_____	healthy environment	_____	other

3. Narrow your list of 10 to the 5 core values you hold most dear in your job/workplace—and list them below.

1. _____
2. _____
3. _____
4. _____
5. _____

4. What can you conclude about your values based on the completed checklist? What kinds of jobs are likely to satisfy the values you've listed as important?

_____
_____
_____
_____

5. How well do your core values fit with your current job, career path, and employer—and what, if anything, are you going to do with these results?

_____

_____

_____

_____

_____

Congratulations! You now have a list of workplace values that represent who you are. It is this core group of workplace values that help determine your level of satisfaction with your job and your career—and which should be used to judge the level of "fit" with any future job, company, or career change.

ASSESSING YOUR INTERESTS

Interests also are excellent indicators of job satisfaction and can guide you in your career choices. **Interests** are the activities you like to engage in, and the topics and concerns that capture your attention. Your interests are evident from the activities you participate in, the subjects you enjoy, and the books you read. Values often underlie your interests. You usually place more value on the things you like to do. However, values tend to be more stable, whereas interests can change more frequently. Interests change with experiences, opportunities, age, and abilities. People desire job changes because of new interests and develop new interests because of new work experiences. If you don't develop or utilize your interests in your work, you may find work to be dull and unfulfilling. The following series of activities will help you get a better picture of your interests.

Exercise 9-2 My interests

List ten activities you love to do. These can be sports, recreation, intellectual pursuits, and hobbies—things you do by yourself or with others.

1. _____
2. _____
3. _____
4. _____
5. _____
6. _____
7. _____
8. _____
9. _____
10. _____

Satisfying jobs can be developed from activities you love to do. Identify jobs that may relate to the top five activity interests you circled.

List Top 5 Activity Interests	Related Jobs
1.	
2.	
3.	
4.	
5.	

What are your three favorite subjects to study in school?

1. _____
2. _____
3. _____

For what areas of work might these subjects help you prepare?

_____
_____
_____
_____
_____
_____
_____
_____

If money were no object, how would you spend most of your time? . . . and how does this relate to job(s) that interest you?

_____
_____
_____
_____
_____
_____

You've identified some of your interests related to your career and personal life. Because interests change with experiences, opportunities, age, and abilities, it's good to reassess your changing interests to help you affirm and revise your career planning. In the next section you will learn about Holland's Occupational Personality types, a well-known theory, designed to assist people in making effective career choices.

ASSESSING YOUR OCCUPATIONAL PERSONALITY TYPE

What kind of job would you prefer? One that allows you to work alone or with people? With your hands or your mind? Leading others or following others? Developing ideas or organizing information? What kinds of occupations would match your personality type? In this section you will identify your occupational personality type using a self-assessment based on John Holland's theory of vocational personalities and work environments.[1] Holland has categorized six personality types and corresponding work environments. Once you identify your occupational personality type, you will be able to discover matching occupations.

According to Dr. Holland's theory, people express their personalities through their vocational choices, and people are attracted to occupations that will provide experiences suitable to their personality type. Job satisfaction, stability, and achievement are more likely if the work environment and the worker's personality are well matched.[2] Holland's theory has gained a lot of credibility, and even the U.S. Department of Labor has adopted Holland's model for categorizing jobs relative to the six occupational personality types.

Holland's personality types are described as a cluster of personal characteristics defining how a person typically copes with life's tasks. Each personality type is based on occupational interests. The six occupational

[1]John Holland and Gary Gottfredson, *Dictionary of Holland Occupational Codes*, 3rd ed. (Odessa, FL: Psychological Assessment Resources, 1996)
[2]John Holland, *Making Vocational Choices: A Theory of Vocational Personalities and Work Environments*, 3rd ed. (Odessa, FL: Psychological Assessment Resources, 1997)
Source: *Holland's Personality Life Styles,* http://advising.wvu.edu/r/download/81583

personality types are: **realistic (R), investigative (I), artistic (A), social (S), enterprising (E),** and **conventional (C)**. No person is entirely one personality type. Actually, you are a combination of all six. However, you are generally dominant in three personality types. Holland classifies occupations using the three highest or strongest personality types. In the assessment below, you will identify your top three occupational personality types, which will ultimately help you to understand more about yourself and how your individual skills and interests are related to your career choice.

Listed below, in Exercise 9-3, are the six Holland Occupational personality types and a list of characteristics common to each. Your personality will most likely combine several personality types to varying degrees. Beneath each occupational personality type is a list of matching occupations, and the three-letter occupational code is given after each occupation. This code identifies the three highest or strongest occupational personality types associated with it.

Exercise 9-3 My occupational personality type

Check the characteristics of each of the six occupational personality types (R, I, A, S, E, C) that best describe you. Check all that apply.

Realistic (R)

Characteristics

_____ Physically strong, rugged, or coordinated

_____ Practical minded

_____ Prefers concrete problems (having exact answers, yes/no)

_____ Shy, has more difficulty expressing feelings

_____ Likes to work with objects, rather than ideas or people

_____ Stable

_____ Persistent

_____ Technical and/or mechanical

_____ Likes to work with hands to make, build, repair, or plant things

_____ Frank/honest/direct

_____ Likes outdoor activities or nature

_____ Would rather do than discuss

_____ Self-reliant

_____ Conforming

_____ Likes to work with tools, machines, plants, animals (as a veterinarian would), or human bodies (as a surgeon would)

Occupations typically included in the realistic type

(The three-letter code following each occupation identifies the three highest/strongest occupational personality types associated with it.)

- Air-conditioning mechanic (RIE)
- Aircraft mechanic (RIE)
- Alteration tailor (RIE)
- Architectural drafter (RCI)
- Automobile body repairer (RIE)
- Automobile mechanic (RIE)
- Automotive engineer (RIE)
- Carpenter (RIE)
- Commercial airplane pilot (RIE)
- Construction worker (REC)
- Cook (hotel and restaurant) (RSE)
- Corrections officer (RES)
- Dental assistant (RES)
- Dental laboratory technician (REI)
- Diesel mechanic (REI)
- Drafter (RCI)
- Electrical engineer (REI)
- Electrical technician (RIE)
- Electrician (REI)
- Embalmer (RIS)
- Exercise careers (RES)
- Farmer (RIS)
- Fiber optics technician (RSE)
- Forester (RIS)
- Furniture upholsterer (RIE)

- Hotel and restaurant cook (RES)
- Industrial supervisor (REI)
- Jeweler (REC)
- Landscape gardener (RIS)
- Machine repairers or operators, or both (RIE)
- Machinist (RIE)
- Mechanical engineer (RIS)
- Mechanical engineer technician (RIS)
- Mining engineer (RIE)
- Nuclear medical technologist (RIS)
- Optician (REI)
- Pharmacist assistant (RIE)
- Plumber (construction) (REI)
- Practical nurse (RSE)
- Quality control manager (RSE)
- Radiochemist (IRE)
- Radio/TV repair (REI)
- Sheet metal worker (R)
- Some wildlife and conservation jobs
- Tailor (RES)
- Tractor mechanic (REI)
- Water quality specialist (REI)
- Welding technician (RES)

Investigative (I)

Characteristics

_____ Curious or likes to explore new ideas or ask why

_____ Likes problem solving (thinking and analyzing)

_____ Independent

_____ Intellectual, scholarly, or studious

_____ Logical or rational

_____ Modest, reserved, or introverted

_____ Methodical or precise

_____ Cautious

_____ Expresses self through the mind

_____ Enjoys solving abstract problems (not having exact answers)

_____ Likes to explore ideas (reading and discussing)

_____ Likes to understand the scientific world

_____ Can get absorbed in things for long periods

_____ Intelligent or desires to understand things thoroughly

_____ Mathematical

Occupations typically included in the investigative type

(The three-letter code following each occupation identifies the three highest/strongest occupational personality types associated with it.)

- Actuary (ISE)
- Anesthesiologist (IRS)
- Archeologist (IRE)
- Biochemist (IRE)
- Biologist (ISR)
- Cardiopulmonary technician (IRE)
- Chemical engineer (IRE)
- Chemical laboratory technician (IRS)
- Chemist (IRE)
- Chiropractor (ISR)
- Civil engineer (IRS)
- Computer engineer (IRC)
- Computer programmer (IRC)
- Computer systems analyst (IER)
- Dentist (ISR)
- Ecologist (IRE)
- Economist (IAS)
- Educational psychologist (IES)
- Electronics technician (IRE)
- General practitioner (ISE)
- Geologist (IRE)
- Geographer (IRE)
- Hazardous waste technician (IRS)
- Horticulturist (IRS)
- Industrial hygienist (IRE)
- Information system programmer (IEC)
- Management consultant (ISR)
- Marketing research analyst (IAS)
- Mathematician (IER)
- Medical lab technologist (IRE)
- Medical technologist (ISA)
- Meteorologist (IRS)
- Nurse practitioner (ISA)
- Pharmacist (IES)
- Physician assistant (ISA)
- Physicist (IRE)
- Psychologist (ISA)
- Radiologist (IRS)
- Research analyst (IRC)
- Research associate (IRC)
- Sociologist (IES)
- Software engineer (IRE)
- Statistician (IRE)
- Surgeon (IRA)
- Technical publications writer (IRS)
- Technical writer (IRS)
- Translator (ISC)
- Veterinarian (IRS)
- Video operator (ISA)

Artistic (A)

Characteristics

_____ Creative or original

_____ Visionary (can envision/picture)

_____ Perceptive or intuitive

_____ Complicated

_____ Imaginative

_____ Idealistic

_____ Impulsive

_____ Likes unstructured situations

_____ Nonconforming or likes to be different

_____ Likes experimenting with new ideas

_____ Solves problems by creating something new

_____ Rather create ideas than study them

_____ Likes to work independently

_____ Expresses self through color, art, theater, music, or writing

_____ Appreciates or enjoys beauty, in nature or other environments

Occupations typically included in the artistic type

(The three-letter code following each occupation identifies the three highest/strongest occupational personality types associated with it.)

- Actor/Actress (AES)
- Advertising art director (AES)
- Advertising manager (ASE)
- Architect (AIR)
- Cake decorator (ARE)
- Cartoonist (AES)
- Choreographer (AER)
- Clothing/fashion designer (ASR)
- Composer (ASE)
- Copywriter (ASI)
- Dancer (AER)
- Editorial writer (AES)
- Furniture designer (AES)
- Graphic designer (AES)
- Humorist (ASE)
- Illustrator (AES)
- Interior designer (AES)
- Journalist/reporter (ASE)
- Landscape architect (AIR)
- Medical illustrator (AIE)
- Museum curator (AES)
- Musician (ASI)
- Photographer (AES)
- Photojournalist (AEC)
- Police artist (ASC)
- Program coordinator (amusement and recreation) (AES)
- Publications editor (AES)
- Stage director (AES)
- Stage technician (ARS)
- Teacher (drama) (ASE)
- Teacher (English) (ASE)
- Teacher (music) (AES)
- Television technician (ASI)
- Wedding consultant (AES)
- Writer/editor (ASI)

Social (S)

Characteristics

_____ Sensitive or attentive

_____ Perceptive or insightful

_____ Unstructured

_____ Idealistic

_____ Generous

_____ Kind, caring, or concerned about others' welfare

_____ Responsible

_____ Solves problems by talking with others

_____ Sociable, friendly, cheerful, or others enjoy talking to you

_____ Cooperative or sharing

_____ Convincing or able to influence

_____ Empathetic (can put yourself in others' shoes) or listens well

_____ Helpful or service-oriented or enjoys teaching

_____ Enjoys people or helping people with their personal problems

_____ Communicates well and is tactful

Occupations typically included in the social type

(The three-letter code following each occupation identifies the three highest/strongest Occupational Personality Types associated with it.)

- Air traffic controller (SER)
- Announcer (radio and TV broadcasting) (SCE)
- Athletic director (SER)
- Athletic trainer (SRE)
- Business teacher (SAE)
- Clergy member (SAI)
- Clinical psychologist (SIA)
- City manager (SEC)
- Coach (SRE)
- College professor (SEI)
- Community planner (SEA)
- Cosmetologist (SEA)
- Counseling psychologist (SIA)
- Counselor (SAE)
- Cruise director (SAE)
- Dental hygienist (SAI)
- Department store manager (SER)
- Detective (SER)
- Dietician (SIE)
- Elementary school teacher (SEC)
- Family and consumer scientist (SAE)
- General duty nurse (SIA)
- Geriatric nurse assistant (SIE)
- Hair stylist (SER)
- High school teacher (SAE)
- Historian (SEI)
- Home economics teacher (SAE)
- Home economist (SEA)
- Home health technician (SRI)
- Hospital administrator (SER)
- Individual/organizational psychologist (SEI)
- Insurance claims examiner (SIE)
- Librarian (SAI)
- Mail carrier (SRC)

- Medical assistant (SCR)
- Medical record administrator (SIE)
- Mental retardation aide (SRI)
- Narcotics investigator (SRE)
- Nurse midwife (SIR)
- Occupational therapist (SRE)
- Paralegal (SCE)
- Park naturalist (SEI)
- Personnel recruiter (SEC)
- Personnel, training, and labor relations specialist (SEC)
- Physical therapist (SIE)
- Physical therapy aide (SIR)
- Police chief (SER)
- Police officer (SER)
- Political scientist (SEI)
- Preschool teacher (SAE)
- Preschool worker (SEA)
- Probation and parole officer (SIE)

- Professional athlete (SRC)
- Public health educator (SEA)
- Psychiatric social worker (SEA)
- Recreation director (SEI)
- Recreation therapist (SEC)
- Registered nurse (SIA)
- Relocation counselor (SAE)
- Respiratory therapist (SIR)
- Retirement counselor (SAE)
- School counselor (SAE)
- School principal/administrator (SEI)
- Social worker (SEA)
- Sociologist (SIA)
- Special education teacher (SEC)
- Speech pathologist (SAI)
- Tax auditor (SER)
- Teacher, deaf students (SEC)
- Vocational-rehabilitation counselor (SEC)
- X-Ray technician (SRI)

Enterprising (E)

Characteristics

_____ Adventurous or risk-taking or impulsive

_____ Ambitious or aggressive worker

_____ Likes recognition or attention-getting or being in charge

_____ Likes control, power, leading or influencing, managing or domineering

_____ Popular or enjoys status and attention

_____ Sociable or extroverted or connects well with people (networker)

_____ Pleasure-seeking or adventurous

_____ Can make decisions quickly or impulsively

_____ Energetic or enthusiastic

_____ Self-confident or optimistic

_____ Impatient with precise work

_____ Likes selling or persuading or bargaining

_____ Likes competition or success or power

_____ Likes or desires wealth or material possessions, or both

_____ Organizes or initiates, then delegates to others to complete tasks

Occupations typically included in the enterprising type

(The three-letter code following each occupation identifies the three highest/strongest occupational personality types associated with it.)

- Advertising, marketing, and public relations managers (ESA)
- Advertising sales representative (ESR)
- Barber (ESR)
- Bartender (ERC)
- Benefits manager (ESA)
- Buyer (ESA)
- Car salesperson (ESR)
- Clown (EAC)
- Construction superintendent (ERS)
- Cook/chef (ESR)
- Credit analyst (EAS)
- Credit manager (ERS)
- Educational administrator (ESA)
- Educational-training manager (EIS)
- Emergency medical technician (ESI)
- Fashion coordinator (EAS)
- Financial manager (ESA)
- Financial planner (ESA)
- Fire marshal (ERS)
- Flight attendant (ESA)
- Food service manager (ESI)
- Foreign service officer (ESA)
- Funeral director (ESR)
- Head coach (ESR)
- Health services manager (ECR)
- Highway patrol pilot (ERS)
- Hotel/motel manager (ESR)
- Housing project manager (EAS)
- Industrial engineer (EIR)
- Insurance adjuster (ESR)
- Insurance sales agent (ESR)
- Interpreter (ESA)
- Kitchen supervisor (ERS)
- Legislative assistant (ESR)
- Lobbyist (ESA)
- Manufacturer's representative (ESA)
- Media director (ESC)
- News writer (ESR)
- Office manager (ESR)
- Park superintendent (ERA)
- Personal shopper (ESR)
- Public relations representative (EAS)
- Real estate agent (ESR)
- Regional manager (ESR)
- Restaurant manager (EAS)
- Sales representative (ERS)
- Social service director (ESA)
- Sports director (ESR)
- Sports instructor (ESR)
- Stockbroker (ESI)
- Tax accountant (ECS)
- Tax attorney (ESI)
- Teacher (ESR)
- Travel agent (ECS)
- Travel guide (ESC)
- Urban planner (ESI)

Conventional

Characteristics

_____ Orderly or neat

_____ Skilled in clerical and numerical tasks

_____ Accurate, precise, careful, or conscientious

_____ Organized or structured

_____ Conservative or practical

_____ Doesn't like responsibility for big decisions

_____ Conforming

_____ Conscientious, persistent, or completes tasks carefully

_____ Efficient or punctual

_____ Sociable

_____ Likes knowing what is expected

_____ Needs to complete details

_____ Likes structure or routine, or both, or follows rules

_____ Carries out tasks initiated by others

_____ Maintains thorough records or attends to details

Occupations typically included in the conventional type

(The three-letter code following each occupation identifies the three highest/strongest occupational personality types associated with it.)

- Accountant (CRS)
- Accounting clerk and bookkeeper (CRS)
- Administrative assistant (ESC)
- Bank teller (CSE)
- Budget analyst (CER)
- Building inspector (CIE)
- Business programmer (CRI)
- Catalog librarian (CSE)
- Computer operator (CSR).
- Computer peripheral equipment operator (CSR)
- Congressional district aide (CES)
- Cost accountant (CSE)
- Court clerk (CSE)
- Court reporter (CSE)
- Customs inspector (CEI)

- Electronic mail technician (CSR)
- Financial analyst (CSI)
- Insurance underwriter (CSE)
- Legal secretary (CSE)
- Medical record technician (CSE)
- Medical secretary (CES)
- Proofreader (CSI)
- Receptionist (CSE)
- Safety inspector (CRS)
- Seamless-hosiery knitter (CRS)
- Secretary (CSE)
- Stenographer (CSE)
- Tax consultant (CES)
- Tax preparer (CSE)
- Ticket agent (CSE)
- Typist (CSE)

Exercise 9-3 My occupational personality Type (continued)

Below you will find a brief description of each of Holland's six occupational personality types. Imagine that you are allowed to design your ideal job. Rank the following statements 1–6 (1 being the highest), noting the way you would like to spend your time on your ideal job.

In my ideal job, I would like to spend most of my time:

_____ **Realistic (R)** working with my hands, in physical activity, out of doors, using tools or machines, or repairing or constructing something.

_____ **Investigative (I)** working with problem solving by thinking and analyzing in abstract, scientific, mathematical, or investigative research pursuits.

_____ **Artistic (A)** working in an unstructured environment, creating new ideas or methods for art forms, or solutions to problems.

_____ **Social (S)** working with people by teaching, helping with personal problems, entertaining, or influencing them. Prefer to solve problems through discussion.

_____ **Enterprising (E)** working in leadership roles to accomplish the objectives of an organization or business. Persuade and motivate others.

_____ **Conventional (C)** working on a job where I know exactly what is expected of me and I can use my organization skills, doing well-defined tasks that require precision and efficiency.

List the personality themes from above in numerical order (do not use the abbreviations).

1st _____
2nd _____
3rd _____
4th _____
5th _____
6th _____

List the initials of your top three occupational personality types. Look at the previous eight pages to see what type of occupations most closely match your top three occupational personality types.

_____   _____   _____
1st   2nd   3rd

The three letters above make up your Holland's code. The initials of your top three personality themes form a code that can be used to discover occupations that match your interests. Holland analyzed up to 12,860 occupational titles and classified them into six occupational personality types as outlined in his dictionary. The three-letter codes provide descriptions of occupations. To illustrate, the code ESC for the job of employment manager means that employment managers resemble people in Enterprising (E) occupations most of all; people in Social (S) occupations somewhat less; and people in Conventional (C) occupations still less. In this way, the codes provide a brief summary of what an occupation is like by showing its degrees of resemblance to three occupational personality types. Your library, learning resource center, or instructor may have a copy of John Holland's *Dictionary of Holland Codes*. You can use this resource to locate additional jobs that match your occupational personality type.

Please note that a few combinations of code letters do not occur at all, or they occur infrequently. In such cases, a person may use a two-letter code, rather than a three-letter code, and study the nature of all the occupations with that code. You can also try switching your code scores around—for example, if you are SEA, you may consider switching the order to ESA or SAE.

How closely does your current career direction match your top three occupational personality types? Were you surprised by the results of your assessment? Has it given you any new ideas regarding career options? Discuss each of the three questions below:

_____
_____
_____
_____
_____
_____

ASSESSING YOUR SKILLS

Skills are the abilities you have that can be applied immediately in specific tasks or functions. They generally are expressed as action words or verbs. Examples of such action words are *instruct, write, repair, motivate*—all things you can do. Some skills, related to the way you manage yourself, are a little harder to describe—you'll learn about those later. It's important to learn about your skills because they are what you contribute to your job. Employers like to know what they are going to get in return for your wages. Identifying your skills and communicating them well is essential to creating a strong resume, networking, having a successful job interview, and landing a job.

In this section, you will learn about three types of skills: transferable, work-specific, and self-management skills. **Transferable skills** can be transferred from one job to another—you can use them in many other types of work with little effort on your part. Probably 80–90 percent of your skills are transferable skills. Transferable skills generally are expressed as verbs.

Exercise 9-4 My transferable skills

Place a check next to each transferable skill you have. Add to the bottom any other transferable skills that you think should be listed.

adapt	design	measure	sketch
administer	detail	mediate	solve
advertise	develop	memorize	study
advise	diagnose	mentor	supervise
advocate	draw	monitor	support
analyze	drive	motivate	survey
anticipate	edit	negotiate	synthesize
appraise	educate	nurture	tabulate
arrange	encourage	observe	teach
assemble	engage	operate	think
assess	entertain	organize	tolerate
audit	evaluate	paint	track
budget	explain	perceive	train
build	file	persuade	transcribe
calculate	guide	plan	translate
chart	hypothesize	present	troubleshoot
classify	illustrate	prioritize	tutor
communicate	imagine	promote	type
compile	improvise	proofread	understand
compose	inspect	question	update
compute	inspire	read	verify
conceptualize	instruct	recruit	visualize
construct	interview	rectify	volunteer
converse	invent	remember	write
cook	investigate	repair	
coordinate	lead	report	
correspond	learn	research	
counsel	liaise	review	
create	listen	schedule	
delegate	log	sell	
demonstrate	manage	sew	

As you read and checked the transferable skills you possess, you probably noticed that they are somewhat vague; they leave questions in your mind: "Repair what?" or "Teach what?" For this reason, transferable skills are seldom expressed alone on a resume or in an interview; instead, they are used to build phrases that communicate work-specific skills. **Work-specific skills** are abilities that you have learned specifically for the job, or perhaps in on-the-job training. Note the following examples of work-specific skills.

Work-Specific Skills

Transferable Skill	Plus	a Specific Job-Related Description
sell		Apple computers
counsel		drug addicts
teach		mathematics
manage		a small business
cook		French food
program		in Javascript
maintain		Cisco routers
design		web pages
provide		PC technical support
write		business correspondence
administer		employee performance appraisals
produce		narrate PowerPoint slides
word process		business correspondence
analyze		statistical data
research		consumer buying trends
utilize		Microsoft Office Professional
repair		small engines
design and deliver		training presentations

As you can see, the work-specific skill is always a phrase. It is begun by stating a transferable skill (a verb), followed by a brief specific description. Since prospective employers want to know specifically what you do, you should list work-specific skills on a resume.

Exercise 9-5 My work-specific skills

1. What are some of your work-specific skills?

   - _____
   - _____
   - _____
   - _____
   - _____
   - _____
   - _____
   - _____

2. What are some of your work-specific skills that you will be expected to perform on the job?

   - _____
   - _____
   - _____
   - _____
   - _____
   - _____
   - _____
   - _____

A third type of skill is the self-management skill. This is the type of skill that does not have to be expressed as a verb. **Self-management skills** relate to how you manage yourself, how well you perform, and your temperament (e.g., being punctual, relating well to co-workers, or being trustworthy). They generally are expressed by adjectives and adverbs that describe your behavior or how well you work, or both.

Self-management skills are important to employers because they want to hire people who are "good workers"—those who will fit with the work group. More people lose jobs because they have poor self-management skills than because they are not competent at their duties. On the other hand, a person with strong self-management skills might get job opportunities even when lacking some of the work-specific skills. Employers tend to figure that, if you can manage yourself, you are well on your way to managing anything else that comes along.

Exercise 9-6 My self-management skills

Check off your self-management skills. Use the blanks to add any you have that aren't listed. Circle those that you would like to acquire or improve.

_____ accurate	_____ energetic	_____ loving	_____ relaxed
_____ adaptable	_____ enjoyable	_____ loyal	_____ reliable
_____ alert	_____ enthusiastic	_____ methodical	_____ reserved
_____ ambitious	_____ fair-minded	_____ meticulous	_____ resourceful
_____ analytical	_____ flexible	_____ motivated	_____ responsible
_____ assertive	_____ forgiving	_____ natural	_____ safety-conscious
_____ calm	_____ friendly	_____ open	_____ self-directed
_____ caring	_____ generous	_____ optimistic	_____ self-starter
_____ cautious	_____ genuine	_____ organized	_____ sensible
_____ cheerful	_____ goal-oriented	_____ original	_____ stable
_____ clear-thinking	_____ handles criticism	_____ outgoing	_____ strong-minded
_____ clever	_____ has common sense	_____ painstaking	_____ supportive
_____ competent	_____ has initiative	_____ patient	_____ tactful
_____ confident	_____ healthy	_____ persevering	_____ team player
_____ considerate	_____ helpful	_____ pleasant	_____ theoretical
_____ cooperative	_____ honest	_____ poised	_____ thoughtful
_____ courageous	_____ imaginative	_____ positive	_____ trustworthy
_____ creative	_____ independent	_____ practical	_____ understanding
_____ curious	_____ industrious	_____ prudent	_____ versatile
_____ customer-focused	_____ informal	_____ punctual	_____ wholesome
_____ demonstrate	_____ innovative	_____ purposeful	_____ wise
_____ dependable	_____ intellectual	_____ quiet	_____
_____ determined	_____ introspective	_____ rational	_____
_____ eager	_____ inventive	_____ reflective	_____
_____ easygoing	_____ kind	_____ relates well	_____
_____ empathetic	_____ light-hearted	to coworkers	_____

Self-management skills can also be phrased in a quantitative fashion to describe how well you perform. Self-management skill phrases like the following can be impressive on a resume.

- Increased sales by 60% in two years

- Maintained a 98% accuracy rate for the last five years as a bank teller

- Maintained a zero absenteeism rate for the last five years

- Maintained a no-lost work day injuries record for the last 3 years

- 7 years experience in fast food management

- Maintained a 3.8 GPA in college

- Process documents at 60 words per minute

Self-management skills can also be phrased in a qualitative fashion to express how well you perform, as in the following examples.

- Positive rapport with teen clientele
- Goal-oriented management style
- Manage time and resources effectively
- Strong technical and reader-friendly writing styles
- Persuasive oral presentations
- Teambuilding for quality service
- Recognized for . . . (select any of these: leadership, integrity, organization, customer service)
- Strong people skills

Self-management skills phrased in either a quantitative or qualitative manner can be placed in a resume under a category called "Key Achievements," "Accomplishments," "Qualifications," or included with your "Work History" or "Education." Resume construction will be discussed in a later section of this section.

When the employer asks you the interview questions, "What are your strengths?" or "What are your skills?", you will have the best of your skills for that job ready in your mind. Also, remember that as you get older, many of your personal characteristics—your values, interests, skills, and so on—may change. Self-awareness is a constant process. Come back to this section of the text from time to time to keep track of changes. Search for some of the free self-assessment tools on the Web. You'll find that self-awareness is a great tool when it comes to planning your career.

INVESTIGATING CAREER OPTIONS

How much do you know about different occupations? Choosing occupations becomes easier not only when you understand yourself but when you are knowledgeable about the occupations available to you. Libraries are full of information on thousands of occupations—just look up the one that interests you. Most college or public libraries have several different computer and printed resources that briefly and concisely outline occupational information: job description, salary, training, advancement, aptitudes required, employment potential, and work performed. The Web has a vast amount of career planning and occupational resources. Try searching the Web with keywords/phrases such as "job search," "employment," "U.S. Department of Labor," or your state's "Department of Labor"; occupational exploration on the Web is almost endless. The following websites will provide you with details about a wide range of occupations:

1. **Occupational Outlook Handbook** (http://bls.gov/ooh), a U.S. Bureau of Labor Statistics publication, is revised every two years and describes what workers do on their job, working conditions, the training and education needed, earnings, expected job prospects, job search tips, job market information for each state, and much more.

2. **Occupational Information Network (O*NET)**
(http://www.onetonline.org), developed under the sponsorship of the U.S. Department of Labor/Employment and Training Administration, is a tool for career exploration and job analysis. O*NET has an occupational database that contains comprehensive information on job requirements and worker competencies. O*NET replaced the Dictionary of Occupational Titles and offers users a more dynamic way of exploring occupations. This resource even identifies Holland's Occupational Personality Type for each occupation, which is referred to as the "interest code" in O*NET.

3. **CareerOneStop** (http://www.careeronestop.org) is sponsored by the U.S. Department of Labor, Employment and Training Administration, and is a comprehensive career resource library, job search center, and provides resume and interviewing help and examples.

Exercise 9-7 Exploring occupations

Directions:

1. Use the available occupational resources in your school, community library, and/or the Web to search for and explore an occupation you're interested in that is related to your course of study.
2. Answer the questions listed in the Occupational Exploration Outline below.

Occupational Exploration Outline

1. *Job title*—Write the name of the job you're investigating.

2. *Job description*—Describe the basic tasks involved in the job.

3. *Necessary skills*—List twenty work-specific skills necessary to perform this job.

4. *Education and training requirements*—List training, apprenticeships, vocational or college education required.

5. *License, certification, examinations required*—Does this job require that you pass an examination (physical or written, or both) or apply for and receive a license/certificate? If so, describe how it is obtained.

6. *Time involved*—How many hours per week are usually spent in this kind of job? Are the hours flexible? Is there a lot of overtime?

7. *National salary level*—List average entry-level salary for the nation. (Can you find a local or state average salary?)

8. *Employment outlook*—What are the prospects for employment during the next five to ten years in this profession? Are there any specific areas of the country with more opportunities for this kind of work?

9. *Professional organizations/unions*—List any unions you would be required to join or any professional organizations available to you, or both.

10. *Career advancement*—List the ladder of occupations you could climb as you gained experience and training.

11. *Holland's Occupational Type*—Use O*NET to identify this occupation's "interest code."

Informational Interviews

Occupational exploration obviously is not limited to the use of printed and Wev resources. You probably have been gathering occupational information for many years simply by asking others about their jobs. Author Richard Bolles, in his annually revised book, *What Color Is Your Parachute?* recommends the use of an informational interview to find out if you would like a job before you commit yourself to preparation for it or apply for it.[3]

To conduct an **informational interview,** you locate people who are involved in work that interests you and arrange to meet and talk with them about it. Be prepared to ask specific questions so you can learn as much as possible without wasting anyone's valuable time. The purpose of an informational interview is to gain job information and broaden your network of contacts for future references.

Tips . . . For Conducting Informational Interviews

- Learn as much as you can about the organization before you conduct the interview. Dress professionally, and bring copies of your resume to give if it seems appropriate.

- Locate someone who is working in a job in which you are interested and courteously explain to her that you are trying to learn more about that field of work. Ask for 15 to 30 minutes of her time to learn more about her job. You may consider asking her for a lunch meeting or asking if you could have a tour of the company. Telephone and email interviews are acceptable, but face-to-face interviews usually are more helpful.

- Prepare a list of specific questions that explore duties, skills, working conditions, problems, hours, and the organization itself. Keep in mind that this is an information-gathering and advice-seeking interview, not an employment interview. Consider using some of the following questions:

    "How did you get into this type of work? What did you study in school?"
    "What do you enjoy most about your job? What are the personal rewards?"
    "What do you enjoy least about your job? What are its drawbacks?"
    "What are some of the most interesting aspects of your job?"
    "What type of educational preparation and training do you recommend for this type of job?"
    "Would you suggest any part-time work experiences that would help me prepare for this type of work?"
    "If you were hiring a person for this position, what qualities, characteristics, and skills would you look for?"
    "What special advice would you give to someone entering this field?"
    "What type of salary range would a person starting in my field expect to make?" Never ask, "How much money would I expect to make?"

- Send a thank-you note. You may want to keep the individual you have interviewed posted on your progress.

- Evaluate the information you have received. How does it relate to your career plans?

---

[3]Richard Nelson Bolles, *What Color Is Your Parachute? 2014 A Practical Manual for Job-Hunters and Career-Changers* (Berkeley, CA: Ten Speed Press, 2009, revised annually).

JOB SEARCH STRATEGIES

Research is a critical part of the job search process. Today, most jobs are found by locating new job openings or vacancies which are posted on the Web and by social and business networking that provides you with contacts from which you can draw job leads, referrals, ideas, or information on businesses, industries, or agencies that may be hiring in your field. If you are still in college, make sure you take advantage of your college's career planning and placement services. In this section, you will explore both traditional and online job searching and networking strategies, and learn what assistance your college may offer.

Job Searching via the Web

The Web has provided employers with the easiest and most far-reaching method for advertising job openings. Some of the best Web sources for the job hunter may include:

1. Company website job ads—you can locate company websites by entering the full name of the business into a search engine such as Google, Bing, or Yahoo!.

2. State job banks—http://www.careeronestop.org/JobSearch/COS_jobsites.aspx.

3. Private sector job sites—such as CareerBuilder (http://www.careerbuilder.com), CoolJobs.com (http://www.cooljobs.com), and Monster.com (http://www.monster.com). You can find others listed at: http://www.careeronestop.org/JobSearch/FindJobs/PrivateSectorJobSites.aspx.

4. Government Sponsored Job Site—such as USAJOBS (http://www.usajobs.gov) and VetSuccess (http://www.vetsuccess.va.gov)

5. Other job sources that can be found on the Web include:

    *   Recruiting and staffing services which focus on matching your skills with the job openings of employers or companies; almost always, the employer pays their fees so there is no cost to you.
    *   Subscriptions to listservs and blogs that post job listings.
    *   Newsletters from professional associations and trade journals.
    *   Newspaper classified ads.
    *   College placement services.
    *   Union hall jobs—may be posted via a variety of web services but you can search for them with the key phrase "union hall jobs."

As you are searching company websites for job openings in your field, you can also gather information that will help you construct your resume and cover letter and prepare for an interview. While on their websites, search for their vision or mission statements, product or service descriptions, and hiring policies. You can locate company websites by entering the full name of the business into a search engine such as Google, Bing, or Yahoo.

There are many job search strategies and resources available to you. If you are looking for your first after-college job, use your college's career services office for job-search assistance. Your college career services office has contacts with business and industry in your local area and may also have contacts nationwide.

Using Your College Career Services Office

Most colleges have a career services office that assists students in locating jobs, as well as in preparing resumes and cover letters. The office also may offer a credentials package service, which allows you to keep an updated file on your employment credentials (transcripts, letters of reference, resumes, and data sheets). The credentials package can be sent to prospective employers with your written consent.

Exercise 9-8 My college's career services office

Make an appointment to speak with a counselor at your school's career services office. Find out as much information as you can—from what hours the office is open to what services are provided. Write the information you find in the following space, where you can refer back to it when you need to.

_____

_____

_____

_____

_____

_____

_____

_____

_____

_____

_____

_____

_____

_____

Networking as Part of Your Job Search

Many jobs are found informally, through personal contact with friends, relatives, acquaintances, and through online social media contacts. Making contacts with others and making use of the contacts you already have to find work and advance your career is called **networking**. Often a friend of a friend knows about a position that's available, or an instructor recommends that a colleague grant you an interview. It may also be by a chance meeting—while attending an event you meet someone who works at a company you are interested in, and by actively listening and asking a few questions, you learn some helpful tips about job openings and how to get your foot in the door.

Remember, when you're networking, you're not yet actually applying for a job—you're inquiring about possible job opportunities and making others aware of your career interests. We can actually learn a lot through networking—career ideas, new potential career paths, understanding of an occupation or company, and learning from the experience of others. The more you network, the more you will realize there's a lot you can learn. Your network is only limited by the company you keep, both on and off the job. Just don't think the only time you are networking is during a job search. You can reap the same networking benefits using social media to network, which will be discussed a little later.

The old fashion (but still very effective) way people network may include:

• Volunteering for Hospice and helping build a home.
• Attending professional meetings and conferences—especially as a student.
• Visiting with other parents during your child's sporting or music events.
• Visiting with other members of your social clubs or religious groups.
• Talking with your neighbors.
• Striking up a conversation with someone else waiting at the veterinarian's office.
• Re-connecting with former colleagues.
• Talking to your parents', uncle's, or grandmother's work colleagues.

Online networking is growing fast and furious. Some of the most popular ways to network online include:

- Re-connecting with former colleagues on one of the many social media sites.
- Posting your career profile on LinkedIn.
- Building your personal "brand" with Twitter, one tweet at a time.
- Searching out friends (current as well as former) on Facebook.

Like most of technology, social media has become a predominant method for job and employee searching. With a decent posting you can "advertise" yourself, career interests, or even your character in a way that you could be favorably seen as a potential job candidate. (Just make sure you have a quality posting so it doesn't have the opposite effect.) Social media has really opened up people's identities beyond what you'd see on a resume and can be used to predetermine whether an applicant should even be considered for employment. Social media networks such as LinkedIn, Facebook, and Twitter are at this writing the three top social media sites for job and employee seekers. Social networks are growing, changing, and new ones are launching offering an abundance of professional and job search networking possibilities. Since you aren't face-to-face with others, the stress of making these new connections is greatly alleviated. It is, however, very important that you make sure the words you use and the ways in which they are presented properly represent your intentions. You don't want to make a mess of a great opportunity to connect with people in hiring places! Social networking gives you the advantage of have a Web presence that highlights you, your work experiences, education and additional training, your work philosophy, and additional items that you want to showcase to the prospective employer or recruiter who is lurking on the sites for potential candidates. According to a recent survey by Reppler,[4] a social media monitoring service, more than 91 percent of employers surveyed stated that they used social networking to screen prospective employees, most often after they had already received an application, with the majority using Facebook, Twitter, and LinkedIn. Sixty-nine percent said they have rejected a prospective employee because of what they say on a social networking site.

At this writing, **LinkedIn** is the most dominant and largest professional network where members connect with each other, participate in groups, provide answers to questions posted by other members, display their career profile, and interact with each other. Many employers and recruiters also post jobs at this recognized site. LinkedIn is also a great site for the person who seems to be continuously on the lookout for new job opportunities. By forming a wide array of contacts, you are able to utilize those connections in your job hunt. Most functions of LinkedIn are free. Upgrades are available for additional functionality. Check the Linkedin website for current details—http://www.linkedin.com.

Facebook is a social networking website that is operated and privately owned by Facebook, Inc. Users can add friends and send them messages or their latest photos, play games, and update their personal profiles to notify friends about themselves. Additionally, users can join networks organized by city, workplace, and school or college. Users and employers can use Facebook to get an alternative look at a potential job candidate. The website's name stems from the informal name of books given at the start of the academic year by university administrations with the intention of helping students to get to know each other better. Check the Facebook website for current details—http://www.facebook.com.

Twitter is a free social networking and micro blogging service that enables its users to send and read messages known as *tweets*. Tweets are text-based posts of up to 140 characters displayed on the author's profile page and delivered to the author's subscribers who are known as *followers*. Senders can restrict delivery to those in their circle of friends or, by default, allow open access. You can use Twitter to announce to the world that you are looking for employment, and many companies post their job openings on Twitter. Check the Twitter website for current details—http://twitter.com.

---

[4]Swallow, Erica. 10-23-2011. *How Recruiters Use Social Networks to Screen Candidates* [INFOGRAPHIC]. Mashable. Retreived Feb. 22, 2012, from http://mashable.com/2011/10/23/how-recruiters-use-social-networks-to-screen-candidates-infographic.

There are many other smaller social media sites, but, at this writing, these are the most popular. Who knows what the future will bring? You can always search the Web for tips on using social media and the best social networks for your job search. You can even find numerous sites like "Social Networking for Dummies" on the Internet. And, the following are some suggestions for successful networking through social media.

Tips . . . For Successful Networking via Social Media

- Explore social network sites and join ones that will help you connect with people in your field. You can showcase your expertise and portray yourself as confident, positive, and professional. Don't post anything you would not want your mother to see. Also know that employers are looking for someone who is well rounded—professional and personable. So be relaxed and also highlight some of your hobbies and activities that display your interests, character, and abilities.

- Be thoughtful when networking online. First impressions are very important, so be very careful with your first public posting.

- Use your career profile to your advantage by creating a positive feel, using solid communication skills, and showing an employer that you can be a good fit for their company.

- Be sure to read each site's privacy policy and user agreement carefully.

- Your online behavior matters more than you think. Don't be an idiot!

- Learn the rules of behavior for a particular social media and follow them.

- Got digital dirt? Clean it up before you begin your job search. Remove any photos, content, and links that can work against you in an employer's eyes.

- Type your name into a search engine to check out what comes up about you.

- Because at this writing, LinkedIn is the network to join for professionals, the remaining tips apply to using LinkedIn for your work, professional networking, and job searching.

  - Establish a non-work, dedicated email address. This is the email account you use for your job search and for social media, and it must be different from your work email address.

  - If you *don't* have a job, think of your social media profiles as "live" versions of your resume. If your online career profile isn't current, update it with the parts of your work history that you enjoyed doing. (If you don't like bookkeeping or some other current or former responsibility, don't include it.)

  - Get a good headshot photo of yourself. Having a complete "profile," which includes a nice photo of yourself, means your profile is many times more likely to be viewed. The photo should not be goofy or silly. It should be a good business-like pose with a clear view of your face—no provocative clothing, poses, or backgrounds. Use that same photo as your "personal logo" across all of your social networks, and do not change it more than once every few years. (Note: the reason for the photo recommendation is to increase viewing; however, photos are not recommended for placement on a resume—more on that later.)

(continued)

– Create your LinkedIn profile. You have seen that LinkedIn is the network used by the majority of employers, so that's the best place for you to focus your attention and begin to build your online reputation. You can locate online guidelines on using LinkedIn for your job search for more details on building your LinkedIn career profile and network.

– Become active and visible. Maintain a professional attitude, demonstrate your skills and knowledge, share good information (all social networks are great for this), and be active. Update your LinkedIn Profile. Tweet about relevant news and information for your profession and/or industry. Post interesting things on your Facebook Wall for others to see, and make relevant, intelligent comments on other Facebook Walls. Share information, promote others, and grow your network.

– Focus on supporting your current job and employer, if you have a job. Social media can help you be more successful in your current job.

– It will probably take a while to get your social media networks established, so even if you are employed, get started.

Tips . . . For Successful Job Search Networking—In Person

• Be friendly when speaking to people and show your appreciation for the time and assistance that they give you.

• Be specific about the skills and abilities you have, as well as for what type of work you're looking. "An entry-level position in an electronics firm" is specific; "Oh, you know, something with computers" is not.

• If one particular person cannot help you, ask if he or she knows of anyone else who might be able to help. Be open to meeting new people; this widens your network of acquaintances.

• Let *everyone* know you're looking for work. You never know who will give you the information that leads to a great job. It might come from the most unlikely source.

• Be ready to return the favor. When friends and family ask you for job leads someday, give them advice and suggestions just as they did for you.

• Join and participate in a professional association in your field. Students can generally join a state, regional, or national professional organization at a student rate. Attending professional organization conferences is an excellent way to learn more about your field and make contacts with those who work in it.

USING YOUR PORTFOLIO TO MARKET YOURSELF FOR THE JOB

Developing a portfolio is not a new concept in marketing yourself for a job. Artists, architects, photographers, models, and others in the arts have used portfolios to show prospective employers examples of their work. Almost any type of professional can use a portfolio as a self-marketing tool for employment. Quality portfolios can give you an edge on the competition because the employer can see samples of your writing, projects, technology skills, and/or products from previous employment or class projects—it shows the prospective employer what kind of work you can do for them. Many colleges require e-portfolios; some job hunters create personal websites to act as their portfolio, and many use social media such as Facebook, LinkedIn, YouTube, and other social media sites to showcase aspects of their portfolio.

You can introduce your portfolio during a job interview, provide a link to your e-portfolio on your resume or cover letter, or offer to send the prospective employer your portfolio. You need to "read" the situation and decide how best to introduce your portfolio. On your resume you may simply write the following statement at the bottom: "Portfolio and references available @ email address/link, or upon request." If you send or leave a print portfolio with an employer, make sure it is a duplicate and not the portfolio containing all your original documents. If you are introducing your portfolio during the interview, it may be a good idea to show your original documents. Keep updating your portfolio with example work from work or class assignments.

You can begin a portfolio when you begin your college education. Collect, photograph, scan, and keep digital samples of noteworthy projects from college or previous employment. When your professor gives you the opportunity to select your own research paper topic, project, or work experience, select assignments that are related to your field. Complete your assignments with a professional effort. Use a computer and quality printer to publish materials. Save and organize these assignments in a quality portfolio, three-ring binder, and in electronic format. Take your portfolio to the job interview to show prospective employers what kind of work you can do for them. Other items you may wish to keep in your portfolio include certificates, licenses, photos of projects, displays, products you have created, printed programs that list your involvement in a service or production, conference booklets (from professional conferences, workshops, and seminars you attended), examples of your technology skills (PowerPoint presentation, podcast, video, or e-publication), and evidence of important memberships (offices held, participation in professional or community organizations). What other items could you place in your portfolio?

Using assignments to place in your portfolio adds a new dimension to completing assignments. Now you have a greater motivation to produce quality work and select work-related projects.

YOUR RESUME

The resume is not going away yet because many employers still want to see it and hold it in their hands, especially during the interview. What has changed about the resume is that applicants are more likely to submit resumes online, reference their online career profile on their resume with a link, and employers and recruiters are increasingly reviewing both resumes and online career profiles, to learn more about the applicants and to determine which ones they will invite for an interview. Resumes are, however, still very functional and they give you the flexibility to customize your resume to fit the position you are seeking. Even employers who post job ads on LinkedIn are still requiring a resume submission; so, nope, the resume is not going away yet and neither is social media! Complete Exercise 9-9, and learn more about what LinkedIn has to offer.

Exercise 9-9 Check out LinkedIn

Describe how LinkedIn can help you search for a job.

_____

_____

_____

_____

_____

Describe the differences between the contents of a resume and a LinkedIn profile.

_____

_____

_____

_____

_____

Large companies and recruiting agencies are inundated every day with resumes from job-seekers, so employers and recruiters have increasingly relied on digitizing resumes. Digitizing resumes involves placing those resumes in keyword-searchable databases, and using software to search those databases for specific keywords that relate to job openings. The bottom line is that if you apply for a job with a company that searches databases for keywords, and your resume doesn't contain the keywords the company seeks for open positions, you are pretty much left off the interview list.

Writing a resume is still the first step to marketing yourself for employment, because as part of this process, you have to determine all the information you need to prepare an exceptional resume—your education and training, work/professional experience, work-specific skills, and achievements. Once you have developed your resume, it can also help you create an online career profile, if desired. You can include a link to your online profile to give the employer a more well-rounded picture of you. The purpose of sending your resume and a link to your online career profile to potential employers is to obtain an interview, not to secure a job offer. Virtually no one will hire a person baed solely on a resume and/or social media profile. Employers will want to invite you to interview and engage you in a discussion about your qualifications, experiences, and problem solving skills, to determine if you are a good fit for the position and the company. A good resume is still at the heart of getting employers interested in meeting you. It's the interview that leads to the job offer.

Resume writing is an art, and it takes time to create an exceptional resume—and who doesn't want an exceptional resume! In the next sections, you will be introduced to a variety of alternatives and ideas for writing your resume, so you can design an exceptional resume that attracts an employer and makes them want to invite you in for an interview.

The following tips are important considerations for you to think about as you create your resume.

Tips . . . For Writing an Effective Resume

- Do your best to highlight how your qualifications and capabilities match the employer's needs. As appropriate, stress your skills and abilities in terms of your potential for solving the employer's problems.

- Organize the information on your resume in accordance with your desired impact on the reader. That's why you usually list your work experience in **reverse chronological** order—because your most important and applicable jobs are likely to be the most recent. Sometimes people decide not to use a strict reverse chronological order so employment gaps are less visible—more on that later.

- If you have past work experience, include accomplishments that will set you apart from other job applicants and show how you may benefit the prospective employer. Consider highlighting accomplishments where you made (or saved) money for your company, improved efficiency/saved time, created solutions to problems, built customer relationships, attracted new customers, expanded services or business, or improved employee performance (or job satisfaction). Of course if you have little work experience, you will probably have some significant college work simulation projects to highlight—that's another good reason to work hard on those projects.

- Be honest; but this does not mean you have to confess your negative attributes or shortcomings on your resume.

- Use clear, concise, impactful language, consistent grammar, and active verbs that will convincingly show the employer that you are a good match for the position requirements—that means your skills, accomplishments, and background clearly match up to the position description. (See a list of active verbs in Table 9-1 that may help you better express your skills and accomplishments.)

(continued)

- Use concise bulleted phrases—no unnecessary words, no pronouns, and avoid abbreviations. Being able to express yourself clearly on paper is a selling point no matter what job you're aiming for.

- Analyze job ads and descriptions to identify and use key words and phrases to include in your resume that will describe your qualifications so they closely match the requirements in the position description. Remember, employers and recruiters use keywords and phrases to select qualified applicants and retrieve e-resumes from databases. If you don't use the appropriate keywords and phrases, your resume will unlikely be included in the interview pile.

- Prioritize the content of you resume with the most important information first. For example, if you have a significant amount of work experience related to the job for which you are applying, you may want to place your work experience ahead of your education. If your degree(s) are a specific requirement for the job, you may want to list your education ahead of your work experience.

- Your resume should let people know that you are a highly responsible and energetic person who gets things done.

- The rule of thumb to determine how long your resume should be as follows:

  - If you have little work experience, or you are applying for an entry-level position, and especially if there is a lot of competition, keep the length of the resume to one page if you can, two pages at the very most. Avoid unnecessary fluff—include only pertinent qualifications that will show the employer that you are a good match for the position.

  - If you have a significant amount of professional work experience and are applying for a higher level position, you are likely to have somewhat less competition and you may need several pages to highlight how well you match the position. This takes some critical thinking. You can also ask for advice at your college's career services office.

  - Note: Some people include add-on pieces to their resume that highlight a particular project or initiative relative to the position.

- Use the following formatting guidelines:

  - Make sure you have plenty of white space for ease in reading where resume category headings can be easily seen and the employer can quickly find the information she is looking for. Keep in mind that employers may spend a few seconds to decide if your resume will get a second look and maybe a minute or two to decide if it warrants an interview.

  - Balance the material on your page.

  - Allow sufficient white space with margins of .75" to 1". Note that Microsoft Word's default margins of 1.25" are generally wider than needed. Avoid a crammed resume. Adequate white space and prominent category headings can be easily seen and the employer can quickly find the information she is looking for.

  - Bulleted lists are extremely reader-friendly.

  - Be consistent with headings so the eye can follow a pattern.

(continued)

- No more than two typefaces should appear on one resume, but if you don't have an eye for good design, stick to one typeface. Times New Roman, Garamond, Arial, Verdana, or Helvetica used alone is a fine choice for your resume. If you want to mix two typefaces, try using Helvetica (or Arial) for headings and Times New Roman for the text. Using larger type (12, 14, or 16 pt.) or boldface for headings can give them necessary prominence. Use italics sparingly; you don't want to overdo emphasis. Avoid underlining—it tends to add clutter.

- Your resume must be legible, and too much fancy type and design will make it harder to read.

- Use parallelism—consistency in grammatical parts of speech. It is usually best (but not always) to begin bullet points with verbs. In most cases, you should avoid mixing nouns and verbs. Be consistent with verb forms for each listing (all "-ed" verbs or all "-ing" verbs, but not a mixture of the two).

- Consult resume-writing websites or books. Your college or local library or career services office will generally have quick resume writing guides or books for you.

- After you prepare what you think is your final copy, very carefully recheck for grammar, spelling, and overall appearance of the resume. Ask an instructor, advisor, or trusted friend to proofread your resume—this is a must for anyone! Make sure there are no typos.

- When you're sure it's perfect, have it printed on high-quality paper in a white or off-white shade. Or, if you plan to email it or submit it through a company website, attach or post it as directed and double check the posting to ensure the proper format is retained. Look for and follow the company's guidelines for submitting resumes through their website.

- Although it is becoming less and less common to send resumes by postal mail, ideally you should mail your resume flat (no folding).

- If you are considering using a Portable Document Format (PDF) resume, it will keep your resume invulnerable to viruses, compatible across computer systems, and appearance consistent from computer to computer. The downside is that it can be more difficult to perform keyword searches on PDF resumes unless they are scanned first or the text is extracted from them. Few employers specifically request PDF resume files.

Thinking Outside the Box Marketing

Large, traditional companies may have more rigid hiring processes and show little interest in out-of-the-box application documents. However, some companies are by nature more creative and versatile, and may expect you to use alternative approaches to get their attention. These companies may require examples of your qualifications using social media, video, podcasts, or a Google Adwords campaign, so they can click on a link and land on your website to learn more about you and see your qualifications. You may also be able to find a way to combine both the traditional resume-cover letter-application route and an alternative route and get yourself ahead of the pack. Organizations want to hire smart, innovative people. Showing how you fall into both those categories can give you a leg up! Again, using college assignments to place in your portfolio gives you greater motivation to select work-related projects to produce quality work.

Table 9-1
Active Verbs

accommodate	consolidate	execute	rectify
achieve	consult	expand	reduce
acquaint	control	expedite	regulate
activate	convert	extend	remove
adapt	coordinate	familiarize	reorganize
administer	counsel	formulate	repair
advise	create	govern	replace
advocate	curtail	group	report
advertise	demonstrate	guarantee	restore
alter	designate	guide	simplify
analyze	design	maintain	solve
appraise	determine	manage	sponsor
approve	develop	measure	stabilize
assemble	direct	merge	strengthen
assist	disclose	minimize	study
assume	discontinue	modernize	supervise
attach	discover	modify	supplement
attain	dispatch	motivate	surpass
augment	display	observe	teach
authorize	distribute	obtain	terminate
balance	economize	operate	train
build	educate	organize	transfer
classify	eliminate	originate	transform
collect	employ	plan	unify
combine	encourage	prescribe	update
command	establish	procure	utilize
communicate	estimate	produce	veto
conceive	evaluate	publicize	write
condense	examine	publish	

Again, resume writing is an art and it takes time to create an exceptional resume! The next section outlines a list of possible components (category headings) used to build a resume. You will probably want to customize each resume you send, at least to some extent, to the job you're applying for. After reviewing the position description, you can determine which components you will want to include in your resume. For the purposes of this course, it will be helpful to you to build a resume with most of the components for the sole purpose of having a compressive resume that will serve as a base to build future resumes. Once you have a comprehensive resume, you can continue to add new education, training, and professional work experiences and modify it to fit the job you're applying for. Ultimately, you should have a resume e-folder with subfolders for the different types of jobs you have applied for. As you read about the following components of a resume, think about how you might use them to design an exceptional resume that attracts the employer and makes them want to call you in for an interview.

Major Components of a Resume

Your name, contact information, education, and experience are must category headings. And the other category headings should be selected to meet your job search needs.

1. **Your full name**

   - **First, last and middle initial**
   - Larger font, bold
   - No Mr., Mrs., or Ms.

2. **Contact Information**

   - Following your name, prominently list **your email address, residence address, and phone number(s).** (Do not use a heading.)
   - If you are away at college, you may want to list your school address and a permanent address. List phone numbers you deem necessary (cell, work, or residence).

3. **Professional or Career Objective**

   - Your objective (if used) should immediately follow your contact information.
   - Objectives should reflect the employer's perspective (not the jobseeker's), be concise and specific but not limiting, help sharpen the focus of your resume, and should tell what you can contribute. An objective should demonstrate the value the candidate will add to the organization. Make sure that it clearly tells employers what you want to do for the organization, using job titles or descriptions that reflect the job you want.
   - You can communicate your willingness to travel or relocate (if appropriate).
   - Some people choose to omit the professional objective because they believe it is limiting.
   - Some employers want to see an objective to size up your intentions, and other employers say objectives are often poorly written and waste space.
   - Modify your objective so it is specific to each job you apply for. If you are handing out copies of your resume at a career fair, consider omitting the objective or have copies with varying objectives appropriate to the variety of positions that you may be eligible for. A qualifications summary which follows is often used instead of the objective.
   - See three example professional objectives below:

     (1) To manage people, interface with customers, and work with highly technical software and hardware applications. (Computer Technology student)
     (2) To pursue my career in management utilizing skills in financial services, administrative procedure, training, and personnel policies. Willing to travel. (Business Management student)
     (3) A retail management position where demonstrated skills in sales and marketing and enthusiasm for innovation will be used for improving customer service and expanding profit margins. Willing to relocate. (Management/Marketing student)

4. **Qualifications Summary**

- A qualifications summary allows you to list statements, especially keywords and phrases relevant to the job you seek such as:
    - Key accomplishments/achievements
    - Transferrable and work-specific skills
    - Your willingness to travel or relocate (if appropriate)
    - Other qualifications that the employer is in search of

- See example qualifications summary statements below and notice the different grammatical approaches:

    - Proficient in Microsoft applications
    - 25 years in sales-related capacities
    - Strong interpersonal and group facilitation skills
    - Professional and concise writing skills
    - Public relations and brand promotion
    - Project management, tracking, and reporting on deliverables

    - Create assessment-based fitness plans
    - Design window displays
    - Plan, coordinate, and execute events including community outreach initiatives
    - Deliver persuasive sales presentations
    - Design and implement custom electronic circuits for signal conditioning, data acquisition and control functions

    - Recognized for leadership, integrity, organization, and customer service
    - Researched consumer needs for AT&T
    - Resolved customer problems satisfactorily while managing exchange and return department
    - Instructed customer relations training program for over 2,000 trainees in 3 years
    - Created an employee incentive program to reduce absenteeism

- A Qualification Summary may also be headed: "Professional Profile," "Profile" "Qualifications in Brief," or "Key Achievements."

5. **Education**

- Credential (degree, diploma, or certificate)—list this first.
- School name, city, and state.
- Major or program of study.
- As appropriate, list your minor, emphasis, or concentration.
- Date of graduation (or expected graduation)—month, year, and once out of school a year or so, omit the month.
- Work-related courses—as appropriate.
- List schools in reverse chronological order.
- This section can appear before or after your experience section, depending on whether your degree or your experience is your best selling point. Always list the most relevant section first. If you are a current college student or about to graduate, generally you would list education first. If you are currently working, generally you would list experience first. The category that qualifies you most for the position you are applying for should go first!

- Once you have completed a college degree/credential, do not list your high school or General Education Diploma (GED).

6. **Experience**

- Sometimes this heading is also stated as "Employment" or "Work Experience." "Experience" is a more inclusive heading because it enables you to list activities other than paid employment, such as volunteer work, internships, sports-team participation, and class projects. If space permits, you could also have both a "Work Experience" and a "Volunteer Work" category. Determine what headings are most fitting.
- List each experience in reverse chronological order. Include full-time, part-time, significant volunteer, club, or organization work, internships, and/or other specific position-related experiences that could help you land the job.
- List job title including the business or company name, city, and state. Stating the company description is optional but may be useful to employers or recruiters.
- List dates of employment (include month or seasonal descriptor and year).
- Bullet list key accomplishments, and quantify accomplishments whenever possible.
- List work-specific skills. Use active verbs when describing your accomplishments. (See a list of active verbs in Table 9-1 that may help you better express your skills and accomplishments.)
- Some prefer to use a job-related functional categorization of work experience—that is arranging work experiences by types of work, instead of using a reverse chronological format. The functional categorization format has been used as a way to deemphasize employment gaps, but note that this format may be unpopular with employers and especially recruiters. As we know, through business closings and downsizing, many have lost jobs. It is important to determine how you can shed a positive light on such gaps in your resume, cover letter, and/or interview. You may also want to highlight how you used this time productively to upgrade your skills and advance your knowledge for future employment. Another approach, if you can legitimately do so, is to frame periods of unemployment as stints of education, training, self-employment, consulting, or project work. Unfortunately, employment gaps may be a red flag, so they should be explained in your resume if you can gracefully do so. Other options include explaining gaps in your cover letter or being prepared to do so in an interview. (However, gaps have eliminated applicants from getting an interview.)
- Avoid placing the following items on a resume:
  - Height, weight, age, date of birth, place of birth, marital status, sex, race, health, social security number.
  - Reasons for leaving previous job(s).
  - Name of boss or supervisor.
  - Street addresses and phone numbers of past employers.
  - Picture of yourself—it can be used to discriminate.
  - Religion, church affiliations, political affiliations—unless you know it will definitely help you, but remember to remove it for a job where it may be used to discriminate against you.
  - Salary information.
  - Specific names of references (more on this issue later).
  - The title "Resume."

7. **Extracurricular and community activities**—This is optional, to be included only if you think it will enhance your desirability in the eyes of the employer.

8. **Other potential category headings** that may help market you for the job:

   - Branding statement—learn what a branding statement is by completing Exercise 9-10.
   - Online career profile link for LinkedIn, Twitter, or other social media networks—could be added as a footer at the bottom of the last page of the resume or part of the header.
   - Licenses/Certifications
   - Affiliations/Memberships (of non-controversial groups)
   - Foreign Travel—if valuable for the position
   - Public Speaking, Presentations
   - Publications
   - Volunteer, Civic/ Community Service, Fund-Raising, Leadership, and Athletic activities.
   - Activities, Hobbies/Interests Publications—ask yourself: Does this information add value to my resume? Is it too risky? Space constraints may also guide your decision.
   - Military—which is usually listed in the "Experience" section.

9. **References**
   - There are a variety of options you may want to consider when addressing references in your resume.
     - End your resume with one of the following statements:
       a. "References available upon request."
       b. "Professional references available upon request."
       c. "Professional references and portfolio available upon request."

     - To save space you may want to leave off "References available upon request" because it is a given that you will be providing a list of references when requested.

   - If references are requested, list them on a separate sheet with a letterhead that matches your resume (and do not volunteer the reference sheet unless asked).
     - List a minimum of 3 business references: People who have direct knowledge of the quality of your daily job performance, your character, and are favorably impressed with you.
     - Always ask permission from those you wish to use for a job reference. It is a good idea to share a job description for the position to which you are applying and your current resume to your references—this will keep them informed about you.
     - List contact's name, title, company, complete address, phone number with area code, and email address (if they use it).

Exercise 9-10 Branding statements

Do your own web search to learn what a branding statement is. In the space below, explain a branding statement and give an example.

_____
_____
_____
_____
_____

Examine the sample resumes in Figure 9-3 and Figure 9-4.

Figure 9-3
Sample Resume (Associate Degree Student)

AYLA K. MADISON

1408 Wilderness Drive • Charleston, WV 23456
(304) 348-2098 • Ayla.Madison@gmail.com

OBJECTIVE

An Ombudsman Coordinator providing supervision and training for volunteer advocates for the elderly.

QUALIFICATIONS PROFILE

- Certified Volunteer Ombudsman
- Confidential complaint investigation
- Facilitative communication skills
- Training in elder abuse awareness
- Wellness promotion and advocacy

- Created client interview process and user's guide
- Knowledgeable of entitlement programs
- Proficiency in Microsoft Office applications
- Business correspondence and newsletter publication
- Research/instruction on nutrition for older adults

EDUCATION

Associate of Applied Science, Gerontology (High Honors)   May 2014
    Kanawha Valley Community and Technical College
    Charleston, West Virginia

Summer Institute on Health Aspects of Aging   August 2013
    American Society on Aging
    Seattle, Washington

Volunteer Ombudsman Certification   February 2012
    Charleston, West Virginia

EXPERIENCE

Volunteer Ombudsman   May 2012–May 2014
    Legal Aid Society of Charleston
    Charleston, West Virginia

- Monitor quality of life and care of residents in nursing homes, board and care homes, personal care homes, and assisted living facilities
- Confidential complaint investigation
- Community education

Activities Director for Alzheimer's Patients   August 2009–August 2013
    Teays Valley Health Care Center
    Scott Depot, West Virginia

- Plan activity calendar
- Publish center newsletter
- Lead activities and exercise
- Maintain patient activity records

PROFESSIONAL ASSOCIATION MEMBERSHIP

- American Society on Aging
- Sigma Phi Omega Gerontology Honor Society

Portfolio and references available upon request.

LinkedIn Profile: http://www.linkedin.com/ayla_madison

Figure 9-4
Sample Resume (Bachelor Degree Student)

ERIKA HYLTON

3802 BALTIC AVENUE • CHARLOTTE, NC 28212
704-439-1174 • ERIKA.HYLTON@GMAIL.COM

PROFESSIONAL SUMMARY

- Creative and critical thinking skills
- Excellent resource management skills
- Data analysis and revenue projection
- Strong interpersonal and group facilitation skills
- Plan, coordinate, and execute events including community outreach initiatives
- Professional and concise writing skills
- Public relations and brand promotion
- Donor and company research

- Budget oversight and cost-effective management
- Proven ability as a creative problem-solver
- Proficient in Microsoft applications
- Positive leadership skills and relationship building
- Project management, tracking, and reporting on deliverables
- Comfortable working across multiple levels within organizations

---

EXPERIENCE

United Way of Central Carolina   May 2010–Present
Charlotte, NC

Donor Relationship Manager
Provide management and oversight of all fundraising activities for assigned territory. This includes building relationship with internal and external stakeholders to develop strategies that align with the goals of United Way.
- Successful implementation of annual fundraising campaign raising $932,812 (104.7% of goal) in 2011.
- Secured 56 new Leadership gifts ($1,000+) resulting in $69,159 new dollars toward the 2011 annual campaign.
- Oversight of revenue forecasting and projection in regard to departmental goals.
- Collaboration of recruitment, orientation, development, management, and communications with volunteers for multiple events, activities, and fundraising efforts.
- Manage volunteers in developing action plans and projects for United Way's strategic priorities.
- Represent and promote United Way to a variety of community organizations and companies.
- Planned, coordinated, and executed two successful golf scrambles and two campaign celebration events.
- Designated Lead for 2012 special events.

Keep NC Beautiful   April 2006–April 2010
Charlotte, NC

Development Director
Supervised all fundraising programs, grants, contributions, deferred gifts, and development plans. Managed efforts to solicit and steward gifts for special fundraising initiatives, including direct mail, email, and Web communications along with the management of volunteer committees.

- Increased revenue 13% over a three-year period.
- Increased in-kind donations by 19% over a three-year period.
- Established and fostered relationships with volunteers, sponsors, donors, and potential donors.
- Prepared and presented funding proposals to individuals, groups, and organizations.
- Solicited support and participation of individuals, corporations, and foundations.
- Conducted event planning, coordination, and management while maintaining constant communication with all stakeholders.
- Increased Keep NC Beautiful visibility through strategic management of media and donor relations while constantly updating branded materials.
- Leveraged negotiations skills to produce discounts or donation of all outsourced services, supplies, and equipment.
- Periodically performed evaluations of programs for effectiveness in achieving strategic goals and objectives.
- Major Events:
    - Green Ball—Planned, managed, and hosted the inaugural event for young professionals, corporate sponsors, volunteers, and community leaders, resulting in a successful annual activity.
    - Keep NC Beautiful Annual Volleyball Tournament—collaborated in planning and execution of the event, additionally securing $40,000 in sponsorships and in-kind donations annually.
    - Keep NC Beautiful/Waste Management Annual Golf Scramble—planned and hosted the event while soliciting sponsorships.

Hylton Page 2

United Way of Central Carolina Charlotte, NC	May 2004–April 2006

Resource Development Division Manager
Provided management and oversight of all fundraising, public relations, and volunteer coordination for assigned accounts. Responsible for assisting in planning, organizing, and implementing fundraising programs, including direct-mail fundraising.

- Implemented successful annual fundraising campaigns raising $3,083,993 in 2005 and $2,904,627 in 2004.
- Analyzed and monitored accounts for opportunities in additional development.
- Contacted new or inactive accounts to obtain commitments for active campaigns.
- Assisted in development and testing of fundraising strategies and programs to improve effectiveness of campaigns.
- Designed and coordinated direct-mail fundraising efforts for corporate and individual donors.
- Recruited and assisted in management of the volunteers involved in the various campaigns, providing motivation and training.
- Solicited annual corporate and individual gifts to achieve yearly set organizational goals.
- Promoted United Way programs and services within various organizations in the Charlotte community.
- Established and fostered relationships with volunteers, donors, and potential donors.
- Regularly executed campaign analysis and presented budget projections for United Way's Executive Board.

Charlotte Observer Charlotte, NC	December 2003–April 2004

Recruitment Sales Assistant
Assisted in overall sales effort of the Classified Advertising Recruitment Team.
- Constantly maintained professional customer relations to ensure repeat business.
- Worked internally and externally to resolve customer issues.
- Meticulously proofread and edited advertisements prior to print.
- Generated leads for classified ads.

EDUCATION

Bachelor of Arts: Communications—Emphasis in Public Relations Coastal Carolina University	May 2010
Associate of Applied Science: Communication Studies Central Piedmont Community College	May 2003

ADDITIONAL TRAINING

- Consultative Sales	- Public Speaking
- Product Definition	- Grant Writing
- Persuasive Presentation Skills	- Sponsorship Proposals
- Business & Professional Communication	- Event Planning & Management
- Business Writing Skills	- Customer Relationship Management

COMMUNITY INVOLVEMENT, ACHIEVEMENTS, & HOBBIES

Habitat for Humanity—Volunteer	2011–Present
Charlotte Rescue Mission—Board Member	2008–2010
Plaza Midwood Neighborhood Association—Board Member	2007–2009
Coastal Carolina University Women's Basketball Team—Member	2000–2003
Hobbies: Basketball, Kickball, and Running	

How to Create a Scannable Resume

Many businesses contract with employment companies to manage job searches including advertising, sorting resumes, and often selecting resumes for interviewing. Employers who receive hundreds of resumes for each advertised opening use scanners to manage the quantity of paperwork. They invest in electronic databases which store resumes and are quickly accessible by a few simple computer commands. Resumes are entered into a system using an optical scanner, and the images are stored, building a database of applicants and relevant skills. Employers then access potential candidates by searching the database for qualifications. A resume that will first be read by a scanner needs to use a standard format and font that is readable by the scanner. Also, if you plan to put your resume on the Internet, it must be in a scannable format, and don't forget to list your email address on it. Many employers list their guidelines for scannable resumes on their company website, so be sure to check for any such guidelines before submitting your resume. Use the following tips so the computer system scanner will be better able to extract your information accurately.

- Begin your scannable resume with your contact information and objective statement. It is good to use an objective statement on a resume that will be scanned. Be sure to indicate the precise job for which you are applying. If your resume has two pages, place your name and a "page two" designation on the second page, and attach with a paper clip—no staples.

- Good scannable fonts are Arial, Calibri, and Times Roman. Avoid ornate fonts where the characters touch. Sizes between 10 points and 14 points work best. Do not use columns.

- Avoid using italics and underlining—they may be difficult for the scanner to read. Bolding is almost always okay.

- For bullets, use either hyphens or solid bullet characters—empty bullet characters could be interpreted as the letter *o,* and other characters could also be misread.

- Use vertical or horizontal lines sparingly. If used, leave at least a quarter of an inch of space around the line. Avoid graphics, shading, or shadowing.

- Do not compress or expand the space between letters or lines. Also, do not double-space within sections.

- Print your resume on white 8$\frac{1}{2}$ x 11 inch paper with a laser printer.

- If sent by mail, send in a manila or similar envelop to avoid folding, and do not staple.

- Describe your skills and accomplishments by using key words and phrases in the language of your profession.

- Keep it concise and simple.

- Place your email address at the top of your resume just below your name, address, and phone number. If you have two phone numbers, list each on its own line.

Many employers list their guidelines for scannable resumes on their company website, so be sure to check for and use the guidelines before submitting your resume. The following guidelines should help you create a resume content that will be captured

- Use enough key words and phrases—terms and phrases that are important in the industry in which you are applying. Identify words that your potential employers would likely use in their database searches, and make sure those terms are in your resume (e.g., B.S., Computer science, supervised, project management) to define your education, experience, and skills.

- Increase your list of key words by including specifics, for example, list the names of software you use
- Describe your experience in specific words rather than vague descriptions
- Use jargon and acronyms specific to your industry
- Avoid using pronouns (e.g, my, I, us)

COVER LETTERS

To put your best effort forward, you should include a cover letter when you submit your resume to an employer. A cover letter is particularly important because it is the first item the employer sees and reads. It does more than introduce your resume to the employer; it tells her or him who you are and why you're sending your resume. It's also an opportunity for the employer to see your writing capabilities and personality, and it distinguishes your application. A well-written cover letter gets the employer interested in seeing your resume, so take the time to write an exceptional cover letter. Infuse your cover letter with energy, personality, and details about your skills and achievements. Even if an employer doesn't request a cover letter, it's still helpful to send one.

Given all the good reasons to send a cover letter, is there ever a time when you should not send one? Evelyn Salvador, a nationally certified resume writer and career coach says: "Skip the cover letter, and you miss out on an opportunity to sell yourself."[5] If the application instructions specifically say not to include a cover letter, or if an online application offers no opportunity, then you can forego the cover letter in these cases. However, some applicants remain determined to send a cover letter (and resume) directly to an employer when the application website provides no opportunity to send a cover letter. This does work for some, but think carefully about this kind of action.

Study the tips for writing strong cover letters, and examine the sample cover letters shown in Figures 9-6 and 9-7.

Tips . . . For Writing Effective Cover Letters

- Send a customized cover letter with each resume you send out. Even if a company is too busy to fully read the cover letter, your letter may make the difference between obtaining a job interview and having your resume ignored. It is generally worth the extra effort.

- The letters you write represent you. Let them be carefully written, well thought out, friendly, perfectly printed, and signed by you unless it is submitted via email. Keep copies of all correspondence related to your job search.

- If possible, address the cover letter to the person in the company who makes the hiring decision or strongly influences the hiring. You don't want your letter lost among many applicants. *Spell that person's name properly*, and include her or his proper title. You can search the company's website to see if this information is available.

- Be businesslike, but be yourself. Write simply and clearly. Get right to the point and write short, targeted letters. Each letter should be one page or less. Each paragraph should contain three or four sentences at most.

- Let the person know why you're sending your resume. Are you responding to an ad, did you research the company yourself, or did someone recommend it? If you are writing on someone's advice, mention that person's name.

(continued)

---

[5]Salvador, Evelyn U. *Step-by-Step Cover Letters: Build a Cover Letter in 10 Easy Steps Using Personal Branding*. Jist Works, an imprint of Jist Publishing, Indianapolis, IN, 2010.

- Emphasize your skills, experiences, and accomplishments as they relate to the specific job you are applying for. Then target your cover letter. Take the job posting and list the criteria the employer is looking for. Then list the skills and experience you have. Either address how your skills match the job in paragraph form **or** create a two-column bullet list that displays the job criteria in one list and your qualifications in an adjacent list. Write a lead-in sentence (prior to the lists) referencing how your qualifications match the position criteria.

- Be polite. Request an interview, and thank the person for her time. Consider mentioning you will follow up your letter with a phone call if you do not hear from her within a certain amount of time. Show the prospective employer that you take an active role in looking for work.

- Spell check and proofread. Then ask someone else to read your letter before you send it. It's often easy not to notice mistakes in our own writing.

Figure 9-6
Sample Cover Letter

57 Maple Road
Richmond, VA 24567

Jane Peterson
Vice President
Hartford Enterprises
8900 Benjamin Road
Handley, Missouri 21446

August 8, 2014

Dear Ms. Peterson:

Jennifer Cartright, the Director of Data Systems at Occidental Engineering, has informed me that you are looking for an executive office administrator with experience in office management and strong computer skills. I have three years of administrative assistant experience and five years of experience as an office manager.

I am also aware that you are about to implement a new data management system. I believe I can assist you with that project. I have implemented electronic data management systems for all five of our Valley Bank branch offices in Richmond, Virginia.

I completed an Associate Degree in Office Administration with a concentration in information systems. Some of the programs which I use fluently include: SharePoint, Microsoft Office applications, and a variety of data management systems.

I believe that my qualifications are a good match for your needs. Enclosed you will find my resume for your consideration.

I would appreciate an opportunity to visit with you and discuss your office needs. I will call your office next week to inquire about an interview. You can reach me on my cell phone at 309-778-9867 or at home 309-776-6789 (evenings).

Thank you for your consideration.

Sincerely,

Ann Morgan

Enclosure

Figure 9-7
Sample Cover Letter

LESLEY G. ASHLEY
2208 Laughing Boulevard   Joyville, New Jersey 60209
lesley.ashley@gmail.com   904-649-8364

November 22, 2014

Dear Mr. Humor,

Please accept this letter as my application for the advertised Engage Life Director position in Joyville, New Jersey. The position description is in line with my aspirations as well as my education, skills, and experience. I hope you will find that I am a good fit for this position because I have a passion for providing older adults with meaningful activities and entertainment opportunities in a comfortable home and community atmosphere.

I have been consistently recognized for my ability to motivate, lead, and instruct. More importantly, you will learn that I smile a lot, use warm humor, and love to modify a variety of games and activities to meet the interests, needs, and abilities of residents. My associate's and bachelor's degrees in Exercise Science with emphases in cardiac/diabetic rehabilitation help me understand disease, fitness, and safety needs. Additionally, my broad work experience in the wellness field and leadership roles, as outlined in my resume, will enable me to make a significant and sustained contribution and help support this important service at Joyville Community Care.

My most relevant experiences include:
- Assisted Living Assistant Activity Director
- Fitness Manager
- Personal Trainer at private fitness clubs and gyms
- Intern at the Cooper Fitness Center in Dallas, Texas
- Two-year internship in Diabetes Exercise and Cardiac Rehabilitation

I enjoy developing and promoting activities and events and inspiring people to take active roles in planning and participation to meet their interests and needs. I am an organized, solutions-oriented person with strong group facilitation and people skills. Additionally, I have experience in managing staff and budgets, and a desire to collaborate to achieve a positive environment for residents, staff, and volunteers.

I am a quick learner of policy, procedures, initiatives, and technologies. I am mechanically inclined which has enabled me to maintain and troubleshoot a variety of exercise equipment in my previous work experiences. I also have strong skills in computer applications including Word, Excel, PowerPoint, and Publisher, and have created my own health website.

Please review my resume for further detail about my qualifications. I would appreciate the opportunity to interview for this position and share with you my enthusiasm for engaging residents in a whole range of leisure activities including creative arts, fitness, intellectual, cultural, social, and spiritual activities.

You can reach me at 904-649-8364 or at my email address (lesley.ashley@gmail.com) if you have further questions.

Thank you for your consideration.

Sincerely,

Lesley G. Ashley

Lesley G. Ashley

JOB APPLICATIONS

Most employers require applicants to complete an application form prior to an interview; in some instances, you may be asked to complete an application instead of sending in a resume. Most companies require both a resume and an application. Many job applications are completed via the Internet. Job applications are convenient for employers to refer to because it is a standard form. Thoroughly complete the application form and double check to make sure that nothing is left unanswered. If the employer wants to see your resume, he'll ask for it.

Be aware that a few employers may use illegal questions on their application forms. It is **illegal to ask** applicants questions about their age, race, sex, dependents, religion, ethnic background, marital status, and possible handicaps. Application forms may ask if you are under or over specific ages to verify your eligibility for work. Using the prefixes Mr., Mrs., or Ms. can identify your sex and these are now illegal, yet they may still be seen on some application forms. You do not have to answer any illegal questions; however, many people do anyway, just to avoid having blank spaces on the application. Additionally, by signing a job application or acknowledging online that the information in the application is accurate, you are attesting to your job and educational history. This means that you can be denied employment or fired in the future if you aren't truthful about your employment record. Read the following suggestions for more information on completing job applications.

Tips . . . For Completing Job Applications

- **Paper Job Applications.** If possible, get an application form in advance to give you adequate time to complete it.

- **Online Job Applications.** Job applications for many companies are available online and can be completed online for available positions. Some employers no longer accept paper applications and require applicants to apply via their company website or the site where they have posted job openings. The remaining tips will discuss considerations for completing paper and online application forms.

- Complete a "model" application with all dates, work history and references. Make a copy to carry with you for easy reference when completing other applications. Another alternative is to keep a "data sheet" (a compilation of information that is normally requested on an application form).

- Should you have to complete the application at the time of your job interview, plan to arrive early to allow time for its completion. Always have your resume and model application or data sheet with you for complete, up-to-date, and accurate information. (Keep these documents in your computer files and keep them up-to-date.)

- Paper forms—type or use a fine-point black or blue ink pen. (Blue ink is more easily read on a form printed in black.) If using a pen, print very neatly.

- Read the instructions and the entire form before writing anything. Many people have begun writing without reading ahead, only to find they have written information in an early section that actually should have been written in a later section of the application form.

- Write "N/A" (not applicable) after questions that do not apply to you.

- Fill out the application completely. Don't leave any blank spaces. If the question is important enough to ask, it's important enough for you to answer. However, if you believe you cannot answer a question because an honest response may jeopardize your chances, you may consider leaving the space blank and be prepared to discuss the subject in an interview or write the following statement: "Will explain in interview."

(continued)

- List your marital status as either married or single; nothing else.

- When you must rate your health, ask yourself: "Will the way I feel keep me from doing the job I want?" If the answer is no, list your health as *excellent*.

- When asked to list the salary you expect, you may list a specific salary, a low-high range, or write "open" or "negotiable."

- For references, list people who are favorably impressed with you and, preferably, those who are familiar with your work. Get permission from those whom you wish to use as a reference.

- If you have been convicted of a crime, write "N/A" in the space provided, unless you were convicted of a felony. In that case, leave the space blank and be prepared to discuss it in an interview.

- If you have little or no formal work history, list any volunteer, charitable, or casual labor jobs in the Work History section of the application. This will show that you know what is expected in the work place.

- If you have gaps of unemployment between jobs, you should offer some explanation. If you have been seeking employment for a while, it is legitimate to write "job hunting." If you have been attending school or training, you should certainly note that.

- Proofread your application before submitting it. Once you've completed the application, sit back and take a moment to thoroughly proofread the document, checking for all errors—especially typos and misspellings.

JOB INTERVIEWS

If you're qualified for the position and you've written an effective cover letter and resume, you'll most likely get to interview for the job. This is the employer's opportunity to meet the person behind the resume and to discover if you are the best candidate for the position.

The interview is also an opportunity for you to meet the employer, to sell yourself, to learn the specifics of the job and of the organization, and to gain all the information you will need to help you decide if this is really the right position for you. Keep in mind that the impression you create during the interview will determine your success in getting the job.

Remember these facts about interviews:

- It is a two-way exchange of information.
- It is your opportunity to present your strengths, skills, and accomplishments in the best possible light to show that you are an excellent match for the position.
- First impressions are important. Interviewers often act more favorably during the interview if the interviewee comes across as warm and personable and uses active listening.

On the following pages, you will find strategies for handling the interview to your best advantage. Your objective is to let the interviewer know that you are the best candidate for the job.

At the Interview

It's important to communicate confidence in yourself on a job interview. If you don't believe you can do the job, how will anyone else believe it? Your body language will communicate volumes about the way you feel about yourself. Hold yourself tall and make eye contact with the interviewer. You're bound to be nervous during the interview—that's to be expected—but let the interviewer know that under the nervousness is a lot of confidence.

Be prepared to make some small talk when you first sit down (read the morning paper before your interview). Make the most of your communication skills—listen intently and answer questions the best way you can. Emphasize your qualifications and desire to work for the company. Answer the interviewer's questions the best way you know how. Some employers will ask you to demonstrate math computation skills, team work, problem-solving, and/or writing skills. If you can, find out how these skills will be assessed and prepare yourself accordingly. Some companies may also require drug tests for applicants for employment.

Whether you're interviewed by one person or a committee, the more prepared you are to respond to questions, the more confident and relaxed you will feel during the interview. Read through the following list of common interview questions and think about what your responses would be. Try to make your responses as specific as possible. If someone asks why you want to work for them, "I just enjoy this type of work" is not a strong answer. A lot more on track is, "I believe my loyalty, sales experience, people skills, organizational skills, and technical skills are just what this agency needs."

Before you go to an interview, determine some potential interview questions that are likely to be asked. Prepare for the interview by using your computer to write thorough answers to the questions. When you are in the interview, you will feel more confident and remember how you planned to respond. Continually save questions and answers in your career e-file for future interviews—eventually you will have a bank of responses that you can improve upon. You may want to use some of the following interview questions.

Common Interview Questions

1.   Why do you want to work for us?
2.   What can you do for us?
3.   Why did you choose this career?
4.   What do you know about this company? How does it fit your interests and talents?
5.   Why should I hire you?
6.   What is your understanding of the nature of this job?
7.   What can you tell me about yourself?
8.   What three words best describe you?
9.   What courses did you like best in college? Why?
10. What experience do you have in this field?
11. What are your three greatest strengths/weaknesses?
12. Discuss the technology skills you possess that would be helpful in this position.
13. What are your greatest accomplishments?
14. What do you consider to be your greatest achievement so far and why?
15. Describe the ideal job.
16. What kind of boss do you like working for?
17. What are your career goals?
18. Why did you leave your last job?
19. What do you do when you're not working?
20. How do you determine or evaluate success?
21. How would you describe your previous employer?
22. How would your previous employer describe you?
23. How do you handle pressure/stress on the job?
24. How do you react to criticism? Give me an example of a specific time you had to handle criticism.
25. What steps do you use to catch mistakes and ensure the quality of your work?
26. What do you perceive will be the outcome of your efforts in this position for our company?
27. What do you believe you can bring to this position that will set you apart from the other candidates?
28. Describe your leadership style and people skills.
29. Describe how you persist to complete a task in spite of a variety of obstacles.

30. Describe your competencies with Microsoft Office or other software programs that may be useful in this position.
31. Where would you like to be five years from now?
32. How would you describe your working style?
33. What has been your biggest challenge on the job/in college?
34. Describe your supervisory (or leadership or management) experience (or style).
35. Describe your people skills that you would apply to this position.
36. Do you prefer working by yourself or with others?
37. What major problem have you had on the job and how did you handle it?
38. What have you learned in previous jobs that will help you here?
39. Describe a time when an unplanned event interrupted your agenda. How did you handle the situation? What was the outcome?
40. How would you solve the following problem? . . .
41. What does your closet look like at home? (Questions like this may surprise you, but they may be asked. How would you respond and put yourself in a favorable light?)
42. If a taxi, shuttle, and a limo were priced exactly the same, which one would you choose to take?
43. What was the most recent book you read, and what did you enjoy about it?
44. Upon your death, what do you think your eulogy would say about you?
45. How would you sell me a hot cup of tea in Florida in the summer?
46. Imagine that in the future a major accomplishment of yours will be featured in a publication and you will be on the front cover. What is the accomplishment, and what is the publication (magazine, newspaper, website, etc.)? Why is this important to you?
47. Is there any professional development that you might need to perform at your best on this job?
48. Discuss any crucial issues related to this position that we have not yet discussed.
49. What questions do you have about the position (or company)?
50. Should you be selected for this position, when could you start?

Tips . . . On Preparing for a Job Interview

- Do your research—search the company's website and further search their products or services on the Web. Know what the company is about and what it does. Put yourself in the interviewer's shoes. Would you hire someone who didn't know what products you made or what services you offered? You don't have to memorize the annual report but, if this is a company you're really interested in, you'll take the time to learn a little about it.

- Know who your interviewer is. What is his/her position within the company?

- Be prepared with a notepad during the interview so you can make notes on any of the interview questions as they're asked. If you are interviewed by a committee, jot their names down and any questions you may want to ask. Also note that it may be helpful to request that a question be repeated. Some questions have several parts and you want to respond to all parts.

- Practice answering possible interview questions with a friend, on tape, or even by yourself. Try to anticipate what questions might be asked. Prepare thoughtful responses.

- Prepare a list of questions that you have about the job or the company. Few things make a worse impression on an employer as when you don't have any questions about the job. Write down your questions and carry them with you if you think you might forget them. You might ask the following: "What would a typical day be like for me at this company?" "What type of orientation or training does your company provide the new employees in this position?"

(continued)

- Be prepared to demonstrate your writing ability. An interviewer may ask you to write a paragraph, memo, or even an essay.

- Know where you're going. If you've never been to the office, make a "dry run" the day before. You don't want to be late for your appointment because you had to stop three times and ask for directions. Leave so you'll get there fifteen minutes early for your interview.

- Take a copy of your resume, a list of references, a completed application (or your data sheet), and a couple of spare pens, in case you're asked to complete an application form.

- Have your driver's license and another picture ID and your Social Security card available in case you're asked to complete additional paperwork required for hiring. Occasionally, some people have received a job offer immediately after the interview.

- Get ready the night before. Put aside the clothes you plan to wear, clean and freshly pressed. Plan to wear a conservative outfit, appropriate to the occasion. No sneakers, white socks, dangling earrings, sandals, shorts, or anything else that would look unprofessional.

- Get plenty of rest the night before and be sure to eat something before your appointment. You can't be at your best on an empty stomach.

- Here's an out-of-the-box tip for your consideration— it's a question that you ask, not one that you answer. If you should decide to use it, do so as early in the interview as possible. It could lay the groundwork for success in the rest of the interview. The question:

   "(Supervisor or hiring manager), I reviewed the job description and based on what I know so far, the job consists entirely of things that I like to do and can do very well. Since this is my first opportunity to talk directly to you about it, would you be willing to tell me exactly what you will expect from me in this position? I would like to hear how you view the job description and your expectations beyond the job description. What's most important? In this position, what would I need to do to earn the highest rating in my first evaluation?" (Don't hesitate to ask clarifying questions.)

   The more you learn from listening to the response, the better you'll know how to respond to the interview questions. While listening, you make a mental outline of the three of four things most important to them. Your job for the rest of the interview is to provide evidence that you can deliver those things.

Be aware of the pitfalls that lead to unsuccessful interviews. Employers list the following as some of the most common reasons they did not offer a job to a candidate after the interview.

- Arriving late
- Exaggerating or lying about your skills/experience/knowledge
- Failing to remember what you wrote on your own resume or an inability to explain any of the accomplishments, skills, or experiences you included on your resume
- Wearing inappropriate clothes and accessories for the workplace
- Poor personal appearance (sloppy, unprofessional dress, unkempt hair)
- Smelling like cigarettes or excessive perfume or aftershave
- Failing to demonstrate enthusiasm and/or attentiveness
- Over-aggressiveness/conceited/know-it-all behavior
- Forgetting to bring a copy of your resume and/or portfolio
- Inability to communicate clearly—little or no eye contact, poor articulation, poor grammar, using slang

- Failing to listen carefully to what the interviewer is saying
- Lack of career plans
- Lack of interest and enthusiasm—being passive or indifferent
- Over-emphasis on money; caring about the salary more than anything else or inquiring about salary and benefits too soon
- Poor academic record
- Evasiveness
- Lack of tact or courtesy
- Badmouthing past employers
- Sloppy application form
- Lack of interest and knowledge in company/organization. Failing to research the company prior to the interview
- Short yes/no responses without explanations for clarification or over sharing

Interview Follow Up—Thank You

Don't forget to follow up after your interview. Send a thank you email to all interviewers or a thank you letter to the employer *as soon as possible*. Your thank you should contain the following:

- An opening paragraph expressing your appreciation for the interview, learning about the position, and that you are further convinced that your interest, background, and skills are a good match for the position.
- A second paragraph that emphasizes key aspects of your background that precisely match what the employer is seeking for the position.
- An optional paragraph that may mention something valuable that you forgot to discuss in the interview. You may also want to address and alleviate one of the employer's concerns mentioned in the interview.
- A last paragraph—again thank the employer or interview committee. You may also want to consider ending with a statement like: "I hope you will favorably consider me for the position," and/or "I look forward to hearing from you soon."

It is important to get your thank you email or letter into the hands of the employer as soon as possible—preferably within 24 hours. Employers appreciate people who follow through and take an active role. If you don't get a particular job, consider calling the interviewer and ask what you might have done better; this can be a source of valuable information that can help you land a job the next time.

HIGHLIGHTS

In this section you've explored a lot about beginning a job search and planning your career after college. You've also learned a lot more about yourself—your values, goals, skills, and interests. You've perhaps begun to consider some job possibilities you didn't know you were suited for. Like college itself, this section has been a process of discovery and planning for the future. Keep in mind that a lot of the information you've learned in this section can be used even before you enter the world of work. Self-assessment tests can help you pinpoint your interests and abilities and, therefore, make better choices about the courses you plan to take. Job interview and networking skills will serve you well in any situation where you meet someone for the first time.

Though you may still be getting used to the routines of college, refer to this section from time to time as you start thinking more about life after you complete your college program. Job searching, networking, and maintaining your career e-files is an ongoing process. Each time you must revise your resume or prepare for a job interview, this section will refresh your memory on how to create a sharp resume and effectivevly market yourself for the job.

DISCUSSION QUESTIONS

Note: Read the following discussion questions and activities before you read Section 9. This strategy will help you look for answers while you read.

1. Define values. How do your values (as assessed in this section) relate to your current career direction?
2. Why is it important to clarify your values in your career planning process?
3. Define interests. How do your interests (as identified in this section) relate to your current career direction?
4. Explain how values relate to interests. How are they different?
5. What is your three-digit Holland's occupational code? Use the *Dictionary of Holland's Occupational Codes* (by John Holland and Gary Gottfredson) to identify five occupations that match your occupational code and that you would consider employment in.
6. How does your occupational code (as assessed in the text) compare to the job you are preparing for?
7. What would you say are your top five work-specific skills?
8. Describe five of your self-management skills as you would on your resume. Under which categories on your resume would you place them?
9. Explain what an informational interview is and its purpose.
10. Does your school have a placement or career services center or other student services that can help you assess your career interest, prepare a resume and/or cover letter, or prepare for a job interview? Of all the services offered at your school, which ones will you most likely use?
11. Explain networking. Discuss its purpose and how you do it.
12. Describe a social media site and how it can be used for the job search. For an employer job candidate search?
13. Explain what a resume is and its purpose.
14. How does an exceptional resume look? Why is it important that you design and compose an exceptional resume?
15. Explain what a professional objective (on your resume) is and its importance. Explain reasons you may or may not want to include an objective on your resume.
16. Thoroughly explain the differences and similarities between your "Qualifications" and your "Work Experience" categories on your resume.
17. Why is it better to have a separate list of references rather than making it part of your resume?
18. What's the purpose of a cover letter? What do you think are the three most important characteristics of a cover letter?
19. What questions are illegal to ask on an application form?
20. With your specific career preparation in mind, write five challenging questions that you think could be asked of you in a job interview. Then write thorough responses to each question.
21. How do you communicate confidence in a job interview?
22. How would you dress for a job interview in your field? (Discuss clothes and accessories.)
23. What do you believe are the five most important things that you can do to prepare for your job interview?
24. How would you negotiate a better salary offer? Explain what you would say and why.
25. What type of individuals would you select for professional references?
26. Make a list of the most important things you would like to accomplish before you die. How can you incorporate the things you would like to do (from your list) in your career planning?
27. What do you think are the most important remarks you should make in a thank you email or letter as a follow up to your interview?

Information Technology

WHAT'S IN IT FOR YOU

In our current age of information technology, we have a great big World Wide Web which contains an enormous collection of webpages all contained on the Internet. Barely a day goes by when we aren't "googling" the Internet for information on something—cheap gas, Groupons, cars, weather, news and movies, homework assignments, services, shopping, old friends, and answers to problems like how to remove Superglue. From desktop and laptop computers, to smart phones and refrigerators and iPads, information technology impacts almost all aspects of our personal, social, school, and work lives. With a few clicks we can connect worldwide. Whether conducting research for a class or a job, the ability to navigate the Internet is essential. This section will highlight basics of the Internet, search skills, security, and technology needs for college and the workforce.

In this section you'll explore:

- The information boom and the information overload.
- Tips for upgrading or purchasing a new computer.
- The basics of the Internet.
- World Wide Web and its offerings.
- Email practices and etiquette for college, career, and life.
- Keeping up with technology to keep up with the changing workplace.
- Safety and security tips for you and your computer.

INFORMATION BOOM TO INFORMATION OVERLOAD

Information technology helps individuals and businesses research, process, and manage information through computerization. There are few jobs that don't use some form of computerization. Even the down-to-earth lawn and garden shops google plant varieties, email customers, and computerize records. Most employers expect that we will bring computer information technology skills to the job and will continue to sharpen them. Today, information technology provides us access to unlimited information and social media connections to our "friends," friends of our friends, and even strangers. Computers have become one of the most empowering tools in our lives and often the most distracting one. Computers are used for practically everything— communication, entertainment, shopping, hunting and applying for jobs and colleges, education, traveling, health care, operating cars, and much, much more. Simply put, we rely on computers. Many stay "connected" daily, hourly, and even while vacationing, especially with the use of smart phones which give us a mini computer in the palm of our hand. The age of information has even given us a new language. For example, "googling" (taken from the popular Google search engine trademark name), now implies searching the Internet. Net lingo, is the creative shorthand/slang (like "gr8" for "great") we use to write our text messages. (A note from your English instructor: Please avoid net lingo on your essays!) Some of us are using computer apps (applications) to track our nutrition intake and log our exercise. But hopefully we don't let computer information technology hinder our body, mind, spirit growth, human relationships, physical activity and recreation, relaxation, and yes, sleep.

Information technology also provides opportunity, assistance, and connectivity to humans who may be miles or oceans apart. Many "skype"—a new verb adopted from the Skype IP (Internet Provider) telephone service that offers free calling between Skype subscribers and low-cost calling to people who don't use the service. This type of Internet phone service allows people a real-time live viewing and voice connection—a great human connection through technology. Information technology provides almost endless opportunities for online learning through numerous commercial learning management systems (LMSs) such as Blackboard, Desire2Learn, and open source (free to the public) LMSs such as Moodle, Sakai, and LRN. A variety of computerized assistive technologies help people with sensory, physical, and learning disabilities improve their lives and increase their independence and productivity. Text to speech and voice recognition software may assist people with disabilities to participate with the world of written information. Communication board apps display the alphabet, yes/no answers, pictures, food selections, and other choices to be selected/pointed to by individuals with speech difficulties to facilitate communication in daily encounters. Information technology can provide many bridges to people and opportunity.

Whether at work or school, the distress may come when we "try" to balance it all by multitasking—doing homework, checking texts and emails, and searching the Web simultaneously—bouncing from one information bite to another. Even with all the technology that is making our lives easier, most of us have been afflicted by information overload. In 1997, the term "Information Fatigue Syndrome" was semi-humorously coined to give a diagnosis to the malady of information overload—more information than our brains can process. Our society has attempted to remedy Information Fatigue Syndrome by speeding things up, packing more and more content in, and adding more technology—are you feeling relieved yet? I doubt it, and the amount of information will continue to increase dramatically—and working harder, faster, and sleeping less is not the solution. As we can see, this bombardment of information can be overwhelming, putting us on overload.

Experts warn us that information overload results in forgetting, not learning, partial attention, stress, and rewiring our brain. As with all learning, whether it is a procedure, terminology, or behavior such as multitasking, our brain remembers our patterns of learning by strengthening neural traces in our brains each time we engage in those patterns of learning. Unfortunately, we probably think we are less productive or lax if we don't multitask. Information overload will not get any easier unless we limit ourselves to dealing with only that information that will help us achieve our goals. Multitasking does not produce the best quality work because our ability to fully concentrate is greatly reduced. We need to stop and think critically about our choices and habits, determine priorities, and set limits. When we don't manage information overload, it can produce symptoms similar to stress such as headaches, fatigue, churning stomach, muscle tightness, mental depression, and/or feeling nervous or anxious. See Section 10 for more problems and symptoms related to stress.

On the positive side, technology has brought a wealth of information, opportunity, people connection, and growth. The Internet has given us a new information marketplace: we can socialize in cyberspace, reach and teach across the world, and use the Internet to sell almost anything to anyone anywhere—what a market! However, in today's information age, we will continue to need some of the same self-help strategies offered in this book to manage our time, our stress, our attitudes, and to help us adapt to our ever-changing lifestyle and demands. Again, the situation will not get any easier unless we limit ourselves to dealing with only that information that will help us achieve our goals. The following exercise will ask you to think about how you will manage your time, stress, and attitudes to cope with information overload.

Exercise 10-1 Coping with information overload

How can the stress management strategies from Section 10 be used to help you manage your (1) time, (2) stress, and (3) attitudes to cope with information overload?

As we have seen, information itself has changed—we have MUCH more of it, more systems and processes to manipulate it, and more services that require accurate and up-to-date information. This changes the way we work, live, and behave. We've moved from the demand for computer literacy to information literacy. As early as 1989, the American Library Association defined the "information literate person," as a person able to recognize when information is needed and have the ability to locate, evaluate, and use the needed information effectively. In essence, we want to be effective users of ideas and information. Technology is affecting almost every aspect of our life—you can work, learn, exercise, play, or even pray online. The next sections will offer tips and suggestions to help you determine your computer needs and more effectively access the Internet and the World Wide Web.

SHOULD I BUY A NEW COMPUTER OR UPGRADE?

Upgrading your old computer or buying a new computer can be a tough task. There are so many choices, and technologies change fast. Whether you're looking for a new computer, or upgrading your existing computer, begin the process by listing everything you'd like that computer to do, e.g., writing college papers, Internet searching, emailing, watching videos, playing games, doing graphics, storing your photos and music, or using a specific type of software for your courses. Once you know what you want your computer to do, it is easier to determine what type of computer to buy or what type of upgrade you'll need. Also, if you're enrolled in a computer course, ask your instructor about your software and computer requirements. Some key things to remember when purchasing/upgrading your desktop or laptop computer are explained below.

Tips . . . For Upgrading or Purchasing a New Computer

- **Type of computer and which CPU (processor)**—A standard mid-range computer will do everything most users need. Seldom does the average user need the latest or fastest computer, and the extra cost does not justify the small gains in performance. There are two main brands of processors, AMD (Advanced Micro Devices) and Intel. Both of these processors are good—just make sure it's a dual-core processor.

- **RAM (memory)**—Computer memory is one of the most important components for performance. 1GB (gigabyte) is the suggested minimum for a new computer but 2GB will ensure that everything runs very quickly.

- **Compatibility**—Make sure your existing software and hardware are compatible; for example, your camera and printer will work with your new computer.

- **Graphics and video capabilities.** If you use your computer for video editing, graphics applications, or playing games, you should get a computer with a separate graphics card rather than an inbuilt graphics card to avoid slow graphics and poor image quality.

- **Backup**—Buy a large volume flash drive or an external drive to back-up all of your valuable photos, videos, and documents.

- **Laptops**—Bear in mind that laptop components may not upgradeable. When you buy a laptop, you need to determine what size screen you need. A smaller screen and keyboard is easier to carry around, while the larger screen laptop may have a more comfortable keyboard and be easier to use. Most laptops come with both a DVD player and wireless technology, but it's always worth checking the specifications just to make sure, especially if you are purchasing a used computer.

- **Finally**—If you buy a reasonably priced computer that serves your needs, you won't feel bad when you buy your next computer in four years.

INTERNET BASICS

The Internet or Net is a worldwide free-broadcast medium for the general public. The Internet is named for its interconnection of computer networks. It is a massive hardware combination of millions of personal, business, and governmental computers, all connected like roads and highways by cables and by wireless signals. Using your PC, Mac, smart phone, Xbox, movie player, and GPS, you can access a vast world of messaging and useful content through the Net. Each college, company, government, or organization that has a network is responsible for maintaining their own network. Unlike the telephone company, no organization owns or controls the Internet, so there is no government regulation and no one censors the information on the Internet. This does not mean that you can break the law on the Internet. This Information Superhighway can send information around the world in less than one second, and most information is free of charge, although access to the Internet may have a nominal monthly charge.

Most Americans pay for unlimited access to the Internet through a local or North American Internet Service Provider (ISP) such as Comcast, AT&T, Verizon, Insight, Hughes Net Systems, or one of the many other ISPs. Other countries around our world also have several ISPs. Many companies have their own computer systems connected to the Internet for employees to access the Web at work or allow their employees to access the company computer system from home. Students may have free Internet access at their colleges and universities, but generally, students have their own access through an ISP.

Some companies don't want outsiders to have access to their website, and they create an **intranet**. An intranet is a company-wide network, closed to public access, that uses an Internet-type technology. Intranets are generally used to publish employee information, business documents and forms, inventory, and internal email.

Observe computer use and abuse policies at your campus or workplace. It can be tempting to do things with computers that are clearly wrong, but we're all better off when we maintain ethical standards.

THE WAY OF THE WEB

The World Wide Web (WWW or W3) is part of the Internet. The Web consists of huge collections of documents stored on computers around the world. As of February 11, 2012, the daily estimated indexed Web contained at least 8.44 billion pages (http://www.worldwidewebsize.com). Webpages are documents on the Web that can include text, graphics, sound, or video, and are written in **HyperText Markup Language (HTML)**, and begin with the following letters on the location line of a web browser—**http**, e.g., http://www.kvctc.edu. A secure version of HTML is **Hypertext Transfer Protocol Secure (HTTPS).** HTTPS allows secure ecommerce transactions, such as online banking. Colleges, universities, companies, government agencies, and many students have websites, or collections of webpages. For businesses today, having their own website on the Internet has become more valuable to their livelihood than the old Yellow Pages. By learning how to create and publish pages on the Web, you gain a skill that could be valuable in your current or future career. If you are working for a larger company, that company will most likely have technical support to create your webpages. However, your knowledge about webpage design will help you make useful contributions to the company's webpage development. If you have more of an entrepreneurial spirit and want to start your own business, creating your own webpages will open your business to the world market. English is the most prominent language used on the Web. If you can create a business website in English, you will reach a large majority of the world users.

Webpages are made available to the entire world with a web server—a computer connected to the Internet. Each webpage has a unique address called the Uniform Resource Locator (URL). All webpage URLs start with **http (Hypertext Protocol)** and contain the computer name, directory name, and name of the webpage. Webpages are hypertext documents—documents containing highlighted text capable of connecting you to other pages on the Web. Web browsers help you explore information on the Web. Some of the most popular web browsers are Firefox, Google Chrome, Internet Explorer, Safari, and Opera. Web browsers are basically software programs that allow you to search for and view various kinds of information on the Web, such as websites, videos, TV, newspapers, magazines, songs, advertisement, historical speeches, animation, famous paintings, games, product demonstrations, simulations for instruction and training, and virtual reality tours. A Merriam-Webster website from the AOL Research Learning Directory defines virtual reality as an "artificial environment which is experienced through sensory stimuli (as sights and sounds) provided by a computer and in which one's actions partially determine what happens in the environment." In other words you could take a visual and sound tour of a museum on the computer and you would select your route. Keep in mind that some files, especially video and animation, may take a while to transfer to your computer, depending on your ISP. A webpage usually shows you the size of a file to give you an indication of how long the file will take to transfer. If you want to hear sound, your computer will also need a sound card and speakers.

Many of you are using your browsers to blog; visit social media sites like Facebook, Twitter, and MySpace; email pictures or videos; or use chat rooms, all which require more speed. It takes a modern browser to make the most of the Web's most modern features, so search the web for information on the best up-to-date browsers. It also takes a reliable Internet connection to handle the size and speed of today's information flow.

Broadband technology provides you with reliable and continuous connection to the Internet and allows you to send and receive mammoth files that include voice, video, and data much faster than before. The more bandwith you have, the bigger pipe for data to flow through and the bigger the pipe, the faster the flow. Your ISP may offer one of the following **broadband technologies:** cable modem, DSL (Digital Subscriber Line), fiber, wireless, satellite, and BPL (Broadband Over Power Lines).

Today's computers and smart phones are equipped with built-in Wi-Fi antennas, and software allows you to connect using the Wi-Fi data signal. In fact, most Wi-Fi software is set up to find and display the available Wi-Fi signals available in your location.

When in question about any of the aforementioned Internet technologies, you can search the Web for comparisons or ask your ISP for assistance.

The following are additional Web and Internet related terms:

App—An app (application) is a software program such as word processing or a spreadsheet. In smart phones, apps are generally designed to focus on smaller tasks like these apps: alarm clock, calendar, e-book reader, locator for best gas prices, Facebook connection, email access, maps, weather forecast, or a scrabble game like "Words with Friends."

Bookmark—The bookmark feature allows readers to mark webpages for later reference.

Blog—A blog (web log) is a website where people post their personal observations on particular subjects such as sports, politics, education, business, and more. Posts are listed in reverse chronological order. Anyone can start one and it costs nothing to start your own personal blog.

Cache—An area of computer memory that stores recently used data. Cache makes browsing the Web faster by storing copies of webpages you have recently viewed. When you want to view a webpage again, the browser retrieves the page from the cache instead of searching for the page on the Internet.

Chat—An online forum offered by many online services or websites that allows participants to "chat" by typing messages that are displayed almost instantly on the screens of other participants who are using the chat room.

Country Code—The part of an Internet address that indicates where the computer system that stores the information is located. For example, the "jp" in "company.com.jp" indicates that the computer system is in Japan. Internet addresses for the United States do not usually display a country code.

Cookie—Information used by a website to keep track of people who visit the site and to remember their preferences and interests. For example, when you visit a website, the site may create a cookie to store your name in. People can set up their browsers to accept or not accept cookies.

DNS Server—The Domain Name System (DNS) server is a computer that translates an Internet name such as "company.com" into a number such as 123.256.1.12. Computers and programs on the Internet need these numbers to understand where to send information. You tell your computer what the name of your DNS server is before you can use the Internet.

GIF—Graphics Interchange Format (GIF) is best used for text, line drawings, screen shots, cartoons, and animations. GIF is limited to a total number of 256 colors or less. It is commonly used for fast loading webpages. It also makes a great banner or logo for your webpage. Animated pictures are also saved in GIF format. For example, a flashing banner would be saved as a GIF file.

Home page—The home page is the main page in a collection of webpages. The home page is usually the first page people read.

Hyperlink—Text, images, or graphics that, when clicked, will connect the user to another webpage, either on the same site or another website. The link is usually obvious, such as underlined text or a button.

Java—A programming language that allows you to create animated and interactive webpages. A Java program in a webpage is called a Java applet.

JPEG—stands for Joint Photographic Experts Group, a format used for color photographs, or any pictures with many blends or gradients. Digital cameras download photos to your computer as a JPEG file which provides quality images that take up less space because it can be compressed for storage.

Keywords—A word that is entered into the search form or search "window" of an Internet search engine to search the Web for pages or sites about or including the keyword and information related to it.

Links—A link allows readers to select an image or highlighted text to display another page on the Web. Generally links are related sites.

Listserv—An email list of email addresses of people with common interests. Software enables people who belong to a list to send messages to the group without typing a series of addresses into the message header. Usually members of the group in the listserv have to subscribe to the mailing list.

Malware—This is malicious software installed on your machine, usually without your knowledge. For example, you may be asked to download an anti-virus software that is actually a virus itself. Or you may visit a webpage that installs software on your computer without even asking. The software is really designed to steal credit card numbers or passwords from your computer, or in some cases, harm your computer. Once the malware is on your computer, it's not only difficult to remove, but it's also free to access all the data and files it finds, send that information elsewhere, and generally wreak havoc on your computer.

Megabyte (MB)—About a million bytes of space. Actually it's 2 raised to the 20th power or 1,048,576 bytes of space. (1024mb equals 1 gigabyte)

PDF—Portable Document Format (PDF) is a file format created by Adobe Systems, Inc., that preserves most attributes (including color, formatting, graphics, and more) of a source document no matter which application, platform, and hardware type was originally used to create it. PDF files can be viewed using Adobe Acrobat Reader, which is a free software application provided by Adobe Systems. PDF documents have a .pdf file extension (myfile.pdf).

Phishing—A modern-day Internet con to defraud you of your personal accounts. Phishing is the use of convincing-looking emails and webpages to lure you into typing your account numbers and passwords/PINs. Often in the form of fake eBay webpages, fake PayPal warning messages, and fake bank login screens, phishing attacks can be very convincing to anyone who is not trained to watch for the subtle clues. As a rule, smart users distrust any email link that says "you should login and confirm this."

Plug-In—A software plug-in is an add-on for a program that adds functionality to it. For example, a browser plug-in (such as Macromedia Flash or Apple QuickTime) allows you to play certain multimedia files within your web browser.

Web Search Query— A search query refers to a word, set of words, or questions a person types into a browser search box to obtain desired information.

Viruses—A program written specifically to cause problems in your computer and to disrupt the normal operation of a computer.

ZIP—Stands for Zone Information Protocol. This is an application that allows for the compression of application files.

EMAIL PRACTICES AND ETIQUETTE FOR COLLEGE, CAREER, AND LIFE

Many of you have been using email, chat rooms, message boards, and instant messages for several years and have relied on this fast, economical, and convenient way to send messages to family, friends, work colleagues, prospective employers, and instructors. Your email can travel around the world in seconds and once you pay a fee to the Internet service provider, there is no charge for sending and receiving email. Email is the major and sometimes only form of written business communication used to announce meetings, submit assignments and reports, create correspondence files, transfer files and books, conduct sales and contracts, and apply for jobs. Because email is a preferred form of business communication, it is important to pay attention to your writing mechanics. Email programs have spell-checking features that will check every word you write against the words stored in their built-in dictionaries—but they don't catch everything. Make sure your messages are clear, concise, and error free. Proof your messages to ensure they will not be misinterpreted—some jokes have been misunderstood and create barriers instead of connections. Try to avoid using CAPITAL LETTERS in your email unless you want to "SHOUT" a positive word or phrase. Using all CAPITAL LETTERS is considered annoying and hard to read.

Your email address consists of two parts (user name and domain name) separated by the @ (at) symbol, and it cannot contain spaces. The **User Name** is the first part of the email address and is the name of the person's account. This can be a real name or a nickname. The **Domain Name** is the second part of the email address and is the location of the person's account on the Internet. Periods (.) separate the various parts of the domain name.

Rex@company.com

(user name)　　(domain name)

You can also customize your emails to have each one end with your **signature**. Your signature adds information about yourself to the end of each email you send. You can include your name, address, workplace and/or department, telephone number, fax number, email address, an image, and even your favorite quote.

Other ways your email program will save you time is by sending a copy (**cc:**) of your email to another person you think needs or wants to be informed of your message. If you don't want people to know you are sending someone else a copy, you can use the "blind copy" option (**bcc:**). You can click on **Reply** and your email program will automatically set up a return message to the sender. You can also click on **Forward** to send a message, video, or pictures you received via email to someone else in your address book. You can use the **attachment** option to send documents in their original format and to send pictures, sound, or videos. If the attachment is very large, you can **compress** it—squeeze it to a smaller size so the file will transfer more quickly over the Internet. You don't want to compress it unless the person receiving the file has a program that **decompresses** your file to expand it to its original form. Additionally, the ability to send many email messages at once, by assigning several addresses to a **group address**, saves you hours of time. And you can create group addresses from your program's **address book** in minutes.

Tips . . . For Email Etiquette and Other Considerations

- Proof your messages for errors and to ensure they will not be misinterpreted. Humor may be misunderstood and create barriers instead of connections, so use humor sparingly. You can use smileys such as :) or :(to indicate facial expressions, but make sure that the recipient understands what they mean.

- Be polite. Terseness can be misinterpreted.

- Avoid excessive email. Too much email can take a lot of time out of your day.

- Make sure that you have a clear and relevant "subject" line, so your reader will not delete your message because he/she couldn't determine the nature of the email.

- Be considerate of your reader's time. Some questions may be better asked over the phone or face-to-face instead of sending an email. "How should I deal with Bob? He never comes to class and our team report is due Friday" may be easier for your instructor to answer by phone or in his/her office.

- Don't reply to every email. When your instructor says, "Thank you, Geoff—I received your report," he is letting you know that he got it. You don't have to reply "thank you" to his "thank you." However, some instructors will request a reply, and some will use email functions that will let them know whether or not you have opened their email.

- Try to avoid using CAPITAL LETTERS in your email unless you want to "SHOUT" a kind word— CONGRATULATIONS! Beware of capitalizing angry words and the consequences. Also note that using all CAPITAL LETTERS IS OFTEN ANNOYING AND DIFFICULT TO READ.

- Pause and think before you send any confidential or private email. Others could accidentally or intentionally "forward" your email to others.

- Be careful when using the reply feature. One common mistake people make is replying to a message that came from a listserv, which may result in a reply to everyone on the list when you only meant to reply to the person who sent the message.

- Wait and think before you send an emotional email or reply to an emotional email. Think about the potential consequences of the email—sometimes an angry email may result in an angrier reply. Once sent, you cannot recover it. Hurt or angry feelings can be aggravated in seconds and take much longer to mend. Wait and think about what you really want to accomplish with your email.

- Don't assume that the minute someone receives your email, the person will read it. Bad assumption. If you schedule a meeting for an hour from now and send an email to each classmate, the chances that all your classmates will read that message within the hour will be pretty small. On the other hand, if you schedule the meeting for the next day, the chances that they will read the message will be pretty high. Remember, email is not designed for immediacy (that's why you have a telephone); it's designed for convenience. Some (not all) email systems have features that try to combat this problem. These features (usually called "notification") will notify you when a person has received your email and may also notify you when the person has read it (really all it can do is assume that the person has looked at the first screen of the message—there is no way to know if the person has read the message). You can check to see who has checked their email before the meeting and then telephone those who have not read it.

(continued)

- Don't keep mail on your server longer than necessary, especially large attachments.

- Don't send chain letters or "make money fast" messages. You may be sending along a virus, and you may be annoying the recipient.

- Don't criticize people's spelling; it is considered petty. Some people have no way of running a spell check on their messages and will make typos. Not all nationalities spell words in the same way.

- Don't make personal remarks about third parties. Email messages can come back to haunt you.

- Don't send unsuitable email or attachments, especially anything of a sexual nature, as they may well be found by an unintended third party.

Your email program will provide you with instructions to use all the aforementioned tasks. If you have trouble locating the instructions, you can often experiment by following the **icons** (symbolic pictures) to create your electronic address book, group addresses, copies, and blind copies. Your computer software and operating system is continually being designed for simplicity and safety features to help you perform functions properly and to keep you from making mistakes.

KEEPING UP WITH TECHNOLOGY TO KEEP UP WITH THE CHANGING WORKPLACE

It's easy to feel left behind with the fast pace of technology improvements. However, one of the most basic computer tools—word processing—once learned, is relatively easy to keep pace with. The basics have been around for a long time and the software updates always have a way of helping you keep abreast of the major changes. The nice thing about some of today's basic computer tools such as word processing, spread sheets (for electronic accounting), data bases (for electronic management of information), PowerPoint (for presentations), Internet search, and email, is that they are not too difficult to learn. With patience, a good instructional book and/or class, and willingness to experiment, you can progressively develop your proficiency. Even better, computer software technology is becoming more intuitive and works like we expect it to.

Software proficiency is already an integral part of life at work, home, and play. When the telephone was first introduced, people questioned its usefulness; now it's a way of life, and it's rare not to have a cell or smart phone.

Businesses, schools, and people are relying more and more on information technology. **Virtualization** or accessibility through technology allows businesses and organizations to conduct business independent of location. We can buy, attend classes and training, and visit libraries without leaving home. We can quickly communicate with people all over the world, play games, find dates, explore rain forests and oceans, access movies and music, explore and locate jobs, find maps, locate people, tour houses on the market, and of course, more technology is continuously invented. With all this capability, jobs will increasingly involve information technology. Employers will increasingly need professionals and paraprofessionals who have advanced skills in using, developing, troubleshooting/repairing, or maintaining software applications, networking, and computerized devices, as well as research and development, information management, and information security. Even today's forest ranger cannot escape technology. She may document wildlife with a digital camera and put it on the Web. She may submit reports by email, and keep updated through an online course or newsletter. Even the marketing profession is dependent on technologies including the Web, social media, digital television, email, smart phones, online coupons, interactive kiosks, and ways to make all this technology hi-touch.

Information Technology is changing the way we work and prepare for our future careers. The term "lifelong learning" was introduced some years ago, and today the need for continuous learning and training for work is a way of life. Colleges integrate technology throughout learning experiences, and students are gaining numerous technology and intuitive skills. As we routinely revise technology and job tasks, how do you see it affecting your future career? The following exercise lets you examine this issue as it may relate to you.

Exercise 10-2 Effects of technology and your future career

Think about the career for which you are preparing. List five ways technology will affect the way you will have to perform your work.

1. _____
2. _____
3. _____
4. _____
5. _____

SAFETY AND SECURITY TIPS FOR YOU AND YOUR COMPUTER

The same skill and innovation that has developed information technology has also developed a criminal side that is malicious and for profit. Below are tips to help you take your online safety and security seriously when you use social networks, email, and the Internet.

1. **Upgrade to a modern browser**—an up-to-date browser helps guard against security threats like phishing and malware attacks that can lead to stolen passwords, malicious software slipped secretly onto your computer, or worse. Search the Internet for names of the best and latest browsers. To check which browser you're using, visit www.whatbrowser.org.

2. Validating Identities Online:

    • Some websites have an **extended validation certificate** that allows you to determine the name of the organization that runs the website.
    • Recognize and avoid email scams. Check the link provided. Does it really go where it appears to go? The best way to prevent this is to copy and paste the link (don't click it) to your address bar. Then look carefully so you don't get tricked by URLs that look legitimate but have one or two letters switched.

3. When making payment, always use sites which have https as protocol in the URL. For example https://asecuresite.com.

4. Always be wary of any message that asks for your personal information, or messages that refer you to a webpage asking for personal information. One thing to be sure of: email programs such as Gmail never ask you to provide this information in an email.

5. Never respond to emails that request you provide your credit card info via email—and don't ever respond to emails that ask you to go to a website to verify personal (and credit card) information. These are called "phishing" scams. Never provide your credit card information on a website that is not a secure site.

6. Always install good antivirus software in your computer and set it to update frequently.

7. When in doubt, delete email attachments from people you don't know (without opening them).

8. Install the latest patches and services packs for your software.

9. Do not follow unsolicited links and be wary of opening unsolicited email messages.

10. Use passwords and make them strong. Search the Web for advice about choosing a strong password.

11. Always log out when you complete an online session on a public computer or terminal.

12. For additional excellent online safety and security tips from the Bureau of Education and Cultural Affairs, go to: http://exchanges.state.gov/pro-admin/pdfs/safety_english.pdf

HIGHLIGHTS

In this section you have been introduced to information technology—technology that helps individuals and businesses research, process, and manage information. You have learned the difference between the Internet and the Web, and web directories, search engines, and metasearch engines. You've become familiar with several popular browsers and the various search options they provide. Most likely, you will continue to experiment with the search tools each time you conduct Internet searches for anything from your coursework to travel searches.

You have become acquainted with the need to question the credibility of the Web, knowing that many website authors use this format to sell their products, ideas, and views, and thus their biases. Although the Internet is also rich in credible resources, you've also been encouraged to avoid the temptation to rely on the Web as your sole source of information. Other resources can help you verify the credibility of your selected websites.

For many of you, email is second nature, but this section also encourages you to pay attention to your writing mechanics since email is now a preferred way to correspond in the business world. As in business and in school, the Internet has become more and more central to our personal lives as a way of searching, processing, communicating, and managing information. Many are beginning to place computers in the kitchen (as a first point of entry to the home) to check for messages, news, daily tips, and recipes. Homes are increasingly networking computers in the kitchen, garage, bedrooms, and family rooms. You have seen that with this technological change there are opportunities to simplify and organize your life, but such change also exposes you to information overload. To manage information overload, we must not forget to use the many stress management strategies we learned. If we don't, we will likely suffer some of the same physical reactions of the stress response. Beyond information overload, we have to take very seriously the safety and security tips to protect ourselves and our computers.

DISCUSSION QUESTIONS

Note: Read the following discussion questions and activities before you read Section 10. This strategy will help you look for answers while you read.

1. List all the ways you currently use the Internet for school, work, and your personal life.
2. Explain the ways you imagine your future use of technology and the Internet changing in your personal life—at school and in your future career.
3. Discuss the ways you see information overload affecting your life and our society. What strategies can you use to better deal with information overload while you are enrolled in school?
4. What is meant by virtual reality?
5. What is the difference between the Internet and the intranet?
6. How has the Internet added value to your life?
7. Imagine that you will someday operate your own business from a website. What business(es) would you consider and why?
9. What is the difference between a cache and a cookie?
10. With your classmates, share experiences that you have had with a virus. What problems did it cause and how did you remedy any problems caused by the virus? What methods are you using to help prevent any such future problems?
11. Which is your favorite web browser and why?
12. Have you ever shopped on the Internet? Discuss good and/or bad experiences you have had with shopping online.
13. Have you ever hunted or applied for jobs on the Internet? Discuss good and/or bad experiences you had with either hunting for or applying for jobs online.
14. Discuss several circumstances that annoy you most about some email that you have received.
15. What courtesies would you like email senders to show you?
16. What technologies do you want to learn more about in order to help you in your career preparation?
17. If you have created a website, share your experiences with your classmates.
18. What do you see as your greatest concern(s) about the age of information? What are the most helpful computer technology and Internet capabilities that you use or plan to use?

APPENDIX

Freshman Orientation
Morgan State University

A-1 SELF-INTRODUCTION EXERCISE
(10 points)

"Do the difficult things while they are easy and do the great things while they are small.
A journey of a thousand miles must begin with a single step."
—Lao Tzu

Hello, my name is _____. I am _____ years old.

I live in _____ (City, State).

I chose Morgan State University because _____.

Some of my hobbies include _____.

A few of my favorite things to do in my spare time are _____.

The one thing that I *don't like* doing is _____.

When I leave MSU, I want to be remembered by _____.

My future career goal is to become a _____.

Freshman Orientation
Morgan State University

A-2 SELF-DISCOVERY EXERCISE I
(25 points)

"I haven't a clue as to how my story will end. But that's all right.
When you set out on a journey and night covers the road,
you don't conclude the road has vanished. And how else could we discover the stars?"
—Anonymous

Where Do I Go from Here?

As a new student you will be exposed to many new experiences, opportunities, and challenges during your first year at Morgan State University. On your journey, it is important that you understand **where you are coming from in order to know where you are going.**

This exercise will help you navigate through this process by allowing you to objectively look at yourself by means of self-analysis. Self-analysis is an ongoing process, which is subject to change—**as you change.**

The following information should be included in your narrative essay:

1. Things you like to do.

2. Things you don't like to do.

3. Things you'd like to improve upon.

4. The best experience (s) you have encountered in your life so far. What did you learn from these experiences?

5. The worst experience(s) you have encountered so far. What did you learn from these experiences?

6. Goal Setting

    a. What are your academic goals for this semester?

    b. What other things would you like to accomplish in 3 months, 6 months, 1 year?

    c. What tools and skill-sets do you need to reach your goals?

    d. What obstacles might you encounter that would prevent you from reaching your goal?

    e. What type of support system do you have in place to help you reach your goals?

Guidelines

1. Paper must be at least two pages (three maximum), 1-inch margins, 12-point font, double-spaced.

2. Be specific.

3. Good format and grammar are essential and will be considered as part of your overall grade.

Freshman Orientation
Morgan State University

A-3 CALCULATING GRADE POINT AVERAGE (GPA) QUIZ

Student Name: _____

Date: _____

True or False
One (1) point each.

1. _____ According to the University grading policy, NA means "not allowed in class."

2. _____ A student must get written approval from their his/her if he/she wants to carry more than 18 credits during a semester.

3. _____ Transfer credit hours are used when calculating cumulative grade point averages for all Morgan students.

4. _____ When a student repeats a class, the cumulated GPA is based on the highest grade received no matter when it was taken.

5. _____ Students are required to repeat DVRD 101, Math 106, and English 101 and 102 if a grade less than a "C" is earned.

6. _____ In order to earn a degree, the number of quality points must be at least half the number of credits pursued at the University.

7. _____ Developmental credit hours earned receive quality points but are not counted toward graduation requirements.

8. _____ Students whose GPA falls below 2.0 will be placed on academic probation and will remain on probation until a GPA of 2.0 or better is reached.

9. _____ If a student is given an "I," the student must complete the work by the end of the next semester of enrollment.

10. _____ Students that are academically dismissed cannot ever return to the University.

Refer to the chart below to answer the next five (5) questions below.
One (1) point each.

Course	Code	Credits	Grade	Quality Points
Biology	101	4	A	_____ (Fill in)
Developmental Math	106	3	B	_____ (Fill in)
Orientation	101	1	A	4
Psychology	101	3	C	6
English	101	3	D	3
		TOTAL =		TOTAL =

11. What is the total number of credits *earned* for the semester?
  a. 11 credits
  b. 14 credits
  c. 10 credits
  d. None of the above.

12. How many quality points are earned for Biology 101?
  a. 16
  b. 12
  c. 4
  d. None of the above.

13. How many quality points are earned for Math 106?
  a. 2
  b. 6
  c. 4
  d. None of the above.

14. The correct number of quality points earned for English 101, Developmental Math, and Orientation are as follows: (Choose only one sequence.)
  a. ENGL. 101 = 6 points, Developmental Math = 6 points, Orientation = 1 point
  b. ENGL. 101 = 3 points, Developmental Math = 9 points, Orientation = 4 points
  c. ENGL. 101 = 6 points, Developmental Math = 3 points, Orientation = 4 points
  d. None of the above.

15. The total number of quality points earned for the semester is:
  a. 42 points
  b. 36 points
  c. 38 points
  d. None of the above.

BONUS QUESTION (10 points) Credit **will not** be given for partial and/or incorrect answers. Calculate the Grade Point Average based on the chart and information above.

*Hint: GPA= Total Quality Points
Total Credits

Freshman Orientation
Morgan State University

A-4 TIME ANALYSIS EXERCISE

Student Name: _____

Date: _____

"So much to do...so little time."

Part 1: Based on a 24-hour day and your current schedule:

1. Estimate the amount of time that you spend on each of the activities listed below.
2. Determine the priority level based on level of importance to you.
3. Determine if the activity is necessary or unnecessary (time waster).

Note: Your answers should be *honest* and *realistic*.

Activity	Estimated Time (Hours/day)	Necessary or Unecessary (Indicate below)	Priority High or Low? (Indicate below)
Sleep			
Eating			
Classes			
Study/School Assignments			
Work			
Relaxation ("Chillin")			
Socialize/Friends/Dating			
Extracurricular/Hobbies			
Personal Hygiene			
Run Errands/Shopping			
Exercise			
Church/Worship			
Driving/Commuting			
Laundry			
Cleaning			
Telephone Calls/Texting			
Volunteer Activities			
Organizations/Clubs			
Watching TV			
Other			
TOTAL HOURS/DAY			

List three (3) things that you learned from this exercise.

1. _____

2. _____

3. _____

**Freshman Orientation
Morgan State University**

A-5 THE JOURNEY BEGINS: DISCOVERING MSU
(25 points)

Student Name: _____

Date: _____

You are about to embark on an exciting and informative ***journey*** to help you become familiar with the student resources and services available at Morgan State University.

(10 points = 1 point each)

1. Where is the Office of Student Retention located? What is the name of the Director of Student Retention?
   _____
   _____

2. What does AEP stand for? What type of services does the program provide? Where is the office located?
   _____
   _____

3. What is the name of your advisor for your major? Where is his/her office located (room, building)? What are his/her office hours and telephone number?
   _____
   _____

4. What is the name of the Interim Dean of the College of Liberal Arts? Where is his office located?
   _____
   _____

5. Where is the office of Records and Registration located? What is the office telephone number?
   _____
   _____

6. Where is the Office of Public Safety located? What are the hours of operation? What types of services does the office provide? Can a student pay for a parking permit in this building? If not, where?
   _____
   _____

7. Where is the Bear Necessity Card Resource Center? What are the hours of operation?
   _____
   _____

8. Where is the Office of Student Health Services located? What are its hours of operation and telephone number?

_____

_____

9. Where is the Office of Financial Aid located? What are the hours of operation?

_____

_____

10. What is the purpose of the Student Accessibility Support Services program? What type of services does the office provide? Where is it located (room number)? Who is in charge of the program?

_____

_____

For each question noted below, you must get a business card and/or a piece of literature from that office in order to receive credit. Please write the question number on the card or piece of literature that it applies. You must place all of the materials that you collected in an envelope prior to submission.

(15 points = 3 points each)

1. Visit the new library. What is the name of the new library? Who is it named after? What are the hours of operation? What is the procedure for borrowing library materials?

_____

_____

2. Where is the Student Government Association (SGA) office located? Who is the President of the (SGA)?

_____

_____

3. What is the name of the Director of the Counseling Center? What building is the center located in?

_____

_____

4. What does ARP stand for? Where is the office located? What services does the office provide? What are the hours of operation?

_____

_____

5. Locate and visit the Center for Academic Success and Achievement. Where are they located, and what are the hours of operation? What services do they provide?

_____

_____

Freshman Orientation
Morgan State University

A-6 MORGAN STATE UNIVERSITY HISTORY QUIZ
(15 points)

Student Name: _____

Date: _____

True or False
One (1) point each.

1. _____ The Centenary Biblical Institute (CBI) was established to provide teacher training for newly freed slaves.

2. _____ The Centenary Biblical Institute was founded in 1867.

3. _____ By act of the State of Maryland, in 1975 Morgan State College became Morgan State University.

4. _____ The first president of the Centenary Biblical Institute was Rev. J. Emory Round.

5. _____ CBI offered its first class to nine male students and one female student on April 30, 1867.

6. _____ Normal School is a nineteenth-century term for teacher-training institutes.

7. _____ Morgan College is named after Rev. Morgan F. Stanley.

8. _____ George W. F. McMechen was the first graduate of Morgan College.

9. _____ Carnegie Hall was the last building to be constructed on the University's current site at Hillen Road and Cold Spring Lane.

10. _____ Dr. Earl S. Richardson, Morgan's current president, was appointed in 1984.

Multiple Choice
Circle the correct answer. One (1) point each.

1. Carnegie Hall was completed in:
   a. 1925
   b. 1919
   c. 1923
   d. None of the above.

2. The first African American president of Morgan College was:
   a. Dr. John Oakley Spenser
   b. Reverend Lyttleton Morgan
   c. Dr. Dwight Oliver Wendell Holmes
   d. Reverend J. Emory Round

3. On November 9, 1939, the State of Maryland officially took over Morgan College and its name was changed to:
   a. Morgan State College of Maryland
   b. Morgan State University
   c. Morgan State College
   d. None of the above.

4. The name of CBI's first female graduate was:
   a. Sharon H. Carson
   b. Sue Ann Carr
   c. Suzette H. Carr
   d. Susie H. Carr

5. Holmes Hall was named in honor of:
   a. Sherlock Holmes
   b. Dr. David Oliver William Holmes
   c. Dr. Dwight Oliver Wendell Holmes
   d. Dr. David Oliver Wendell Holmes

**Freshman Orientation
Morgan State University**

A-7 ACADEMIC ADVISING AND REGISTRATION
(50 points)

Student Name: (Please print) _____

Major: _____

Academic Advisor: _____

Office Hours: _____

Phone Number: _____

*Signatures Required

Student: _____ Date:_____

Academic Advisor: _____ Date:_____

*Note: Student and Advisor signatures and copy of student registration/schedule are required in order to receive credit/points for this assignment.

Advisement and Responsibility
A Case Study: Brandon's Advisement

In the spring, Brandon received his MSU acceptance letter and invitation to participate in the summer Access Orientation Program. Although he had mixed emotions about starting his college career in Computer Engineering, he was sure that he was up to the task.

The night before his scheduled advisement session, Brandon's "homeboys" called to see if he wanted to go to the "club" for a few hours. Needless to say the club was "hot" and the music was "on." When he finally got back to his dorm, it was 3:00 AM; he was tired and his head hurt.

Brandon's advisement session was scheduled for 8:00 AM the next morning. Arriving nearly a half hour late, he tried to sneak past the student mentors without being noticed. Dr. McMillan and Dr. Brunson asked if "there were any questions about the placement results." Brandon had quite a few but was too embarrassed to ask. He thought to himself, "I'll get with Shante; she can explain it to me tomorrow."

Brandon's girlfriend Shante was also a MSU student majoring in Psychology. She suggested that he make his schedule the same as hers so that they could spend more time together. "What about my developmental reading and math courses?" Brandon asked. "Just chill," she said. "I can help you with them since we're in the same classes. Trust me, I know what I'm doing." Brandon took the same schedule Shante gave him when he went to meet with his advisor.

Dr. Johnson, Brandon's academic advisor, was very confused about the schedule that he had selected. Brandon did not have any of the required courses for his major for the next term. Dr. Johnson only allowed 30 minutes for each student to discuss placement test results and the program requirements. However, most of that time was used up trying to figure out where Brandon was "coming from." Brandon would now have to schedule another appointment to further discuss his classes and to register for the upcoming semester. Unfortunately, Dr. Johnson would be out the next week enjoying a well-deserved vacation in Aruba. Now Brandon would have to wait until Dr. Johnson returned to complete his schedule and registration.

By the time Dr. Johnson returned, the final 250 students had participated in the Access Orientation Program and all of the developmental reading and math classes were closed.

Dr. Johnson called Professor Howard for permission to "override" Brandon into the class. Professor Howard could not accommodate Dr. Johnson's request due to lack of class space and timeliness.

Brandon was angry and disappointed. He thought to himself, "Now I have to wait another semester to get the courses I need. More money! More money! More money!!!"

Listed below are the players in Brandon's advisement story. Rank them in the order of responsibility for Brandon's disastrous advisement experience.

_____ Brandon, the student

_____ Dr. Johnson, his advisor

_____ Shante, his girlfriend

_____ Brandon's "homeboys"

_____ Professor Howard

_____ No one

**Freshman Orientation
Morgan State University**

**A-8 SELF-DISCOVERY EXERCISE II
(25 points)**

*"The longest journey of any person is the journey inwards. Of him who has chosen his destiny,
Who has started upon his quest for the source of his being?"*
—Dag Hammarskjold

Are We There Yet?

In your first self-discovery exercise, you were asked to write a self-analysis paper designed to help you **discover** your likes and dislikes, personal strengths and weaknesses, and how they might affect your academic and professional growth.

As you move forward to the end of the semester, you have experienced many new opportunities and challenges that may impact your continued matriculation at Morgan State University.

As you near the end of your journey, many of you will find that much has changed.

Guidelines

Using your first self-discovery exercise, class assignments, and Morgan experiences as points of reference, in **Narrative format** please address the following:

a. How you incorporated the things that you do well into your academic curriculum.

b. How the things that you don't do well have affected your academic success.

c. How things that you have improved upon have helped you at MSU.

d. Have your *career goals* changed since the beginning of the semester? If so, why?

e. What things you would like to do differently next semester, next month, next year. What is your plan?

Reminders

1. Paper must be at least two pages (three maximum), 1-inch margins, 12-point font, double-spaced.

2. Be specific.

3. Good format and grammar are essential.

Notes

Notes

Notes